ZAGAT®

Boston
Restaurants
2010/11

Including Cape Cod,
Martha's Vineyard, Nantucket
and The Berkshires

LOCAL EDITORS
Naomi Kooker and Lynn Hazlewood with Eric Grossman

LOCAL COORDINATOR
Maryanne Muller

STAFF EDITOR
Bill Corsello

Published and distributed by
Zagat Survey, LLC
4 Columbus Circle
New York, NY 10019
T: 212.977.6000
E: boston@zagat.com
www.zagat.com

ACKNOWLEDGMENTS

We thank Jack Dew, Dave Krugman, Kit Krugman, Gerrish Lopez, Chelsey Minnis, Ellen Roberts, Ian Turner, Brit Withey and The Culinary Guild of New England, as well as the following members of our staff: Christina Livadiotis (assistant editor), Brian Albert, Sean Beachell, Maryanne Bertollo, Danielle Borovoy, Jane Chang, Sandy Cheng, Reni Chin, Larry Cohn, Alison Flick, Jeff Freier, Curt Gathje, Justin Hartung, Roy Jacob, Garth Johnston, Natalie Lebert, Mike Liao, Andre Pilette, Becky Ruthenburg, Jacqueline Wasilczyk, Sharon Yates, Anna Zappia and Kyle Zolner.

The reviews in this guide are based on public opinion surveys. The ratings reflect the average scores given by the survey participants who voted on each establishment. The text is based on quotes from, or paraphrasings of, the surveyors' comments. Phone numbers, addresses and other factual data were correct to the best of our knowledge when published in this guide.

Maps © Antenna Audio

Contents

Ratings & Symbols

Zagat Top Spot	Name	Symbols	Cuisine	Zagat Ratings			
				FOOD	DECOR	SERVICE	COST

Area, Address & Contact

🏆 **Tim & Nina's** ◖ *Eclectic*   ▽ 27 | 4 | 13 | $15

Waterfront | 1000 Thatcher St. (Margin St.) | 617-555-1234 | www.zagat.com

Review, surveyor comments in quotes

The site of the first tea party, this "weird, wonderful" Waterfront bastion of intense politics and "Eclectic fodder comes with gourmet twists" – think "scrumptious truffled grits", "Beluga-infused polenta" and "sea urchin muffins"; the fare has foodies "dreaming" happily, but the "ramshackle" digs in a converted ATM vestibule and "slow service" cause aesthetes "nightmares."

Ratings

Food, Decor and **Service** are rated on the Zagat 0 to 30 scale.

0 – 9	poor to fair
10 – 15	fair to good
16 – 19	good to very good
20 – 25	very good to excellent
26 – 30	extraordinary to perfection
▽	low response | less reliable

Cost

Our surveyors' estimated price of a dinner with one drink and tip. Lunch is usually 25 to 30% less. For unrated **newcomers** or **write-ins**, the price range is shown as follows:

I	$25 and below	E	$41 to $65
M	$26 to $40	VE	$66 or more

Symbols

🏆	highest ratings, popularity and importance
◖	serves after 11 PM
S̸	closed on Sunday
M̸	closed on Monday
⌿	no credit cards accepted

Maps

Index maps show restaurants with the highest Food ratings in those areas.

About This Survey

This **2010/11 Boston Restaurants Survey** is an update reflecting significant developments since our last Survey was published. It covers 1,263 restaurants in Boston and its surroundings, as well as in Cape Cod, Martha's Vineyard, Nantucket and The Berkshires, including 90 important additions. To bring this guide up to the minute, we've also indicated new addresses, phone numbers, chef changes and other major alterations. Like all our guides, this one is based on input from avid local consumers – 6,767 all told. Our editors have synopsized this feedback and highlighted (in quotation marks within reviews) representative comments. You can read full surveyor comments – and share your own opinions – on **ZAGAT.com,** where you'll also find the latest restaurant news plus menus, photos and more, all for free.

OUR PHILOSOPHY: Three simple premises underlie our ratings and reviews. First, we've long believed that the collective opinions of knowledgeable consumers are more accurate than the opinions of a single critic. (Consider, for example, that as a group our surveyors bring some 900,000 annual meals' worth of experience to this Survey. They also visit restaurants year-round, anonymously – and on their own dime.) Second, food quality is only part of the equation when choosing a restaurant, thus we ask surveyors to separately rate food, decor and service and report on cost. Third, since people need reliable information in a fast, easy-to-digest format, we strive to be concise and to offer our content on every platform.

ABOUT ZAGAT: In 1979, we started asking friends to rate and review restaurants purely for fun. The term "user-generated content" had not yet been coined. That hobby grew into Zagat Survey; 31 years later, we have over 375,000 surveyors and cover everything from airlines to shopping in over 100 countries. Along the way, we evolved from being a print publisher to a digital content provider, e.g. **ZAGAT.com, ZAGAT.mobi** (for web-enabled mobile devices), **ZAGAT TO GO** (for smartphones) and **nru** (for Android phones). We also produce customized gift and marketing tools for a wide range of corporate clients. And you can find us on Twitter (twitter.com/zagatbuzz), Facebook and other social media networks.

JOIN IN: To improve our guides, we solicit your comments; it's vital that we hear your opinions. Just contact us at **nina-tim@zagat.com.** We also invite you to join our surveys at **ZAGAT.com.** Do so and you'll receive a choice of rewards in exchange.

THANKS: We're grateful to our local editors: Naomi Kooker, deputy editor of *Boston Common* magazine; Lynn Hazlewood, former editor-in-chief of *Hudson Valley* magazine; our coordinator, Maryanne Muller, a personal chef and cooking instructor; and Eric Grossman, a Boston-based food and travel writer. We also sincerely thank the thousands of surveyors who participated – all of our content is really "theirs."

New York, NY
April 14, 2010

Nina and Tim Zagat

What's New

Even in the worst of economies, at least one brave restaurateur usually throws caution to the wind and opens a luxury-priced destination. Not so this year. Of the nearly 70 new Greater Boston restaurants highlighted in this guide, not one is pegged as expensive, much less very expensive. Indeed, value-seeking diners have an embarrassment of affordable riches, many of which are flat-out bargains. (Boston's average per-meal cost, $33.64, is slightly below the national mean of $35.25.) For a list of the city's Best Buys, see page 17.

SURVIVAL OF THE SMARTEST: Swanky brand names continue to modify their M.O. for modern times, and leading the pack is über-chef Ken Oringer. Normally you need bank approval before hitting his highly rated **Clio** or **KO Prime,** but at cozy South End enoteca **Coppa,** a partnership with Jamie Bissonnette, a couple of courses can cost just a couple of Hamiltons. Kenneth A. Himmel, owner of expense-accounter **Grill 23 & Bar,** goes the American comfort-food route at **Post 390** in the Back Bay, while also investing in **Bistro du Midi,** a classy French spot with prices that are pleasant at dinner and peasant at lunch. Dante de Magistris provides a trip to Italy without the euros at **Il Casale** in Belmont, and the One World Cuisine group, purveyor of midpriced Indian fare at **Kashmir** and **Mela,** among others, is even more cash-conscious at **Dosa Factory** in Cambridge, where all the street eats hover around the $10 mark.

INN STYLE: Hoteliers are enticing lodgers and locals alike with an impressive array of smart newcomers. World-class toque Jean-Georges Vongerichten presents a generally moderately priced round-up of his greatest culinary hits at stylish **Market** in the Theater District's W; sophisticated tavern **Woodward** anchors the chic scene at the Ames Hotel; and **Twenty8 Food & Spirits** is a classy addition to Foxboro's Rennaissance. Boston Harbor Hotel transformed its waterfront dining room into airy **Rowes Wharf Sea Grille,** and Millennium Bostonian reconceived its first-floor lounge into a full-fledged restaurant, **North 26,** a minimalist source of New England staples. In the same overhaul vein, **Pairings,** offering food-and-wine matchmaking services, lightens up the formerly dim Bonfire space in the Park Plaza Hotel & Towers, just as The Lenox's **City Table** goes easier on the wallet than its erstwhile Azure. In the Checking Out department, summer 2009 saw the closure of Four Seasons classic Aujourd'hui, which is now a private banquet room.

 LOCAL LEANINGS: Though they involve ingredients that can be costlier to procure, the local, sustainable and seasonal trends soldier on. Among the "green"-leaning newcomers are **East by Northeast,** a Cambridge Chinese, **Nourish,** a Lexington American, and Newton's **Prana Café,** whose vegan eats are made with provender from area farms. For American classics, there's **Farm Bar & Grille** in Essex, which cultivates veggies in its own garden, plus Somerville's **Teele Square Cafe,** whose proprietors grow their own herbs and raise egg-supplying hens.

Boston, MA
April 14, 2010

Naomi Kooker

Most Popular

Plotted on the map at the back of this book.

BOSTON

1 Legal Sea Foods | *Seafood*	21 Lumière | *French*
2 Blue Ginger | *Asian*	22 Sel de la Terre | *French*
3 L'Espalier | *French*	23 Ruth's Chris | *Steak*
4 No. 9 Park | *French/Italian*	24 Fugakyu | *Japanese*
5 Hamersley's Bistro | *French*	25 Rialto | *Italian*
6 Abe & Louie's | *Steak*	26 Petit Robert Bistro | *French*
7 Oleana | *Mediterranean*	27 Union Oyster* | *Seafood*
8 Capital Grille | *Steak*	28 Sorellina | *Italian*
9 B&G Oysters | *Seafood*	29 Olives | *Mediterranean*
10 Mistral | *French/Mediterranean*	30 Davio's | *Italian/Steak*
11 Oishii | *Japanese*	31 Radius | *French*
12 Grill 23 & Bar | *Steak*	32 Helmand | *Afghan*
13 EVOO | *Eclectic*	33 Il Capriccio | *Italian*
14 Cheesecake Factory | *American*	34 Giacomo's | *Italian*
15 Craigie on Main | *French*	35 Morton's | *Steak*
16 Clio/Uni | *French*	36 Upstairs on the Sq. | *Amer.*
17 Anna's Taqueria | *Tex-Mex*	37 Aquitaine | *French*
18 Elephant Walk | *Cambodian*	38 Eastern Standard | *Amer./Euro.*
19 La Campania | *Italian*	39 P.F. Chang's | *Chinese*
20 East Coast | *BBQ/Seafood*	40 Dalí | *Spanish*

CAPE COD, MARTHA'S VINEYARD & NANTUCKET

C=Cape Cod; M=Martha's Vineyard; N=Nantucket

1 Abba/C | *Mediterranean/Thai*	11 Cape Sea Grille/C | *American*
2 Brewster Fish/C* | *Seafood*	12 28 Atlantic/C | *Amer.*
3 21 Federal/N | *American*	13 Arnold's Lobster/C | *Seafood*
4 Chillingsworth/C | *French*	14 Topper's/N | *American*
5 American Seasons/N | *Amer.*	15 Wicked Oyster/C* | *Amer./Sea.*
6 Chatham Bars Inn/C | *American*	16 Chatham Squire/C | *Pub Food*
7 Mews/C | *American*	17 Nauset Beach Club/C | *Italian*
8 Lobster Pot/C | *Eclectic/Seafood*	18 Straight Wharf/N | *Seafood*
9 Ocean House/C | *American*	19 Red Pheasant | *Amer./French*
10 Impudent Oyster/C | *Seafood*	20 Black Dog Tav./M | *American*

---

* Indicates a tie with restaurant above

KEY NEWCOMERS

Farm Bar & Grille — Essex

Teele Square Cafe

Dorado Tacos

Boston

Robinwood

88 Wharf

Bistro Chi

Abby Park

Kama Lounge

Suffolk Grille

Nourish

Il Casale

Prana Cafe

Bobby's

Singh's

Big Papi's

Milestone

Forty Carrots

Twenty8 Food & Spirits

Tavolino

Lowell

North 26

Rowes Wharf Sea Grille

Woodward

Bistro du Midi

Pairings

Market

Coppa

Ginger Park

Courtyard at the Boston Public Library

Post 390

City Table

Six Burner

Teranga

Stork Club Boston

Technique

East by Northeast

Trina's Starlite Lounge

Lord Hobo

Ginger Exchange

Dosa Factory

Tajine

Tory Row

Corner Tavern

Pazzo

Cafe 47

Lansdowne Pub

Symphony 8

Menus, photos, voting and more - free at ZAGAT.com

Key Newcomers

Our editors' take on the year's top arrivals. See page 252 for a full list.

Abby Park | *American*

Big Papi's Grille | *American*

Bistro Chi | *Chinese*

Bistro du Midi | *French*

Bobby's | *American*

Cafe 47 | *American*

City Table | *American*

Coppa | *Italian*

Corner Tavern | *American*

Courtyard/Public Library | *Amer.*

Dorado Tacos & Cemitas | *Mexican*

Dosa Factory | *Indian*

East by Northeast | *Chinese*

88 Wharf | *American*

Farm Bar & Grille | *American/BBQ*

Forty Carrots | *American*

Ginger Exchange | *Asian/Japanese*

Ginger Park | *Asian*

Il Casale | *Italian*

Kama Lounge | *Spanish*

Lansdowne Pub | *American/Irish*

Lord Hobo | *American*

Market | *American*

Milestone | *Mediterranean*

North 26 | *New England*

Nourish | *American*

Pairings | *American*

Pazzo | *Italian*

Post 390 | *American*

Prana Café | *Vegan*

Robinwood | *American*

Rowes Wharf Sea Grille | *Seafood*

Singh's Café | *Indian*

Six Burner | *American*

Stork Club Boston | *American*

Suffolk Grille | *American*

Symphony 8 | *American*

Tajine | *Moroccan*

Tavolino | *Italian*

Technique | *New England*

Teele Square Cafe | *American*

Teranga | *Senegalese*

Tory Row | *American*

Trina's Starlite Lounge | *American*

Twenty8 Food & Spirits | *American*

Woodward | *American*

In the year to come, veteran restaurateurs are expected to continue expanding their empires, starting with Barbara Lynch (**B&G Oysters, No. 9 Park,** et al.), who will combine "French technique and Italian soul" at **Menton** in the Seaport District's Fort Point Channel. Elsewhere, Jasper White is planning a yet-to-be-named eatery at the Hynes Convention Center in the Back Bay, and chef Chris Chung and manager Christian Touche, both late of **Clio/Uni,** will do their own French/ sushi thing at **Aka Bistro** in Lincoln. As for new branches of old favorites, there will be a **Flour Bakery** in Cambridge, an offshoot of the North End's **Strega Ristorante** on Fan Pier in the Seaport District and a second **Za** attached to **EVOO,** which has moved to Kendall Square.

Top Food

See also Cape Cod, Martha's Vineyard and Nantucket Top Spots on pages 176, 198 and 206, respectively.

BOSTON, CAMBRIDGE, NEARBY SUBURBS

28 L'Espalier | *French*
    Oleana | *Mediterranean*
    O Ya | *Japanese*
    La Campania | *Italian*
    No. 9 Park | *French/Italian*

27 Ten Tables | *Amer./Euro.*
    Bistro 5 | *Italian*
    Clio/Uni | *French*
    Neptune Oyster | *Seafood*
    Troquet | *American/French*
    Oishii | *Japanese*
    Hamersley's Bistro | *French*
    EVOO | *Eclectic*
    Meritage | *American*
    Taranta | *Italian/Peruvian*
    Sorellina | *Italian*

Hungry Mother | *American*
Lumière | *French*
Il Capriccio | *Italian*
Delfino | *Italian*
Prezza | *Italian*
Craigie on Main | *French*
Mistral | *French/Med.*

26 Carmen | *Italian*
    Trattoria di Monica/
      Vinoteca | *Italian*
    Trattoria Toscana | *Italian*
    Galleria Umberto | *Italian*
    Toro | *Spanish*
    Terramia | *Italian*
    Flour Bakery | *Bakery*

OUTLYING SUBURBS

29 Duckworth's | *American*

27 Oishii | *Japanese*
    Sichuan Gourmet | *Chinese*

26 Ithaki | *Mediterranean*

Square Café | *American*
Blue Ginger | *Asian*
Maxwell's 148 | *Asian/Italian*
Clam Box | *Seafood*
Caffe Bella | *Mediterranean*
Capital Grille | *Steak*

BY CUISINE

AMERICAN (NEW)

29 Duckworth's
27 Ten Tables
    Troquet
    Meritage
    Hungry Mother

AMERICAN (TRAD.)

25 Oak Room
24 Mr. Bartley's
    Oceana
    NewBridge Cafe
    Summer Winter

ASIAN

26 Blue Ginger
23 Myers + Chang
20 Billy Tse
    Grasshopper
    Ma Soba

BARBECUE

25 East Coast Grill
    Blue Ribbon BBQ
24 NewBridge Cafe
22 Redbones BBQ
    Soul Fire

BURGERS

24 Mr. Bartley's
23 UBurger
21 Audubon Circle
19 Miracle of Science
    B. Good

CAMBODIAN/ VIETNAMESE

23 Elephant Walk
    Pho Pasteur
21 Le's
    Wonder Spice
    Lam's

Excludes places with low votes

CHINESE

- 27 Sichuan Gourmet
- 25 Peach Farm
- 24 Qingdao Garden
- Bernard's
- East Ocean City

ECLECTIC

- 27 EVOO
- 25 Blue Room
- Centre St. Café
- 23 Scutra
- Metropolis Cafe

FRENCH

- 28 No. 9 Park
- 27 Mistral
- 26 Salts
- 25 Butcher Shop
- 24 Sandrine's

FRENCH (BISTRO)

- 27 Troquet
- Hamersley's Bistro
- Craigie on Main
- 26 Pigalle
- 24 Pierrot Bistrot

FRENCH (NEW)

- 28 L'Espalier
- 27 Clio/Uni
- Lumière
- 26 Radius
- T.W. Food

INDIAN

- 25 Punjab
- 24 Kebab Factory
- India Quality
- Himalayan Bistro
- Mela

ITALIAN

- 27 Sorellina
- Taranta
- Delfino
- Prezza
- 26 Carmen

ITALIAN (NORTHERN)

- 27 Bistro 5
- Il Capriccio
- 26 Trattoria Toscana
- Bridgeman's
- 25 Tosca

JAPANESE

- 28 O Ya
- 27 Oishii
- 26 Oga's
- 25 Fugakyu
- Sakurabana

MEDITERRANEAN

- 28 Oleana
- 27 Mistral
- 26 Ithaki Med.
- Caffe Bella
- Chiara

MEXICAN

- 25 Tacos Lupita
- El Sarape
- 24 Olecito/Olé
- Tu y Yo
- Cantina la Mexicana

MIDDLE EASTERN

- 26 Sofra Bakery & Café
- Helmand
- 25 Café Mangal
- 24 Byblos
- Sultan's Kitchen

NEW ENGLAND

- 24 Gibbet Hill Grill
- Green Street
- 23 Henrietta's Table
- Woodman's
- 22 Parker's

PIZZA

- 26 Galleria Umberto
- 25 Santarpio's Pizza
- Za
- 24 Emma's Pizza
- Pizzeria Regina

PUB FOOD

- 22 Matt Murphy's
- 21 Audubon Circle
- Publick House
- 20 Sunset Cantina
- 19 Mission B&G

SEAFOOD (AMERICAN)

- 27 Neptune Oyster
- 26 Clam Box
- B&G Oysters
- 25 East Coast Grill
- 24 Oceana

SEAFOOD (ETHNIC)

25 Giacomo's
   Peach Farm
24 Tamarind Bay
   Daily Catch
   East Ocean City*

SPANISH

26 Toro
25 Dalí
23 Taberna de Haro
   Solea
   Tasca

STEAKHOUSES

26 Capital Grille
   Abe & Louie's
25 Morton's
   Grill 23 & Bar
   Davio's

THAI

25 Brown Sugar/Similans
24 Dok Bua
   House of Siam
   Khao Sarn Cuisine
23 Thai Basil

BY SPECIAL FEATURE

BRUNCH

27 Meritage
25 Centre St. Café
23 Henrietta's Table
   Metropolis Cafe
22 Tryst

CHILD-FRIENDLY

26 Clam Box
   Flour Bakery
25 Blue Ribbon BBQ
21 Jasper White's
20 Full Moon

CHOWDER

27 Neptune Oyster
26 B&G Oysters
22 Legal Sea Foods
21 Turner Fisheries
20 Union Oyster House

DESSERT

26 Flour Bakery
24 Bristol Lounge
   Hi-Rise
23 Finale
22 Picco

HOTEL DINING

27 Clio/Uni
   (Eliot Hotel)
   Meritage
   (Boston Harbor Hotel)
26 Rialto
   (Charles Hotel)
25 Oak Room
   (Fairmont Copley Plaza)
24 Bristol Lounge
   (Four Seasons Hotel)

LANDMARKS

24 Locke-Ober
23 Charlie's Sandwich
20 Union Oyster House
17 Jacob Wirth
   Durgin-Park

LATE DINING

26 Franklin Café
25 Fugakyu
24 Peach Farm
22 Eastern Standard
21 Chau Chow

PEOPLE-WATCHING

25 Butcher Shop
22 Scampo
   Parish Cafe
20 Stephanie's
   Sonsie

POWER LUNCH

26 Radius
   Abe & Louie's
25 Harvest
24 Bristol Lounge
23 Smith & Wollensky

WINNING WINE LISTS

28 L'Espalier
   La Campania
   No. 9 Park
27 Troquet
   Hamersley's

BY LOCATION

BACK BAY

- 28 L'Espalier
- 27 Clio/Uni
  - Sorellina
- 26 Capital Grille
  - Abe & Louie's

BEACON HILL

- 28 No. 9 Park
- 25 Grotto
- 24 Pierrot Bistrot
  - Rist. Toscano
  - Mooo . . .

BROOKLINE/
CHESTNUT HILL

- 27 Oishii
- 26 Capital Grille
- 25 Fugakyu
  - Orinoco: A Latin Kitchen
- 24 Pomodoro

CENTRAL/
INMAN SQS./
EAST CAMBRIDGE

- 28 Oleana
- 27 Craigie on Main
- 26 Baraka Cafe
  - Salts
  - Helmand

CHARLESTOWN

- 25 Olives
- 24 Tangierino
- 23 Figs
  - Navy Yard Bistro
- 16 Warren Tavern

CHINATOWN

- 25 Peach Farm
- 24 East Ocean City
- 23 Kaze
  - Taiwan Cafe
  - Jumbo Seafood

DOWNTOWN CROSS./
FINANCIAL DICTRICT

- 26 Radius
- 25 Sakurabana
- 24 Ruth's Chris
  - Sultan's Kitchen
  - Locke-Ober

FENWAY/KENMORE SQ.

- 26 Trattoria Toscana
- 24 India Quality

  Petit Robert Bistro
- 23 Elephant Walk
  - UBurger

HARVARD SQ.

- 27 Ten Tables Cambridge
- 26 Rialto
- 25 Garden at The Cellar
  - Harvest
- 24 Darwin's Ltd.

JAMAICA PLAN

- 27 Ten Tables
- 25 Centre St. Café
- 24 El Oriental de Cuba
- 23 JP Seafood
  - Bukhara

NEEDHAM/NEWTON/
WELLESLEY

- 27 Lumière
- 26 Blue Ginger
- 25 Blue Ribbon BBQ
  - Sweet Basil
  - Café Mangal

NORTH END

- 27 Neptune Oyster
  - Taranta
  - Prezza
- 26 Carmen
  - Trattoria di Monica/Vinoteca

PARK SQ.

- 25 Via Matta
  - Davio's
- 24 Fleming's Prime
- 23 Finale
- 22 Da Vinci

SEAPORT/
WATERFRONT

- 27 Meritage
- 26 Flour Bakery
- 25 Morton's
- 24 Oceana
  - Daily Catch

SOMERVILLE

- 25 Dalí
  - Tacos Lupita
- 24 Kebab Factory
  - Tu y Yo
  - Gargoyles

SOUTH END

27 Oishii Boston
   Hamersley's Bistro
   Mistral
26 Toro
   Flour Bakery

THEATER DISTRICT

27 Troquet
26 Pigalle
24 Avila
   Teatro
21 Blu

WALTHAM/
WATERTOWN

28 La Campania
27 Il Capriccio
24 New Ginza
   Tuscan Grill
23 Solea

CAPE COD

27 Inaho
   Front Street

Pisces
Red Pheasant
Bramble Inn

MARTHA'S VINEYARD

27 Détente
   Larsen's Fish Mkt.
26 Bite
   L'Étoile
25 Atria

NANTUCKET

28 Company/Cauldron
27 Topper's
26 Le Languedoc
   Black-Eyed Susan's
25 Straight Wharf

THE BERKSHIRES

28 Old Inn/Green
27 Wheatleigh
   Blantyre
25 Gramercy Bistro
   Elizabeth's

Top Decor

<u>28</u>	Sorellina
<u>27</u>	Meritage
	Oak Room
<u>26</u>	Top of the Hub
	Gibbet Hill Grill
	Bristol Lounge
	Tangierino
	Mistral
	J's at Nashoba
	Square Café*
	Cuchi Cuchi
	Clio/Uni
<u>25</u>	La Campania
	Clink
	Radius
	28 Degrees
	Locke-Ober
	Rialto
	Bravo
<u>24</u>	No. 9 Park
	Bistro 5

Parker's
Dalí
Beehive
Scarlet Oak Tavern
Oceanaire
Maxwell's 148
Hungry I
Longfellow's Inn
Rocca
Scampo
L'Andana
Mooo . . .
Davio's
Chiara
Barker Tavern
Upstairs on the Square
Avila
Eastern Standard
Tosca

OUTDOORS

B&G Oysters
Barking Crab
Casa Romero
Hamersley's Bistro
Harvest
Henrietta's Table

J's at Nashoba
Oleana
Red Rock Bistro
Stella
Stellina
Stephanie's

ROMANCE

Carmen
Casa Romero
Dalí
Hungry I
Il Capriccio
Lala Rokh

L'Espalier
Mamma Maria
Oleana
Pigalle
Tangierino
Taranta

ROOMS

Beehive
Bridgeman's
Clink
Clio/Uni
Cuchi Cuchi
Dalí

La Campania
Mistral
Oak Room
Radius
Sorellina
Tangierino

VIEWS

Anthony's
Back Eddy
Barking Crab
Bristol Lounge
Dante
J's at Nashoba

Meritage
Oceana
Red Rock Bistro
Tavern on Water
Top of the Hub
Upstairs on the Square

Top Service

<u>28</u> L'Espalier

<u>27</u> Trattoria Toscana
Maxwell's 148
No. 9 Park

<u>26</u> Bistro 5
Bristol Lounge
Meritage
Sorellina
Oak Room
EVOO
O Ya
Lumière
Clio/Uni
Duckworth's
Salts
La Campania

<u>25</u> Marco Romana
Mistral
Hamersley's Bistro
T.W. Food

Craigie on Main
Gibbet Hill Grill
Capital Grille
Troquet
Blue Ginger
Hungry Mother
Il Capriccio
Abe & Louie's
Grapevine
Oleana
Mooo . . .
Radius
Rialto
Ten Tables

<u>24</u> Flora
Pigalle
Grill 23 & Bar
Davio's
Morton's
Locke-Ober

Best Buys

In order of Bang for the Buck rating.

1. 1369 Coffee Hse.
2. Anna's Taqueria
3. Baja Betty's
4. Boloco
5. B. Good
6. Galleria Umberto
7. UBurger
8. Sofra Bakery & Café
9. Boca Grande
10. Tacos Lupita
11. Athan's Café
12. Darwin's Ltd.
13. Flour Bakery
14. Oxford Spa
15. Paris Creperie
16. UFood Grill
17. Charlie's Sandwich
18. Cantina la Mexicana
19. Bottega Fiorentina
20. Punjabi Dhaba
21. Picante Mexican
22. Il Panino Express
23. Mr. Crepe
24. Hi-Rise Bread Co.
25. All Star Sandwich
26. Rami's
27. Sound Bites
28. Deluxe Town
29. Blue Ribbon BBQ
30. Shawarma King
31. Pie Bakery & Café
32. El Oriental de Cuba
33. Dok Bua
34. Mr. Bartley's
35. Cafe Jaffa
36. South End Buttery
37. Veggie Planet
38. Upper Crust
39. Basta Pasta
40. Rosebud Diner

OTHER GOOD VALUES

Addis Red Sea
Border Cafe
Boston Burger
Boston/Salem Beer
Brown Sugar Café
Bukowski Tavern
Café Polonia
Cambridge Common
Carlo's Cucina
Centre St. Café
Delux Café
Demos
Dorado Tacos
Dosa Factory
Fajitas & 'Ritas
Farm Bar & Grille
Federal
Giacomo's
Ginger Exchange
Halfway Café
Hot Tomatoes
India Quality/Punjab
Johnny's Lunch.
Kebab Factory
Koreana
Le's
Mike's City Diner
Miracle of Science
Muqueca
NewBridge Café
Other Side Café
Palio's
Paramount
Pho Lemongrass
Pizzeria Regina
Redbones BBQ
Robinwood
Santarpio's Pizza
Silvertone B&G
Six Burner
South St. Diner
Steve's Greek
Sultan's Kitchen
Sunset Grill/Cantina
Sweet Basil
Taqueria Mexico
Teele Square
Vinny's at Night
Za
Zaftigs

PRIX FIXE MENUS

Call for availability. All-you-can-eat options are for lunch and/or brunch.

PRIX FIXE LUNCH

28 L'Espalier ($24)
26 Radius ($29)
24 Kayuga II ($9)
   Punjab Palace ($7)
   Sandrine's ($20)
   Sel de la Terre ($22)
   Upstairs on the Square ($20)
23 Elephant Walk ($17)
22 Lotus Blossom ($11)

PRIX FIXE DINNER

27 EVOO ($38)
   Lumière ($35)
26 Pigalle ($40)
   Rendezvous ($38)
25 Grotto ($36)

24 Sandrine's ($40)
   La Morra ($35)
   Pierrot Bistrot ($34)
   Chez Henri ($39)
23 Lineage ($36)

ALL YOU CAN EAT

26 J's at Nashoba ($23)
25 Blue Room ($23)
   Kebab Factory ($8)
24 Bristol Lounge ($39)
   Himalayan Bistro ($8)
   Mela ($10)
   Tamarind Bay ($9)
23 Kashmir ($10)
   Henrietta's Table ($45)
   Bukhara ($9)

BEST BUYS: CAPE COD

In order of Bang for the Buck Rating.

1. Betsy's Diner
2. Sir Cricket's
3. Captain Frosty's
4. Dunbar Tea Room
5. Liam's at Nauset Bch.
6. Cobie's Clam Shack
7. Stir Crazy
8. Catch of the Day
9. Captain Kidd
10. Clancy's

BEST BUYS: MARTHA'S VINEYARD

1. Art Cliff Diner
2. Sharky's Cantina
3. Net Result
4. Bite
5. Larsen's Fish Mkt.
6. Offshore Ale
7. Newes From America
8. Zapotec
9. Black Dog Tavern
10. Jimmy Seas Pan Pasta

BEST BUYS: NANTUCKET

1. Fog Island Cafe
2. Black-Eyed Susan's
3. Brotherhood of Thieves
4. Even Keel Cafe
5. Sushi by Yoshi
6. Queequeg's
7. Arno's
8. Sea Grille
9. Sconset Café
10. Le Languedoc

BEST BUYS: BERKSHIRES

1. Baba Louie's
2. Barrington Brewery
3. Siam Square
4. Aroma B&G
5. Sushi Thai Garden
6. Bombay
7. Elizabeth's
8. Route 7 Grill
9. Truc Orient
10. Xicohtencatl

BOSTON/
CAPE COD & THE ISLANDS
RESTAURANT
DIRECTORY

Boston

Abbondanza Ristorante Italiano 🖂 *Italian* ▽ 23 | 16 | 21 | $31

Everett | 195 Main St. (bet. Appleton St. & Forest Ave.) | 617-387-8422
"In the wilds of Everett", this "quintessential" "old-school" Italian doles out "large portions" of "simple, delicious" and "consistently fresh seafood and pasta" that admirers aver "hold their own" against any "red-sauce royalty"; relatively "low prices" match the "quaint but not kitschy" atmosphere, which feels "welcoming" thanks to a "friendly staff."

NEW Abby Park *American*   - | - | - | M

Milton | 550 Adams St. (Franklin St.) | 617-696-8700 | www.abbypark.com
Sexy and casual all at once, this New American newcomer in East Milton Square sports masculine dark-wood wainscoting below cream-colored walls, hardwood floors and stretches of red upholstery in the booths; the affordable meals are whipped up in a semi-open kitchen, and the central lounge is home to a fully stocked bar, a rarity for the area.

Z Abe & Louie's *Steak*   26 | 22 | 25 | $61

Back Bay | 793 Boylston St. (Fairfield St.) | 617-536-6300 |
www.abeandlouies.com
"You'll swear you died and went to fat-cat heaven" at this "manly" Back Bay steakhouse where the "melt-on-your-tongue" beef served with "all the bells and whistles" is "worth every penny", especially if you "go on someone else's expense account"; while the "'in' crowd" downs "fantastic wines" at the bar, others enjoy the "elegant" (if "noisy") dining room where "top-notch", "seasoned" staffers help make any meal feel "celebratory."

Addis Red Sea *Ethiopian*   22 | 19 | 18 | $26

South End | 544 Tremont St. (Clarendon St.) | 617-426-8727 |
www.addisredsea.com
Porter Square | 1755 Massachusetts Ave. (Linnean St.) |
Cambridge | 617-441-8727 | www.addisredseacambridge.com
"Leave your fork at home" when heading to one of these Porter Square and South End "bargain" Ethiopians where "spongy" injera bread is used to sop up "delectable morsels" of "authentic" fare cooked with "amazing spices" and "served family-style"; the "traditional settings" come complete with "evocative decor", seats that can be "uncomfortable" (because you're practically "sitting on your haunches") and "friendly" though "somewhat slow service."

Aegean *Greek*   21 | 19 | 20 | $28

Watertown | 640 Arsenal St. (Coolidge Ave.) | 617-923-7771
Framingham | 257 Cochituate Rd. (bet. Caldor Rd. & Greenview St.) |
508-879-8424
www.aegeanrestaurants.com
The "homestyle", "well-seasoned" Greek fare "made with love" at this duo is offered in "generous portions" and at "wallet-friendly" prices, just like the "affordable" Hellenic wines; the Framingham location,

boasting a "great bar", is "more chichi", the one in Watertown is "spacious" yet "homey" and both employ "friendly" staffs.

Alchemist Lounge   *American* | 17 | 17 | 18 | $27 |
Jamaica Plain | 435 S. Huntington Ave. (Centre St.) | 617-477-5741 | www.alchemistlounge.com

"Funky" digs plus "swanky drinks" plus "live music at times" is this Jamaica Plain bar/eatery's formula for an "unpretentious" "neighborhood hangout"; but there are minuses in the equation: the New American "comfort food" with a "twist" is "inconsistent", just like service can be "iffy" (still, the "hipster" staffers are "generally happy to be there"); P.S. "sitting outside" for "brunch is nice."

Al Dente   *Italian* | 22 | 17 | 22 | $34 |
North End | 109 Salem St. (Cooper St.) | 617-523-0990 | www.aldenteboston.com

A "bountiful selection" of "always-pleasing", "homestyle red-sauce Italian" dished out in "huge portions" "at reasonable prices" makes this North Ender "a good value"; plus, the "nice peeps" who work here "treat you as family", making up for the "tight quarters."

All Star Sandwich Bar   *Sandwiches* | 23 | 15 | 18 | $16 |
Inman Square | 1245 Cambridge St. (Prospect St.) | Cambridge | 617-868-3065 | www.allstarsandwichbar.com

"Awesome" "concoctions", often filled with "unexpected ingredients" that "challenge the imagination", make this Inman Square storefront a "sandwich-lover's paradise"; the "friendly" staff can get "understandably overwhelmed" at peak times, but it's "worth the wait" in "simple", somewhat "squished" surroundings for such "ample" (albeit "overpriced") eats; P.S. "no wraps allowed", so carbo-phobes should skedaddle.

Alta Strada   *Italian* | 21 | 18 | 20 | $39 |
Wellesley | 92 Central St. (Weston Rd.) | 781-237-6100 | www.altastradarestaurant.com

Chef Michael Schlow brings a "hip vibe" and "stylish" Italian fare focusing on "imaginative" small plates to Wellesley via this eatery, but numbers-crunchers can't decide whether it's "overpriced" or "affordable for what you get"; however, everyone's in concert when it comes to the "bustling", "modern"-"minimalist" setting: it's "noisy beyond belief" ("glad there's takeout available" at the "gourmet market in the basement").

Amarin of Thailand   *Thai* | 22 | 19 | 20 | $27 |
Newton | 287 Centre St. (Jefferson St.) | 617-527-5255
Wellesley | 27 Grove St. (bet. Central & Spring Sts.) | 781-239-1350
www.amarinofthailand.com

There may be "no surprises" at these Newton and Wellesley Thais, but there's "never a dud" on the "wide"-ranging menu thanks in part to "high-quality" ingredients and "reasonable prices"; "pleasant", "casual atmospheres" that "invite conversation" and "efficient", "kid-friendly" service mean they're "much more than just take-out joints."

	FOOD	DECOR	SERVICE	COST

Amelia's Kitchen *Italian* | 22 | 16 | 18 | $27 |

Somerville | Teele Sq. | 1137 Broadway (Curtis St.) | 617-776-2800 | www.ameliaskitchen.com

"If you live in Somerville", it's "worth the trip to Teele Square" for this "understated", "family-owned" storefront – or so say regulars who find "value" in the selection of "reliable" pizzas, pastas and other Italian staples; on the other hand, some dollar-watchers deem it "pricey for the portions" and perhaps too "ordinary."

Amelia's Trattoria ⑤ *Italian* | 22 | 17 | 19 | $32 |

Kendall Square | 111 Harvard St. (Portland St.) | Cambridge | 617-868-7600 | www.ameliastrattoria.com

"MIT techies" and Kendall Square locals hit this "quaint" "hole-in-the-wall" for "killer pastas", "unique pizzas" and other Italian "goodies" ranging from "light to hearty"; the "cozy" space with "tiny aisles" gets "packed" at key times and service varies between "efficient" and "bored", but "decent prices" make it "fantastic", especially for lunch.

Amrheins *American* | 18 | 17 | 18 | $28 |

South Boston | 80 W. Broadway (A St.) | 617-268-6189 | www.amrheinsboston.com

"Commune with old South Boston" at this "casual" "standby" serving "hearty, flavorful", "reasonably priced" American grub amid "dark" yet "pleasant" environs; there's "outdoor dining in the summer", but "sports enthusiasts" prefer hunkering down around the "large", "beautiful" hand-carved bar and its "big TVs."

Anchovies ● *Italian* | 20 | 14 | 18 | $24 |

South End | 433 Columbus Ave. (bet. Braddock Park & Holyoke St.) | 617-266-5088

"Always busy" with "straights, gays" and South Enders "old and new", this "salty hideout" attracts with a "noisy bar" pouring "strong", "cheap drinks" and "affordable" fare from Italy brought to table until late into the night; highlights of the "flea-market" decor include "moose heads, road signs and voodoo masks", while service proves to be a bright spot when it's "friendly" (as opposed to "cranky").

Angela's Café *Mexican* | - | - | - | M |

East Boston | 131 Lexington St. (Brooks St.) | 617-567-4972 | www.angelascaferestaurant.com

Rich moles, prepared by a chef from Puebla, Mexico, are the signatures of this tiny East Boston cafe whose authenticity extends to the cute, festive red-and-yellow setting and Mexican music playing in the background; moderate prices abound, especially at breakfast, which is served seven days a week; N.B. beer and wine only, although a full-liquor license is expected.

Angelo's ⑤ *Italian* | ▽ 26 | 17 | 22 | $44 |

Stoneham | 237 Main St. (bet. Elm & William Sts.) | 781-279-9035 | www.angeloristorante.com

Even if there were more dining options in Stoneham, this "tiny" spot would still be a "treasure", as its "authentic" Italian fare is "cooked to order", "fantastic" and complemented by a "good wine selection"; prices on the "tablecloth side" are "commensurate with the quality of the food", those in the "pizzeria area" are more "reasonable", while the decor in both "leaves lots to be desired" (post-Survey renovations may help with that).

☑ Anna's Taqueria *Tex-Mex*   22 | 10 | 18 | $9

Beacon Hill | 242 Cambridge St. (Garden St.) | 617-227-8822
Cambridgeport | MIT Stratton Student Ctr. | 84 Massachusetts Ave.
(Vassar St.) | Cambridge | 617-324-2662 ●⇄
Porter Square | Porter Exchange Mall | 822 Somerville Ave. (Mass. Ave.) |
Cambridge | 617-661-8500 ⇄
Brookline | 1412 Beacon St. (Summit Ave.) | 617-739-7300 ⇄
Brookline | 446 Harvard St. (bet. Coolidge & Thorndike Sts.) |
617-277-7111 ⇄
Somerville | 236 Elm St. (bet. Bower Ave. & Chester St.) |
617-666-3900 ●⇄
www.annastaqueria.com

"Starving students" and other "deal"-seekers flock to these "no-frills" Tex-Mex taquerias where "lightning-fast" "burrito cowboys" whip up "gut-busting" "bundles of joy" along with "fresh, hot and filling" tacos and quesadillas at "easy-to-digest" prices; though doubters deem them "not worthy of the hype", everyone else admits to being "totally addicted."

Anthony's Pier 4 *Seafood*   18 | 18 | 18 | $49

Seaport District | 140 Northern Ave. (Pier 4) | 617-482-6262 |
www.pier4.com

Supporters say this Seaport District "stalwart" is a "reliable" "step back in time" for "quintessential" "New England seafood" ferried by "career waiters"; true, being a stop for "hordes" of tourists on "drive-by-eating excursions" may have caused it to have "lost its luster", but it's still "worth the wait and the bucks", "at least once", for the "dynamite popovers" and "spectacular views of the harbor."

Antico Forno *Italian*   23 | 17 | 19 | $32

North End | 93 Salem St. (bet. Cross & Parmenter Sts.) | 617-723-6733 |
www.anticofornoboston.com

"One of the better deals in the North End", this "Southern Italian stalwart" "amazes" with "hearty", "ultrafresh" "red-sauce basics", plus pizzas and pastas "finished in a brick oven", then served by "unfussy" staffers; while the "simply decorated" "space is tight", "noisy" and "crowded" with "a lot of families", "all is forgotten after that first bite of bubbling cheese."

Antonio's Cucina Italiana ☒ *Italian*   22 | 13 | 21 | $27

Beacon Hill | 288 Cambridge St. (bet. Anderson & Grove Sts.) |
617-367-3310 | www.antoniosofbeaconhill.com

"Bringing North End" "real-deal" Italian to Beacon Hill without the "dressed-up prices", this "mundane storefront" "surprises" with "more-than-generous portions" of "homestyle" eats that "never fail to deliver"; the "tight quarters" are "always packed" (hence "noisy"), but the "friendly" "staff makes it work" by being "prompt" too.

Apollo Grill & Sushi ◑ Ⓜ *Japanese/Korean* ▽ 17 | 13 | 15 | $33

Chinatown | 84-86 Harrison Ave. (Kneeland St.) | 617-423-3888
Though "not on the radar" when the sun shines, this open-till-4 AM Chinatownie becomes a "hidden gem" "after a long night of party-ing" "when you need sushi" or "average" Korean barbecue; the "de-cor could use a little touch-up", but that matters not to clubbers for whom "affordability" and "availability" trump ambiance.

Appetito *Italian* 19 | 17 | 19 | $36

Newton | 761 Beacon St. (Langley Rd.) | 617-244-9881
When "not aiming for fancy", Newton Center locals head to this "re-liable neighborhood restaurant" for "ample portions" of "solid" Italian that some suspect is "more sophisticated" than the norm and others lament is "a bit heavy at times"; "smallish" digs with "tables too close together" and "erratic service" don't prevent it from being "al-ways busy" – and "loud."

Ⓩ **Aquitaine** *French* 23 | 22 | 22 | $46

South End | 569 Tremont St. (Clarendon St.) | 617-424-8577 | www.aquitaineboston.com

Ⓩ **Aquitaine Dedham at Legacy Place** *French*

Dedham | Legacy Pl. | 950 Providence Hwy. (Elm St.) | 781-471-5212 | www.aquitainededham.com
"A little trip to France" is as easy as booking this South End bistro where steak frites are "the must" at dinner, mussels ("use bread to soak up every drop of sauce") reign at lunch and "out-of-this-world waffles" rule at brunch – and though everything's slightly "pricey", it's "fair" for the "high quality"; the elevated noise level "remains both exciting and annoying", but the "stylish" setting and "polite, prompt" service make it "impressive" "for business and romance" alike; N.B. the Dedham branch opened post-Survey.

Aquitaine Bis *French* 23 | 21 | 21 | $45

Chestnut Hill | Chestnut Hill Shopping Ctr. | 11 Boylston St. (Hammond St.) | 617-734-8400 | www.aquitainebis.com
At this "smaller version" of the South End original, the "biggest issue" is the "intrusive noise" – but that only adds to the "chic", "you're-in-France" vibe (indeed, "you totally forget" you're in a Chestnut Hill strip mall); likewise, the "traditional bistro" fare is "way above what you would expect" in the 'burbs, and though it's "not cheap", it's "worth it", especially factoring in "plenty of free parking."

Ariadne Ⓢ *American* 21 | 22 | 20 | $47

Newton | 344 Walnut St. (Washington Park) | 617-332-4653 | www.ariadnerestaurant.com
For "romance" and "sophistication", Newtonians know this New American offers "old-school luxe" by way of "plush", "comfortable booths", "tall ceilings, big curtains" and "soothing colors and fab-rics"; the "Mediterranean-influenced" menu is itself "wonderful", as are the "well-chosen wines", and while they're "pricey", more "ca-sual bites" are available at the "gorgeous bar" (where one is more likely to find less "glacial service").

Artú *Italian*
21 | 16 | 20 | $32

Beacon Hill | 89 Charles St. (Pinckney St.) | 617-227-9023
North End | 6 Prince St. (Hanover St.) | 617-742-4336
www.artuboston.com

"Simple", "moderately priced" "Italian standards of consistent quality" make this pair a "go-to" for "to-go" lunches and dinners; they're dine-in destinations too: if you hope to "impress a date", hit the "quaint", "spare" Beacon Hill "basement" where "exposed brick abounds", or if you're with "friends and family", the "long and narrow" North End locale has "more space" and a "wonderful bar."

Asana *American/Asian*
- | - | - | E

Back Bay | Mandarin Oriental | 776 Boylston St. (Fairfield St.) | 617-535-8888 | www.mandarinoriental.com/boston

Open for breakfast, lunch and dinner, the signature restaurant of the Back Bay's Mandarin Oriental hotel puts the spotlight on pricey New American and Asian fare; during the day, light floods in from floor-to-ceiling windows overlooking Boylston Street, while at night, dark bamboo floors, aquatic blues, earth tones and a glassed-in wine room create a sexy vibe.

Ashmont Grill *American*
22 | 19 | 22 | $31

Dorchester | 555 Talbot Ave. (Ashmont St.) | 617-825-4300 | www.ashmontgrill.com

At this "urban oasis" in Dorchester, the "high-quality" American "comfort food" leans toward the "gourmet", but the "modest prices", "lively", "casual" vibe and "diverse mix" of clientele ensure that it "remains a neighborhood joint"; the "dot-themed" interior boasts a "great bar" where "fun, attentive" 'tenders mix "amazing cocktails", which can also be enjoyed on the "beautiful", "private-and-cozy-feeling" patio.

Asmara *Eritrean/Ethiopian*
∇ 21 | 16 | 20 | $24

Central Square | 739 Massachusetts Ave. (bet. Pleasant & Prospect Sts.) | Cambridge | 617-864-7447 | www.asmararestaurantboston.com

For "delicious" fare that seems "unusual and familiar at the same time", adventurers head to this Central Square spot for "authentic", "spicy" Eritrean-Ethiopian cuisine that you "eat with your hands" (bring a new friend – it's "a real ice breaker"); despite the spare surroundings, it's "worth a visit" for such "warm service" and "affordable" prices.

Assaggio ● *Italian*
24 | 21 | 22 | $36

North End | 29 Prince St. (Hanover St.) | 617-227-7380 | www.assaggioboston.com

"Why spend a fortune" in the North End when "huge plates" of "reasonably priced" "old-country" Italian and "inventive specials" can be found here? – or so wonder this "dependable" eatery's backers who also appreciate that the "friendly" servers "stay out of your hair" when appropriate so you can enjoy the "warm, inviting", statue-filled ground level or the "romantic", "vine-covered" cellar in peace.

	FOOD	DECOR	SERVICE	COST

Atasca *Portuguese*   23 | 22 | 22 | $32

Kendall Square | 50 Hampshire St. (Webster Ave.) | Cambridge |
617-621-6991 | www.atasca.com

"Earthy", "flavorful" Portuguese dishes starring "jumping-fresh"
seafood are whipped up for "reasonable prices" at this "bustling"
Kendall Square site whose "vibrant atmosphere" and "friendly, efficient service" are "great for groups of friends" or "families"; it can
be "romantic" too, especially on the summertime patio where "it's
all about drinking *vinho verde*."

Athan's European   23 | 19 | 18 | $14
Bakery & Café *Mediterranean/Bakery*

Brighton | 407 Washington St. (bet. Leicester & Parsons Sts.) |
617-783-0313
Brookline | 1621 Beacon St. (Washington St.) | 617-734-7028
www.athansbakery.com

This "sun-filled" "sanctuary" in Brighton may serve "delicious"
Mediterranean meals, but the "decadent", "visually stunning" desserts ("buttery", "flaky pastries", "yummy gelato" and an
"enormous selection of baklava") are the "main" events here and at
the bakery-only Brookline original; some tally it's "a little overpriced" for what it is, but then again, if you're going to "blow your
diet and then some", wouldn't you rather go "gourmet"?

Atlantica Ⓜ *Seafood*   ▽ 15 | 24 | 17 | $40

Cohasset | 44 Border St. (Summer St.) | 781-383-0900 |
www.cohassetharborresort.com

"Lovely", "magical" "views of Cohasset Harbor" are "alone worth the
visit" (and what "you're paying for") at this "cavernous" seafooder;
"unfortunately, that's all" that wows, as the "food is just ok" – in fact,
you may prefer to "sit at the bar" with a glass of wine; N.B. from
October to May, it's open Wednesday–Saturday for dinner only.

Atlantic Fish Co. *Seafood*   23 | 21 | 22 | $45

Back Bay | 761 Boylston St. (bet. Exeter & Fairfield Sts.) | 617-267-4000 |
www.atlanticfishco.com

"Many tourists" and "after-workers" hit this Back Bay fish house for
"dependable", "high-quality" seafood "simply but tastily prepared";
it's "no bargain", but the "professional" – "if youthful" – staff, "warm
atmosphere" and "great people-watching" from the outdoor dining
area make it "worth what you pay."

Audubon Circle *Pub Food*   21 | 19 | 18 | $23

Kenmore Square | 838 Beacon St. (Arundel St.) | 617-421-1910 |
www.auduboncircle.us

"Somewhere between grad-school shindig and real life" lies this
"funky"/"classy" Kenmore Square venue with a "limited but choice
menu" of American pub grub ("heavenly burgers", "always popular
potstickers") whose "inexpensive" tabs belie their "high-end" preparations; "go here before a Red Sox game for little-to-no waits", "after
work" for the "extensive drinks list and many kinds of beer" or "in
the summer" for the "awesome patio."

	FOOD	DECOR	SERVICE	COST

Aura *American* `22` `19` `21` `$50`

Seaport District | Seaport Hotel | 1 Seaport Ln. (bet. Congress St. & Northern Ave.) | 617-385-4300 | www.aurarestaurant.com

"Hidden in the convention jungle" that is the Seaport District, this "respectable" all-day establishment makes its mark with "refined", sometimes "whimsical" (and pricey) New American preparations as well as a "terrific bar"; the "intimate" setting, however, proves to be "unmemorable" – after all, it's "still a hotel lobby"; N.B. a post-Survey renovation may outdate the Decor score.

Avenue One *American* `▽ 18` `17` `18` `$40`

Downtown Crossing | Hyatt Regency Boston | 1 Ave. de Lafayette (bet. Chauncy & Washington Sts.) | 617-422-5579 | www.avenueoneboston.com

Though the mid- to upper-priced New American fare at this all-day venue in Downtown Crossing's Hyatt Regency straddles the line between "outstanding" and "weak", it's still not a bad choice for pre-theater; however, for every ticket-holder who appreciates the "bright, open" feel of the spacious room, there's another who can't escape the feeling they're "eating in a hotel lobby", causing them to "quickly eat and leave."

Avila *Mediterranean* `24` `24` `23` `$51`

Theater District | 1 Charles St. S. (Boylston St.) | 617-267-4810 | www.avilarestaurant.com

The "colorful, high-style surroundings" and "upbeat atmosphere" of this "hip" "oasis" in the Theater District complement an "imaginative", "pricey" Mediterranean menu enhanced by specials that "are in fact special" and an "expansive wine list" ("the sommelier hits the mark every time"); what's more, the "professional", "attentive" servers "get you in and out if you let them know" you've got a show.

Bacco *Italian* `21` `19` `20` `$38`

North End | 107 Salem St. (Cooper St.) | 617-624-0454 | www.bacconorthend.com

"Watch the world go by" from an upstairs window or join the "chatty" crowd below at this North Ender offering "dependable" Italian fare whose value splits surveyors ("a little pricey" vs. "reasonable for the quality and quantity"); the "bustling" atmosphere is bolstered by "quite a large bar" where locals perch to "watch the game" with drinks poured by "friendly" 'tenders.

Back Eddy, The Ⓜ *Seafood* `22` `21` `20` `$40`

Westport | 1 Bridge Rd. (Rte. 88) | 508-636-6500 | www.thebackeddy.com

Dining on "fresh", "not-fancy" seafood alfresco or "having cocktails on the dock" at this Westport "pearl" is "what living in New England in summertime is all about" ("you pay for the view", but "watching the sunset over the water" alone is worth it); the service, while "friendly", can be "uneven", and though the somewhat "stark interior" can get "loud", what's a "party" without "buzz"?; N.B. closed January–March.

Baja Betty's Burritos *Mexican*
20 | 13 | 20 | $11

Brookline | 3 Harvard Sq. (Davis Ave.) | 617-277-8900 |
www.bajabettys.com

"Always fun" for "cheap, fast" eats, this Brookliner rolls out "Californian-style Mexican" fare like "big, sloppy and delicious" burritos stuffed with "fresh", relatively "healthy ingredients" by a "friendly staff"; it's just a small "storefront", but it's so "relaxed", not to mention such an "excellent value", you won't mind bringing the kids.

Bakers' Best Cafe *American*
22 | 13 | 16 | $19

Newton | 27 Lincoln St. (Walnut St.) | 617-332-4588 |
www.bakersbestcatering.com

"Soccer moms" and other "well-heeled suburbanites" crowd into this "much-loved" Newton New American bakery/cafe to "see and be seen" while "waiting in line forever" for "sensational" breakfasts, lunches, brunches and desserts ("on the pricey side for what" it is, but "worthwhile" nonetheless); those who can't cotton to the "chaotic" "cafeteria-style seating" opt for "wonderful takeout."

Bambara *American*
20 | 22 | 19 | $40

East Cambridge | Hotel Marlowe | 25 Edwin H. Land Blvd. (Rte. 28) |
Cambridge | 617-868-4444 | www.bambara-cambridge.com

"Modern" decor is "the most striking feature" of this "funky restaurant in a funky hotel" in Cambridge, but the "inventive" New American fare, "spiked with interesting colors and flavors", holds its own; it's especially "useful for business dining" (prix fixe lunches are "great deals", dinner tabs run toward the "high end"), while "after work", "exotic" cocktails "with unique spirits" render it a "great place to meet friends."

Bamboo *Thai*
23 | 18 | 20 | $23

Brighton | 1616 Commonwealth Ave. (Washington St.) | 617-734-8192 |
www.bamboothairestaurant.com

"Everything is fresh and dee-lish" at this Brighton Thai known for "cheap", "healthy dishes" and "lots of specials"; while surveyors split on whether the "small" environment is "warm and cozy" or "long in the tooth", the majority of folks finds the service "prompt" and "attentive", with bonus points bestowed on staffers who "recognize familiar faces."

☒ B&G Oysters *Seafood*
26 | 20 | 22 | $46

South End | 550 Tremont St. (Waltham St.) | 617-423-0550 |
www.bandgoysters.com

"Hipsters and yuppies slurp" up a "fabulous variety of freshly shucked oysters" and "deeply satisfying" (though "awfully pricey") "New England–style" seafood washed down with "smart wines" at this "Barbara Lynch hit" "tucked under a brownstone" in the South End; the "tight quarters" are "always crowded", but the "knowledgeable" service and "lively atmosphere" make it feel like you're "crammed into someplace special"; P.S. try for the "gorgeous garden out back" in warm weather.

	FOOD	DECOR	SERVICE	COST

Bangkok Bistro *Thai*
| 22 | 13 | 18 | $21 |

Brighton | 1952 Beacon St. (Chestnut Hill Ave.) | 617-739-7270
At this Brighton Thai, the "nondescript" dining room is "a little dark" and the service is only "somewhat attentive", but "the taste of the food outweighs any concerns", as do the "hefty portions" and "reasonable prices"; "great lunch specials" and "quick takeaway" are two more reasons it's "not a bad choice" when in "hectic" Cleveland Circle.

Bangkok Blue *Thai*
| 21 | 13 | 16 | $23 |

Back Bay | 651 Boylston St. (bet. Dartmouth & Exeter Sts.) | 617-266-1010 | www.bkkblueboston.com
Desk jockeys call this Back Bay Thai an "awesome lunch spot", but it's "just right when you need a good, quick" dinner too; it may appear to be a "dubious" "hole-in-the-wall", but the "flavorful" fare ("delicious noodles", "curries with just the right spice") and "value" prices "more than make up for" that – still, you might be more comfortable on the "patio in the summer."

Bangkok City *Thai*
| ▽ 20 | 20 | 20 | $29 |

Back Bay | 167 Massachusetts Ave. (Belvidere St.) | 617-266-8884 | www.bkkcityboston.com
"A nice meal before the symphony" can be had at this Thai "next to Berklee" in the Back Bay, where the "extensive menu" displays the "usual" suspects, "some different choices" and "reasonable costs"; a "pleasant atmosphere" and "pretty" decor (featuring Asian artifacts and an atrium) further make it "a good bet."

Baraka Cafe Ⓜ🍴 *African*
| 26 | 18 | 17 | $25 |

Central Square | 80½ Pearl St. (bet. Auburn & William Sts.) | Cambridge | 617-868-3951 | www.barakacafe.com
"Exquisite" North African cuisine is "prepared with love" at this "quaint", "family-run" "gem" in Central Square; it "doesn't take reservations" or credit cards and you'll have to "make do without alcohol" and with "borderline negligent service", but just come early, "bring the greenbacks" (you won't need many), order the "to-die-for rose-petal lemonade" and take the "time to enjoy" the "exotic" experience.

Barker Tavern Ⓜ *American*
| 23 | 24 | 24 | $48 |

Scituate | 21 Barker Rd. (bet. Brookline & Wellesley Rds.) | 781-545-6533 | www.thebarker.com
The "charming Colonial atmosphere" that permeates this "rambling", "lovely old house" overlooking Scituate Harbor fosters "romantic, cozy" meals consisting of "well-prepared and -presented" American dishes ("the swordfish is a must"); "gracious service" abounds, both in the "pricey" main room and the adjoining pub, which "serves a lighter menu" and "generous cocktails."

Barking Crab *Seafood*
| 16 | 16 | 14 | $28 |

Seaport District | 88 Sleeper St. (Northern Ave.) | 617-426-2722 | www.barkingcrab.com
"Rowdy young professionals" and "out-of-towners" "defy you not to have fun" at this "salt-of-the-earth" Seaport District "clam shack",

| | FOOD | DECOR | SERVICE | COST |

an open-air tent known for "long waits", "shared" picnic tables, "ok" seafood and "frosty brews"; while it may have "all the ambiance of a listing ship" and service is sometimes "invisible", "as long as expectations are not high", you too will have a "rocking" time.

BarLola ● *Spanish* | 18 | 21 | 18 | $34 |

Back Bay | 160 Commonwealth Ave. (Dartmouth St.) | 617-266-1122 | www.barlola.com

An "amazing" "sunken outdoor patio" ("beautifully appointed with flowering plants"), a "low-lit bar area that's cozy during the colder months" and a location "off-the-beaten" Back Bay path make this Spanish small-plates purveyor "seem like a secret" "romantic" "respite"; the "sangria is a must", and while many find the tapas "terrific", some connoisseurs deem them "too expensive" for being "lackluster."

Bar 10 ● *Mediterranean* | 17 | 21 | 19 | $36 |

Back Bay | Westin Copley Pl. | 10 Huntington Ave. (Dartmouth St.) | 617-424-7446 | www.westin.com

"Those who know" this "sophisticated" lounge "hidden" within the Westin Copley Place realize "it's all about being seen" "cuddling" "in high back booths" amid "dim lights" and a "gorgeous bouquet of brown" tones with "innovative", "expensive" martinis in hand; to facilitate the transition from "after work" to "late night", there's also a "limited menu" of "light" Mediterranean "munchies."

Basta Pasta *Italian* | 24 | 8 | 17 | $16 |

Central Square | 319 Western Ave. (Putnam Ave.) | Cambridge | 617-576-6672 | www.bastapastacambridge.com

It's "not much to look at", but this "no-atmosphere" "sub shop"-style Central Square "hole-in-the-wall" serves a "vast menu" of "delectable" Italian fare (featuring "homemade pastas") "cooked with impeccable skill" and offered for "amazingly low prices"; service is "decent at best" and "seating is limited", so many regulars "opt for takeout" and "savor every flavor" in the comfort of their own homes.

Bayside, The Ⓜ *Seafood* | - | - | - | I |

Westport | 1253 Horseneck Rd. (3rd. St.) | 508-636-5882 | www.thewestportbayside.com

You'll feel like you've stepped into Jimmy Buffett's backyard at this low-cost family-run seafooder a quick drive from Horseneck Beach in Westport; a prime spot to kick back seaside with a margarita while dining on the likes of fried clams, lobster rolls and homemade fruit pies, it offers ample outdoor seating under awnings in addition to a charming dining room.

Beacon Hill Bistro *French* | 22 | 21 | 20 | $42 |

Beacon Hill | Beacon Hill Hotel | 25 Charles St. (bet. Beacon & Chestnut Sts.) | 617-723-1133 | www.beaconhillhotel.com/bistro

With a "quaint", "long and narrow dining room", this "elegant yet unpretentious" French bistro in the Beacon Hill Hotel is a "charming", "date-night haunt", despite the fact that "service can vary"; though the selections and portions feel "limited" to some (and "a bit pricey" to others), they're "solid" and "satisfying", not to mention "delicious", to most.

Beacon Street Tavern *American*
20 | **20** | **20** | **$31**

Brookline | 1032 Beacon St. (bet. Carlton & St. Marys Sts.) | 617-713-2700 | www.beacon1032.com

The "same" "friendly vibe" as its Washington Square Tavern sibling permeates this Brookline offshoot serving "fairly easy on the wallet" American pub fare alongside "great beers", "amazing drinks" and an "extensive wine list" that's "better than you could hope for" at such a "bustling pub"; "on a nice day", "ask for a seat on the patio."

Beehive *American*
18 | **24** | **18** | **$36**

South End | Boston Center for the Arts | 541 Tremont St. (Clarendon St.) | 617-423-0069 | www.beehiveboston.com

When they're the recipients of "friendly, professional" service, South End "over-30s" buzz about this "artistic" restaurant/club's "sassy bordello vibe", "outstanding" live music, "amazing drinks" and "reasonably priced" New American menu that "changes regularly"; however, when the staff's "slow" and "too cool for you", they're "disappointed" they "waited" on the "ridiculous line" to get in.

Bella Luna Restaurant & Milky Way Lounge *Italian*
- | **-** | **-** | **M**

Jamaica Plain | The Brewery | 284 Amory St. (Boylston St.) | 617-524-6060 | www.milkywayjp.com

This Jamaica Plain icon has relocated to the Sam Adams brewery complex, where its midpriced Italian menu is served in a sexy, dimly lit setting with local artwork hanging on lipstick red walls; naturally, beer is the drink of choice at the large bar, and the adjacent Milky Way Lounge offers entertainment – running the gamut from local bands to karaoke to trivia – seven nights a week.

Bella's *Italian*
▽ **19** | **16** | **22** | **$39**

Rockland | 933 Hingham St. (Commerce Rd.) | 781-871-5789 | www.bellasrestaurant.com

Rocklanders "always get" what they "expect" at this "comfy" Italian: a "great" staff vending "fantastic" "make-your-own" grilled pizzas and a "wide variety" of "traditional" "red-sauce" dishes at "not-over-the-top" prices; because it "can be a mob scene" - especially in the "fun lounge" - it "lacks" as a "first-date choice", but for vino and Keno with a "big local crowd", it's on the ball.

Bernard's *Chinese*
24 | **15** | **21** | **$35**

Chestnut Hill | The Mall at Chestnut Hill | 199 Boylston St. (Hammond Pond Pkwy.) | 617-969-3388

"Lots of imagination" is evident in the "fresh, flavorful", "upscale Chinese" cuisine served at this "delightful surprise" with a "solicitous" staff that "fawns" over everyone ("regulars get the royal treatment"); the "wine list is mountains above average" too, making it easier to "get over" that the "not-pretty" digs - with a "strange location" in The Mall at Chestnut Hill - get "crowded and noisy" with "grandparents, youngsters and large shopping bags."

	FOOD	DECOR	SERVICE	COST

Bertucci's *Italian*   17 | 14 | 16 | $22

Faneuil Hall | Faneuil Hall Mktpl. | 22 Merchants Row (State St.) | 617-227-7889

Kenmore Square | 533 Commonwealth Ave. (Brookline Ave.) | 617-236-1030

Central Square | 799 Main St. (bet. Cherry & Windsor Sts.) | Cambridge | 617-661-8356

Harvard Square | 21 Brattle St. (Mt. Auburn St.) | Cambridge | 617-864-4748

Huron Village | 5 Cambridgepark Dr. (Alewife Brook Pkwy.) | Cambridge | 617-876-2200

Braintree | 412 Franklin St. (West St.) | 781-849-3066

Brookline | 4 Brookline Pl. (Washington St.) | 617-731-2300

Chestnut Hill | Atrium Mall | 300 Boylston St. (Florence St.) | 617-965-0022

Newton | 275 Centre St. (Pearl St.) | 617-244-4900

Framingham | 150 Worcester Rd. (Caldor Rd.) | 508-879-9161

www.bertuccis.com

Additional locations throughout the Boston area

"For a fancy night out", this "ubiquitous chain" is "not the place" – however, it "hits the spot" for "solid brick-oven pizza" "on the fly", "especially for families" in need of "reasonable prices" but "not top-notch service"; Italian aficionados deem the other entrees merely "ok", but even they won't turn down the "highly addictive", "piping-hot rolls" "served pre-meal."

Betty's Wok &   19 | 16 | 18 | $25
Noodle Diner *Asian/Nuevo Latino*

MFA | 250 Huntington Ave. (Mass. Ave.) | 617-424-1950 | www.bettyswokandnoodle.com

With a locale "convenient" to the MFA, this Asian–Nuevo Latino "'50s-style" diner with a "perky" staff and "loud oldies" provides a "funky" prelude to "the theater or the symphony"; "control"-freaks appreciate that you get to "customize your meal" by "choosing the meat, sauce" and vegetables to mix with your "oodles of noodles", even though it can seem "a little overpriced" for "doing the chef's work."

B. Good *Health Food*   19 | 13 | 19 | $11

Back Bay | 131 Dartmouth St. (bet. Columbus Ave. & Stuart St.) | 617-424-5252

Back Bay | 272 Newbury St. (bet. Fairfield & Gloucester Sts.) | 617-236-0440

Harvard Square | 24 Dunster St. (bet. Mass. Ave. & Mt. Auburn St.) | Cambridge | 617-354-6500

Brookline | 455 Harvard St. (bet. Columbia St. & Thorndike St.) | 617-232-4800

Dedham | Legacy Pl. | 950 Providence Hwy. (Elm St.) | 781-251-0222

www.bgood.com

"Be good to your waistband and your wallet" at this "unpretentious", "healthy alternative" to other fast-food joints doling out "a variety of low-calorie, low-fat" fare like "fresh burgers and sandwiches", "air-baked fries" and "surprisingly good milkshakes" that "cost a little more" than the standard, but are still pretty "cheap"; those who've sampled the sporadic menu "miss", however, say it buoys "the cliché that healthy food doesn't taste good."

Bhindi Bazaar Indian Cafe *Indian*   22 | 13 | 18 | $21

Back Bay | 95 Massachusetts Ave. (bet. Commonwealth Ave. & Newbury St.) | 617-450-0660 | www.bhindibazaar.com

Subcontinental connoisseurs say this Back Bay Indian's "bountiful portions" of "out-of-the-ordinary" cuisine from "different corners of the country" fall "above the mark", thanks in part to "helpful recommendations" from the "friendly staff"; even those who "have yet to experience the 'wow' factor" ("yawn"-inducing environs don't help) admit it's "consistent", not to mention "cheap."

Bia Bistro Ⓜ *French/Italian*   ▽ 24 | 17 | 20 | $41

Cohasset | 35 S. Main St. (Elm St.) | 781-383-0464 | www.biabistro.com

Chef Brian Houlihan is "keen on pleasing" at this "cozy, rustic" Cohasset "gem", and he succeeds with "more than adequate" portions of "well-prepared" Italian–Southern French dishes complemented by a "varied wine list" and "thoughtful service"; it continues to "fly under the radar", but locals "would like to keep it that way", even though it can bia bit "pricey" (it's "worth it").

🆕 Big Papi's Grille *American*   - | - | - | M

Framingham | Worcester Rd./30 Rte. 9 E. (Shoppers World Dr.) | 508-620-9990 | www.bigpapisgrille.com

Too-cool-for-school Red Sox slugger David 'Big Papi' Ortiz is a partner at this family-friendly New American in Framingham, where the dinner-only menu includes nods to his Dominican roots such as a chimichurri burger; the casual, clubby environs offer several dining areas (including a semi-private room, Table 34, named for Big Papi's uniform number), a handsome, long bar with TVs and red banquettes throughout.

Billy Tse *Asian*   20 | 14 | 20 | $27

Revere | 441 Revere St. (Pierce St.) | 781-286-2882 | www.billytse-revere.com ◗

North End | 240 Commercial St. (Atlantic Ave.) | 617-227-9990 | www.billytserestaurant.com

If you're in the North End and "not in the mood" for pasta, this Asian "diamond in the Italian rough" (with a Revere sibling) offers "yummy" if "Americanized" Chinese, Thai and sushi at "decent prices"; the "kitschy decor" "could be improved", but the more "fun drinks" you have from the "hopping bar", the less you'll care; P.S. it's "dependable for takeout" too.

Biltmore Bar & Grille, The *American*   18 | 15 | 18 | $30

Newton | 1205 Chestnut St. (Oak St.) | 617-527-2550 | www.thebiltmoregrill.com

"With an eye toward the upscale", this nonetheless "casual" watering hole/grill brings "slightly fancy", "reliable and reasonable" American fare to the "outer reaches of Newton"; with pressed-tin ceilings, the decor leans toward the "retro", which gives patrons something to look at if it's "too loud" to converse and it "takes forever to get served"; N.B. the dinner menu was updated and the mahogany bar and dining area were expanded post-Survey, possibly outdating the Food and Decor scores.

Bina Osteria & Alimentari *Italian* ‎ - | - | - | M

Downtown Crossing | 571-581 Washington St. (Avery St.) | 617-956-0888 | www.binaboston.com

A frosted glass wall separates the dual concepts at this midpriced Italian in Downtown Crossing from the team behind Bin 26 and Lala Rokh; one side is a full-service restaurant with mother-of-pearl-specked terrazzo floors, a bar and a communal table, and the other is an upscale gourmet food-and-wine shop (the alimentari), which serves breakfast fare, panini and homemade gelato for takeout.

Bin 26 Enoteca *Italian* ‎ 21 | 22 | 21 | $42

Beacon Hill | 26 Charles St. (Beacon St.) | 617-723-5939 | www.bin26.com

"Tucked away" on Beacon Hill, this "lively" "wine lover's delight" whose decor "uses corks and bottles" in "creative" ways (don't forget to "look up" in the "cool bathrooms") is known for a "dizzying array" of vino complemented by "sophisticated" Italian nibbles; the "small servings" are "steeply priced" for random pairings, so be sure to consult the "informative" (if slightly "arrogant") staff first.

Birch Street Bistro *American* ‎ 19 | 20 | 19 | $34

Roslindale | 14 Birch St. (bet. Belgrade Ave. & Corinth St.) | 617-323-2184 | www.birchstbistro.com

An "anchor in the Roslindale eating scene", this "friendly neighborhood bistro" proffers "reasonably priced" American fare ("some inventive dishes, some comfort food"), and though it occasionally "varies" in execution, "most everything comes out fine"; the "warm", "pleasant" space – all "dark" tones and exposed brick – benefits from a "cool bar", a patio and "nice music on Thursdays."

Bison County Bar and Grill ❶ *BBQ* ‎ 18 | 12 | 16 | $24

Waltham | 275 Moody St. (Crescent St.) | 781-642-9720 | www.bisoncounty.com

"Dependable", "reasonably priced" ribs, brisket, pulled pork and other "smoked stuff", plus "unique and tasty bison burgers", fuel "fun times" at this Waltham joint with a "decent selection of draft beers" and an appropriately "no-fuss atmosphere"; BBQ buffs, however, warn "don't get buffaloed" into thinking the eats are authentic.

NEW Bistro Chi 🏖️Ⓜ️ *Chinese* ‎ - | - | - | M

Quincy | 37 Cottage Ave. (bet. Chestnut St. & Dennis Ryan Pkwy.) | 617-773-3000 | www.bistrochi.com

At this Chinese arrival in Quincy, authentic, midpriced cuisine is proffered in a subdued, minimalist setting outfitted with bamboo, cream-colored tables and chairs, fabric-covered banquettes and softly glowing hanging lamps; there's also a small bar serving everything from beer to Scorpion Bowls, plus an adjacent lounge called Kama.

	FOOD	DECOR	SERVICE	COST

NEW **Bistro du Midi** M *French* | – | – | – | M |

Back Bay | 272 Boylston St. (bet. Arlington St. & Hadassah Way) | 617-426-7878 | www.bistrodumidi.com

This airy, rustic Back Bay French bistro serves a classic, mid-priced menu of small plates, entrees and housemade pâtés on two levels; downstairs boasts exposed ceiling beams, a zinc bar and floor-to-ceiling windows that open onto outdoor seating (and views of the Boston Public Garden), while upstairs, past the glass-enclosed wine cellar, there's a semi-open kitchen and a dining room with a cozy fireplace.

☑ **Bistro 5** ⑤M *Italian* | 27 | 24 | 26 | $50 |

West Medford | 5 Playstead Rd. (High St.) | 781-395-7464 | www.bistro5.com

An "unprepossessing exterior" hides this West Medford "jewel" where chef-owner Vittorio Ettore takes "great pride" in his "consistently wonderful" "gourmet" Northern Italian dishes bolstered by "local" ingredients with "explosive" flavors (he also "frequents" the "elegant" dining room to "chat" with his guests); adding to the "amazing" – and yes, "pricey" – experience are "fabulous" staffers who "offer great pairing" ideas from the "well-chosen wine list."

Bistro 712 ⑤M *French* | ▽ 24 | 20 | 22 | $42 |

Norwood | Norwood Ctr. | 712 Washington St. (Day St.) | 781-769-7712 | www.bistro712.com

The "sure hand" in this Norwood kitchen produces "sophisticated", frequently "changing" French cuisine, which in turn is ferried by "great" staffers to the "intimate" converted-storefront dining room decked out in burgundy walls and cream accents; indeed, not least of all because it's "unique" for the 'burbs (and not even that expensive), it remains "a keeper."

Black Cow Tap & Grill *Pub Food* | 19 | 20 | 18 | $38 |

South Hamilton | 16 Bay Rd. (bet. Linden St. & Railroad Ave.) | 978-468-1166
Newburyport | 54R Merrimac St. (Green St.) | 978-499-8811
www.blackcowrestaurants.com

"Warm and welcoming atmospheres" draw "convivial" crowds of hops-hounds to these "hopping" pubs serving "solid" American bar grub at "appropriate prices"; the "lively bar scenes" can make for "noisy" meals, however they could be quieter if you "opt for the deck" "overlooking the harbor" in Newburyport or "get a booth" in South Hamilton.

Black Sheep Restaurant *American* | ▽ 21 | 20 | 15 | $27 |

Kendall Square | Kendall Hotel | 350 Main St. (Anne St.) | Cambridge | 617-577-1300 | www.kendallhotel.com

"Charming" and downright "adorable", this red Kendall Hotel restaurant filled with firefighter memorabilia proffers a "varied and appealing" menu of "most satisfactory" American classics from breakfast to dinner; "service is erratic", but the prices please every time.

	FOOD	DECOR	SERVICE	COST

Blarney Stone, The *Pub Food*   16 14 15 $23
Dorchester | 1505 Dorchester Ave. (Park St.) | 617-436-8223 | www.blarneystoneboston.com

"Reinvented" from an "old-time pub" to a "somewhat hip after-work spot", this Dorchester "hangout" serves "basic" American grub to an "eclectic crowd" – and if the clientele brands the fare "nondescript", well, "you get what you pay for"; the lunch menu is merely "adequate" too, but "the patio is a bonus."

Blu *American*   21 21 20 $46
Theater District | Millennium Complex | 4 Avery St. (bet. Tremont & Washington Sts.) | 617-375-8550 | www.blurestaurant.com

In "a nondescript gym" lies this "chic", "unusual" space with "great views" of the Theater District, where folks both "dressed up for the night and tumbling in after a workout" come for the "smallish", "pricey" menu of "healthy-tasting" American fare with "occasional flashes of inspiration"; some servers are "warm", others are "cold", but word is the bartenders – who mix "interesting drinks" – are "fun."

Blue Fin *Japanese*   22 16 19 $33
Porter Square | Porter Exchange Mall | 1815 Massachusetts Ave. (Roseland St.) | Cambridge | 617-497-8022
Middleton | 260 S. Main St. (Lonergan Rd.) | 978-750-1411 | www.bluefin-restaurant.com

"Crowds of all kinds" rush these "simple" Middleton and Porter Square "Japanese food houses" for "fantastic quality" sushi and "authentic" "cooked items" that most feel are "reasonably priced" (lunch offers some real "deals"); even when others are "waiting" for your table, you won't "feel rushed" by the "courteous servers" – you may, however, grow tired of the "below-par decor."

☑ Blue Ginger *Asian*   26 23 25 $58
Wellesley | 583 Washington St. (Church St.) | 781-283-5790 | www.ming.com

"As good as the hype" suggests, this "Wellesley wonder" stars Ming Tsai's "palate-popping" "East-meets-West" Asian-fusion "miracles" – and the best part is that the "gifted" "star chef" is "actually there" ("what a novelty!"), further rendering it "well worth" the "expensive" tabs; the "calming blue" environs feature a "phenomenal" bar area where folks can "drop in for a light meal without having made a reservation a month in advance."

Blue on Highland *American*   17 20 19 $34
Needham | 882 Highland Ave. (West St.) | 781-444-7001 | www.blueonhighland.com

This "somewhat trendy" Needham New American features "quiet booths" in the "mod" dining room and an "upbeat atmosphere" at the bar; the "fun drinks list" is suitable for "girls' night out" or "watching the Sox", and while some find the fare "respectable", for others, the "uneven" menu "does not measure up", no matter how "relatively low priced" it is.

	FOOD	DECOR	SERVICE	COST

Blue Ribbon BBQ *BBQ*

25 | 12 | 19 | $17

Arlington | 908 Massachusetts Ave. (Highland Ave.) |
781-648-7427
Newton | 1375 Washington St. (Elm St.) | 617-332-2583
www.blueribbonbbq.com

"A rare find north of the Mason-Dixon Line", the "heaping platters"
of "lip-smacking", "fork-tender", "slow-cooked" BBQ at this "rowdy"
pair in Arlington and Newton are "hands-down" "wow-wow-wow",
as are the "fantastic sauces" and "out-of-this-world sides" dished
out by "friendly" staffers; the "dinerlike settings" are "elbow-to-
elbow", so "program the number into your speed dial" to get takeout
"lickety-split quick" (and "for not a lot of money").

Blue Room, The *Eclectic*

25 | 21 | 22 | $42

Kendall Square | One Kendall Square Complex | 1 Kendall Sq.
(Hampshire St.) | Cambridge | 617-494-9034 | www.theblueroom.net
"Feel in-the-know for having found" this "almost hidden"
Kendall Square purveyor of "truly Eclectic" fare featuring "complex", "inventive", "delicious oddities" "based on what's fresh";
"warm and pleasant decor and staff" facilitate the "come as you are"
vibe, and if it's a smidge "pricey", the "fabulous" Sunday brunch buffet "won't break the bank" (while converting even "the most
die-hard breakfast-skipper").

Bluestone Bistro ❶ *Pizza*

∇ 17 | 11 | 17 | $18

Brighton | 1799 Commonwealth Ave. (Chiswick Rd.) | 617-254-8309 |
www.bluestonebistro.com
"It's your typical college pizza and sub shop", "nothing more" admit
"students" who deal with this Brighton joint's "so-so" chow because
its requires from them so few bucks; those who only "get takeout" in
the winter sometimes try the patio in summer "since there are very
few in the area."

Blue22 Bar & Grille *American/Asian*

∇ 19 | 13 | 20 | $24

Quincy | 1237 Hancock St. (Saville Ave.) | 617-774-1200 |
www.blue22-barandgrille.com
Sports fans "watch games" on "big-screen TVs", "trendy" "singles"
"have a blast" at karaoke and trivia nights and everyone downs
"well-priced drinks" sopped up with a "fun mix" of "American bar
food" and "Asian snacks" at this "interesting place in Downtown
Quincy"; those perturbed that their "conversation was strained" due
to all the activity scoff it's "still trying to settle on its identity", but
"variety"-seekers dig the "unique" approach.

🆕 Bobby's 🚭Ⓜ *American*

- | - | - | M

Wellesley Hills | 11 Washington St. (River St.) | 781-235-2345 |
www.bobbysgrille.com
American through and through, this Wellesley Hills arrival offers a
midpriced menu of traditional fare in a spacious setting that continues the patriotic theme with paintings of a bald eagle and the U.S.
flag; the comfy, high-ceilinged space also includes a sleek wooden
bar with a few high-top tables nearby.

	FOOD	DECOR	SERVICE	COST

Boca Grande *Tex-Mex* | 19 | 10 | 14 | $10 |

Kenmore Square | 642 Beacon St. (Commonwealth Ave.) | 617-437-9700
East Cambridge | 149 First St. (Bent St.) | Cambridge | 617-354-5550 ⑤
Porter Square | 1728 Massachusetts Ave. (Linnaean St.) | Cambridge | 617-354-7400
Brookline | 1294 Beacon St. (bet. Harvard & Pleasant Sts.) | 617-739-3900
www.bocagranderestaurant.com

"When you need a fix" of Tex-Mex, this quartet "won't knock your socks off", but will provide "well-prepared" "basics" from "overstuffed burritos and quesadillas" to "real-deal" tamales and tacos; there's "no decor", "limited seating" and "typical counter service" ("some days on, some days lacking"), but it's "fast and cheap", which is just one reason why "there's always a line."

Bokx 109 American Prime *Steak* | ▽ 23 | 27 | 21 | $60 |

Newton Lower Falls | Hotel Indigo | 399 Grove St. (Rte. 128) | 617-454-3399 | www.bokx109.com

"You'd never guess" to find such a "dynamic hot spot" in Newton Lower Falls, but that's exactly where the "glam" Hotel Indigo has constructed this modern/retro, brown-and-red steakhouse serving "large portions of grilled meats" alongside "creative" entrees and "innovative sides"; there are reports of "spotty" service ("kinks" that will surely be "ironed out"), but most deem it a "treat on every level" – "ridiculously expensive" tabs notwithstanding.

Boloco *Eclectic* | 18 | 11 | 16 | $9 |

Back Bay | 137 Massachusetts Ave. (Boylston St.) | 617-369-9087
Back Bay | 247 Newbury St. (bet. Fairfield & Gloucester Sts.) | 617-262-2200
Downtown Crossing | 27 School St. (Province St.) | 617-778-6750
Fenway | 283 Longwood Ave. (Blackfan Circle) | 617-232-2166
Fenway | Marino Ctr. | 359-369 Huntington Ave. (bet. Forsyth St. & Opera Pl.) | 617-536-6814
Financial District | 133 Federal St. (Matthews St.) | 617-357-9727 ⑤
Financial District | 50 Congress St. (bet. Exchange Pl. & Hawes St.) | 617-357-9013 ⑤
Theater District | 2 Park Plaza (bet. Boylston & Charles Sts.) | 617-778-6772
Harvard Square | 71 Mt. Auburn St. (Holyoke St.) | Cambridge | 617-354-5838
Medford | Tufts University | 340 Boston Ave. (bet. Bellevue & Winthrop Sts.) | 339-674-9740
www.boloco.com
Additional locations throughout the Boston area

"Smart" bo-locals "who like to eat light" patronize this counter-serve chain for "customizable", "grab-and-go" "Mexican-esque" Eclectic wraps and "addictive smoothies" made from "fresh", "healthy" ingredients; "inconsistency" in both preparation and service from store to store makes for "good and bad days", but it "won't hurt your wallet."

	FOOD	DECOR	SERVICE	COST

Bombay Club *Indian*

20 | 17 | 18 | $28

Faneuil Hall | Faneuil Hall Mktpl. | 1 Faneuil Hall Mktpl.
(bet. N. Market & S. Market Sts.) | 617-723-6001 ✏
South End | 1415 Washington St. (bet. Pelham & Union Park) |
617-247-2500
www.bombayclub.com
Post-Survey, this supplier of "standard but well-prepared Indian"
fare packed up its antique Hindu statues and moved from Harvard
Square into South End digs sporting hardwood floors, dim red lighting,
a long bar and gold-brushed walls (not reflected in the Decor score);
while a few find it "a little pricey" for the genre, most calculate it "a
good value", especially the "bottomless lunch special", and fans
also "enjoy eating" at the "pleasant" Faneuil Hall take-out outpost.

Bon Caldo *Italian*

22 | 20 | 20 | $38

Norwood | 1381 Providence Tpke. (Sumner St.) | 781-255-5800 |
www.boncaldo.com
"Convenient" for Norwood Italian-cravers looking to save themselves "a trip to the North End", this midpriced "red-sauce" site plies
"authentic", "well-prepared" "standards" supplemented by "enough
extras" so one "won't get bored"; it's all conveyed by "friendly" servers, who also proffer a "nice selection of wines", both in the "comfortable" main room and in the "beautiful bar area."

Bond *Eclectic*

- | - | - | M

Financial District | Langham Boston | 250 Franklin St. (Oliver St.) |
617-451-1900 | www.boston.langhamhotels.com
Gourmands looking for an upscale yet moderately priced escape in
the Financial District find it at this Eclectic inside the luxurious
Langham hotel, where a bygone era is evoked by original crystal
chandeliers hanging from vaulted ceilings and a beautiful rosewood
bar; casual lunch fare, small plates at dinner and a mezzanine
lounge bring this classy act into the 21st century.

Bon Savor *French/South American*

▽ 20 | 19 | 19 | $26

Jamaica Plain | 605 Centre St. (Pond St.) | 617-971-0000 |
www.bonsavor.com
The "welcoming owners" and "capable staff" of this "little" Jamaica
Plain bistro provide "delectable", "reasonably priced" French–South
American breakfasts and lunches in "attractive", "sunny" environs,
which at dinnertime take on a "romantic", "candlelit" glow (the menu
was reconcieved post-Survey, outdating the Food score); "wonderful brunches" make it "usually crowded on weekend mornings."

Border Cafe ● *Cajun/Tex-Mex*

19 | 17 | 18 | $21

Harvard Square | 32 Church St. (Palmer St.) | Cambridge |
617-864-6100
Saugus | 356 Broadway (Lynn Fells Pkwy.) | 781-233-5308
Burlington | 128 Middlesex Tpke. (3rd Ave.) | 781-505-2500
www.bordercafe.com
"Never-ending baskets of chips", "strong", "icy margaritas" and
"quick", "reliable" Tex-Mex–Cajun "without the frills" leave "hordes

of students" "satisfied" "for cheap" at these "happy zoos" in Burlington and Harvard Square; on the other hand, "every night is family night" at the Saugus iteration, and even though it moved to new digs post-Survey, you should still "be prepared" for the same "grueling seating process" and "tacky decor" (just like the others).

Boston Beer Works ● *Pub Food* | 18 | 16 | 17 | $23 |

Fenway | 61 Brookline Ave. (Lansdowne St.) | 617-536-2337
West End | 112 Canal St. (Causeway St.) | 617-896-2337

Salem Beer Works *Pub Food*

Salem | 278 Derby St. (bet. Congress & Lafayette Sts.) | 978-745-2337
www.beerworks.net

Inexpensive American pub grub (mostly "predictable", occasionally "surprising", always "filling") soaks up the "big selection" of beers made in-house ("try a sampler" of the seasonal ales) at this pack of microbreweries; "with all the TVs", they're "always filled to capacity" with "lively" "Sox fans", and if that can lead to "inattentive" staffers, at least they "make great recommendations" when you catch them.

NEW Boston Burger Company *Burgers*

Somerville | 37 Davis Sq. (College Ave.) | 617-440-7361 | www.bostonburgerco.com

Whether you order the Jumbo (double-stacked), the Texan (with chili) or build your own burger, there's a plethora of options at this quick-serve joint in Somerville's Davis Square, which also offers salads, boneless chicken wings and other comfort foods; the small, simple setting is adorned with Boston skyline prints, and there's patio seating in warm weather.

Boston Sail Loft *Seafood* | 15 | 14 | 16 | $25 |

Waterfront | 80 Atlantic Ave. (Commerical Wharf) | 617-227-7280
Forever to be "described as a shack", this "nautical"-themed "old standby" on the Waterfront may serve "decent enough" seafood, but the kitchen is no match for the bar: "friendly 'tenders" pouring "reasonably priced" beers and cocktails make it "popular in the evenings" among "recent grads" and "young professionals" who try to "get a seat by the window and watch the boats go by" when not partaking in the "singles scene."

Bottega Fiorentina *Italian* | 24 | 14 | 18 | $16 |

Back Bay | 264 Newbury St. (bet. Fairfield & Gloucester Sts.) | 617-266-0707 | www.botteganewbury.com
Brookline | 313B Harvard St. (Babcock St.) | 617-232-2661 | www.bottegabrookline.com

"True neighborhood gems", these Italian delis augment "hearty sandwiches" with "unforgettable" pastas and "amazing sauces", all at "bargain basement prices"; "seating is limited" at the "unassuming", counter-serve Brookline original ("takeout is your best option"), while the Back Bay offshoot has true "sit-down service" and a patio overlooking always-hopping Newbury Street.

	FOOD	DECOR	SERVICE	COST

Bouchée *French*

21 | 22 | 21 | $42

Back Bay | 159 Newbury St. (bet. Exeter & Dartmouth Sts.) |
617-450-4343 | www.boucheebrasserie.com

Francophiles applaud the "authentic brasserie" fare served at this
"lively" Back Bay spot, just as grape groupies toast the "extensive
wine menu" – and though "you pay for it", it's "worth" the cost;
further making it "feel like a Parisian cafe" is a "stylish" interior
("dark woods, nice lighting"), while the "lovely" patio with its "prime
people-watching", not to mention "skilled, friendly" service, is
pure Newbury Street.

Brasserie Jo *French*

20 | 20 | 20 | $42

Back Bay | Colonnade Hotel | 120 Huntington Ave. (W. Newton St.) |
617-425-3240 | www.brasseriejoboston.com

With its "casually elegant", "art deco-ish" setting, "uniformed staff"
and "classic French cuisine" – "well executed", from the "succulent
mussels" to the "heavenly profiteroles" – this Back Bay brasserie
"takes you straight to Paris"; true, you'll find "no surprises" (except
perhaps that "it's not cheap"), but it manages "reliability" while "filling the dining void in the Symphony Hall vicinity."

Bravo *Eclectic*

21 | 25 | 21 | $47

MFA | Museum of Fine Arts | 465 Huntington Ave. (bet. Forsyth Way &
Museum Rd.) | 617-369-3474 | www.mfa.org

"The perfect ending to a visit to a great art museum", this Museum
of Fine Arts "class act" offers Eclectic lunches that "often echo" special exhibits, all "beautifully presented" by an "attentive staff";
"overlooking the courtyard", the "sophisticated", "modern" dining
room is usually filled with "museum members taking advantage of
their discount" (it's "pricey" otherwise); N.B. dinner served
Wednesday–Friday only.

Brenden Crocker's
Wild Horse Cafe *American*

▽ 25 | 22 | 23 | $37

Beverly | 392 Cabot St. (Colon St.) | 978-922-6868 |
www.wildhorsecafe.com

Beverly locals always "have a good time" "relaxing" on the "comfy
chairs and sofas" while digging into "fun, interesting", midpriced
New American dishes – recommended by "knowledgeable" staffers
who ferry them from the open kitchen – at this cozy, folksy venue
with a bar that's an "atmospheric" spot for "excellent drinks."

Bricco ● *Italian*

25 | 21 | 21 | $51

North End | 241 Hanover St. (bet. Cross & Richmond Sts.) | 617-248-6800 |
www.bricco.com

"Outrageous views" of the North End, "especially in summer" when
the windows are open, and often "rowdy" revelers "packed in like
sardines" cause almost as big of a "commotion" as the "amazing",
"artistically presented" "modern Italian" fare whipped up at this
"tiny place"; "wonderful wines" and generally "attentive" service are
two more reasons why fans "go back and go back again", despite the
fact that it's "an expensive evening."

	FOOD	DECOR	SERVICE	COST

Bridgeman's *Italian*
26 | 23 | 23 | $44

Hull | 145 Nantasket Ave. (bet. Berkley Rd. & Park Ave.) | 781-925-6336 | www.bridgemansrestaurant.com

Head to Hull to "dine by the sea" at this "sophisticated yet unpretentious" "gem" where the service is "attentive" and the reasonably priced Northern Italian cuisine features "out-of-site seafood" and "awesome specials"; though it's so "noisy" you should "bring your earplugs", a "stroll along the ocean" makes for a soothing ending to a "delicious" experience.

Brighton Beer Garden ● *Pub Food*
- | - | - | M

Brighton | 386 Market St. (Washington St.) | 617-562-6000 | www.brightonbeergarden.com

This clubhouse-style jock bar in Brighton is a sports fan's Shangri-la, with 40 HDTVs and a large menu that goes beyond pub grub while staying easy on the wallet.

☑ Bristol Lounge, The *American*
24 | 26 | 26 | $53

Back Bay | Four Seasons Hotel | 200 Boylston St. (Charles St.) | 617-351-2053 | www.fourseasons.com/boston

"Money can buy happiness!" exclaim guests of the Back Bay's Four Seasons, who've shelled out for "informal dining at its regal best" in its "beautifully appointed", "sedate" lounge; whether for a "dignified afternoon tea", champagne and "dessert after a show" or a New American bite before (such as the "phenomenal burger"), "you can't go wrong" with a "romantic" table "overlooking the Public Gardens"; P.S. "don't miss" the "over-the-top" Viennese dessert buffet on Friday and Saturday evenings.

Brookline Family Restaurant *Turkish*
21 | 9 | 19 | $19

Brookline | 305 Washington St. (Harvard Sq.) | 617-277-4466 | www.brooklinefamilyrestaurant.com

"You'd never guess" from its "generic name" or "hole-in-the-wall" decor, but this Brookline storefront is a "haven of Turkish delights", with "enormous" portions of "exotic cuisine" that exhibits "all the right flavors" and "cheap" tabs; the "quirky" setup goes from "cafeteria-style" lunches to "table service for dinner", while the "helpful staff" helps to create a "real family atmosphere"; P.S. the American breakfasts are "popular" too.

Brownstone ● *American*
15 | 17 | 16 | $25

Back Bay | 111 Dartmouth St. (Columbus Ave.) | 617-867-4142

A true "locals' place", this wood-and-leather tavern on the Back Bay–South End border offers New American pub fare that may be merely "mediocre" (and served by "spotty" staffers) but it's "cheap"; it's also a "relaxing" setting to "just have a drink" while "catching the Sox or Pats" on the "large TVs" – except when it gets "loud" with "spillover from the bar next door."

Brown Sugar Cafe *Thai*
25 | 17 | 21 | $24

Boston University | 1033 Commonwealth Ave. (bet. Alcorn & Babcock Sts.) | 617-787-4242

(continued)

Similans, The *Thai*
East Cambridge | 145 First St. (bet. Bent & Rogers Sts.) | Cambridge |
617-491-6999
www.brownsugarcafe.com

"Downright delicious" Thai "classics and originals" that "pack a
punch" come from a "huge menu", for "affordable prices" and via
"cheerful", "super-fast" staffers at these BU and East Cambridge
siblings; those irked by "tight", "forgettable" quarters appreciate
that "delivery is quick and efficient."

Bukhara *Indian*   23 | 19 | 18 | $25
Jamaica Plain | 701 Centre St. (Burroughs St.) | 617-522-2195 |
www.bukharabistro.com

Jamaica Plainers in search of "amazing" Indian cuisine at "reasonable prices" know to hit up this "quaint", "pleasant-enough" spot for
both "standard" and "unusual" dishes, especially during the "wonderful lunch buffet"; though they never know whether they'll be saddled with "rushed" or "indifferent" service, the faithful claim it'd be
"naan-sense" to pass it by.

Bukowski Tavern ●⇗ *Pub Food*   17 | 15 | 17 | $17
Back Bay | 50 Dalton St. (Boylston St.) | 617-437-9999
Inman Square | 1281 Cambridge St. (Prospect St.) | Cambridge |
617-497-7077

With a "surly staff", "rowdy" regulars ("not college kids") and the
music "volume [turned up] to 11", these Back Bay and Inman
Square taverns literally scream "dive"; "basic pub fare" fills folks up
"for a fair dime", but it's really "all about" the "noteworthy" beers
on a list with so much "depth", you'd do well to consult the
"well-versed" bartenders – or spin the "wheel of indecision" at the
Dalton Street branch.

Bullfinch's *Eclectic*   21 | 21 | 23 | $38
Sudbury | 730 Boston Post Rd./Rte. 20 (bet. Lafayette Dr. & Stone Rd.) |
978-443-4094 | www.bullfinchs.com

"Small and large groups receive equal attention" from a "wonderful"
staff at this "charming, quirky" "suburban family place" in a Sudbury
strip mall, offering moderately priced Eclectic eats prepared with
"imaginative" "flair"; the "warm atmosphere" ensures "a good time
is had by all", especially on the "fun patio" and at the "fantastic"
Sunday jazz brunch.

Burren, The *Pub Food*   14 | 16 | 14 | $20
Somerville | 247 Elm St. (Chester St.) | 617-776-6896 |
www.burren.com

"Jovial at all times", this bit of "Dublin" in Somerville's Davis
Square is all "about draft beer" and "great entertainment, with
live music every night of the week"; it's "no culinary beacon",
"but if you're just looking for some" "cheap", "quick" Irish pub
"munchies" served by "brogue"-sporting staffers in "standard" tavern environs, it's "fine."

	FOOD	DECOR	SERVICE	COST

Burtons Grill *American* `21` `20` `21` `$39`

Fenway | 1363 Boylston St. (Kilmarnock St.) | 617-236-2236
North Andover | Eaglewood Shops | 145 Turnpike St. (Peters St.) |
978-688-5600
Hingham | The Derby Street Shoppes | 94 Derby St. (Cushing St.) |
781-749-1007
www.burtonsgrill.com

"Swarming" with the "ballgame crowd", this Fenway outpost of the
suburban New American franchise lures with a "diverse menu" of
"classy" meats and such "without [high] prices" or an overly "manly
atmosphere"; though many staffers also seem like "students",
they're "friendly", "eager" and help keep the joint "jumping";
N.B. the Hingham and North Andover branches were not surveyed.

Butcher Shop, The *French/Italian* `25` `22` `23` `$45`

South End | 552 Tremont St. (Waltham St.) | 617-423-4800 |
www.thebutchershopboston.com

At Barbara Lynch's French-Italian vino bar/butcher shop, South Enders
jockey for "spots at the butcher block" or small tables for "high-
quality", "carefully prepared" meats and cheeses served by "passionate", "knowledgeable" servers; the chance to get their "socks
rocked" by an "ever-changing" selection of "interesting" wines gets
them to "come back frequently", even though there's often a "wait"
and the eats are "priced like entrees and sized like canapés."

Byblos ☑ *Lebanese* `24` `16` `20` `$30`

Norwood | 678 Washington St. (Vernon St.) | 781-278-0000 |
www.byblosrestaurant.com

"Plentiful" portions of "superb", "authentic Lebanese" cuisine is
served for "reasonable prices" at this Norwood Middle Eastern with
an "easy atmosphere" and "fun" weekend entertainment; the decor
may be a tad "tacky" and the "friendly" service "can be a little slow",
but fans say those should be no cause for concern: "go for the food,
go for the belly dancing, just go!"

Cactus Club *Tex-Mex* `16` `16` `16` `$25`

Back Bay | 939 Boylston St. (Hereford St.) | 617-236-0200 |
www.cactusclubboston.com

"After-workers", lively "singles" and "college students" descend
upon this "rather predictable" Back Bay Tex-Mex "party place",
making its bar, "gimmicky" dining room and sidewalk patio "packed"
and "very loud"; while they're there and "wrecked on delicious frozen
margaritas", they say the "fair-priced" "pseudo-Mexican food"
"tastes good" – but the morning after, it's often a different story.

Café Algiers *Mideastern* `18` `20` `14` `$19`

Harvard Square | 40 Brattle St. (Church St.) | Cambridge |
617-492-1557

Students and "beatniks" get lost in "long", "deep discussions" over
"strong Arabic coffee" and "well-prepared, well-priced" Middle
Eastern "basics" at this "venerable", "bohemian" "Harvard Square
hangout" with "North African"–inspired decor; in warm weather, the

"beautiful but tiny roof deck" is "great", but be warned: "the higher you sit, the slower the service" from the sometimes "snarky" staffers.

Café at Taj Boston *Eclectic*

20 | 22 | 21 | $51

Back Bay | Taj Boston | 15 Arlington St. (Newbury St.) | 617-536-5700 | www.tajhotels.com/boston

All sorts of French, Indian, Italian and New England dishes can be found on the Eclectic menus proffered all day by a "warm staff" at this "elegant, peaceful" Back Bay hotel cafe boasting "great views" of Newbury Street through a wall of windows; numbers-crunchers calculate it's "way too expensive for what you get", but history buffs pronounce it "a Boston tradition that's well worth experiencing"; P.S. the lounge hosts a "wonderful" afternoon tea.

Cafe Barada 🗷 *Mideastern*

∇ 23 | 12 | 23 | $19

Porter Square | 2269 Massachusetts Ave. (Dover St.) | Cambridge | 617-354-2112 | www.cafebarada.net

"Delicious", cheap Middle Eastern eats are "hard to find" – that's why Cambridgians are "so happy" to have this "small" bastion of "authentic Lebanese" "home cooking" right in Porter Square; the sparseness of the "too-brightly-lit" environs are of no concern when the "sweet", "adorable owner" is around.

Café Belô *Brazilian*

∇ 20 | 11 | 17 | $13

Allston | 177 Brighton Ave. (bet. Parkvale & Quint Aves.) | 617-202-6816
Somerville | 120 Washington St. (Franklin St.) | 617-623-3696 ◗
Everett | 158 School St. (Broadway) | 617-544-3772
www.cafebelo.com

"Fill your plate and pay by weight" at these Brazilians where "genuine" "homestyle" meats and other "delicious delights" are set out "buffet-style"; the "cafeteria"-like settings are "not glamorous", to put it mildly, but where else can you "stuff yourself" for such "an incredibly low price"?

Café Brazil *Brazilian*

23 | 14 | 22 | $24

Allston | 421 Cambridge St. (Harvard Ave.) | 617-789-5980 | www.cafebrazilrestaurant.com

"Real Brazilian food cooked by real Brazilians" is the stock in trade of this Allston spot where it's "hard to spend a lot of money" on the mounds of "impeccable meats" (there's plenty for "vegetarians" to fill up on too); "warm service" and frequent "live entertainment" "add to the charm", even when the somewhat "tacky decor" (there's a "mural of Copacabana Beach") does not.

Cafe Escadrille 🗷 *Continental*

19 | 18 | 19 | $47

Burlington | 26 Cambridge St. (Wayside Rd.) | 781-273-1916 | www.cafeescadrille.com

"Consistent for 35-plus years", this Burlington "standby" provides "traditional" Continental fare in two settings: the "fancy", "special-occasion worthy" Gourmet Room and the casual, more forward-thinking Greenhouse Cafe; while the latter serves as a "pleasant" "escape", the former gets the brunt of the criticism, with naysayers focusing on "overpriced" tabs for "outdated" dishes.

	FOOD	DECOR	SERVICE	COST

Café Fleuri *Mediterranean*   22 | 23 | 23 | $48

Financial District | Langham Hotel | 250 Franklin St. (bet. Oliver & Pearl Sts.) | 617-451-1900 | boston.langhamhotels.com

"The place to be seen" in the Financial District for a "power breakfast", this "bright", "lovely" Med "oasis" beneath a six-story glass atrium in the Langham Hotel is also a "great corporate lunch spot"; cocoa connoisseurs come for the "sinfully delicious chocolate buffet" on Saturdays (September–June), while music lovers rave about the "awe-inspiring Sunday jazz brunch" (if not the "over-the-top prices").

NEW Cafe 47 *American*   - | - | - | M

Back Bay | 47 Massachusetts Ave. (bet. Marlborough St. & Public Alley 905) | 617-536-1577 | www.cafe47.net

Missing home, Massachusetts native Beth Panagos moved back from Rhode Island, bought a scruffy Back Bay pizzeria blocks from Berklee College and opened this midpriced Traditional American serving to-go and sit-down lunches and affordable dinners; its setting features cranberry-wood floors, graphic prints on brick walls, a partially open kitchen and a chic granite bar dispensing wine and beer.

Cafe Jaffa *Mideastern*   22 | 13 | 17 | $16

Back Bay | 48 Gloucester St. (bet. Boylston & Newbury Sts.) | 617-536-0230 | www.cafejaffa.net

"Astoundingly affordable" considering its location "just steps from tony Newbury Street" in the Back Bay, this "Middle Eastern pit stop" offers "authentic, tasty" kebabs, falafel and the like in "ample" portions; despite "courteous", "cheerful" service, the "far-from-fancy", "low-lit" environs get many to opt for takeout.

Café Mangal 🅂 *Mediterranean*   25 | 19 | 22 | $37

Wellesley | 555 Washington St. (Grove St.) | 781-235-5322 | www.cafemangal.com

Wellesleyans anoint this "family-run" restaurant "neighborhood-gem" status for its "exotic menu" of "amazing" Med-Turkish fare served in a "shotgun-style" dining room that's "busy and boisterous for lunch" (when American options round out the menu) and "cozy and warm at night"; "attentive" servers are "happy to tell you about the dishes", while "BYO makes the expensive entrees [seem] more reasonable."

Cafe of India *Indian*   22 | 17 | 18 | $26

Harvard Square | 52A Brattle St. (Hilliard St.) | Cambridge | 617-661-0683 | www.cafeofindia.com

Harvard Square suppers say you can "bring the family or bring a date" to this Indian for the "value" lunch buffet and "reliable" dinners; a location "near the A.R.T." makes it "convenient for pre-theater", and if the "cozy" interior could use a redecorating "rescue", it's "nice in summer" when the "front windows are open."

Cafe Podima *Sandwiches*   ▽ 19 | 4 | 9 | $12

Beacon Hill | 168 Cambridge St. (Hancock St.) | 617-227-4959

Beacon Hill residents and workers appreciate this "convenient", inexpensive "stop-in" for its "yummy sandwiches", "excellent smoothies" and "awesome frozen yogurt" "with about 100 toppings"; those displeased over the "seen-better-days" setting (with only a handful of seats) and "slow", "cranky" service call for "free delivery."

Café Polonia Polish

24 | 16 | 21 | $24

South Boston | 611 Dorchester Ave. (Southampton St.) | 617-269-0110 | www.cafepolonia.com

Nearly "hidden" in South Boston, this eatery dishes out "large portions" of "low-cost", "home-cooked" Polish "goodness" to cravers of kielbasa, pierogi and potato pancakes; "warm, knowledgeable" servers patrol the "tiny", "cottage"-like space, taking the time to "thoroughly explain" the menu when asked.

Café St. Petersburg M Russian

19 | 17 | 18 | $40

Newton | 57 Union St. (Langley Rd.) | 617-467-3555 | www.cafestpetersburg.com

"A touch of Russia in Newton" is found at this "cozy", colorful spot serving "wonderful" blini, "mouthwatering borscht" and other "authentic" fare, best paired with "ice-cold" "infused vodkas"; complaints include "Cold War–era service" (especially to outsiders) and somewhat "high" tabs – however, caviar is offered at "a decent price", while a live piano player is a weekend bonus.

Cafe Sushi Japanese

∇ 17 | 11 | 18 | $26

Harvard Square | 1105 Massachusetts Ave. (Putnam Ave.) | Cambridge | 617-492-0434

"Students on a budget" appreciate that they "never have to wait" for the "great deals" on "basic" sushi – especially on Sunday nights when most selections are $1 per piece – available at this low-key storefront outside of Harvard Square; but that's not enough to draw opponents of "unremarkable" quality and "small portions."

Cafeteria Mediterranean

17 | 16 | 16 | $31

Back Bay | 279A Newbury St. (bet. Fairfield & Gloucester Sts.) | 617-536-2233 | www.cafeteriaboston.com

Situated on a high-profile corner of Newbury Street, this Back Bay canteen receives its "stylish" clientele on a large sidewalk patio ("good people-watching") and in a "trendy", minimalist dining room – which "modern"-decor detractors deem "a bit uncomfortable"; the "prices are reasonable", but many would welcome "more oomph" both in the "predictable", "passable" Mediterranean victuals and "inattentive service."

Z Caffe Bella Z Mediterranean

26 | 19 | 23 | $46

Randolph | 19 Warren St. (Main St.) | 781-961-7729

For possibly "the best meal you'll ever have in a strip mall", program your GPS for this "unassuming" Randolph restaurant where "wonderful" servers proffer "huge portions of hearty", "exceptional" Med fare and an "awesome wine list"; it's "a little expensive" for the 'burbs, "deafeningly loud" and the "no-reservations policy" often yields "extraordinary waits", but in spite of all that, "if you haven't been, you're missing out."

	FOOD	DECOR	SERVICE	COST

Caffe Paradiso ● *Coffeehouse* | 17 | 16 | 15 | $19 |

North End | 255 Hanover St. (bet. Cross & Richmond Sts.) | 617-742-1768 |
www.caffeparadiso.com

"Tourists" take "light-lunch" breaks at this "dependable", "busy" Italian coffeehouse with a "classic" old-world atmosphere in the North End, while locals like to "unwind after a long day" with "reasonably priced wines" and *"futbol"* "playing on multiple screens"; its 2 AM closing time also renders it "great for dessert, espresso and people-watching" "after dinner."

Caffe Tosca ⊠ *Italian* | 24 | 21 | 23 | $37 |

Hingham | 15 North St. (Cottage St.) | 781-740-9400 |
www.eatwellinc.com

Known for a "fantastic" assortment of wood-fired Italian meats, pastas and pizzas, not to mention a "nice patio", this "casual" "offshoot of Hingham's Tosca restaurant" offers "real bargains" "compared to its big sister across the street"; partisans also sing the praises of the "reasonably priced wine list", which helps fuel the "lively bar scene."

Caliterra *Californian/Italian* | ▽ 16 | 18 | 17 | $41 |

Financial District | Hilton Boston Financial Dist. | 89 Broad St. (Franklin St.) | 617-556-0006 | www.caliterrarestaurant.com

"Before setting out" for the day, guests of the Hilton Boston Financial District enjoy "leisurely" breakfasts at this "contemporary" Cal-Ital eatery also known as a "lively business-lunch rendezvous" among area workers; a "broad menu" is offered at dinner – which some suspect is "overpriced" given the somewhat "unoriginal" fare.

Cambridge Common ● *Pub Food* | 17 | 14 | 17 | $18 |

Harvard Square | 1667 Massachusetts Ave. (bet. Sacramento & Shepherd Sts.) | Cambridge | 617-547-1228 |
www.cambridgecommonrestaurant.com

One of the "best values in all of Cambridge", this "homey" Harvard Square pub serves "cheap" plates of comfort grub ("tasty burgers", fried pickles) alongside "local brews" to everyone "from famous professors" to "undergrads"; but many of them get frustrated by "slow-as-molasses" service and "noise" – both from fellow patrons and downstairs' Lizard Lounge – that makes "tables and heads vibrate."

Cambridge 1 ● *Pizza* | 22 | 18 | 19 | $21 |

Fenway | 1381 Boylston St. (bet. Kilmarnock St. & Park Dr.) | 617-437-1111
Harvard Square | 27 Church St. (Palmer St.) | Cambridge |
617-576-1111
cambridge1.us

"Fancy" "wood-grilled pizzas" that are "light in texture, big on flavor" and loaded with "unusual", "funky" "topping combinations" are the draws at these "hip", "reasonably priced" parlors (there's also a "limited range of appealing salads"); the "roomier" Fenway operation is a destination to "grab a beer and a bite before a game", while the "sharp-looking" Harvard Square original can get "insanely crowded" – thankfully, "service is prompt once seated."

Menus, photos, voting and more – free at ZAGAT.com

	FOOD	DECOR	SERVICE	COST

Canestaro *Italian* ▽ 19 | 14 | 16 | $24

Fenway | 16 Peterborough St. (Park Dr.) | 617-266-8997 |
www.canestaro.com

Cheered for its "dependability", this Fenway Italian provides "good values" on "filling" sandwiches, "nice pasta dishes" and "delicious" pizzas; "friendly service", both in the simple, "cozy" dining room and "quaint" sidewalk area, makes it a "great bet" for "a relaxing meal without the huge crowds" "before a Red Sox game."

Cantina Italiana *Italian* 22 | 16 | 20 | $36

North End | 346 Hanover St. (Fleet St.) | 617-723-4577 |
www.cantinaitaliana.com

With a "reasonably priced" menu "full of red-sauce favorites" offered in "really big portions" amid "old-school comforts" (read: "old decor"), this "cozy joint" "charms" patrons who can "accept it" on its own "throwback" terms; while "attentive" staffers and "lively" company abound, "you can usually get a table without reservations on weekends" – a large plus in the North End.

Cantina la Mexicana *Mexican* 24 | 14 | 20 | $15

Somerville | 247 Washington St. (Union Sq.) | 617-776-5232 |
www.lataqueria.us

This "festive" cantina located in Somerville boasts "authentic", "fresh and tasty" south-of-the-border fare, "friendly" staffers who "treat you like family" and "bargain-basement prices"; what's more, there's the "added benefit of a full bar" with a "Mexican beer menu" and, of course, lots of tequila.

⬛ Capital Grille, The *Steak* 26 | 24 | 25 | $65

Back Bay | 359 Newbury St. (bet. Hereford St. & Mass. Ave.) |
617-262-8900
Chestnut Hill | 250 Boylston St. (bet. Hammond Pond Pkwy. &
Langley Rd.) | 617-928-1400
Burlington | 10 Wayside Rd. (Cambridge St.) | 781-505-4130
www.thecapitalgrille.com

Even those who "don't like chains" agree these "clubby" beef emporiums do "fantastic" jobs when it comes to delivering "fabulous steaks", "spectacular sides" and "terrific wines"; it's "so unbelievably crowded and noisy" though, some "can't hear" the "attentive", "knowledgeable" servers describe the offerings – which are so "expensive", "it's best if your boss is paying."

Captain's Table & - | - | - | I
Take Away *Seafood*

Wellesley | 279 Linden St. (Kingsbury St.) | 781-235-3737 |
www.captainmardens.com

You can't get closer to the sea in the suburbs than at this casual diner-style Wellesley hot spot owned and operated by adjacent Captain Marden's Seafoods, one of Boston's top fishmongers; boosters roll up their sleeves to crack lobster or dig into inexpensive daily specials that seem like an even better deal when factoring in the BYO policy.

Carlo's Cucina Italiana *Italian* | 25 | 12 | 22 | $26 |

Allston | 131 Brighton Ave. (bet. Harvard Ave. & Linden St.) |
617-254-9759 | www.carloscucinaitaliana.com

"The secret's out" lament acolytes who have to suffer increasingly
"long waits" (not to mention a "lack of parking") to get into this
Allston "hole-in-the-wall" Italian's "snug", "noisy" digs; but it's
"worth it" for such "generous portions" of "easy-on-the-pocket",
"consistently excellent" fare, which is "delivered hot to table"
by "friendly" servers.

☑ Carmen Ⓜ *Italian* | 26 | 19 | 23 | $46 |

North End | 33 North Sq. (Prince St.) | 617-742-6421 |
www.carmenboston.com

"Small space, huge flavors" are how fans describe this North End
"closet" and its "creative", "expensive but magnificent" Italian
dishes, which are served amid "romantic" lighting and decor; "gracious" servers ferry selections from the "wide-ranging wine list" to
eager diners, many of whom first had to "wait outside", "even with
reservations"; P.S. "no coffee or dessert", but there's plenty
of cannoli nearby.

Casablanca *Mediterranean* | 22 | 21 | 20 | $36 |

Harvard Square | Harvard Sq. | 40 Brattle St. (Church St.) | Cambridge |
617-876-0999 | www.casablanca-restaurant.com

A "rare holdover from old-school Harvard Square", this
Mediterranean "fixture" "tucked underground" plies an "interesting
crowd" with "always delicious" "small and large plates" from a "reasonably priced", "small but varied menu"; festooned with
Casablanca movie frescoes", the "terrific atmosphere" features a
"fun bar" (a "noisy, crowded" "place to spot celebrities") as well as
a "cool dining room."

Casa Portugal *Portuguese* | 21 | 14 | 19 | $28 |

Inman Square | 1200 Cambridge St. (bet. Prospect & Tremont Sts.) |
Cambridge | 617-491-8880 | www.restaurantcasaportugal.com

Inman Square's "many Portuguese residents" can't get enough of
the "authentic", "reliable" dishes, featuring lots of "delicious seafood preparations", which are "efficiently served" at this "longtime
neighborhood" "standby"; though the digs may be looking a "bit
dowdy these days", it matters not when taking into account tabs
that "won't break the bank."

Casa Romero *Mexican* | 23 | 22 | 22 | $36 |

Back Bay | 30 Gloucester St. (bet. Commonwealth Ave. & Newbury St.) |
617-536-4341 | www.casaromero.com

"Truly a hidden gem", this "intimate" "cave" "tucked away" in a Back
Bay alley vends "authentic", "refined" Mexican fare; indeed, the
"upscale menu "disappoints only those looking for a burrito" (probably the same folks who find it "a little pricey" for the genre), while
the "tasty margaritas" knock everyone "for a loop"; P.S. "wonderful
service" helps to make it a "great date spot", especially on the
"romantic back patio."

Central Kitchen *American*

24 | 21 | 21 | $37

Central Square | 567 Massachusetts Ave. (Pearl St.) | Cambridge | 617-491-5599

"Cambridge date night" often begins at this "hip", "warm and homey" Central Square spot where "amazing wines" pair with a "well-edited", "frequently rotating menu" of "delectable" New American fare that some calculate as "reasonably priced" and others deem "expensive"; "solo diners" also feel welcome, especially at the bar, which is usually "lively" and "crowded" (good thing, since "it's too dark to read").

Centre Street Café *Eclectic*

25 | 16 | 22 | $23

Jamaica Plain | 669A Centre St. (bet. Burroughs & Myrtle Sts.) | 617-524-9217 | www.centrestcafe.com

"What a way to start the day" cheer the "folks who wait outside" in "long lines" "in all sorts of weather" for this Eclectic "Jamaica Plain jewel's" "amazing", "value"-priced weekend brunch; inside, "friendly, caring" staffers make themselves heard over "loud" crowds to tout the venue's "commitment" to "local and organic ingredients" before ferrying "massive portions" of "inventive", "wholesome" fare, which is also served daily for lunch and dinner.

Chacarero *Chilean*

- | - | - | I

Downtown Crossing | 101 Arch St. (bet. Franklin & Summer Sts.) | 617-542-0392

Downtown Crossing | 26 Province St. (bet. Bosworth & School Sts.) | 617-367-1167

www.chacarero.com

Downtown Crossing worker bees are abuzz about this duo's "excellent Chilean sandwiches", piled high on homemade bread with fresh ingredients and a secret recipe hot sauce (if you dare); "prices that can't be beat" have them arriving "early to avoid lines" at the takeout-only Arch Street storefront and the Province Street location, which offers limited seating, while both are only open through lunch and on weekdays; P.S. "yummy" breakfast items are also available.

Changsho *Chinese*

20 | 19 | 19 | $28

Porter Square | 1712 Massachusetts Ave. (bet. Linnaean & Martin Sts.) | Cambridge | 617-547-6565 | www.lotuscuisine.com

You'll "never have to wait" to get into this "reliable" Cambridge "cavern" (set between Harvard and Porter squares) sporting a plethora of tables, a "classy" design and "somewhat suburban Chinese food" that may be "more expensive than most" of its ilk, but is "generally worth it" (the lunch buffet is a "good deal"); it's a "great place for Sunday dim sum", not least of all because it boasts "free parking."

Charley's *American*

18 | 17 | 18 | $29

Back Bay | 284 Newbury St. (Gloucester St.) | 617-266-3000

Chestnut Hill | The Mall at Chestnut Hill | 199 Boylston St. (Hammond Pond Pkwy.) | 617-964-1200

www.charleys-restaurant.com

"Take the kids, grandparents, first dates, illicit lovers", anyone to these "casual" "saloons" for a "wide variety" of "affordable"

American "comfort fare" (weekend brunches, which come with a "complimentary cocktail", are especially "great"); the Back Bay branch's patio is a "people-watching" paradise, while the Chestnut Hill locale is a "homey and relaxed" "mall favorite", despite service being a "crap-shoot" here.

Charlie's Kitchen ● *Diner*

| 17 | 13 | 15 | $16 |

Harvard Square | 10 Eliot St. (Winthrop St.) | Cambridge | 617-492-9646

One of the "last holdouts from the yuppie-fication of Harvard Square", this "old college hangout" still plies its "cheap, cheap, cheap" diner fare, including the "famous double cheeseburger", in a "boisterous" atmosphere ("punk kids singing Kenny Rogers karaoke" anyone?); if the service is "iffy" and the victuals "forgettable", the "cool" "beer garden is perfect."

Charlie's Sandwich Shoppe ⊠⇗ *Diner*

| 23 | 13 | 20 | $15 |

South End | 429 Columbus Ave. (bet. Dartmouth & W. Newton Sts.) | 617-536-7669

Travel "back to a time when egg yolks were acceptable" by joining the "long line" to get into this inexpensive, idiosyncratic South End breakfast-and-lunch "landmark" whipping up "awesome" "greasy diner food" ("turkey hash is the standout") for "local pols and celebs" who "share tables" with the hoi polloi; there's "no alcohol, no bathroom, no attitude", and if you're one of the "scores of people who turn up" on Sunday, prepare for "disappointment", because it's closed.

Chart House *Seafood*

| 21 | 22 | 20 | $47 |

Waterfront | 60 Long Wharf (Atlantic Ave.) | 617-227-1576 | www.chart-house.com

"Expensive" tariffs for "delicious fish" are blunted by a "classic Boston seaside" atmosphere (it "doesn't feel like the chain that it is") at this "scenic", "upscale" Waterfront outpost; though the patrons skew "touristy" and the staff gets "inconsistent" marks, most report "enjoyable" experiences.

Chau Chow City ● *Chinese*

| 21 | 10 | 15 | $22 |

Chinatown | 83 Essex St. (bet. Chauncy & Oxford Sts.) | 617-338-8158

"If you're looking for a beautiful restaurant with personal service, go somewhere else", but if you're just seeking an "extensive" array of "amazing" daily dim sum from "authentic push carts" at "bargain" prices, choose this "huge" Chinatown staple (it's "dingy" and "unfriendly", but "who cares?"); "big groups" descend for dinner, while "post-club-goers" keep it "always crowded" until 2 or 3 AM nightly.

Cheers *Pub Food*

| 14 | 18 | 16 | $27 |

Beacon Hill | 84 Beacon St. (bet. Arlington & Charles Sts.) | 617-227-9605 ●

Faneuil Hall | Faneuil Hall Mktpl. | Quincy Mkt. (bet. Commercial & Congress Sts.) | 617-227-0150

www.cheersboston.com

"Die-hard *Cheers* fans" "don't care" if the Beacon Hill "bar that inspired the TV show" and its Faneuil Hall facsimile are "total tourist

| | FOOD | DECOR | SERVICE | COST |

traps" that "look nothing like the sitcom" – they "take a picture", "grab a T-shirt" and leave happy; however, non-"sentimental" types who "get dragged here when relatives visit" are "totally disappointed" by "character-themed" pub grub that "tastes like a prop" and staffers who "don't want to know your name, just your wallet."

☒ Cheesecake Factory ◐ American   18 | 17 | 17 | $28

Back Bay | Prudential Ctr. | 115 Huntington Ave. (Belvedere St.) | 617-399-7777

East Cambridge | Cambridgeside Galleria | 100 Cambridgeside Pl. (bet. 1st St. & Land Blvd.) | Cambridge | 617-252-3810

Braintree | 250 Granite St. (Forbes Rd.) | 781-849-1001

Chestnut Hill | Atrium Mall | 300 Boylston St. (Florence St.) | 617-964-3001

Peabody | North Shore Mall | 210 Andover St. (Cross St.) | 978-538-7599

Natick | Natick Collection | 1245 Worcester St. (Speen St.) | 508-653-0011

Burlington | Burlington Mall | 75 Middlesex Tpke. (Rte. 128) | 781-273-0060

www.thecheesecakefactory.com

The menu's "mammoth" – and "so are the crowds" – at this "family-pleasing" chain where the "endless" American options arrive in equally "colossal" portions (ironically, "they give you so much there's no room" for their "heavenly" namesake desserts); despite "ordinary" settings, "spotty" staffing and "lots of commotion", these "well-oiled machines" are so "busy, busy, busy" that they're best accessed "off-hours" to avoid a "long wait."

Chef Chang's House Chinese   20 | 14 | 19 | $25

Brookline | 1004 Beacon St. (St. Marys St.) | 617-277-4226 | www.chefchangshouse.com

"Chang's still got it" assure advocates of this nearly 30-year-old Brookline Chinese praised for its "perfectly prepared Peking duck" and other "delicious", "reasonably priced" classics; those with an eye on design feel the "tired" interior "needs a major redo", but "reliable" service ensures they get in and out "quick."

Chef Chow's House Chinese   20 | 16 | 21 | $22

Brookline | 230 Harvard St. (Webster St.) | 617-739-2469 | www.chefchowshouse.com

Coolidge Corner's "neighborhood standby" for "fresh" and "great tasting", if "typical", Chinese fare employs a "prompt", "friendly staff" that brings "smiles" to Brookliners' faces; the decor boasts "nothing special except a fish tank", but that feature makes it "kid-friendly", just like the "inexpensive" tabs.

Chez Henri Cuban/French   24 | 20 | 22 | $45

Harvard Square | 1 Shepard St. (Mass. Ave.) | Cambridge | 617-354-8980 | www.chezhenri.com

"Charmingly French and amusingly Cuban", the "interesting twists" imbued in this Harvard Square spot's fare are as much a "joy" as its "cozy" dining room is "romantic" ("share plates" for a "great" "foodie date"); the "convivial" bar offers a "completely different", "less expensive menu" on which the "to-die-for Cuban sandwich" and "awesome drinks" are stars, while "engaging service" can be found throughout.

| | FOOD | DECOR | SERVICE | COST |

Chiara ☒ *Mediterranean* — 26 | 24 | 24 | $50

Westwood | 569 High St. (Barlow Ln.) | 781-461-8118 | www.chiarabistro.com

Westwood's fine diners are "thrilled" with this "classy" establishment's "sophisticated", "well-executed" Mediterranean menu, which is served alongside "wonderful wines" by an "attentive staff" in "lovely", "tastefully furnished" digs ; indeed, they assure it's "as good as Boston's best" – and just "as expensive."

Chilli Duck *Thai* — 21 | 13 | 18 | $21

Back Bay | 829 Boylston St. (I-90) | 617-236-5208

Both "authentic" dishes "made with care" and "yummy" "American-friendly versions" reward "all levels of Thai enthusiasts" at this "easy-to-miss", "cozy basement secret" in the Back Bay; indeed, there's "far better food" than the "odd" "tiki-room" decor "would suggest", but it's as "light on the wallet" as one could hope.

China Pearl *Chinese* — 21 | 11 | 14 | $20

Chinatown | 9 Tyler St. (Beach St.) | 617-426-4338
Quincy | 237 Quincy Ave. (bet. Circuit & Faxon Park Rds.) | 617-773-9838
Woburn | Woburn Mall | 288 Mishawum Rd. (Ryan Rd.) | 781-932-0031
www.chinapearlrestaurant.com

For a dim-sum "adventure", devotees "go early" to this "aging" Chinatown "factory", and they still must endure "long", "claustrophobic" lines that go "down the stairs and out to the street" – but it's "worth it" for such "super-inexpensive", "delectable treats", which "keep coming one after another" via "little carts"; for best results, those in-the-know suggest "ordering off the menu"; P.S. the Quincy and Woburn iterations offer similar "real-deal" experiences.

China Sky *Chinese/Japanese* — 19 | 19 | 18 | $29

Wellesley | 11 Forest St. (Rte. 16) | 781-431-2388 | www.chinaskyrestaurant.com

"Well-to-do" Wellesleyans "pay a bit of a premium" for the "white-tablecloth Chinese cuisine" and "respectable sushi" served at this "elegant", "restful" venture; it also provides "fast service", which ensures "easy take-out" service too.

Christopher's ◑ *Eclectic* — 17 | 15 | 18 | $21

Porter Square | 1920 Massachusetts Ave. (Porter Rd.) | Cambridge | 617-876-9180 | www.christopherscambridge.com

"First and foremost a bar", this "Porter Square icon" supplements "loads" of beer on tap and "Bloody Marys the size of your head" with a "nifty variety" of Eclectic comfort stuff; servers can either "smile" or act "bored", but the "great prices" help to leave the "multiculti, multigenerational" regulars "feeling that the world is a good place."

Church ◑ *American* — 20 | 21 | 19 | $30

Fenway | 69 Kilmarnock St. (bet. Peterborough & Queensberry Sts.) | 617-236-7600 | www.churchofboston.com

"Oh my Goth", Fenway folks totally dig this "dark", "cool" haunt, and "not just for the irony" of sipping "creative" signature cocktails inspired by the "seven deadly sins" in a "hook-up joint" with a hallowed name – the New American fare is quite "tasty", and "priced reasonably" to boot; the "restaurant side" sports stained-glass windows and velvet drapery, "the club side is kind of hardcore" and there's a "lovely outdoor area when the weather's nice."

Ciao Bella *Italian* 19 | 18 | 18 | $37

Back Bay | 240A Newbury St. (Fairfield St.) | 617-536-2626 | www.ciaobella.com

"Sitting outside watching all the characters walk by" makes for a "picturesque" respite at this Back Bay Italian offering "traditional" fare that, though "not memorable", is "decent" enough; if the service can be "spotty" and the "decor could use some updating", maxedout shoppers respect it as that rare "affordable" option on Newbury Street (though it might seem "a bit overpriced" elsewhere).

Cilantro Ⓜ *Mexican* ∇ 18 | 18 | 18 | $35

Salem | 282 Derby St. (bet. Hawthorne Blvd. & Lafayette St.) | 978-745-9436 | www.cilantrocilantro.com

Salemites craving "flavorful", "upscale Mexican" cuisine and an "excellent tequila selection" say this "lovely little place" punctuated by exposed-brick walls and regional artwork does the trick; however, *enemigos* exclaim the "overpriced" fare "sounds better than it is."

🆕 City Table *American* - | - | - | M

Back Bay | The Lenox | 61 Exeter St. (Boylston St.) | 617-933-4800 | www.lenoxhotel.com

This Back Bay New American replaces Azure as The Lenox's premier dining destination, and though it's kept the same chef – and retained many menu items – it's offering more variety (including dinner sandwiches) and a lower price point all-around; it also sports a more casual, comfortable look, with banquettes, hardwood floors, earth tones, votive candles and an expansive bar area with high-top tables.

CK Shanghai *Chinese* 22 | 13 | 18 | $28

Wellesley | 15 Washington St. (bet. Mica Ln. & River St.) | 781-237-7500 | www.ckshanghai.com

Toting "great credentials", chef C.K. Sau "brings Chinatown to the 'burbs" at this Wellesley venture via his "delicious" Shanghainese cuisine featuring lots of "fantastic sauces" and "fresh veggies"; the strip-mall setting is "bland" and the interior is "cramped" and "noisy", but you can always "call in a take-out order" to "avoid the crowds."

🅩 Clam Box of Ipswich ⌿ *Seafood* 26 | 10 | 16 | $22

Ipswich | 246 High St. (bet. Haverhill St. & Mile Ln.) | 978-356-9707

"Clams raise their hands to get fried" at this "legendary" "roadside attraction" in Ipswich, a "giant box-shaped" "shack" where "tender", "sweet" seafood is cooked till "golden" in "the lightest batter you've ever tasted"; there's one "heck of a long line" to order and another to get a seat (inside or out on the picnic tables), but "bivalve lovers" say it's "worth the wait"; N.B. BYO.

Clink *American*
19 | 25 | 19 | $51

Beacon Hill | Liberty Hotel | 215 Charles St. (Cambridge St.) |
617-224-4004 | www.clinkboston.com

In an "ingenious" "building reuse", the old Charles Street Jail at the
foot of Beacon Hill has been transformed into the Liberty Hotel's
"stylish" New American where the "super cool" wash down "inventive" "small" entrees and "extremely small tapas" with "creative
drinks" amid "old cell doors"; but it's too focused on "the wannabe
seen, not foodies" complain "gimmick"-phobes who'd rather be
"locked up" than pay "highway-robbery" prices for "average"
taste and service.

☑ Clio/Uni *French*
27 | 26 | 26 | $81

Back Bay | Eliot Hotel | 370A Commonwealth Ave. (Mass. Ave.) |
617-536-7200 | www.cliorestaurant.com

Within the "gracious confines" of the Back Bay's Eliot Hotel, this
"tranquil enclave" continues to make foodies "swoon" over both
the "bold, complex flavors" of chef Ken Oringer's "exceptional"
New French fare ("with touches of molecular gastronomy") and
the "heavy blow dealt to the wallet"; "more casual" yet just as
"outrageously expensive", neighbor Uni does "spectacular" sashimi, and if a few find the staffers throughout to be "snooty", most
cheer them as "professional" escorts to "ethereal" "heights
of expectation fulfillment."

Club Cafe *American*
▽ 18 | 18 | 18 | $33

South End | 209 Columbus Ave. (Berkeley St.) | 617-536-0972 |
www.clubcafe.com

Catering to a "captive gay audience" "for decades", this South End
New American is "welcoming" to a "mixed crowd nowadays", which
comes as much for the "solid", reasonably priced wares as they do
for the "steady" social scene; the service occasionally comes "with
attitude", but all in all, it's a "neighborhood joint" "everyone" "can
count on"; P.S. a post-Survey renovation may have helped with decor some folks found "dated."

Coda ◑ *American*
22 | 20 | 22 | $29

South End | 329 Columbus Ave. (Dartmouth St.) | 617-536-2632 |
www.codaboston.com

Though "small", this South End American "has plenty to offer": a
"convenient", "genteel" setting (with a "tasteful, modern interior"
marked by "warm exposed brick" and "local art") "where you don't
have to spend a fortune for a tasty meal"; tipplers toast the "beers
galore", "well-made drinks" and "extensive wine list" with its "extremely helpful descriptions", while everyone appreciates the
"no-attitude" staff.

Columbus Café *Eclectic*
19 | 16 | 20 | $30

South End | 535 Columbus Ave. (Claremont Park) | 617-247-9001 |
www.columbuscafeandbar.com

"You always feel welcome" at this "unpretentious" South Ender where
the "homey" dining room and "sunny patio" (a "great place to people-

watch") are often packed with "symphony and Huntington Theatre-goers" munching on "tasty", "reasonably priced" Eclectic comfort dinners; the "knowledgeable" staff remains "calm, even when it's packed", which is the norm on weekends when brunch is the "draw."

Comfort ☒Ⓜ *American* | - | - | - | M |

Watertown | 5 Spring St. (Main St.) | 617-924-3220 |
www.eatcomfortfood.com

In chain-heavy Watertown, advocates of "the little guy" "would like to see" this "tucked-away" American succeed, not least of all to support the "personable owner" and "helpful" staff; the "tasty", "reasonably priced" fare and casual atmosphere "both live up to the name", while live weekend music is a welcome embellishment.

Coolidge Corner Clubhouse ● *Pub Food* | 17 | 14 | 17 | $21 |

Brookline | 307A-309 Harvard St. (bet. Babcock & Beacon Sts.) |
617-566-4948 | www.thecoolidgecornerclubhouse.com

The "menus are entertainment in themselves", as the sandwiches are named after athletes at this "small" Brookline sports haven offering a "huge variety" of "basic", "bang-for-the-buck" American pub grub in "massive portions"; "noisy" parents cram "cheek-to-jowl" to get a gander at one of "several TVs" "during football season or any major" game, while their offspring peruse what is a "surprisingly large kids' menu for a bar."

NEW Coppa *Italian* | - | - | - | M |

South End | 253 Shawmut Ave. (Milford St.) | 617-391-0902 |
www.coppaboston.com

Housemade charcuterie, pasta and wood-oven pizza, plus an extensive menu of small plates, define this midpriced Italian enoteca in the South End run by chef-partners Ken Oringer and Jamie Bissonnette; the space is romantic and rustic with reclaimed wood floors, high ceilings, subway tile and a small wooden bar where beer, wine and inventive cocktails made from cordials are served.

Coriander Bistro *Indian/Nepalese* | - | - | - | I |

Sharon | 5 Post Office Sq. (bet. Billings & S. Main Sts.) | 781-784-2300 |
www.corianderbistro.net

Though the name remains the same, a new owner (who also runs West Roxbury's Himalayan Bistro) has converted this former French gem in Sharon into an Indian-Nepalese, dressing the white-tablecloth dining room with handicrafts and a photo of the Taj Mahal; in addition to budget-friendly dinners (complemented by a full bar), it offers a weekday lunch buffet, weekend brunch and patio dining.

NEW Corner Tavern, The ● *American* | - | - | - | M |

Back Bay | 421 Marlborough St. (Mass. Ave.) | 617-262-5555

The owners of the legendary Back Bay watering hole Last Drop renamed it, ditched the dartboards, spruced up the space with track lighting and a paint job, and added a kitchen for whipping up midpriced New American fare; there's also a wider selection of libations, but the 2 AM closing time remains unchanged.

Cornwall's ● *Pub Food*
| 15 | 16 | 18 | $21 |

Kenmore Square | 654 Beacon St. (Commonwealth Ave.) | 617-262-3749 | www.cornwalls.com

"Fun after work" or "before a game", this often "crowded" Kenmore Square "hangout" employs a "friendly staff" to oversee an "encyclopedic beer list" and "simple", "fine" British pub grub; those put off by the "stale" decor can focus instead on pool tables, dartboards and a "wall of classic American board games", which "stands waiting to entertain you on cold, rainy nights."

Cottage, The *Californian*
| 19 | 21 | 19 | $31 |

Wellesley | 190 Linden St. (bet. Everett St. & Pine Tree Rd.) | Wellesley Hills | 781-239-1100 | www.cottagewellesley.com

An "import from La Jolla", this "delightful" Wellesley transplant serves "true Californian cuisine" (starring "real-deal fish tacos") in a setting "reminiscent of a Nantucket cottage", with "crisp white wood and comfortable booths with pillows"; while it can be "laid-back" – with the aid of "refreshing" cocktails and "gracious" staffers – singletons say "don't go before 7 PM unless you want an upscale Chuck E. Cheese experience": its "kid-friendliness" is off the charts.

Cottonwood ● *Southwestern*
| 18 | 17 | 17 | $30 |

Back Bay | 222 Berkeley St. (St. James Ave.) | 617-247-2225 | www.cottonwoodboston.com

"It's all about the chips, dips and margaritas" (especially the latter) at this "loud" and "crowded" Back Bay "after-work scene" serving "satisfying" if "not memorable" Southwestern noshes "priced right"; the "decor has not changed in decades", but more interesting visuals can be found on the "nice patio in the summer" – "inconsistent service", unfortunately, is perennial.

Courthouse Seafood ▣ *Seafood*
| ▽ 22 | 9 | 16 | $18 |

East Cambridge | 498 Cambridge St. (6th St.) | Cambridge | 617-491-1213 | www.courthouseseafood.com

It feels like a "neighborhood pizza place" ("paper plates", "no alcohol"), but this East Cambridge luncheonette dishes out "extremely fresh", "well-prepared" seafood (the same owners run the "fish market next door") at "wonderful-bargain" prices; a staff that "keeps the line moving" "even when busy" is another plus – "ah, if only it were open for dinner."

🆕 Courtyard at the Boston Public Library, The ▣ *American*
| - | - | - | M |

Back Bay | Boston Public Library | 700 Boylston St. (bet. Dartmouth & Exeter Sts.) | 617-859-2251 | www.bpl.org

This elegant American overlooking the central library's outdoor courtyard is ideal for a Back Bay business lunch or leisurely afternoon tea (with food from one of the city's most respected caterers); prints from the art collection, linens and a cascading orchid centerpiece give a sense of grandeur to the high-ceilinged room, while the adjoining, more casual Map Room Café offers takeaway.

Ⓩ Craigie on Main Ⓜ *French*   27 | – | 25 | $64
(fka Craigie Street Bistrot)

Central Square | 853 Main St. (Allen St.) | Cambridge | 617-497-5511 |
www.craigieonmain.com

"Knowledgeable, serious" chef Tony Maws knows what his fans want –
"wildly inventive", "truly adventurous" French cuisine "emphasizing
local ingredients", fashioned into "innovative presentations" and
conveyed by "helpful, cheerful" servers – and now he delivers it in
Central Square, having moved from the old "tiny" Harvard Square
"basement" post-Survey; nervous Nellies who "hope he can maintain
the quality" in "bigger digs" most likely have nothing to worry about,
but dollar-watchers who "pray for lower prices" shouldn't bet on it.

Ⓩ Cuchi Cuchi Ⓢ *Eclectic*   22 | 26 | 21 | $38

Central Square | 795 Main St. (Windsor St.) | Cambridge | 617-864-2929 |
www.cuchicuchi.cc

"Pin-up waitresses" dressed in "flamboyant" "vintage" "costumes"
are just as "sexy" as the "decadent" "speakeasy" decor at this "over-
the-top" Central Square "hot spot"; "fun, flirty drinks" (props to the
"sassy mixologists") "kick off" many a "girls' night out", while "diverse" "international tapas" "designed to give you a food-gasm"
prove to be "fabulous" aphrodisiacs for "romantic evenings *à deux*."

Cygnet *American*   ▽ 21 | 22 | 22 | $42

Beverly | 24 West St. (Hale St.) | 978-922-9221 |
www.cygnetrestaurant.com

"Business meetings and quiet conversations" fill the "warm, relaxing"
dining room of this Beverly Farms American, but it's a "recommended" choice for "elegant" parties too; "graceful", "helpful" servers
convey the somewhat expensive, "reasonably good" fare, while
"professionals" "remember" what regulars drink in the "cozy" bar.

Daedalus *American*   17 | 19 | 18 | $28

Harvard Square | 45½ Mt. Auburn St. (bet. Bow & DeWolfe Sts.) |
Cambridge | 617-349-0071 | www.daedalusharvardsquare.com

"Let's face it", the main attraction of this pubby Harvard Square
"hangout" is its "beautiful roof deck" – so it's a good thing that the
American fare is "affordable", because it's "average at best"; the
"grad students and teaching assistants" who summer there say they
"wouldn't go out of their way" in winter, but they "always seem to
end up coming back because it's so damned convenient."

Daily Catch *Italian/Seafood*   24 | 11 | 17 | $35

North End | 323 Hanover St. (bet. Prince & Richmond Sts.) |
617-523-8567 ⊄

Seaport District | Moakley Federal Courthouse | 2 Northern Ave.
(Sleeper St.) | 617-772-4400

NEW Brookline | 441 Harvard St. (bet. Coolidge & Thorndike Sts.) |
617-734-2700
www.dailycatch.com

"Probably no bigger than your kitchen", this "garlic-scented" North
End storefront attracts "long lines" of folks waiting to pay "cash

only" for "amazing", "abundant" Italian seafood-and-pasta dishes "served piping hot" "in the skillet they were cooked in", judiciously washed down with "wine in juice glasses" (there are "no bathrooms"); the larger Seaport District offshoot, boasting an "incredible view" from the patio, is a "different experience" altogether, but it still "packs a punch"; N.B. after a years-long hiatus, the Brookline branch reopened post-Survey.

Daily Grill *American*   19 | 19 | 19 | $36

Back Bay | Prudential Ctr. | 105 Huntington Ave. (Bolyston St.) | 617-424-4400 | www.dailygrill.com

The Back Bay link of this ever-expanding national chain proffers a "wide-ranging menu" of "consistently good" New American fare in an "attractive setting" ("big booths, lots of dark wood, stately bar") that's as suitable for a "casual" "business lunch" as it is for just "watching the game"; in the long run, it's "nothing spectacular", but "large portions" and "decent prices" place it pretty much beyond reproach.

Dalia's Bistro &   ∇ 19 | 19 | 17 | $37
Wine Bar 🅢 *American*

Brookline | 1657 Beacon St. (Winthrop Rd.) | 617-730-8040 | www.daliasbistro.com

With the "right amount of subtle lighting" and "lots of good wines that aren't offered everywhere", this "small", "pleasant neighborhood bistro" in Brookline is appropriate for a "romantic", moderately priced New American meal; its perpetual tranquility indicates it's a "well-kept secret" – which it could remain say those who find "nothing wrong, but nothing memorable."

Dalí Restaurant &   25 | 24 | 23 | $39
Tapas Bar ● *Spanish*

Somerville | 415 Washington St. (Beacon St.) | 617-661-3254 | www.dalirestaurant.com

Drop yourself "into a Dalí painting" when you drop into this "surreal" Somerville Spaniard, an "endearingly kitschy, unabashedly romantic" tapas bar whose "amazing array" of "exquisite", "pretty pricey" small plates comes from "gorgeous" staffers with "genuine" "knowledge"; masses of "friends", "families", "dates" and "birthday celebrations" keep the atmosphere "festive", and while that often leads to "lines" to get in, "beautiful people" "wait it out" with the aid of "awesome sangria."

Dalya's 🅢 *American*   23 | 21 | 22 | $43

Bedford | 20 North Rd. (Rte. 62) | 781-275-0700 | www.dalyas.com

A "bit of sophistication" in Bedford, this New American attracts "ladies who lunch" and "romance"-seekers with its "homey" farmhouse setting ("like eating at a friend's home") and a "wide-ranging menu" of "wonderful" fare "tastefully presented" by a "personable" staff that "tries hard to please"; it's "a little spendy", but it's "dependable", which keeps locals "coming back."

Dante *Italian*

24 | 22 | 22 | $48

East Cambridge | Royal Sonesta Hotel Boston | 40 Edwin H. Land Blvd. (Cambridgeside Pl.) | Cambridge | 617-497-4200 | www.restaurantdante.com

The "devastatingly delicious", "imaginative" Italian creations, "lively wine list" and "assiduous" service at this "modern", "airy" spot in East Cambridge's Royal Sonesta "exceed expectations for a hotel restaurant", even though the "modest" food portions make it somewhat "overpriced"; on the other hand, the "unbelievable Sunday brunch" is a "value", especially on the "sublime" patio with its "wonderful views of the Charles River."

Darwin's Ltd. *Coffeehouse/Deli*

24 | 14 | 15 | $13

Harvard Square | 148 Mt. Auburn St. (Brewer St.) | Cambridge | 617-354-5233
Harvard Square | 1629 Cambridge St. (bet. Roberts Rd. & Trowbridge St.) | Cambridge | 617-491-2999
www.darwinsltd.com

Offering a bevy of "inventive", "superb" sandwiches, salads, pastries and "fabulous coffee", this Harvard Square deli duo incites "long lines", especially at lunchtime (it's a bit "costly" for what it is, but the "portions are hearty"); seating can be "hard to find" in the "loud, brick-walled rooms", so many customers ask the "knowledgeable" though sometimes "unfriendly" counter help to bag it for takeout.

Davide Ristorante *Italian*

∇ 24 | 18 | 23 | $50

North End | 326 Commercial St. (bet. Battery & Clark Sts.) | 617-227-5745 | www.daviderestaurant.com

"Without a flashy/trendy environment", this North End basement draws clients celebrating "special occasions" or on "hot dates" solely via the promise of "good portions" of "classic Italian" cuisine in a "comfortable", "not jam-packed" setting – which is just a little too "drab" for some (not factoring in the "welcoming staff", of course).

Da Vinci 🗷 *Italian*

22 | 23 | 22 | $50

Park Square | 162 Columbus Ave. (Arlington St.) | 617-350-0007 | www.davinciboston.com

The "name befits the artistry of the chef-owner" applaud diners who've discovered this "charming", "warm" Park Square Italian where "wonderful pastas" are the "specialty" and the rest of the offerings are "presented beautifully" ("don't be surprised" if the toque "comes to your table to greet you personally"); though many find the prices "reasonable", dissenters deem them "expensive" for the portions.

🗷 Davio's *Italian/Steak*

25 | 24 | 24 | $55

Park Square | Paine Furniture Bldg. | 75 Arlington St. (Stuart St.) | 617-357-4810
Foxboro | Gillette Stadium | 290 Patriot Pl. (Washington St./Rte. 1) | 508-339-4810
www.davios.com

"Treat yourself" to a "fabulous" Northern Italian meal "presented with panache" by an "impeccable" staff at these "busy, noisy" and ultimately "awesome" steakhouse siblings: the "tasteful", "clubby" "see-and-be-seen" "famous-folk" magnet in Park Square and its "well-appointed" offshoot, a "top choice" in Foxboro; the "expansive wine list" completes the experience – now, how about a "scholarship fund" to help pay for it?

Deep Ellum ❶ *Eclectic*   ▽ 18 | 17 | 19 | $25

Allston | 477 Cambridge St. (Brighton Ave.) | 617-787-2337 | www.deepellum-boston.com

There's "something for everyone" at this "cute, cozy", "grown-up" Allston address: a "deep" selection of "stellar beers", "fantastic cocktails" and inexpensive Eclectic "fun food" (try the "amazing pretzels") all doled out by "friendly" servers; inside gets "loud", while the "great" "deck out back" is a warm-weather sanctuary.

☒ Delfino Ⓜ *Italian*   27 | 17 | 24 | $37

Roslindale | 754 South St. (bet. Belgrade Ave. & Washington St.) | 617-327-8359 | www.delfinorestaurant.com

Regulars of this "casual" Roslindale Italian spot "treasure" its "generous portions" of "fresh and delightful" fare as much as they do the "accommodating" staff; indeed, the "drawbacks" of a "no-reservations policy" ("call ahead and put your name on the list"), "long waits", "crowds", "noise" and "tight seating" are "small prices to pay", especially considering the "quite reasonable" tabs.

Delux Cafe ❶☒⌂ *Eclectic*   21 | 18 | 16 | $21

South End | 100 Chandler St. (Clarendon St.) | 617-338-5258

A "funky" "alternative" to some of "the pricier restaurants" in the South End, this "divey hole-in-the-wall" serves a "short menu" of "damn tasty" Eclectic eats to "posh" people, "hipsters", "bicycle messengers" and anyone else who digs a "crazy" space "festooned with Elvis memorabilia and Christmas lights year-round"; servers can become "distracted" "when it's crowded", but "great cocktails" and "not-your-average beers" provide "cheap" comfort – for which you must pay cash.

Deluxe Town Diner *Diner*   22 | 16 | 19 | $17

Watertown | 627 Mt. Auburn St. (Bigelow Ave.) | 617-926-8400 | www.deluxetowndiner.com

A "unique Watertown landmark", this "restored" diner's "interesting, adventurous" and "cheap" menu "goes far beyond greasy burgers and fries"; while it's "great all the time", weekend brunch is the real "scene", as boosters "brave" "lines out the door" (and then "uncomfortable" booths) for "amazing" pancakes and waffles "of all kinds", served in "sizable portions" by a "friendly, fun" staff.

Demos *Greek*   21 | 7 | 15 | $15

Waltham | 146 Lexington St. (Pond St.) | 781-893-8359
Watertown | 60-64 Mt. Auburn St. (Main St.) | 617-924-9660

As a "healthy alternative to traditional fast-food joints", these "crazy-busy" Waltham and Watertown drop-ins "can't be beat" for "ample servings" of "delicious" Greek classics at "rock-bottom prices"; those who can't get past the "bare-bones", "cafeteria-style" settings make it their "choice take-out destinations."

Devlin's *American* | 20 | 21 | 19 | $30 |

Brighton | 332 Washington St. (Market St.) | 617-779-8822 |
www.edevlins.com

Catering to a "young professional crowd", this "refined" "neighbor-hood spot" wins raves for an "interesting" menu of New American fare and "tasty designer drinks", as well as an "awesome patio" ("you'd never know you're sitting in the middle of Brighton"); inside, the "comfortable, contemporary" dining area is slightly "more for-mal" than the bar, which "can be loud and crowded", while "prompt", "friendly" servers are found throughout.

Dillon's *American* | 16 | 16 | 15 | $24 |

Back Bay | 955 Boylston St. (Mass. Ave.) | 617-421-1818

With a "nice patio" outside and "vintage oversized ceiling fans" and "big TVs" in, this Back Bay hang pulls in "happy-hour" crowds, "game-watchers" and dudes "looking for digits"; as far as the "typi-cal" American grub goes, some's "enjoyable", some's "subpar" ("good pricing" though).

District 🄢🄼 *American* | ▽ 17 | 25 | 18 | $36 |

Leather District | 180 Lincoln St. (bet. Beach & Kneeland Sts.) |
617-426-0180 | www.districtboston.com

"High class and tasteful all the way", this leather-and-birch lounge lures after-workers and night owls to the sleepy Leather District for "good" New American fare that's heavy on the small plates and rea-sonably priced; "the staff pulls everything together effortlessly", particularly for the many "events" that are held here, but the whole endeavor comes off as "a little pretentious" to some attendees.

Diva Indian Bistro *Indian* | 22 | 20 | 16 | $27 |

Somerville | 246 Elm St. (Chester St.) | 617-629-4963 |
www.divabistro.com

Among Davis Square's Indian haunts, this Somervillean stands out with a "contemporary space" in which to serve its "wonderful" cuisine (don't skip the "giant", "crispy, delicious dosas"); surveyors split over whether the tabs are "affordable" or comparatively "overpriced", but most everyone agrees on the service issue: "slow", "brusque" and dripping with "attitude" ("why?"); P.S. the "architecturally fascinating" lounge next door concocts "truly unique, scrumptious" cocktails.

DJ's 🄼 *American* | - | - | - | M |

West End | 222 Friend St. (Valenti Way) | 617-723-3222 |
www.djsbarboston.com

Twenty-five HDTVs in multiple rooms have sports fans cheering this West End bar/eatery as a "great place to watch the game" while tackling a large menu of "slightly upscale" yet moderately priced American grub; on non-game days, frequent live bands score points from music lovers.

Dog Bar at 65 Main St. Ⓜ *American*
▽ 23 | 21 | 23 | $34

Gloucester | 65 Main St. (bet. Porter & Short Sts.) | 978-281-6565 | www.dogbarcapeann.com

This "casual" Gloucester tavern serves a "delightful" assortment of American classics in "cozy" digs marked by exposed brick and vintage-looking photos; "friendly" servers deliver designer cocktails from the bar, which "rocks" with "live music several nights a week."

Dok Bua *Thai*
24 | 11 | 20 | $17

Brookline | 411 Harvard St. (bet. Fuller St. & Naples Rd.) | 617-232-2955 | www.dokbua-thai.com

"Welcome to Kitschville!" – this Brookline Thai is as known for its "funky"/"fun" decor ("Christmas lights, travel posters", shelves from its past "grocery-store" life) as it is for "delicious, plentiful" "lunch and dinner specials" from an "encyclopedic menu with pictures of every dish" and "unbeatable prices"; what's no joke is the "courteous" staff.

Dolphin Seafood *Seafood*
18 | 15 | 17 | $30

Harvard Square | 1105 Massachusetts Ave. (Remington St.) | Cambridge | 617-661-2937

Natick | 12 Washington St. (Rte. 135) | 508-655-0669
www.dolphinseafood.com

Taking folks "back to a simpler era in American seafood joints", these "old-school" eateries with outposts in Harvard Square and Natick (mostly) broil "big quantities" of "fresh fish" "without all the doctoring up"; if epicures dis the preparations as "boring" and the settings as "unimaginative", even they have to admit "at least it's cheaper" than the big chains.

Donatello *Italian*
24 | 19 | 21 | $48

Saugus | 44 Broadway/Rte. 1 (Rte. 95) | 781-233-9975 | www.donatellosaugus.com

"Right out of *The Sopranos*" and onto Saugus' strip-mall-heavy Route 1 comes this "nice surprise" offering "wonderful", "authentic" Italian fare in a setting that's "perfect for celebrations"; though the "prices are aggressive", not so the "accommodating" servers, "fun, chatty bartenders" and "low-pressure" ambiance.

Don Ricardo's Ⓩ *Brazilian/Peruvian*
▽ 23 | 14 | 26 | $24

South End | 57 W. Dedham St. (bet. Shawmut Ave. & Tremont St.) | 617-247-9249

A "hidden gem", this "reliable" spot serves "delicious", "authentic" Brazilian-Peruvian "treats" alongside "super sangria" at "significantly cheap" prices considering its South End address; the "lovely", "welcoming" staff makes it "feel like home", even though there's "not much atmosphere" to speak of.

NEW Dorado
Tacos & Cemitas *Mexican*
- | - | - | I

Brookline | 401 Harvard St. (Naples Rd.) | 617-566-2100 | www.doradotacos.com

Anyone looking for authentic Mexican – or an introduction to the street-food sandwich known as *cemita* – will find an inexpensive fix at this cheery counter-service Brookline haunt done up in orange, blue and yellow tones; N.B. a beer and wine license is in the works.

NEW Dosa Factory *Indian* — | — | — | I

Central Square | 571 Massachusetts Ave. (Pearl St.) | Cambridge | 617-868-3672 | www.dosa-factory.com

One World Cuisine, operator of Kashmir, Mela and many more, brings South Indian–style street eats indoors at this dosa diner tucked behind the Shalimar Gourmet Foods & Spices store in Central Square; with most items under $10, the prices are in sync with the modest surroundings, which feature orange booths, photos of outdoor vendors and counter service; N.B. a Waltham location is slated for April 2010.

Douzo ◐ *Japanese* 24 | 23 | 20 | $41

Back Bay | 131 Dartmouth St. (Stuart St.) | 617-859-8886 | www.douzosushi.com

"Everyday" sushi "classics are reinvented" at this Back Bay "sophisticate" whose "innovative" rolls befit the slightly "expensive" tabs and "trendy, modern" environs (design mavens can't help comparing it to a "West Elm" showroom); while you never know if you'll get a "responsive" or "underwhelming" server, you can usually "expect a bit of a wait" for a table, which goes quicker with "well-crafted cocktails" at the bar.

Doyle's Cafe *Pub Food* 15 | 18 | 18 | $21

Jamaica Plain | 3484 Washington St. (Williams St.) | 617-524-2345

Since 1882, this Irish pub "institution" has been "everyone's" Jamaica Plain "hangout", especially "politicians" who meet to deal alongside "townies and Sox fans", amid "famous and infamous faces staring down from the walls" and other "Boston lore decor"; the "stick-to-your-ribs" grub can be rather "undistinguished" (at "prices that haven't changed since your grandfather" was young), but the "substantial beer selection" is "outstanding."

Drink ◐ *American* — | — | — | M

Seaport District | 348 Congress St. (bet. Farnsworth St. & Thomson Pl.) | 617-695-1806 | www.drinkfortpoint.com

With a "cool", "attractive" setting marked by a meandering woodblock bar and a "museumlike" display of mounted beetles, plus a "limited" yet "interesting" menu of "retro" American canapés by noted toque Barbara Lynch, this subterranean gastro-lounge brings "buzz" to an "iffy" stretch of the Seaport District; but with relatively "expensive" tabs for what amounts to "finger food" and rather "small drinks" (granted, they're concocted with "scientific flair" by "real pros"), for dollar-watchers, it fizzles when the check comes.

NEW Ducali Pizzeria & Bar ◐ *Italian* — | — | — | I

North End | 289 Causeway St. (bet. Commercial & Prince Sts.) | 617-742-4144 | www.ducalipizza.com

Concertgoers and sports enthusiasts heading to TD Garden have another option for grabbing a freshly made panini or artisan

Neapolitan pizza pie thanks to this family-run North End casual Italian; serving lunch and dinner and beer and wine only, it features an open kitchen, tiled floor and vintage signage that gives the no-frills space welcoming character.

☑ Duckworth's Bistrot 🅜 *American*   `29` `20` `26` `$48`

Gloucester | 197 E. Main St. (Plum St.) | 978-282-4426 |
www.duckworthsbistrot.com

"Run, don't walk" to this "absolute gem in the most unexpected place" – Gloucester – for chef Ken Duckworth's "exceptional", seasonal New American fare "prepared with flair", featuring "entrees available in half portions" that can be paired with "excellent wines" "by the half glass", both "godsends for exploring" (and more "budget"-friendly to boot); the "casual" digs are "elbow-to-elbow" and often "noisy", but those are minor inconveniences for an experience to which "nothing on the North Shore compares."

Durgin-Park *New England*   `17` `14` `15` `$33`

Faneuil Hall | Faneuil Hall Mktpl. | 340 N. Market St. (Congress St.) |
617-227-2038 | www.durgin-park.com

Famous for its "immense portions" of "New England favorites" like "tasty prime rib", this Faneuil Hall "blast" from 1826 is also "notable for surly", "sassy" waitresses who "put you in your place" (it also "prides itself" on "below-par decor" featuring "long tables" with "red-checked cloths"); yes, it's kind of an "overpriced" "tourist trap", but "everyone should go once", at least to "say you've done it."

🆕 East by Northeast 🅜 *Chinese*   `–` `–` `–` `M`

Inman Square | 1128 Cambridge St. (Norfolk St.) | Cambridge |
617-876-0286 | www.exnecambridge.com

At this newcomer just outside of Inman Square, a chef who cut his teeth at T.W. Food and others is serving midpriced seasonal and sustainable Chinese fare, including hand-rolled dumplings; the restaurant's name is written on the dining-room wall in Chinese, and there's a four-seat bar dispensing a short list of signature cocktails.

☑ East Coast Grill & Raw Bar *BBQ/Seafood*   `25` `18` `22` `$39`

Inman Square | 1271 Cambridge St. (Prospect St.) | Cambridge |
617-491-6568 | www.eastcoastgrill.net

"The thrill of the Grill" is "still strong", as evidenced by the "wicked crowds" who "endure" "long waits" to "explore the world of heat" via Chris Schlesinger's "seriously hot BBQ" and "killer" "fresh seafood" at this "boisterous" Inman Square "classic"; a "seasoned staff" works the "zany" tropical-themed setting like a "well-oiled machine", delivering "cutting-edge cocktails" and checks that are only "slightly on the pricey side"; P.S. for the "ultimate" "fiery" "challenge", come for the regularly scheduled Hell Nights.

☑ Eastern Standard ☻ *American/European*   `22` `24` `22` `$40`

Kenmore Square | Hotel Commonwealth | 528 Commonwealth Ave.
(Brookline Ave.) | 617-532-9100 | www.easternstandardboston.com

From a "wonderful breakfast" to a "casual, inexpensive" American lunch complemented by "intriguing", "innovative" cocktails (the "mixologists are geniuses") to an "elegant, pricey" European dinner paired with "well-chosen wines", there's "something for everyone" at this "cavernous", "glamorous" Kenmore Square "grande cafe" with a "gorgeous marble bar", "high ceilings" and an "excellent heated patio"; always "buzzing", it's especially "noisy" on "game day" – "like the Gare du Nord filled with Sox fans."

East Ocean City *Chinese/Seafood*   24 | 12 | 17 | $28

Chinatown | 25 Beach St. (bet. Harrison Ave. & Washington St.) | 617-542-2504 | www.eastoceancity.com

For fish "flapping one moment" in "tanks by the door", "delicately cooked and on your plate 10 minutes later", this "delicious" Cantonese canteen is the place in Chinatown; "locals" frequent it ("so you know it's good") for lunch and dinner, "bar-hoppers" are "forever indebted" to its "late hours" and "moderate" prices, and no one seems to mind the "brusque service" and "drab surroundings."

Ecco *American*   - | - | - | M

East Boston | 107 Porter St. (bet. Chelsea & Paris Sts.) | 617-561-1112 | www.eccoboston.com

Part restaurant, part nightlife hot spot, this sexy, affordable East Boston New American (with Latin and Asian influences) offers a quiet dining room with black leather banquettes and a bar area that hops after-hours; N.B. the wall scrawled with sports-figure signatures is a leftover from the space's former occupant, Sablone's.

ⓃⒺⓌ 88 Wharf   - | - | - | M
Riverfront Grill *American*

Milton | Residences at Milton Landing | 88 Wharf St. (Adams St.) | 857-598-4826 | www.88wharf.com

At this classy yet casual American perched on the Neponset River in Milton, locals and city dwellers enjoy midpriced meals in the spacious dining room with marina-themed photos, or gather for a drink at the marble bar sporting two TVs; during warmer months, the leafy patio feels far removed from the city – even though the Red Line stop is just a quick walk away.

Ⓩ Elephant Walk *Cambodian/French*   23 | 20 | 20 | $36

Fenway | 900 Beacon St. (Park Dr.) | 617-247-1500
Porter Square | 2067 Massachusetts Ave. (bet. Hadley & Russell Sts.) | Cambridge | 617-492-6900
Waltham | 663 Main St. (Moody St.) | 781-899-2244
www.elephantwalk.com

"Still amazing after all these years", these triplets serve a "well-executed" menu (with many "lovely vegetarian options") of "mouthwatering" Cambodian and French fare – although the fact that it's "not fusion" per se, "rather two distinct cooking traditions", makes for a "strange concept" to some; the "handsome decor" "captures the imagination" of diners – that is, when they're not having to snag the "rushed, inattentive" members of the otherwise "professional" serving fleet.

	FOOD	DECOR	SERVICE	COST

El Oriental de Cuba *Cuban*
24 | 14 | 19 | $17

Jamaica Plain | 416 Centre St. (S. Huntington Ave.) | 617-524-6464 |
www.elorientaldecuba.com

"Justly famous" 'round Jamaica Plain, this "warm and welcoming"
spot earns "institution" status thanks to its "huge portions" of
"amazing" Cuban cuisine offered at "low prices"; the "decor's nothing special", but there's plenty else to look at since it's "almost
always filled to capacity."

El Sarape *Mexican*
25 | 15 | 21 | $26

Braintree | 5 Commercial St. (Union St.) | 781-843-8005 |
www.elsarape.com

South-of-the-border specialists say this Braintree cantina serves the
"most authentic Mexican on the South Shore", with "zesty", "consistently amazing" preparations complemented by "dynamite margaritas" and "unreal sangria", all at reasonable rates; the "gracious
staff" and occasional live music pleases, even when the colorfully
"cliché decor" and heavy "weekend crowds" do not.

Emma's ☒ *Pizza*
24 | 13 | 18 | $18

Kendall Square | 40 Hampshire St. (Portland St.) | Cambridge |
617-864-8534 | www.emmaspizza.com

Kendall Square subjects hail this "queen" of "gourmet thin-crust pizzas", as she lets them eat "divine" pies topped with "creative combinations" of "inventive" ingredients for "reasonable prices"; but the
"small space with only a handful of tables" makes them work for it
("be prepared to wait if you don't come early"), so many head
instead for the "quick" "to-go counter."

Emperor's Garden *Chinese*
21 | 13 | 14 | $20

Chinatown | 690 Washington St. (Kneeland St.) | 617-482-8898

Upon entering this "old theater" in Chinatown, dim sum lovers are
"bombarded with a continuous flotilla of carts" manned by "noncha-
lant" staffers handing out the "remarkable" "value" eats; the
"shabby" setting "could definitely use a visit from HGTV", but with
seating for roughly 800, "you can always get in" during the "crowded"
weekend rush ("if you enjoy a meal in solitude, show up for dinner").

Equator *Eclectic/Thai*
∇ 18 | 14 | 19 | $29

South End | 1721 Washington St. (Mass. Ave.) | 617-536-6386 |
www.equatorrestaurantma.com

A "strange mix" of Thai standards, Italian pastas and steaks makes
this South End eatery "hard to define", especially since everything's
"average"; but "if you're in the area" for lunch or "the symphony", its
"convenient" location, "efficient service" and "fairly reasonable
prices" make it a "pleasant" option.

Erawan of Siam *Thai*
22 | 23 | 20 | $26

Waltham | 469 Moody St. (High St.) | 781-899-3399 |
www.erawanofsiam.net

"Wood carvings, decorative artwork" and traditional floor seating
adds to the "charming" "authenticity" of this "spacious" Waltham

Thai; the "reasonably priced", "well-prepared" fare comes "attractively presented" by "gracious", "receptive" staffers, mirroring their kitchen counterparts who "will accommodate 'Thai hot' if you ask for it – just be prepared for some serious heat."

Erbaluce ☑ *Italian*

| | | | M |

Park Square | 69 Church St. (Shawmut St.) | 617-426-6969 | www.erbaluce-boston.com

Word on this "calm" Park Square Italian is its "ever-changing" fare is "flavorful" and "inventive", the wines are "well chosen" and the prices are "competitive"; service is mostly "friendly and informed", and while the proprietors "didn't blow the budget" on the decor (cappuccino walls, terra-cotta floors), the simple, "tiny" space feels "warm", thanks in part to "views into the kitchen."

Estragon ☒ *Spanish*

| | | | M |

South End | 700 Harrison Ave. (bet. E. Brookline & E. Canton Sts.) | 617-266-0443 | www.estragontapas.com

Authentic, moderately priced tapas are served at this South End Spaniard from the former owner of Brookline's Taberna de Haro; its sleek and sexy art deco–inspired setting features a small lounge area with antique settees, a long bar and two large communal tables, and there's an affiliated gourmet shop next door.

Euno *Italian*

| 24 | 22 | 21 | $37 |

North End | 119 Salem St. (Cooper St.) | 617-573-9406 | www.eunoboston.com

Tucked "away from the craziness of Hanover Street", this "intimate" North Ender serves "tasty", "traditional" Italian cuisine at "affordable prices" in a "cute", brick-lined ground level with "windows that open to the street" and a downstairs that feels "like dining in a private wine cellar"; words of caution for winter: while the "staff is accommodating", some report "having to wait" outside ("there's no bar"), even with reservations.

☑ EVOO ☒ *Eclectic*

| 27 | 22 | 26 | $47 |

Kendall Square | 350 Third St. (Potter St.) | Cambridge | 617-661-3866 | www.evoorestaurant.com

At this "gem", which relocated from Somerville to Kendall Square in March 2010 (thereby outdating the Decor score), devoted regulars say the "sophisticated" Eclectic fare with "great emphasis on local ingredients" "scores every time", particularly with the assistance of the "stellar" servers' "helpful" explanations of the "unique combinations" and "wonderful wine" pairings; for "this caliber", the prices are "completely reasonable", especially the "incredible-bargain" three-course prix fixe.

Exchange Street Bistro *Eclectic*

▽ | 20 | 21 | 20 | $35 |

Malden | 67 Exchange St. (Main St.) | 781-322-0071 | www.exchangestreetbistro.com

As "hip" and "modern" as any city venue, but without the "Boston expense", this red-and-black Malden bistro attracts a "great local crowd" for "delicious" "seasonal" Eclectic eats brought by "pleasant", "accommodating" staffers; drivers appreciate that there's "lots of parking", while the driven toast the "awesome martini bar."

Fajitas & 'Ritas *Tex-Mex*
16 | 14 | 14 | $20

Downtown Crossing | 25 West St. (bet. Tremont & Washington Sts.) | 617-426-1222 | www.fajitasandritas.com

"The young, the cheap and the hungry" habituate this "dark, dingy", "graffiti-splashed" Downtown Crossing Tex-Mexer (especially "after work") for "sizzling platters" of "inexpensive" fajitas and "huge pitchers" of "killer" margs; the staffers can swing from merely "spotty" to "appalling", but since they "don't even have to take your order" (you "fill out" a "checklist"), there's minimal interaction.

NEW Farm Bar & Grille *American/BBQ*
- | - | - | I

Essex | 233 Western Ave. (Scotts Way) | 978-768-0000 | www.farmbargrille.com

Rustic American comfort classics and house-smoked BBQ are cultivated at this inexpensive, down-home Essex newcomer that's got a barroom with high-top tables and flat-screens in addition to its open dining room, which is festooned with dancing-pig drawings, old farm equipment and specials-laden chalkboards; adding to its reputation as an adult funfest are a patio that's set alongside a vegetable garden and volleyball and horseshoe courts, not to mention weekend live music; N.B. a tiki bar is slated as a spring 2010 add-on.

NEW Federal, The ❶ *Pizza/Sandwiches*
- | - | - | I

Beacon Hill | 204 Cambridge St. (S. Russell St.) | 617-391-0025 | www.thefederalboston.com

This affordable Beacon Hill lunch and dinner spot offers a variety of sandwiches (everything from housemade classic roast beef to a Cuban) along with pies baked in a stone oven, all served in a brick-and-wood dining room equipped with TVs; late hours (till 2 AM Thursday–Saturday) attract night owls; N.B. no booze.

51 Lincoln *American*
23 | 20 | 22 | $49

Newton | 51 Lincoln St. (Columbus St.) | 617-965-3100 | www.51lincolnnewton.com

"A surprise in Newton Highlands", this "gem" vends "scrumptious" New American cuisine loaded with the "seasonal delights" and "innovation" ("you will never look at watermelon quite the same after you taste the grilled appetizer") of chef Jeffrey Fournier, also creator of the "beautiful" abstract artwork that bedecks the "inviting setting"; a vocal minority proclaims the experience "overrated", but most find it worth the "somewhat pricey" tabs.

Figs *Italian*
23 | 17 | 19 | $31

Beacon Hill | 42 Charles St. (bet. Chestnut & Mt. Vernon Sts.) | 617-742-3447
Charlestown | 67 Main St. (bet. Monument Ave. & Winthrop St.) | 617-242-2229
www.toddenglish.com

Todd English may no longer spend much time at his Beacon Hill and Charlestown "designer pizza" parlors, but his presence is felt in pies that feature "unusual ingredients and flavor combinations", supplemented by "amazing salads" and other "glorious" Italian eats; when the "cramped" environs get "loud and crowded", it can make the otherwise "thoughtful staff" seem "rushed" – which further irks folks who find the relatively "reasonable" tabs "overpriced for what you get."

Filippo Ristorante Ⓜ *Italian*   ▽ 21 │ 15 │ 18 │ $34

North End | 283 Causeway St. (Endicott St.) | 617-742-4143 |
www.filipporistorante.com

"Within walking distance of the Boston Garden", this old-school Italian "on the far end of the North End" is a "great option prior to the game" – but it's also sort of a "cheesy" one due to its "overthought" interior complete with ceiling frescoes; at least the "authentic", reasonably priced fare pleases, as do the "great wines" and service.

Finale ● *Dessert*   23 │ 20 │ 20 │ $23

Park Square | 1 Columbus Ave. (Park Plaza) | 617-423-3184
Harvard Square | 30 Dunster St. (bet. Mass. Ave. & Mt. Auburn St.) |
Cambridge | 617-441-9797
Brookline | Coolidge Corner | 1306 Beacon St. (Harvard St.) | 617-232-3233
www.finaledesserts.com

"Dreams are made of" the "decadent" works of "gourmet" "art" whipped up at these "divine" desserteries where "chocoholics" "go with a big group" to create their own "buffet of deliciousness", coupled with "unusual coffees" and an "extensive" cordial selection ("small savory lead-ins" are also available, as are "yummy lunch sandwiches and salads"); while foes complain of "trying waits", "slow service" and "high prices", friends get the final say: "well worth" it, no matter any irritation.

Finz *Seafood*   20 │ 19 │ 19 │ $37

Dedham | 910 Washington St. (Fay Rd.) | 781-329-0097
Salem | Pickering Wharf | 76 Wharf St. (Derby St.) | 978-744-8485
www.hipfinz.com

With a "terrific" patio and "beautiful water views" in Salem, a "large", brightly colored, "open" feel in Dedham and "upbeat atmospheres" at both, these siblings reel in cravers of "fresh", "creative" seafood; tough cookies call it "nothing exceptional" for tabs that are a smidge "pricey" (and with service that's merely "average"), but they can usually be swayed with the aid of "robust cocktails."

Fire & Ice *Eclectic*   16 │ 15 │ 15 │ $26

Back Bay | 205 Berkeley St. (St. James Ave.) | 617-482-3473
Harvard Square | 50 Church St. (bet. Brattle St. & Mass. Ave.) |
Cambridge | 617-547-9007
www.fire-ice.com

A "fun", "interactive" concept to some, a "laughably fake" "take on Mongolian barbecue" to others, these Back Bay and Harvard Square "novelties" – "essentially buffets" where you choose Eclectic "meats, veggies and sauces", then watch "teenagers cook" them all on large, circular grills – are "often jammed" with "groups and families", making for "noisy, hectic" meals; since it's "all you can eat", it may seem "too expensive" if you don't "come hungry."

Firefly's *BBQ*   20 | 16 | 18 | $25

Quincy | 516 Adams St. (bet. Alrick Rd. & Furnace Brook Pkwy.) | 617-471-0011
Framingham | Super Stop N' Shop Plaza | 235 Old Connecticut Path (Rte. 126) | 508-820-3333
Marlborough | 350 E. Main St. (Concord Rd.) | 508-357-8883
www.fireflysbbq.com

"Pretty darn good barbecue for a bunch of Yankees" reckon pit aficionados about these "hoppin'", "family-friendly" joints smoking up "enormous quantities" of "amazing ribs" and other "juicy meats" available with a "wide range of sauces" and "tasty sides"; the decor and service are, in a word, "chain-y", but so is the "tremendous value"; P.S. "remember to get the red velvet cake" for dessert.

Fireplace, The *New England*   21 | 21 | 20 | $40

Brookline | 1634 Beacon St. (Washington St.) | 617-975-1900 | www.fireplacerest.com

"Yes, there is a real fireplace" at this "intimate", "friendly" Brookliner, but it's the "New England comfort food" featuring "innovative uses of local ingredients" that keeps it on the radar year-round; if "some dishes are just too convoluted" and "too pricey", "excellent wine tastings", "historical theme nights", regularly scheduled live music and other "interesting special events" "keep the community happy."

Flash's ● *American*   18 | 16 | 18 | $21

Park Square | 310 Stuart St. (Arlington St.) | 617-574-8888 | www.flashscocktails.com

"Nothing fancy" is offered at this Back Bay hangout, but for "after work or to just hang with friends" while scarfing down "quick, cheap" American fare (the "garlic fries are super-yum" – "just don't eat them on a date"), it's "lively and convenient"; like the rest of the staff, "the bartenders are all smiles and know their stuff", as is evident in "sure-bet signature cocktails" both "retro" and "imaginative."

Flat Iron Tapas   ▽ 22 | 20 | 18 | $36
Bar & Lounge *American*

West End | Bulfinch Hotel | 107 Merrimac St. (Causeway St.) | 617-778-2900 | www.flatironboston.com

"Offering fresh twists on the genre", this "dark, sophisticated" New American tapas lounge with "limited seating" in a West End hotel pairs its "high-quality finger food" with "creative cocktails"; but the fact that the "small plates are smaller than usual" (and "pricey" to boot) steams some noshers, as does service that "needs to wake up."

Fleming's Prime Steakhouse *Steak*   24 | 22 | 24 | $57

Park Square | 217 Stuart St. (bet. Arlington & Charles Sts.) | 617-292-0808 | www.flemingssteakhouse.com

"Not as stuffy" as the competition, this "inviting" chophouse chain purveys "classic" steaks and sides in "relaxed", "clubby" Park Square digs conducive to both "business and romance"; "low-profile" service and an "excellent wine-by-the-glass program" add to its allure, but since "everything's à la carte", be prepared for "high-end" tabs.

Floating Rock ⇗ *Cambodian*
▬ ▬ ▬ I

Revere | 144 Shirley Ave. (Nahant Ave.) | 781-286-2554

"Hard-core" Cambodian cuisine calls the adventurous to this "backwater storefront" near Revere Beach, where a "kind family" makes the fare "with a lot of care" amid "nonexistent decor"; there's "no liquor, but they do make a mean Thai iced tea" to counteract the "marvelous tiger tears" – "ask for them authentically hot" and be prepared yourself to be "brought to tears"; N.B. it's moving in spring 2010 to 485 Massachusetts Avenue in Cambridge's Central Square.

Flora Ⓜ *American*
24 23 24 $48

Arlington | 190 Massachusetts Ave. (Lake St.) | 781-641-1664 | www.florarestaurant.com

Having "done wonders" creating a "comfortable, modern space" out of a "former bank" (it "could be the one from *It's a Wonderful Life*"), this Arlington New American inspires more "revelations" in "inventive" "seasonal" fare "prepared with style and skill" and "never-fussy service"; longtime customers calculate "prices are getting a bit high", but they're "balanced" by "great wine specials."

Florentine Cafe *Italian*
21 20 20 $36

North End | 333 Hanover St. (Prince St.) | 617-227-1777 | www.florentinecafeboston.com

It's "too loud for an intimate conversation", and that's just how the "enthusiastic clientele" prefers things at this North End Italian known for its "happening bar scene" and "divine atmosphere" in the summer when "a wall of windows" "opens to the street"; but "reasonably priced", "well-prepared" "classic dishes" and "pleasant service" ensure it's much more than just a "fun place to see and be seen."

Flour Bakery & Café *Bakery*
26 16 18 $14

Seaport District | 12 Farnsworth St. (Congress St.) | 617-338-4333
South End | 1595 Washington St. (Rutland St.) | 617-267-4300
www.flourbakery.com

It's "hard to choose" from the "scrumptious" assortment of "impeccable" soups, salads and sandwiches served at these Seaport District and South End bakery/cafes, and it's just as "difficult to resist" the "moan-producing" pastries like "to-die-for homemade Oreos" and "sinful sticky buns"; the "overwhelming crowds", "cramped" digs and "besieged staff" can make joining the "neverending lines" "daunting", so be sure to "bring your patience" – and a lot of dough ("it's a little pricey").

Forest Café *Mexican*
20 10 17 $23

Porter Square | 1682 Massachusetts Ave. (Sacramento St.) | Cambridge | 617-661-7810 | www.theforestcafe.com

"Still amazing and exotic after all these years" aver advocates of this "shop-worn" "sports bar"/eatery thought of as a "pioneer" in "spicy", "seriously authentic" "regional Mexican" fare in its "easy-to-miss" location between Porter and Harvard squares; but detractors say it's "gone south", "cheap" tabs and drinks that "kick like a mule" notwithstanding.

NEW Forty Carrots *American*

| - | - | - | I |

Chestnut Hill | Bloomingdale's at The Chestnut Hill Mall | 225 Boylston St./Rte. 9 W. (bet. Dunster St. & Hammond Rd.) | 617-630-6640

Tucked inside Bloomingdale's in Chestnut Hill, this New American cafe is open during store hours, offering a spot for morning coffee, lunch or an early dinner (when beer and wine are served); the cheery, full-service dining room is decked out in orange, green and white, and there's a take-out section specializing in its famous fro-yo.

Franklin, The ❍ *American*

| 26 | 20 | 21 | $35 |

South Boston | 150 Dorchester Ave. (bet. 4th & 5th Sts.) | 617-269-1003

Franklin Café ❍ *American*

South End | 278 Shawmut Ave. (Hanson St.) | 617-350-0010

Franklin Cape Ann *American*

Gloucester | 118 Main St. (bet. Center & Hancock Sts.) | 978-283-7888 www.franklincafe.com

Some of "the best deals in town" are found in this "always crowded" trio's "superb", "gourmet-at-a-bargain" New American comfort fare – which only becomes "expensive" when "the bar tab racks up" with "killer drinks" during the "endless wait" for a table ("no reservations", except at Cape Ann); the "cozy" South End "late-night gem" boasts a "dark, sultry ambiance", the Gloucester branch is "larger" with a "little outdoor deck", while the South Boston iteration opened post-Survey.

Frank's Steak House *Steak*

| 18 | 14 | 19 | $33 |

Porter Square | 2310 Massachusetts Ave. (Rice St.) | Cambridge | 617-661-0666 | www.frankssteakhouse.com

"Remember when we had sour cream on baked potatoes, blue cheese dressing" on "iceberg lettuce" and steak that didn't "require a home-equity loan"? – well, "the good old days" are alive and well at this "reliable, reasonable" beefery in Porter Square that further evokes "a bygone era" with its "gigantic", "no-frills" space and weekend "lounge singer"; all in all, it's quite the "throwback" "experience" – just "don't expect any wows."

☑ Fugakyu ❍ *Japanese*

| 25 | 22 | 21 | $39 |

Brookline | 1280 Beacon St. (Harvard St.) | 617-738-1268

☑ Fugakyu Café *Japanese*

Sudbury | 621 Boston Post Rd./Rte. 20 (Horse Pond Rd.) | 978-443-1998 www.fugakyucafe.com

"A sushi-lover's dream", this "fin-tastic" Brookliner – with a "minimalist", cafe-style Sudbury offshoot – "always bustles" with "huge crowds" sampling "innovative" rolls and other "high-quality" "Japanese delicacies" listed on a "varied", "creative menu"; mostly "efficient" servers navigate two floors featuring a "flashy" lounge, "sushi bar, private screened rooms and booths", and while it all "comes at a price", it's "worth the expense" (conversely, "lunch is a steal").

	FOOD	DECOR	SERVICE	COST

Full Moon *American* | 20 | 18 | 22 | $24 |

Huron Village | 344 Huron Ave. (bet. Chilton & Fayerweather Sts.) | Cambridge | 617-354-6699 | www.fullmoonrestaurant.com

"Foodie adults" enjoy "sophisticated" New American fare and a much-needed "glass of wine" while their "sippy-cup"-toting kids "entertain" themselves with "toys, crayons and a play space" at this Huron Village "original" charging budget-friendly prices; "don't go" unless you can "tolerate hordes" of children the way the "continually cheery staff" can – for their patience, they "deserve early retirement."

Ⓩ Galleria Umberto 🖼✄ *Italian* | 26 | 10 | 17 | $12 |

North End | 289 Hanover St. (bet. Prince & Richmond Sts.) | 617-227-5709

Newcomers are "dumbfounded by how delicious" and "astonishingly cheap" this "unique" North End "lunch-only" classic's "few items" are – most notably the "splendid" "thick-crust" pizza "blanketed with cheese" and "tangy fresh tomato sauce", "delicious" calzones and "amazing arancini" ("beautiful little deep-fried rice balls"); but if they don't "get there early", they're also stupefied by the "lines around the corner" – and the fact that "when it's out of food", "it closes."

Garden at The Cellar Ⓜ *American* | 25 | 17 | 20 | $33 |

Harvard Square | The Cellar | 991 Massachusetts Ave. (Dana St.) | Cambridge | 617-230-5880 | www.gardenatthecellar.com

"Tucked away a little outside Harvard Square", this "unassuming" "gem" offers a "varied" menu of "amazingly seasoned" New American fare made with "straight-from-the-farm" ingredients and served in portions that seem "huge" in light of the "moderate prices"; while the upstairs dining room splits surveyors ("comfortable" vs. "awkward and sterile"), everyone toasts the "great downstairs bar."

Gardner Museum Cafe Ⓜ *American* | 20 | 21 | 19 | $28 |

MFA | Isabella Stuart Gardner Museum | 280 Fenway (Palace Rd.) | 617-566-1088 | www.gardnermuseum.org

The "incredible" Gardner Museum "caters to all your senses", and its "lovely" New American midday cafe is "no exception"; "off a grand atrium", the "charmingly intimate", "relaxing" spot with a "glorious" garden proffers "light items" on a "brief menu" that offers "something for everyone" – and while it's "a bit pricey for lunch", it's "usually worth it."

Gargoyles on the Square Ⓜ *American* | 24 | 21 | 22 | $43 |

Somerville | 219 Elm St. (Grove St.) | 617-776-5300 | www.gargoylesrestaurant.com

"Always creative" and "sometimes sublime" cheer fans of the New American fare served at this "hip", "intimate" Davis Square spot where every "fairly priced" dish contains "an unusual ingredient" and "extraordinary flair"; a minority decries that the "over-ambitious" combinations "don't always work" while falling "short on value" – but at least they "outshine the strangely curtained decor"; P.S. don your "halter top" for the Sunday disco brunch – "the funnest!"

	FOOD	DECOR	SERVICE	COST

Gaslight Brasserie du Coin ● *French* | 21 | 23 | 20 | $39 |

South End | 560 Harrison Ave. (Waltham St.) | 617-422-0224 |
www.gaslight560.com

"Succulent" French brasserie cuisine comes for "surprisingly decent
prices" – considering the "swanky" South End location – at this "hip,
fresh" Aquitaine sibling whose "classic", "elegant" decor looks imported from the "Left Bank"; "friendly, knowledgeable" staffers tend
to the "lively" "hordes of young professionals" who truly appreciate
that the "solid" wine *carte* offers both "great high- and low-end" selections; P.S. "gotta love the free parking!"

G Bar & Kitchen ▧ *American* | ▽ 21 | 23 | 18 | $55 |

Swampscott | 256 Humphrey St. (Blaney St.) | 781-596-2228 |
www.gbarandkitchen.com

"Finally, some good food in 'the Swamp'" applaud samplers of this
spot's "interesting", "seasonal" American fare, which is served
alongside "great drinks" in "warm, cozy", "sharp-looking" environs
marked by a tiled floor, high ceilings and fancy chandeliers; it still
needs to "work out kinks" in the service department, but on the
whole, Swampscott suppers say it's "worth going back", even with
such "expensive" pricing.

Gennaro's Five North Square *Italian* | - | - | - | M |
(fka Five North Square)

North End | 5 North Sq. (Prince St.) | 617-720-1050 |
www.5northsquare.com

New owners have taken over this cozy Italian in the North End, giving it a sexier look by sprucing up the hardwood floors and adding a
small granite bar to the buzzing downstairs, drapes to the quieter,
more romantic upstairs and setting faux candles on the clothed tables and colorful paintings on the beige walls throughout; though
more refined versions of the red-sauce fare and an updated wine list
have also been implemented, it still offers the promise of a special
evening without busting the bank.

Geoffrey's Cafe ● *American* | 19 | 19 | 21 | $29 |

Roslindale | 4257 Washington St. (bet. Kittredge & Poplar Sts.) |
617-325-1000 | www.geoffreyscafebar.com

"Thank goodness it's back" cheer supporters of this much-
transplanted eatery, now a "welcoming" "neighborhood spot" in
Roslindale, where "tasty", "satisfying" New American "comfort-
food updates" are sold for "reasonable prices"; but "what really
makes this place special" is the "patient, knowledgeable" staff, with
"fun outdoor seating" coming in a close second.

Ghazal ● *Indian* | - | - | - | M |

Jamaica Plain | 711 Centre St. (bet. Burroughs St. & Harris Ave.) |
617-522-9500 | www.ghazalboston.com

This affordable contemporary Indian in Jamaica Plain boasts a warm
dining room with wood floors, granite tabletops and a portrait of the
Taj Mahal; a classic Indian buffet at lunch gives way to a more romantic mood for dinner with candlelit tables, low lighting and wine.

	FOOD	DECOR	SERVICE	COST

⚡ Giacomo's ∌ *Italian* — 25 | 15 | 20 | $31

North End | 355 Hanover St. (bet. Fleet & Prince Sts.) | 617-523-9026
South End | 431 Columbus Ave. (bet. Dartmouth & W. Newton Sts.) |
617-536-5723

"Long lines" "form well before the evening opening" of this "cash-only" North End Italian "mainstay" where patient patrons are "blown away" by "rich, bold", "wonderful-value" pasta and seafood, paired with "inexpensive wines", before being "rushed out" to make way for the "people outside with their noses pressed against the glass"; the South End offshoot serves the same "scrumptious" fare in similarly "cramped", "frenetic" digs, but here it "takes reservations" (you'll still "wait").

⚡ Gibbet Hill Grill *New England/Steakhouse* — 24 | 26 | 25 | $45

Groton | 61 Lowell Rd. (Rte. 119) | 978-448-2900 | www.gibbethill.com

After driving through "rolling hills and small towns", travelers are delighted to come upon this "amazing" 100-year-old "wooden-post-and-beam" Groton barn with "a central fireplace", serving "high-style" New England steakhouse fare amid "views of grazing cattle"; "attentive, timely" service and a "lively bar" also make it a "special" destination for "date night, a family outing" or a private party in rooms set in a silo.

NEW Ginger Exchange, The *Asian/Japanese* — - | - | - | I

Inman Square | 1287 Cambridge St. (bet. Oakland & Prospect Sts.) |
Cambridge | 617-250-8618 | www.thegingerexchange.com

It takes two storefronts to house everything this Inman Square Japanese has to offer; indeed, in addition to its main attractions (sushi, noodles, bento boxes), there's a panoply of Pan-Asian tastes, plus a bar with a full complement of alcoholic beverages; the prices are as mild as the contemporary setting with hardwood floors and bamboo tables is soothing – that is, until you're jolted by the red accent wall and its bold artwork.

NEW Ginger Park *Asian* — - | - | - | M

South End | 1375 Washington St. (Union Park St.) | 617-451-0077 |
www.gingerparkboston.com

NYC expat chef Patricia Yeo has brought her Southeast Asian street food to the South End, where she's serving a midpriced menu of small plates accompanied by wine and sake; the expansive, elegant setting includes an undulating wood ceiling and a bar backed by windows that offer a view of the bustling cityscape.

Ginza *Japanese* — 23 | 16 | 20 | $36

Chinatown | 16 Hudson St. (bet. Beach & Kneeland Sts.) | 617-338-2261
Brookline | 1002 Beacon St. (St. Marys St.) | 617-566-9688
www.bostonginza.com

"Nothing will surprise you" at these separately owned Brookline and Chinatown "mainstays", but all their patrons "care about" is that the sushi "never misses": it's "always fresh", "tasty" and presented in a "timely" fashion; the "environments lack" and some of the servers can be "intimidating", but as long as they continue to offer lunch "steals" and "very late dining" on weekends (till 3:30 AM on Hudson Street), they're bound to remain "stalwarts."

Glenn's ☑ Eclectic   ▽ 23 | 19 | 22 | $45

Newburyport | 44 Merrimac St. (Green St.) | 978-465-3811 | www.glennsrestaurant.com

The "cozy", "dimly lit interior is rather nice", and the pervasively "pleasant" atmosphere even more so at this Newburyport spot to "chill out, munch out" on "wonderful" Eclectic eats and, on Sundays, veg out to "delightful" live jazz; those concerned the regular *carte* is "overpriced" join the "local crowd at the bar" "for a light dinner" via the "extensive appetizer menu."

Glory American   ▽ 21 | 19 | 19 | $46

Andover | 19 Essex St. (bet. Brooks & Central Sts.) | 978-475-4811 | www.gloryrestaurant.com

"A treat" for locals and travelers "en route from NH to MA" alike, this "dark", "happening" Merrimack Valley venue serves "quality" (if "a bit overpriced, even for Andover") New American cuisine in a "romantic", "fireplace"-blessed dining room – which contrasts with the lounge, a "real scene" starring a "young crowd."

Golden Temple ● Chinese   21 | 20 | 20 | $32

Brookline | 1651 Beacon St. (bet. University & Winthrop Rds.) | 617-277-9722 | www.healthyfreshfood.com

"High-quality" ingredients, "healthier" preparations and "costlier" tabs don't disguise the fact that this Brookliner serves "the Chinese food you grew up with" (read: "Americanized") – what you're really "paying extra" for is its "architecturally interesting design", something akin to the "belly of a fish" or "Thunderdome"; "aging high rollers" come early, while the "disco-fever"-afflicted arrive when it "turns into a nightclub", with a "bumping dance floor" and "terrific drinks."

Good Life ☒ American   17 | 17 | 16 | $27

Downtown Crossing | 28 Kingston St. (bet. Bedford & Summer Sts.) | 617-451-2622 | www.goodlifebar.com

If you take a seat in the somewhat "cramped" dining room ("with white cloths and roses on the tables") of this Downtown Crossing American, you "have to remember it's a bar at heart" so as to not think it "a weird paradox" when "drunk after-workers spill" from its dueling lounges; the "gussied-up" "pub food" is "nothing to write home about", but it's "value" priced and "decent" enough for a business lunch.

Grafton Street Pub & Grill American   17 | 18 | 17 | $28

Harvard Square | 1230 Massachusetts Ave. (Holyoke St.) | Cambridge | 617-497-0400 | www.graftonstreetcambridge.com

"Young professionals and grad students" frequent this Harvard Square grill for "after-work" drinks and "quick" "pseudo-Irish" New American dinners that are a "notch above pub grub" (and "priced high for what you get"); you never know whether service will be "fine" or "sloppy", but the place is "always crowded" and "noisy", so it

	FOOD	DECOR	SERVICE	COST

may be best to just come for the "preppy" "minglefest after 9 PM" – or in summer, when the "nice patio" and "large windows" open.

Grain & Salt *Indian/Pakistani*
| - | - | - | M |

Allston | 431 Cambridge St. (Denby Rd.) | 617-254-3373 | www.grainnsalt.com

A red-and-gold dining room with hardwood floors, tables draped in black and low-lit sconces sets a romantic, dramatic tone for this Allston Indian-Pakistani eatery owned by a native of Mumbai; the modest prices seem even more so thanks to the nearby parking lot.

Grand Chinatown *Chinese*
| - | - | - | M |

North Quincy | 21A-25 Billings Rd. (Hancock St.) | 617-472-6868

The owners of East Chinatown in North Quincy have opened this 'grander' Chinese around the corner, which serves authentic, mid-priced Cantonese fare in an expansive dining room; N.B. it's beer-and-wine-only.

Grapevine *American/Italian*
| 25 | 20 | 25 | $46 |

Salem | 26 Congress St. (Derby St.) | 978-745-9335 | www.grapevinesalem.com

"Wonderful for a celebration dinner", this "lively" Salem "destination" "always satisfies and sometimes inspires" with "superbly executed" New American fare flourishing "creative" Italian flair and paired with "fantastic wines"; if the eggplant-and-cranberry digs "have seen better days", they're "easily overlooked" in light of the "spirited" service and "real treat" of a warm-weather courtyard.

Grasshopper *Asian/Vegan*
| 20 | 10 | 16 | $19 |

Allston | 1 N. Beacon St. (Cambridge St.) | 617-254-8883 | www.grasshoppervegan.com

"Hard-core" vegans "delight" that this "mellow" Allston Asian even "exists", and they're further "delighted" to report the "extensive menu" boasts "innovative" combinations, "wonderful flavors" and "unbeatable value" (thus "excusing" the "low-budget decor"); confirmed carnivores, on the other hand, opine only a "die-hard tofu lover" could enjoy the "weird pseudo meats."

Green Briar *Pub Food*
| ▽ 17 | 16 | 18 | $21 |

Brighton | 304 Washington St. (Cambridge St.) | 617-789-4100 | www.greenbriarpub.com

Pay cheap tabs for Irish breakfasts on weekends or PM pub grub any day at this "authentic" Brighton "neighborhood spot" with brogue-sporting servers, live music, televised soccer and a "great back patio"; but even the "college kids and grads" for whom it's a home away from home wonder "why would you go here for anything other than drinking beer?"

Green Papaya *Thai*
| 20 | 12 | 19 | $24 |

Waltham | 475 Winter St. (2nd Ave.) | 781-487-9988

Don't let the "nondescript strip-mall" setting or "bland interior" "dissuade you from trying" this Waltham Thai – the "basic" dishes are "fresh", "tasty" and "fairly inexpensive", plus the cooks are "always willing to adjust to individual tastes"; "speedy service" keeps it "crowded" with "business" folk at lunch and take-out diners at dinner.

Green Street *New England* | 24 | 19 | 22 | $31 |

Central Square | 280 Green St. (bet. Magazine & Pearl Sts.) | Cambridge | 617-876-1655 | www.greenstreetgrill.com

Sure, the "mind-blowing", "inventive cocktails" "get all the attention" ("and deservedly so – you'll "wish you never wasted time with a Cosmo") at this Central Square spot, but the kitchen exudes a real "enthusiasm for food" with "fabulous", "reasonably priced" "New England–style comforts" (the "offal of the day" is "always a winner"); just "don't judge" it by its "divey" facade: the "intimate" interior's as "classy" as the staff is "friendly."

Greg's Restaurant 🖾 *American/Italian* | ▽ 19 | 11 | 19 | $24 |

Watertown | 821 Mt. Auburn St. (Belmont St.) | 617-491-0122

"Popular with the early-bird crowd", this "checkered tablecloth" Watertown "hangout" churns out "midcentury" Italian-American fare featuring "red sauce everywhere" and "durably coated fried food"; "great prices" and a "friendly" staff are two more reasons fans have been going for more than 40 years, but honestly, the decor "could use some updating"; P.S. hit the bar for "buckets" of "bright-orange 'cheese' dip" and "crackers" – an "amusing plus!"

Grezzo *Vegan* | ▽ 23 | 21 | 23 | $42 |

North End | 69 Prince St. (Salem St.) | 857-362-7288 Ⓜ
NEW Newburyport | 25 State St. (bet. Essex & Middle Sts.) | 978-961-1676
www.grezzorestaurant.com

"Holding its own" in Italian stronghold North End, this vegan venture presents "an innovative approach" to "raw, organic cuisine" with "tasty, nutritious" preparations that are as "beautiful to look at" as the "cozy, plush" surroundings, "colorful with oversized veggie and fruit paintings"; "knowledgeable" staffers add to an "interesting" (albeit "expensive") "new dining experience" – of course, the expected holdouts scoff "there's a reason cooking was invented"; N.B. the Newburyport offshoot premiered post-Survey.

Ⓩ Grill 23 & Bar *Steak* | 25 | 24 | 24 | $66 |

Back Bay | 161 Berkeley St. (Stuart St.) | 617-542-2255 | www.grill23.com

"Just the right blend of old-world steakhouse" and "new-world trendy" goes into this "opulent" Back Bay "hall of famer" where "the usual suspects" – "suits", "Brahmins", "celebrities" – flock for "bigger-than-life portions" of "phenomenal" meats, "fabulous sides" and an "enormous wine list"; "exemplary service" is par for the course, as are "premium prices" and "noise" that "leaves your ears ringing."

Grotto *Italian* | 25 | 19 | 22 | $41 |

Beacon Hill | 37 Bowdoin St. (bet. Beacon & Cambridge Sts.) | 617-227-3434 | www.grottorestaurant.com

"If you're not careful" you might pass this "hidden jewel" in a Beacon Hill basement – so keep your eyes peeled, because its "indulgent"

Northern Italian fare is "not to be missed", especially considering the "high quality-to-cost" ratio (the three-course prix fixe is a particularly "awesome" "bargain"); while some can't get past the "cramped" seating, most happily succumb to its "darkly lit", "ultraromantic" "charms" – with the help of "personal service" and "spectacular wines", of course.

Haley House Bakery Café ☒ *American* ▽ 24 | 16 | 20 | $13

Roxbury | 12 Dade St. (Washington St.) | 617-445-0900 | www.haleyhouse.org

Have a "great breakfast" or lunch with a side of "instant karma" at this American cafe/"bakery with a heart" in Roxbury, which "turns lives around" by offering residents in need "training for culinary careers"; a "diverse" clientele appreciates that the "real treats" are made "using local, organic and seasonal produce" (props to the "rotating art displays" too), but that's just icing on a cake whose "service to the community is beyond belief"; N.B. dinner is now served Wednesday–Friday until 9 PM.

Halfway Cafe ◑ *Pub Food* 17 | 11 | 18 | $19

Dedham | 174 Washington St. (VFW Pkwy.) | 781-326-3336
Watertown | 394 Main St. (Lexington St.) | 617-926-3595
Marshfield | 1840 Ocean St. (Library Plaza) | 781-834-3040
Holbrook | 200 S. Franklin St. (bet. Adams St. & Technical Park Dr.) | 781-767-2900
Canton | Cobbs Corner Plaza | 95 Washington St. (Cobbs Corner) | 781-821-0944
Marlborough | 820 Boston Post Rd./Rte. 20 (bet. Farm & Wayside Inn Rds.) | 508-480-0688
www.thehalfwaycafe.com

They're really "sports bars", but feel free to "take the kids" to these "laid-back" "pub-grub" purveyors for "flavorful steak tips" (the "signature dish") and other reliable "cheap eats"; they're "nothing fancy" – the decor's pretty much just "multiple televisions" and the service is "typical" for a "family-friendly" chain – but "who can afford fancy all the time?"

☒ Hamersley's Bistro *French* 27 | 23 | 25 | $61

South End | 553 Tremont St. (Clarendon St.) | 617-423-2700 | www.hamersleysbistro.com

"Maestro" Gordon Hamersley remains "very visible" at this "light, airy" South End "institution", just as his "not-trendy", "seasonally changing" country French fare "still lives up to its well-deserved reputation", particularly the "luscious" "signature roast chicken" (rumored to trigger "out-of-body experiences"); the "top-notch" fare and "superior service" command upper-tier pricing, but the "thoughtful wine list" displays "some good buys."

Harry's Restaurant ◑⊅ *Diner* 20 | 10 | 18 | $24

Westborough | 149 Turnpike Rd./Rte. 9 (Lyman St.) | 508-366-8302 | www.harrysrestaurant.com

"Everything a diner should be", this "small" "all-American" "riot" in quiet Westborough plies an "eclectic mix of customers" with "great breakfasts", plus "excellent" fried clams, "pies to die for" and other inexpensive "greasy-spoon" plates; a "happy, homey" vibe pervades, and the "rapid" staffers keep it all flowing smoothly until the AM ("go here for a good time late-night").

Haru ● *Japanese*   20 | 21 | 19 | $40

Back Bay | 55 Huntington Ave. (Ring Rd.) | 617-536-0770 | www.harusushi.com

"Prudential Mall masses" make this "very Zen" Back Bay outpost (bamboo, slate, water features) of the NYC-based chain their choice for "innovative, delicious maki" and nigiri, plus some "cooked" Japanese fare, all offered at "prices on the high end of reasonable"; but said tabs are "unwarranted" warn more discerning palates who judge the sushi "so-so", the portions "small" and the service "a little slow."

Harvard Gardens ● *American*   17 | 15 | 17 | $28

Beacon Hill | 316 Cambridge St. (Grove St.) | 617-523-2727 | www.harvardgardens.com

More a "bar with food than a restaurant", this "dark" "meat market for the Mass. General post-shift crowd" ("meet a doctor or nurse!") serves American pub grub to soak up its "infused martinis" - unfortunately, the fare's "generally a disappointment for the price"; it's often "jammed", "making it hard to get around" for both patrons and servers, the latter "doing their best under difficult circumstances."

Harvest *American*   25 | 22 | 23 | $53

Harvard Square | 44 Brattle St. (Church St.) | Cambridge | 617-868-2255 | www.harvestcambridge.com

A Harvard Square "institution for more than 30 years", this "oasis" "gracefully serves" "refined", "exquisitely prepared" New American cuisine with "local produce" to "Nobel Prize winners", "classy" "parents" and "employers wooing graduates" (read: "this is not a place to go slumming"); the "warm", "quietly elegant" setting, featuring a "lovely patio" and "stylish", "well-stocked" bar, furthers the feeling that the "pricey" tabs are "worth every penny."

Haveli *Indian*   - | - | - | I

Inman Square | 1248-1250 Cambridge St. (Prospect St.) | Cambridge | 617-497-6548 | royalbharatinc.com

With "tapestry-covered walls" and other "fantastic" decor touches, this Inman Square Indian imparts "the true feeling of a haveli [private residence]", albeit quite a "romantic" one; "great deals" can be found throughout the "reliable, standard" menu, including a daily lunch buffet and "dinner specials that fill you up without emptying your wallet."

☑ Helmand *Afghan*   26 | 22 | 21 | $35

East Cambridge | 143 First St. (Bent St.) | Cambridge | 617-492-4646 | www.helmandrestaurantcambridge.com

"Who knew Afghani cuisine is so wonderful?" goes the common refrain from first-timers to this "exquisite" East Cambridge eatery where the "unusual, delicious" "food from another world" includes "plenty of vegetarian options" and "scrumptious bread" that comes from a "large oven in the center" of the "warm, romantic main room"; everything is "extremely well priced" and "arrives quickly" – too fast for thwarted lingerers who feel the staff "can't wait to get you out."

Henrietta's Table *New England*   23 | 20 | 21 | $41

Harvard Square | Charles Hotel | 1 Bennett St. (Eliot St.) | Cambridge | 617-661-5005 | www.henriettastable.com

There's "always something new on the menu" at this hotel venue in Harvard Square, where the "hearty", "locally sourced" "comfort food" is "just like" "your New England grandmother" made – only "fancier" and "more expensive"; the ambiance in the "large, well-populated" "farmhouse-style" interior and "lovely patio" is forever "cheery", regardless of the "inconsistent" service; P.S. "don't miss the fabulous Sunday brunch."

Highland Kitchen *American*   23 | 19 | 21 | $31

Somerville | 150 Highland Ave. (Central St.) | 617-625-1131 | www.highlandkitchen.com

"The word is out!" – this "intimate joint" in "increasingly yuppified" Somerville offers "stellar", occasionally "triumphant" New American cuisine with "delicious" "Southern twists" for "reasonable" rates; indeed, it's "always crowded", especially with a "younger crowd" downing "funky cocktails" while programming the "groovy jukebox" in the bar – but somehow, "friendly service makes it seem less noisy."

Hilltop Steak House *Steak*   16 | 12 | 16 | $34

Saugus | 855 Broadway/Rte. 1 (Lynn Fells Pkwy.) | 781-233-7700 | www.hilltopsteakhouse.com

"Your very elderly relative's favorite" Saugus steakhouse – the one with the "seasonally attired" "plastic cows out front" – still draws "enormous volumes of people" who "don't mind" "waiting" for their tables to be called ("fawty-foah to Cah-son City!") before "being herded" to "huge" "theme rooms" with "out-of-date cowboy decor" for "big portions" of "value" beef; while many young 'uns will "never understand" its appeal, the "curious" admit it's "worth at least one trip."

Himalayan Bistro *Indian/Nepalese*   24 | 17 | 22 | $26

West Roxbury | 1735 Centre St. (Manthorne Rd.) | 617-325-3500 | www.himalayanbistro.net

"For a change of pace", this West Roxbury "alternative" augments "fresh" Indian eats with "unique" "Nepalese specials", many delivering "quite a kick", all offering "good value"; the setting is "not enticing at all", but it's "quiet" and sufficiently "comfortable" thanks to "friendly" servers who clearly "take pride in serving their national fare."

Hi-Rise Bread Co. *Bakery/Sandwiches*   24 | 14 | 14 | $14

Harvard Square | 56 Brattle St. (Church St.) | Cambridge | 617-492-3003 ⊘
Huron Village | 208 Concord Ave. (Huron Ave.) | Cambridge | 617-876-8766

"Long lines" and "scant" seating don't deter Harvard Square and Huron Village hordes from these bakery/cafes' "innovative" sandwiches "piled high on heavenly fresh-baked bread" and "bursting with flavor" ("pricey" but almost "big enough for two meals"), plus "tasty soups" and "to-die-for pastries"; yes, "everything's delicious" – it's only the "grouchy", "snotty" counter help that "puts a bitter taste in your mouth."

Hot Tomatoes *Pizza*

22 | 15 | 17 | $19

Downtown Crossing | 45 Kingston St. (bet. Bedford & Otis Sts.) | 617-292-0233
North End | 261 North St. (Lewis St.) | 617-557-0033
The "small kitchen" of this "cute", "cramped" North End storefront "manages to produce incredible pizzas" with "fancy ingredients", "amazing soups and salads" and "innovative sandwiches" ("there's a sub to suit any taste bud"); some cost-assessors feel it's "expensive" for a deli, but "for the amount of food you get, it's a great value"; N.B. the lunch-only Downtown Crossing locale opened post-Survey.

House of Siam *Thai*

24 | 17 | 19 | $27

South End | 542 Columbus Ave. (Worcester St.) | 617-267-1755
South End | 592 Tremont St. (Dartmouth St.) | 617-267-7426
houseofsiamboston.com
"Mouthwatering dishes" listed on a "menu so big, you get lost in it" are "served with a smile" "for reasonable prices" at these South End Thai "go-tos" for both eat-in and takeout; the Columbus Avenue "staple" "could use a spruce" (good thing it's "dimly lit"), while its slightly smaller Tremont Street sibling opened post-Survey.

House of Tibet Kitchen Ⓜ *Tibetan*

- | - | - | I

Somerville | Teele Sq. | 235 Holland St. (Broadway) | 617-629-7567
"What a find" marvel Somervilleans of this simple, "friendly", "reliable" restaurant when they first sample its "amazing, unique" Tibetan menu, which features "endless options for vegetarians" (it's also quite "comforting" in "cold weather"); "the portion sizes are just right", a real bonus considering how "cheap" it is.

Houston's *American*

22 | 20 | 21 | $35

Faneuil Hall | Faneuil Hall Mktpl. | 60 State St. (Congress St.) | 617-573-9777 | www.hillstone.com
A "chain that doesn't feel like one", this "reliable" national franchise's Faneuil Hall outpost "clicks" thanks to a "pretty darn good" menu of "all-American comfort" items (including a notoriously "addicting spinach dip") and a "modern metropolitan" ambiance that brings in "mingling singles" and "consistent after-work crowds"; despite debate on the cost – "reasonable" vs. "overpriced" – most report "solid quality" here.

Hungry I, The *French*

24 | 24 | 22 | $55

Beacon Hill | 71½ Charles St. (bet. Mt. Vernon & Pinckney Sts.) | 617-227-3524 | hungryiboston.com
"Many engagements have been sealed" at this "wildly romantic" "cove under Beacon Hill" with "cozy tables" next to three fireplaces, lots of "interesting nooks" and a "secret garden out back"; the "pricey", "outstanding country French fare" exhibits "innovation" while remaining "faithful to tradition", and the "attentive" servers

can offer "good advice about" it to "serious foodies" who think it "has nothing to offer."

☑ Hungry Mother ⓜ *American*   27 | 22 | 25 | $41

Kendall Square | 233 Cardinal Medeiros Ave. (Binney St.) | Cambridge | 617-499-0090 | www.hungrymothercambridge.com
Settle in for some "high-end Southern comfort" at this "terrific" Kendall Square spot where a "small, innovative menu" of "elegant" New American cuisine gets a "Virginia spin" courtesy of "great", "dedicated" chef Barry Maiden (ex Lumière); but don't try it "without a reservation", because the "chic, homey" and "cramped" space gets "insanely busy" with folks keen on the "unique whiskey-based cocktails", "appreciable wine list" and "knowledgeable", "energetic staff."

☑ Il Capriccio Ⓢ *Italian*   27 | 22 | 25 | $58

Waltham | 888 Main St. (Prospect St.) | 781-894-2234 | www.ilcapricciowaltham.com
"Waltham's foodie paradise" "impresses" with "luxurious", "magical-at-times" Northern Italian cuisine ("don't miss" the "incredible" mushroom soufflé) – but it's "incomparable" sommelier Jeannie Rogers' "superb", "voluminous wine list" that really "makes the evening special"; some dub the setting a "cold", "tight" "maze", but most say it's "sophisticated", just like the "intelligent service" – "as you should expect for a restaurant in this [upper] price range."

NEW Il Casale ⓜ *Italian*   - | - | - | M

Belmont | 50 Leonard St. (Moore St.) | 617-209-4942 | www.ilcasalebelmont.com
Chef Dante de Magistris (Dante) draws inspiration from his childhood summers spent in Southern Italy for small plates and family-style dinners served in a renovated 1899 Belmont firehouse, where handcrafted Vermont wood tables and hand-blown Venetian glass lanterns evoke the restaurant's name (*casale* means 'rural home'); the dining room features a communal table overlooking the open kitchen, and there's sidewalk seating in warmer months.

Il Panino Express ⌀ *Italian*   23 | 12 | 17 | $15

North End | 264-266 Hanover St. (Parmenter St.) | 617-720-5720 | www.depasqualeventures.com
North Enders pop into this "little", "no-frills" stop for "quick", "cheap", "homemade Italian" bites like "*bene* slices" and "hearty, tasty sandwiches"; the atmosphere's strictly "cafeteria", but it's "nicer" on a "summer night when they open the windows."

Incontro ● *Italian*   22 | 22 | 17 | $43

Franklin | 860 W. Central St. (Forge Pkwy.) | 508-520-2770 | www.incontrorestaurant.com
The folks behind this Franklin Italian have done a "beautiful job fixing up an old mill", outfitting it with a "modern, comfortable" downstairs dining area (it gets "noisy", so "ask for one of the round banquettes" for "an intimate meal") and a "funky" "see-and-be-seen" bar with billiards upstairs; the fare, especially the wood-fired pizza, is also "superb" (if "a bit pricey for the area") – it's just service that "needs work."

	FOOD	DECOR	SERVICE	COST

Independent, The *American* | 18 | 19 | 16 | $30 |

Somerville | 75 Union Sq. (Washington St.) | 617-440-6022 |
www.theindo.com

"Two environments – one for eating" a "diverse menu" of
"dependable", "occasionally innovative" New American "pub
standards" and some "serious entrees" ("alright for the price"),
and "one for drinking" an "excellent selection of craft beers and
classic cocktails" – define this hangout located in Somerville;
the service is somewhat "erratic", but the crowd makes it "an
oasis of conviviality."

India Pavilion *Indian* ▽ 20 | 13 | 16 | $24 |

Central Square | 17 Central Sq. (Western Ave.) | Cambridge |
617-547-7463 | www.royalbharatinc.com

"Central Square has no shortage of Southwest Asian" eateries, but
this "old reliable" "makes a name for itself" with "pretty generous
portions" of "typical", "traditional" Indian fare at "modest" prices;
area workers deem it easy "to grab lunch with coworkers", despite
having to occasionally "flag down" service (and that it "could
use new decor").

India Quality *Indian* | 24 | 15 | 21 | $23 |

Kenmore Square | 484 Commonwealth Ave. (Kenmore St.) |
617-267-4499 | www.indiaquality.com

"Despite its dreary location" in a "cramped" "Kenmore Square
basement", this Indian eatery "obsesses" "curry lovers" with its
"generous portions" of "out-of-this-world", "value"-priced
"staples", all of which "can be tailored to mild, medium or hot";
"quick" "service with a smile" is another reason it has so
many "regular customers."

Isabella *American* | 24 | 20 | 22 | $40 |

Dedham | 566 High St. (bet. Eastern Ave. & Washington St.) |
781-461-8485 | www.isabellarestaurant.com

You can really "taste the fresh ingredients" in the "imaginative" New
American cuisine created at this Dedham "keeper" whose "high
quality" is even more notable for its "reasonable prices"; a
reputation as an "oasis of sophistication" is bolstered by "elegant
yet casual" environs, characterized by a "nice mural of Isabella
Stewart Gardner" and an "accommodating" staff that "always
makes you feel welcome."

Island Hopper *Asian* | 19 | 17 | 18 | $24 |

Back Bay | 91 Massachusetts Ave. (bet. Commonwealth Ave. &
Newbury St.) | 617-266-1618 | www.islandhopperboston.com

What a "great idea" marvel "deal"-seekers who happen upon this
"solid" Back Bay bastion of all things Asian – Malaysian,
Singaporean, Vietnamese, Thai, Chinese (including "hard-to-find
Hainanese dishes") and others – where "quick", "friendly" meals are
the norm since it's "usually not crowded"; but "be wary of a restaurant that tries to squeeze in too many cuisines" warn detractors who
also shun "cheesy" "island" decor.

	FOOD	DECOR	SERVICE	COST

☑ Ithaki Mediterranean Cuisine ☒ *Mediterranean*

26 | 21 | 24 | $43

Ipswich | 25 Hammatt St. (Depot Sq.) | 978-356-0099 | www.ithakicuisine.com

Ipswich Greek groupies tell their Boston counterparts it's "definitely worth the trek" for this "sophisticate's" "expertly prepared and presented", "modern" Med cuisine; they further point toward the "gracious", "attentive" service and "lovely" fresh-flower-festooned environment as reasons it's not only a "guaranteed positive experience", but deserving of the "expensive" cost.

Ivy Restaurant *Italian*

20 | 20 | 17 | $35

Downtown Crossing | 49 Temple Pl. (bet. Tremont & Washington Sts.) | 617-963-1534 | www.ivyrestaurantgroup.com

"Come with friends and share" this "stylish", "loud" Downtown Crossing spot's "delicious, interesting" Italian tapas while perusing the "nice range" of *vini* priced under $30 (it "falls short for wine snobs", but it's a "great value" to everyone else) and the "young", "scantily clad crowd clustered at the bar"; but "make sure to leave enough time for the relaxed" servers – "just eye candy apparently", when they're not "rude."

Jacob Wirth *American/German*

17 | 18 | 17 | $28

Theater District | 31-37 Stuart St. (bet. Tremont & Washington Sts.) | 617-338-8586 | www.jacobwirth.com

One of the Theater District's longest-running attractions, this "landmark" 1868 "beer hall" stars "saucy" servers and "the only authentic German menu in Boston" (tempered with some "less hearty" New American fare, none of it overpriced); ok, it may be wholly "mediocre" and a smidge "shabby", but it's "interesting" from a "historical" perspective, plus the brew list is "a thing to behold", as is the "amazing Friday night sing-along."

Jae's *Asian*

20 | 16 | 18 | $31

South End | 520 Columbus Ave. (Concord Sq.) | 617-421-9405 | www.jaescafe.com

With an "interesting menu" of "dependable sushi" and other Japanese offerings, "spicy Thai" and "traditional Korean fare", this South Ender "satisfies" all sorts of Asian hankerings in one fell swoop and for a "reasonable price"; the fact that it "could use some sprucing" doesn't keep the "crowds" away, which in turn leads to occasionally "slow service."

Jake's Dixie Roadhouse *BBQ*

17 | 13 | 16 | $25

Waltham | 220 Moody St. (bet. Main & Pine Sts.) | 781-894-4227 | www.jakes-bbq.com

"BBQ, blues and beer" are what this "real roadhouse" in Waltham is all about, and its "grubby"-"comfy" atmosphere proves a fitting setting for "good" live music and "different regional" styles of cheap albeit "mediocre" 'cue served in "big portions"; to say it's "so loud" is an understatement, which is why it works "better as a bar scene."

James's Gate Ⓜ *American/Irish*

▽ 16 | 16 | 18 | $23

Jamaica Plain | 5-11 McBride St. (South St.) | 617-983-2000 |
www.jamessgate.com

This "cozy" "place to hang" employs an "Irish-accented staff" that
tends a "blazing fire in the winter" as it vends "unpretentious, satisfying" pub grub and "copious" amounts of beer in the bar (there's also
a patio come summer); the separate dining room boasts its own
"charm and character", but a few foodies conclude that ordering from
its seemingly "more upscale" American menu could be a "mistake."

Jamjuli *Thai*

19 | 16 | 18 | $24

Newton | 1203 Walnut St. (Centre St.) | 617-965-5655 | www.jamjuli.com
"Darn reliable", "quick" Thai for "reasonable prices" makes this "easy-
to-drive-past" Newton spot a stop, and while its flavor may be "run-
of-the-mill" (despite a "strong range of selections"), you can always
"ask" the "friendly people" who work there "to increase the spice" –
who knows, that might also make up for the setting's "lack of warmth."

Jasmine Bistro *French/Hungarian*

▽ 24 | 16 | 25 | $39

Brighton | 412 Market St. (Washington St.) | 617-789-4676 |
www.jasmine-bistro.com

The "extremely personable" family that operates this "cozy" Brighton
"treasure" "treats you like one" of its own while plying "spectacular"
renditions of "multiple cuisines": French, Middle Eastern and "true
Hungarian" ("hard to find in Boston"); it's arguable that "home
cooking shouldn't cost this much", but to the loyal regulars who
make it a "destination", it "never disappoints."

Jasper White's Summer Shack *New England*

21 | 14 | 18 | $37

Back Bay | 50 Dalton St. (Boylston St.) | 617-867-9955
Huron Village | 149 Alewife Brook Pkwy. (Cambridge Park Dr.) |
Cambridge | 617-520-9500
NEW **Hingham** | Derby Street Shoppes | 96 Derby St. (Cushing St.) |
781-740-9555
www.summershackrestaurant.com

Have an "adult meal" of "fresher-than-fresh" "New England seafood"
like "to-die-for clam bakes" while the kids nosh on "great corn dogs"
("if you don't come with a toddler, you're in the minority") at these
"noisy" "airplane hangars" whose "campy" "decor conjures the
coast" with "sticky" "picnic benches and paper tablecloths"; but the
fact that it's "probably the most expensive 'shack' you'll ever visit" ran-
kles "pooh-poohing foodies" who call it "completely unremarkable."

Jer-Ne *American*

20 | 22 | 20 | $54

Theater District | Ritz-Carlton Boston Common | 10 Avery St.
(Tremont St.) | 617-574-7176 | www.ritzcarlton.com

"Pretty laid-back" for the upscale Ritz-Carlton Boston Common, this
stylish, loungey eatery – in which "modern art" hangs below "soaring ceilings" – is a place to go "if you want to sit quietly at a bar and
enjoy" "great drinks and snacks" in the Theater District; as for the
New American meals, though "elegant", they're too "uninspired" to
command checks for which "you need to jer-ne for more money."

	FOOD	DECOR	SERVICE	COST

Jerusalem Pita *Israeli*

-	-	-	M

Brookline | 10 Pleasant St. (bet. John & Waldo Sts.) | 617-739-2400 | www.jerusalempita.com

There's an uptown urban feel to this small Brookliner that imports pita and spices for its midpriced kosher Israeli fare, including shawarma, falafel and grilled meats; guests can cozy up to the granite bar for a glass of wine or beer or sit at tables surrounded by murals and shimmering hanging lights.

Jimmy's Steer House *Steak*

20	16	20	$27

Arlington | 1111 Massachusetts Ave. (Quincy St.) | 781-646-4450 | www.jimmysarlington.com
Saugus | 114 Broadway (bet. Rte. 129 & Walnut St.) | 781-233-8600 | www.jimmyssaugus.com

"Older folks and families" "mob" these "not-fancy" Arlington and Saugus "standby" steakhouses for "fair-sized portions" of "consistent" beef that, while "not prime", lies "as close as you can come" for such "modest costs"; "you might need to wait" for a table, although the "harried staff" does its best to get the early birds "home by 6 PM."

Joe's American Bar & Grill *American*

16	16	17	$29

North End | 100 Atlantic Ave. (Commercial Wharf) | 617-367-8700
Braintree | South Shore Plaza | 250 Granite St. (I-95, exit 6) | 781-848-0200
Dedham | 985 Providence Hwy. (bet. Rtes. 1 & 128) | 781-329-0800
Peabody | North Shore Mall | 210 Andover St./Rte. 114 (Rte. 128) | 978-532-9500
Woburn | 311 Mishawum Rd. (Commerce Way) | 781-935-7200
Hanover | Merchants Row | 2087 Washington St./Rte. 53 (Rte. 123) | 781-878-1234
Franklin | 466 King St. (Union St.) | 508-553-9313
Framingham | Shoppers World | 1 Worcester Rd./Rte. 9 (bet. I-90 & Rte. 30) | 508-820-8389
www.joesamerican.com

"When in doubt, go to Joe's" for "large portions" of "decent-value" "straight American" chain fare (a "step up from bar food" and "reliable"); it's "noisy" and the "decor is kind of generic"/"corporate", but many branches' "outdoor seating" – especially the one in the North End, where it comes "for a fraction of the cost" of its neighbors – are "crowd-pleasing" "pluses."

Joe Tecce's *Italian*

19	17	18	$36

North End | 61 N. Washington St. (Cooper St.) | 617-742-6210 | www.joetecces.com

"For a taste of old-school Italian" "red sauce", head to this "North End institution" where "accommodating" servers bring it in "huge portions" for "reasonable prices"; "every square inch is decorated" with grapes, "urns, mosaics and statues", and though quite a few peg it as a "tacky cliché", still, "it's been around so long, you have to pay it some respect – but not very often."

	FOOD	DECOR	SERVICE	COST

John Harvard's Brew House ● *Pub Food*   16 | 16 | 17 | $25

Harvard Square | 33 Dunster St. (bet. Mass. Ave. & Mt. Auburn St.) |
Cambridge | 617-868-3585
Framingham | Shoppers World | 1 Worcester Rd./Rte. 9 (bet. I-90 &
Rte. 30) | 508-875-2337
www.johnharvards.com

The "inexpensive" American pub grub's merely "mediocre", but the
"brewed on-site beers" are "terrific" at this "casual gathering place"
for "tourists and students" in Harvard Square and its offshoot, "the
salvation of suburbanites who don't have much choice" in
Framingham; "lots of TVs" distract "sports-watchers" from
the "inconsistent service."

Johnny D's Uptown ●Ⓜ *American*   19 | 15 | 17 | $24

Somerville | 17 Holland St. (College Ave.) | 617-776-2004 |
www.johnnyds.com

"Great" live music "every night of the week" is "definitely the draw"
to this Somerville "icon" with "record covers on the walls" and service that swings between "friendly" and "obnoxious"; the "reasonably priced" American pub fare is strictly "concomitant", except at
the "crowded, loud" and "awesome weekend" jazz brunch when
"slow-cooked oatmeal" and other AM alimentation "stand out."

Johnny's Luncheonette *Diner*   18 | 14 | 17 | $19

Newton | 30 Langley Rd. (bet. Beacon & Centre Sts.) | 617-527-3223 |
www.johnnysluncheonette.com

"Gigantic portions" of "retro" American diner food – especially all-
day "breakfast items beyond belief" – "at affordable prices" incite
"long lines at peak times" for this "cool little '50s-style" "staple" in
Newton Center; it's so packed and "noisy" with "multigenerational
crowds", you shouldn't be surprised if you have to "chase the
staff for everything."

José's *Mexican*   19 | 16 | 20 | $20

Huron Village | 131 Sherman St. (bet. Rindge Ave. & Walden St.) |
Cambridge | 617-354-0335 | www.josesmex.com

Lots of tequila buffs consider it "worth the schlep" to this "colorful,
slightly rickety" Mexican "on a quiet street" near Huron Village because it always "feels like a party", helped no doubt by "second margaritas that always [seem] way stronger than the first"; as for the
fare, it's "reliable", "cheap" and plentiful, if "a tad underspiced."

Joshua Tree *Pub Food*   15 | 14 | 15 | $21

Allston | 1316 Commonwealth Ave. (bet. Griggs & Redford Sts.) |
617-566-6699 | www.joshuatreeallston.com
Somerville | 256 Elm St. (Davis Sq.) | 617-623-9910 |
www.joshuatreesomerville.com

"Younger" folks, including "lots of students", descend on these Allston
and Somerville sports bars for their "tons" of "high-def flat-
screens"; "as a side" to the "excellent beers", the "basic", inexpensive pub grub does the trick, but "as a main meal", it "leaves much
to be desired", just like service that "isn't always the quickest."

	FOOD	DECOR	SERVICE	COST

JP Seafood Cafe *Japanese/Korean*

| 23 | 15 | 20 | $26 |

Jamaica Plain | 730 Centre St. (Harris Ave.) | 617-983-5177 |
www.jpseafoodcafe.com

A "solid choice for no-nonsense", "high-quality sushi", this "reliable"
Jamaica Plain Japanese also offers "moderately priced" Korean
delivered by a "welcoming" staff; the "casual, kid-friendly", "fish-
themed" digs can feel like a "noisy" "school cafeteria", which leads
non-parents to decree "all in all, it's probably better for takeout."

❷ J's at Nashoba Valley Winery ⓂAmerican

| 26 | 26 | 23 | $44 |

Bolton | 100 Wattaquadock Hill Rd. (Berlin Rd.) | 978-779-9816 |
www.nashobawinery.com

"You'll think you're in a farmhouse in Normandy" at this Bolton hilltop
"romantic" with "breathtaking" views of "aromatic orchards" – even
though the "delicious", "adventurous" fare, featuring "produce
grown on the premises", is all (New) American; the "wonderful" staff
does "an excellent job pairing the food with the vineyard's own fruit
wines", and while the cost is "high", the portions make it "a value";
P.S. bring "a group for brunch" on the "beautiful" patio, "come early
for apple picking" and remain for *vin* "tastings afterward."

Jumbo Seafood *Chinese/Seafood*

| 23 | 15 | 18 | $28 |

Newton | 10 Langley Rd. (Centre St.) | 617-332-3600 |
www.jumboseafoodrestaurant.com

New Jumbo Seafood ❶ *Chinese/Seafood*

Chinatown | 5 Hudson St. (bet. Beach & Kneeland Sts.) |
617-542-2823 | www.newjumboseafoodrestaurant.com

When it comes to Cantonese fare, this separately owned pair is "a
step above most" (and "a bit more expensive", but "worth it")
thanks to "fresh seafood" you "choose from a tank", supplemented
by "well-prepared" dim sum at weekend brunch; with "white tablecloths and high-definition TVs" "over the bar", the Newton location
sports more of a "modern feel" than the "basic", "cramped"
Chinatown original, while both offer "adequate service."

🆕 Kama Lounge *Spanish*

| - | - | - | M |

Quincy | 39 Cottage Ave. (bet. Chestnut St. & Dennis Ryan Pkwy.) |
617-773-3002 | www.kama-lounge.com

Settle in for the night at this Quincy club (from the owners of Bistro
Chi next door) serving tapas and specialty cocktails amid a sea of
sofas, coffee tables and cozy nooks – perfect for date nights or a
hang with the gang; the black walls, black seating and low lighting
are offset by gold ceilings, a DJ pumping house tracks, dancing and
the occasional live performance.

Karoun 🚫Ⓜ *Armenian/Mideastern*

| 22 | 18 | 21 | $34 |

Newton | 839 Washington St. (Walnut St.) | 617-964-3400 |
www.karoun.net

"It's all about the belly dancing" say Newtonians who frequent this
"family-run" establishment's "amazing" weekend shows – but it's
also "reliable" for a "kebab fix", as the midpriced Middle Eastern

fare, coupled with "authentic Armenian" dishes, "never disappoints"; "the decor could use a bit of modernizing", while the staff is dependably "lovely and welcoming."

Kashmir *Indian* | 23 | 19 | 19 | $32 |

Back Bay | 279 Newbury St. (Gloucester St.) | 617-536-1695 | www.kashmirrestaurant.com

As "classy" and "civilized" as the Back Bay itself, this venue offers "brilliant" Indian cuisine in a "well-decorated" interior where "there's almost never a wait" (because everyone knows the "outdoor seats in nice weather are the way to go"); it's "a bit pricey" for the genre, but it "costs more because it's on Newbury Street" – indeed, the "lunch buffet is the only bargain", but it's "a magnificent one."

Kathmandu Spice *Nepalese* | 22 | 16 | 19 | $24 |

Arlington | 166 Massachusetts Ave. (Lake St.) | 781-316-1755 | www.kathmanduspice.com

"Easily one of the more interesting restaurants in Arlington", this eatery offers "reasonably priced" Nepalese fare featuring a "nice variety of vegetarian and meat dishes", "unusual textures and spices" and "outside influences", especially from "India and Tibet"; the "great" "deal" lunch buffet in particular often draws "noisy crowds" to the "dreary, dull" digs, which the "warm staff" does its best to offset.

Kayuga ● *Japanese/Korean* | ∇ 24 | 15 | 20 | $31 |

Brookline | 1030 Commonwealth Ave. (Babcock St.) | 617-566-8888

Kayuga II *Japanese/Korean*

Arlington | 444 Massachusetts Ave. (Medford St.) | 781-648-7878

"Unpretentious", "satisfactory" Japanese and Korean eats, including low-priced sushi, and late hours make this spot a destination for students in Brookline, nondescript atmosphere notwithstanding; meanwhile, the "delightful" Arlington offshoot adds Chinese and Thai dishes while keeping the portions "generous" and the prices "fair."

Kaze ● *Japanese* | 23 | 16 | 16 | $26 |

Chinatown | 1 Harrison Ave. (Essex St.) | 617-338-8283 | www.kazeshabushabu.com

"Great for a date", "healthy eating" or to just "show off your boiling skills", this Chinatown "change of pace" offers "a nice range of ingredients and broths" to do shabu-shabu, Japan's more wholesome version of fondue; the "clean, modern", "spacious" space loses points for a "garish" facade, but it matters not to seekers of "fun" "without breaking the bank."

Kebab Factory *Indian* | 24 | 16 | 19 | $22 |

Somerville | 414 Washington St. (Beacon St.) | 617-354-4996 | www.thekebabfactory.net

"Both the skewered and non-skewered" Indian dishes at this "tiny", "distinctive" Somerville spot come "innovatively presented" with "adventurous" "spins" via "friendly, attentive" servers; the somewhat industrialized "decor does little" to attract, but the "nice prices" and "oh-so-yummy lunch buffet" "blow [folks] away."

	FOOD	DECOR	SERVICE	COST

Khao Sarn Cuisine 🗷 Ⓜ *Thai* | 24 | 20 | 21 | $29 |

Brookline | 250 Harvard St. (Beacon St.) | 617-566-7200 |
www.khaosarnboston.com

"Exotic" for Brookline, the Northern Thai cuisine offered at this
"comfortable" storefront is "delicious, fresh" and "fills your belly
without emptying your wallet"; takeout is as "pleasant" as eating in
the "elegant, minimalist setting", which features a full bar where
"capable", "attentive" servers procure "luscious mango martinis
and delicious mai tais."

King & I *Thai* | 22 | 14 | 21 | $24 |

Beacon Hill | 145 Charles St. (Cambridge St.) | 617-227-3320 |
www.kingandi-boston.com

"Year after year", this "classic Thai" "in the heart of Beacon Hill"
doles out "generous portions" of "inexpensive", "fresh and
delicious" fare, which is "prepared to your taste" "fast" by "friendly"
servers; patrons who shun "fairly small" spaces with "unremarkable
decor" "stick to takeout."

KingFish Hall *Seafood* | 22 | 20 | 20 | $46 |

Faneuil Hall | Faneuil Hall Mktpl. | 188 Faneuil Hall Mktpl. (Chatham St.) |
617-523-8862 | www.toddenglish.com

"Due to its Faneuil Hall location", this "large place" is "filled with
tourists", but locals get "reeled in" too due to celebrity chef "Todd
English's mastery of seafood" prepared with boatloads of "delicious
twists", which "friendly, efficient" servers deliver alongside "fun
cocktails" on two "noisy" floors with "riotous clam-shaped booths",
a "splendid patio" and "terrific raw bar"; if only it weren't "such a hit
on the wallet."

Kingston Station ❶ *American* | 20 | 18 | 19 | $29 |

Downtown Crossing | 25 Kingston St. (bet. Bedford & Summer Sts.) |
617-482-6282 | www.kingstonstation.com

"Short money" gets Downtown Crossing lunch-goers and after-
workers "solid" American fare, "inventive drinks" and
"unpretentious wines" from a "focused list" ("love that it serves
by the glass, half-carafe, full-carafe" or bottle) at this "laid-
back" bistro; though the "cool" decor's tiled surfaces make a
"noisy" first impression, the "personable" staff engenders the
intended "cozy atmosphere."

KO Prime *Steak* | 24 | 22 | 23 | $66 |

Downtown Crossing | Nine Zero Hotel | 90 Tremont St. (Beacon St.) |
617-772-0202 | www.koprimeboston.com

"Ken Oringer has outdone himself" at his "exciting" "nontraditional
steakhouse" in Downtown Crossing's "boutique-y Nine Zero Hotel",
which "delivers what the masses expect" ("handsome presentations" of "amazing" beef) alongside more "cutting-edge" fare (the
"chef likes to use all of the animal", so expect plenty of offal); the
"sexy scene", "plush" environs, "trendy" cocktail "concoctions" and
"beautiful", "young" crowd are expectedly "over the top" – is it any
wonder the prices are "sky high" too?

Koreana Ⓜ *Japanese/Korean*   21 | 14 | 17 | $30

Central Square | 154-158 Prospect St. (Broadway) | Cambridge |
617-576-8661 | www.koreanaboston.com

An "authentic" "grill-your-own" Korean barbecue experience awaits
at this spot between Central and Inman Squares, where the "intense, exotic flavors" of "incredible marinades" and "interesting
sides" can be coupled with hot pots and sushi; despite "nothing-
special decor", it's usually "lively" with "students" for whom "fair
prices" trump "mediocre service."

Kouzina ⊠Ⓜ *Greek/Mediterranean*   23 | 16 | 21 | $37

Newton | 1649 Beacon St. (Windsor Rd.) | 617-558-7677 |
www.kouzinarestaurant.com

"Such a prize" is this storefront's "consistently delicious", "fairly
priced" Greek and Mediterranean fare (with "some innovative
takes") and "personalized service" that fans "don't want anyone
else to know about it"; but it's obviously too late since the "tiny"
space located in Newton's Waban neighborhood with "very close"
tables "fills up fast" despite the promise of "noise", "uncomfortable
seating" and "drafts when the door opens" in winter.

Kowloon ◗ *Asian*   17 | 17 | 15 | $26

Saugus | 948 Broadway/Rte. 1 (Main St.) | 781-233-0077 |
www.kowloonrestaurant.com

"Gloriously tacky", this "huge", "always packed" 1950 Saugus
"institution"/"food factory"/exercise in "frivolity" offers the "spec-
tacle" of "throwback Polynesian decor" (like a "tiki party" on
"acid"), plus a "dizzying array" of Asian fare; but it's "rather greasy"
say foodies who are "amazed" what people "drunk" on "scorpion
bowls" will "put in their mouths"; P.S. weekend music and "comedy
shows upstairs" make for complete nights of "entertainment."

🆉 La Campania ⊠Ⓜ *Italian*   28 | 25 | 26 | $59

Waltham | 504 Main St. (bet. Cross & Heard Sts.) | 781-894-4280 |
www.lacampania.com

For a "special" "event", "reserve well in advance" for this "sublime"
Waltham "experience" where "wonderfully flavorful, well-plated
and inventive Italian cuisine" is conveyed by "exquisite, unobtrusive" staffers in a "charmingly rustic", "romantic" dining room; a
"stellar wine list" completes the nearly "flawless package", and
though you may be "surprised at how expensive" it is, this is one
"splurge" that's "worth every penny."

La Cantina Italiana *Italian*   ▽ 20 | 13 | 19 | $24

Framingham | 911 Waverly St. (Winter St.) | 508-879-7874 |
www.golacantina.com

"Huge plates of pasta like your nona used to make" are the linchpins
of the "hearty" "old-time Italian" menu that's been drawing
Framingham "parm fans" to this kitchen for more than 50 years;
because the proprietors "don't gouge you" and "treat you like family", "seniors" and folks with "kids" just grin and bear the "less
than desirable" decor.

	FOOD	DECOR	SERVICE	COST

La Casa de Pedro *Venezuelan*

| 21 | 20 | 20 | $31 |

Watertown | 343 Arsenal St. (School St.) | 617-923-8025 | www.lacasadepedro.com

"Pedro himself" "keeps a close eye" on the "spicy", "scrumptious", "reasonably priced" Venezuelan vittles (featuring lots of "memorable meat dishes") and "potent mojitos" served at his "bustling", "cavernous" Watertown *casa*; the "bright", "colorful" interior ("you have to see the palm trees") hosts "fun" live music Thursday–Saturday, while the patio is a "great place to sit" in the summer.

La Famiglia Giorgio *Italian*

| 23 | 14 | 22 | $27 |

North End | 112 Salem St. (bet. Cooper & Prince Sts.) | 617-367-6711 | www.lafamigliagiorgio.com

"Go on an empty stomach" and down as much of the "ridiculously enormous portions" of "hearty" "red-sauce Italian" cuisine as you can at this "family-style" "strong value" in the North End; the mural-bedecked digs are "too crowded and noisy" for some, but the "friendly, efficient" staff "knows how to make customers feel right at home."

La Galleria 33 *Italian*

| ∇ 26 | 22 | 22 | $40 |

North End | 125 Salem St. (Prince St.) | 617-723-7233 | www.lagalleria33.com

"Huge portions" of "fine Italian cuisine" are offered for prices that most consider "reasonable" at this venue with a "hot location" in the North End; the service is as "relaxed" as the setting, a "pretty room" with an open kitchen, French doors and exposed brick that peeks from behind large-scale art pieces.

Lala Rokh *Persian*

| 23 | 21 | 22 | $43 |

Beacon Hill | 97 Mt. Vernon St. (Cedar St.) | 617-720-5511 | www.lalarokh.com

"Exotic" yet "subtle flavors" born of "unusual ingredients" are the hallmarks of the "refined" Persian cuisine offered at this Beacon Hill destination – and it's elevated to a "ceremonial level" via "professional, eager" staffers that "guide diners through the sophisticated menu"; most agree the "intimate", "subdued" setting abets "romance", while a cadre of critics admit to being "a little underwhelmed" in the wake of such "high expectations", calculating you must be "paying for the address."

La Morra *Italian*

| 24 | 20 | 23 | $47 |

Brookline | 48 Boylston St. (bet. Cypress St. & Harvard Ave.) | 617-739-0007 | www.lamorra.com

"Give us more of La Morra" beg Brookline Villagers of this "upscale neighborhood" "charmer" (with an "odd location" "on the highway"), not least of all because its "superb" Northern Italian entrees, "yummy small plates" and "wonderful wine selection" are "fairly priced" for the "high quality"; "hands-on owners" patrol the "warm", "rustic" "multilevel environment" (admittedly, it "can be noisy"), ensuring that the "informal yet gracious" servers "hustle" when need be.

	FOOD	DECOR	SERVICE	COST

Lam's Thai/Vietnamese
| 21 | 15 | 20 | $24 |

Newtonville | 825 Washington St. (Walnut St.) | 617-630-5222 | www.lamsrestaurant.com

Newton "families" "keep coming back" to this "relaxing" "pleaser" because they "know what they're going to get every time": Thai and Vietnamese fare "deliciously prepared" with "colorful, fresh ingredients" by a "charming", "friendly" staff; as for the "modest surroundings", they just don't matter vis-à-vis the "fairly inexpensive" tabs.

L'Andana Italian
| 25 | 24 | 23 | $55 |

Burlington | 86 Cambridge St. (Arlington Rd.) | 781-270-0100 | www.landanagrill.com

"Suburban foodies" turn up at this "vibrant" Burlingtonian from chef-owner Jamie Mammano (Mistral, Sorellina, Teatro) for "fancy", wood-grilled Italian dishes presented in rustic, "barnlike" digs; the "cavernous" setting may "take away from some of the intimacy" and prices can be "out of sight", but most find it an "excellent option" when you "don't want to drive into the city."

Landing, The American
| ∇ 16 | 21 | 20 | $36 |

Manchester-by-the-Sea | 7 Central St. (School St.) | 978-526-7494 | www.thelandingat7central.com
Marblehead | 81 Front St. (State St.) | 781-631-1878 | www.thelandingrestaurant.com ●

These "picturesque" venues in Manchester-by-the-Sea and Marblehead are dining "staples", offering "standard" American comfort chow for "reasonable" sums; while the "old-school" cooking "may not approach the quality found in Boston's greatest restaurants", "fun locations", "water views" and "good bar scenes" compensate.

NEW Lansdowne Pub, The ● American/Irish
| - | - | - | M |

Fenway | 9 Lansdowne St. (Ipswich St.) | 617-247-1222 | www.lansdownepubboston.com

If it weren't for the sea of Fenway fans on game nights, you might think you're in Ireland at this affordable arrival with Emerald Isle and American pub eats, a handcrafted wood bar, rustic chandeliers and about 45 beers, including Irish imports and local microbrews; N.B. there's live music Thursday–Sunday and food until 1 AM nightly.

La Paloma Ⓜ Mexican
| 21 | 15 | 19 | $24 |

Quincy | 195 Newport Ave. (Hobart St.) | 617-773-0512 | www.lapalomarestaurant.com

With help from an "efficent" staff, this "festive" Mexican brings "authentic" eats and "fantastic" margaritas to Quincy; despite "tacky decor", "long lines" and "strip-mall" atmospherics, those who "like it hot" dub it a "good cheap-eats destination."

La Summa Italian
| ∇ 22 | 18 | 22 | $35 |

North End | 30 Fleet St. (bet. Atlantic Ave. & Hanover St.) | 617-523-9503 | www.lasumma.com

For "no-frills", "reasonably priced" Southern Italian dining, you can't go wrong at this "old-world" North Ender where a "friendly" crew ferries "good-sized portions" in a "warm" room that's "like being at your grandmother's"; snobs sneer it's "second tier", yet admit the chow is "solid" – and "you'll always leave full."

Laurel *American*

| 20 | 18 | 20 | $34 |

Back Bay | 142 Berkeley St. (Columbus Ave.) | 617-424-6711 | www.laurelgrillandbar.com

Though the New American food "looks expensive", the pricing is actually "decent" at this "nonpretentious spot" that's "definitely a switch" from the usual in the Back Bay; some say the menu and setting are beginning to "show their age", but most laud it for the "generous" portions, "aim-to-please" service and "relaxed, peaceful" air.

Lavender Asian Cuisine *Asian*

| - | - | - | I |

Sudbury | Sudbury Plaza | 519A Boston Post Rd. (Rte. 20) | 978-579-9988 | www.lavenderasiancuisine.com

Fresh ingredients are the hallmark of this suburban eatery inside the Sudbury Plaza shopping center, serving inexpensive, MSG-free Asian cuisine, including Chinese, Thai, Malaysian and Japanese (*sans* sushi); its carpeted dining room features white-clothed tables, a Great Wall of China illustration and a resplendent blue-pearl–topped bar.

La Verdad 🅱🅜 *Mexican*

| 22 | 14 | 15 | $27 |

Fenway | 1 Lansdowne St. (Ipswich St.) | 617-421-9595 | www.laverdadtaqueria.com

Fans of "amazing" Mexican chow "on the cheap" cheer Ken Oringer's "bright spot in the Fenway", vending "authentic" street eats in a dining room and via the taqueria's take-out counter; cynics dis "teeny-tiny" portions, "uneven" service and "way too loud" acoustics – especially "when the Sox are in town" – but agree that the "great tequila list" knocks it out of the park.

La Voile

| 23 | 23 | 22 | $55 |

Boston Brasserie *French/Mediterranean*

Back Bay | 259 Newbury St. (bet. Fairfield & Gloucester Sts.) | 617-587-4200 | www.lavoileboston.net

"Real French waiters" with "Cannes-do" attitudes serve "outstanding" Gallic classics (as well as Mediterranean dishes that are "true to their origins") at this *"très belle"* Back Bay room with a "sailing theme"; sure, it's a bit "pricey" and many "wish it were easier to get a table", but overall it's a "wonderful" "brasserie translation."

NEW Ledge

| - | - | - | M |

Kitchen & Drinks *American*

Dorchester | 2261 Dorchester Ave. (Adirondack Pl.) | 617-698-2261 | www.ledgeboston.com

Located in the gentrified Lower Mills section of Dorchester, this New American gastropub offers wood-grilled flatbread pizzas, seafood, steaks, chops and other moderately priced fare, plus a kids' menu; the spacious, upscale environs feature hardwood floors, banquettes and soft spot lighting, and there's also a large granite bar and a stone patio.

	FOOD	DECOR	SERVICE	COST

Left Bank *American* ▽ 21 | 20 | 20 | $66

Tyngsboro | Stonehedge Inn | 160 Pawtucket Blvd. (Rte. 113) | 978-649-4400 | www.stonehedgeinnandspa.com

Somewhat "more casual" than its predecessor, Silks, this "reinvented" New American in Tyngsboro's Stonehedge Inn "continues its tradition" of "leisurely dining" with a "creative" menu paired with an "extensive wine list"; but with such "high prices", it may be more appropriate for "special occasions" and "romantic" trysts.

☑ Legal Sea Foods *Seafood* 22 | 18 | 20 | $41

Back Bay | Copley Pl. | 100 Huntington Ave. (bet. Dartmouth & Exeter Sts.) | 617-266-7775

Back Bay | Prudential Ctr. | 800 Boylston St. (Fairfield St.) | 617-266-6800

Park Square | 26 Park Plaza (Columbus Ave.) | 617-426-4444 ●

Waterfront | Long Wharf | 255 State St. (Atlantic Ave.) | 617-227-3115

Harvard Square | 20 University Rd. (Eliot St.) | Cambridge | 617-491-9400

Kendall Square | 5 Cambridge Ctr. (bet. Ames & Main Sts.) | Cambridge | 617-864-3400

Chestnut Hill | Chestnut Hill Shopping Ctr. | 43 Boylston St. (Hammond Pond Pkwy.) | 617-277-7300

Peabody | North Shore Mall | 210 Andover St./Rte. 114 (Rte. 128) | 978-532-4500

Framingham | 50-60 Worcester Rd./Rte. 9 (bet. Concord & Speen Sts.) | 508-766-0600

Burlington | Burlington Mall | 75 Middlesex Tpke. (Rte. 128) | 781-270-9700

www.legalseafoods.com

Additional locations throughout the Boston area

"Chain shmain!" – this seafood "institution" again earns Boston's Most Popular restaurant title not (only) due to its "ubiquity", but because of its "consistent" delivery of "guaranteed-fresh, well-prepared" fish, from the "basic" to the "ambitious", plus a "surprisingly decent wine list"; the "big, bustling" settings swing from "plain-Jane" to "upscale" ("service varies" too), and while even admirers admit it's "perhaps a little overpriced", it's "worth it" for such "quality."

Le Lyonnais Ⓜ *French* ▽ 23 | 18 | 23 | $42

Acton | 416 Great Rd./Rte. 2A (Rte. 27) | 978-263-9068 | www.lelyonnaisacton.com

The "pleasant setting" for this "quaint" bistro located in Acton is a "well-appointed", circa-1850 house where "classic" Gallic cuisine reminiscent of "the France of yesterday" is served for "reasonable" prices; while the "cozy" mood and "good service" make it an "old standby" for some, others report "dated ideas" that yield "uninspired" fare.

Le's *Vietnamese* 21 | 13 | 16 | $17

Allston | 137 Brighton Ave. (Harvard Ave.) | 617-783-2340

Harvard Square | 36 Dunster St. (Mt. Auburn St.) | Cambridge | 617-864-4100

	FOOD	DECOR	SERVICE	COST

(continued)

Le's

Chestnut Hill | Atrium Mall | 300 Boylston St. (Florence St.) | 617-928-0900
www.lesrestaurant.com

"Amazing bargains" "under any name", these Vietnamese siblings – once known as Pho Pasteur – offer "giant bowls" of pho "with all the fixin's" plus other "traditional dishes" for "college budget" tabs; despite "bland" decor and "spotty" (albeit "lightning fast") service, they're "reliable" choices for a "quick" bite.

⊠ L'Espalier *French*

28	–	28	$95

Back Bay | 774 Boylston St. (bet. Exeter & Fairfield Sts.) | 617-262-3023 | www.lespalier.com

"An extraordinary culinary adventure" awaits at this Back Bay "legend" where the "unforgettable textures, flavors and scents" of its "inventive" New French cuisine – once again "soaring above the rest" to earn Boston's No. 1 Food rating – are "matched" to "world-class wines" by "extremely well-informed", equally highly ranked staffers; post-Survey, it moved into "more spacious", "modern" digs connected to the Mandarin Oriental, and while "the jury's out as to how it translates" ("can a hotel have the warmth and charm of the old brownstone?"), "as long as" "genius" chef Frank McClelland is "in the kitchen", longtime fans with "fat wallets" will "be in the dining room."

Les Zygomates ◐⊠ *French/Mediterranean*

22	20	20	$44

Leather District | 129 South St. (Essex St.) | 617-542-5108 | www.winebar.com

Imagine "Paris at South Station" at this "relaxed yet upscale" Leather District bistro where "classic" French-Med dishes "done with panache" are served by "welcoming" staffers in "brick-and-beam"-lined digs; "good value", "great live jazz" and "interesting wines by the glass" further make it a "treasure."

Lexx *American*

17	18	17	$37

Lexington | 1666 Massachusetts Ave. (bet. Grant St. & Wallis Ct.) | 781-674-2990 | www.lexx-restaurant.com

With its "homey" bar, "pleasant atmosphere" and "dependable" cooking, this somewhat "upscale" New American is a "solid" alternative to the sea of "chain restaurants" in Lexington; while "not bad for a suburban place", locals shrug it's "safe if somewhat boring", citing "spotty service" and "above-average prices for just average food."

Lil Vinny's Ristorante *Italian*

▽ 20	13	19	$30

Somerville | 525 Medford St. (Broadway) | 617-628-8466 | www.lilvinnys.com

"Home-cooked" Southern Italian fare, a "warm" vibe and "friendly" service make this "family-run" Somerville "red-sauce" specialist a "nice neighborhood" option (it's a sibling of the popular Vinny's at Night); given its "small" dimensions and "good value for the money", don't be surprised by a "busy" scene on weekends.

	FOOD	DECOR	SERVICE	COST

Limoncello *Italian*

22 | 19 | 21 | $42

North End | 190 North St. (Richmond St.) | 617-523-4480 | www.ristorantelimoncello.com

This North End Italian on the Freedom Trail "feels like home", with its "welcoming" atmosphere and "entertaining" staffers, and boasts an "interesting" back story – the place was bankrolled from lotto winnings; though a minority finds things a bit "ordinary", they admit the food arrives in "generous portions" and the "large" dining room "accommodates groups" easily.

Lineage Ⓜ *American*

23 | 20 | 23 | $45

Brookline | Coolidge Corner | 242 Harvard St. (Beacon St.) | 617-232-0065 | www.lineagerestaurant.com

Brookline's Coolidge Corner is home to this neighborhood "hideaway", a "top-notch" destination for "seasonal", "farm-fresh" New Americana (though insiders hint it's "best for fish"); sure, it may be "a bit on the expensive side", but "informative" service, a "warm" setting and a "cool crowd" make for "always pleasant" dining.

Littlest Bar, The *Pub Food*

- | - | - | I

Financial District | 102 Broad St. (Wharf St.) | 617-542-8469

Once tucked inside a shoebox of a space in Downtown Crossing and now in not-so-little digs in the Financial District, this legendary watering hole offers American pub grub (lunch and dinner) to go with the dozen-plus beers on tap; the handsome wood bar is adorned with two TVs, though the overall effect is still cozy.

Living Room, The ☽ *American*

15 | 19 | 15 | $29

Waterfront | 101 Atlantic Ave. (Richmond St.) | 617-723-5101 | www.thelivingroomboston.com

A no-brainer for "after-work drinks", this "yuppie" Waterfront lounge-cum-eatery is better known for its "great nightlife" scene – so long as you're "under 25" – than its "subpar" New American grub; indeed, sluggish service and "small portions for big prices" lead many to sigh it "could be so much better."

Local, The *American*

- | - | - | M

West Newton | 1391 Washington St. (bet. Elm St. & Mass. Tpke.) | 617-340-2160 | www.thelocalnewton.com

This West Newton gastropub stays true to its name with New England–brewed beers on tap and sustainable, moderately priced New American comfort food; sleek and open yet invitingly dark, it's the kind of upscale watering hole where you can settle into the dining room for a meal or catch a game on TV at the bar.

Locke-Ober Ⓩ *American/Continental*

24 | 25 | 24 | $66

Downtown Crossing | 3 Winter Pl. (bet. Tremont & Washington Sts.) | 617-542-1340 | www.lockeober.com

"Important" dining lives on at this Downtown Crossing "institution", a circa-1875 "trip back in time" that "lives up to its reputation" as a perennial "business" and "special-occasion" dinner destination; "classic clubroom" looks and "old-world service" set the tone for the

	FOOD	DECOR	SERVICE	COST

"reimagined" Continental classics and "creative" New American dishes by chef Lydia Shire, and the overall "outstanding" quality leads "blue bloods" to declare it's "still a grande dame" – despite a few rumbles that it "could be better for the prices charged."

Longfellow's Wayside Inn *New England*   18 | 24 | 21 | $38

Sudbury | Longfellow's Wayside Inn | 72 Wayside Inn Rd. (Rte. 20) | 978-443-1776 | www.wayside.org

Set in one of America's oldest inns, this "historic jewel" in Sudbury transports you to "Colonial Massachusetts" with its ultra-"traditional" New England menu and "time-warp" decor ("rustic tables, uneven floors"); granted, it's "not the place for haute cuisine", but the food is "solid Yankee" all the way and its "gorgeous grounds" and "homey service" make it a "family" destination if nothing else.

NEW Lord Hobo *American*   - | - | - | M

East Cambridge | 92 Hampshire St. (Windsor St.) | Cambridge | 617-250-8454 | www.lordhobo.com

Lament no more the loss of B Side Lounge and welcome this spiffed-up American gastropub in East Cambridge, where the midpriced menu offers brew-friendly fare like hand-cut fries with curry and lobster mac 'n' cheese; the classy, upscale setting includes velvet curtains and dark-red walls sporting local artwork, plus a horseshoe bar made from African wood and issuing an impressive list of draft beers.

L'Osteria *Italian*   23 | 16 | 21 | $34

North End | 104 Salem St. (Cooper St.) | 617-723-7847 | www.losteria.com

This longtime North End staple "hasn't changed a bit", plating "plentiful" portions of "classic", "honest" Italian food in a setting that's "fine for families" and "large groups" (but "not romantic enough for a date"); a "jovial" mood, "great prices" and "wonderful husband-and-wife" owners have fans purring this one "fits like an old slipper."

Lotus Blossom *Chinese/Japanese*   22 | 21 | 21 | $30

Sudbury | 394 Boston Post Rd./Rte. 20 (Station Rd.) | 978-443-0200 | www.lotuscuisine.com

Sudbury diners in search of "upscale Chinese" head to this "popular" spot offering a "varied", "Westernized menu" alongside sushi; "pleasant" service and "tasteful" decor compensate for "long waits" on weekends and the fact that it's "a bit pricey" for the genre.

LTK *Eclectic*   20 | 19 | 17 | $37

Seaport District | 225 Northern Ave. (D St.) | 617-330-7430 | www.ltkbarandkitchen.com

"Definitely different" and "more edgy" than its parent, Legal Sea Foods, this Seaport District Eclectic aims for a "younger demographic" with an "expansive menu" of "innovative" dishes with an Asian influence; it's "loud but fun" and particularly "great before a show at the nearby Bank of American Pavilion", but "overworked" staffers and "noisy" acoustics lead some to report "hit-or-miss" experiences – still, supporters say "that's why it's a test kitchen."

	FOOD	DECOR	SERVICE	COST

Lucca ● *Italian*　　　　　　| 25 | 22 | 22 | $50 |

North End | 226 Hanover St. (Richmond St.) | 617-742-9200 |
www.luccaboston.com

This "sleek" yet "comfortable" North End Northern Italian is just the
place for an "upscale night out" with a "wonderful", "not-your-
standard-red-sauce" menu, "exceptional service" and a "prime"
Hanover Street location (the "front windows are great for people-
watching"); it's "noisy upstairs, more romantic downstairs", but
wherever you wind up, it's fairly "pricey."

Lucca Back Bay ● *Italian*　| 21 | 23 | 22 | $53 |
(fka Sasso)

Back Bay | 116 Huntington Ave. (Garrison St.) | 617-247-2400 |
www.luccaboston.com

With soaring "high ceilings" and a "sophisticated" air, this "lovely"
Back Bay Italian (formerly called Sasso and sibling to North End's
Lucca) proffers "upscale" fare in an "impressive" formal dining room or
a "quiet mezzanine"; admirers find it "super all the way" – so long as
you bring someone "paying with euros" to settle the "expensive" bill.

Lucia *Italian*　　　　　　| 21 | 16 | 19 | $40 |

North End | 415 Hanover St. (Charter St.) | 617-367-2353 |
www.luciaboston.com
Winchester | 5-13 Mt. Vernon St. (bet. Main & Washington Sts.) |
781-729-0515 | www.luciaristorante.com ●

"Old timey" to the hilt, this North End and Winchester duo offers
Italian "the way it used to be", with all the "usual offerings", "fresh
ingredients" and "good wine" pairings, plus some culinary updates;
if sometimes it takes a while for the staff to "notice you", at least the
Sistine Chapel–inspired "frescoes provide visual entertainment
while you wait" in otherwise "tired" digs (post-Survey renovations
to both branches may have helped with that).

Lucky's Lounge *American*　| 18 | 20 | 17 | $27 |

Seaport District | 355 Congress St. (A St.) | 617-357-5825 |
www.luckyslounge.com

A Fort Point Channel "hideout" with a "very '50s" vibe, this Seaport
"retro lounge" serves "delicious" American comfort grub for a "reasonable price" – "if you can find it" (there's "no sign" and it's "subterranean"); still, "twentysomething" fans say it's "not about the
food", rather the "late-night" scene, "cocktails-are-king" mood and
live entertainment, including Sunday night's "Sinatra" homage
(which also plays at weekend brunch).

❷ Lumière *French*　　　　| 27 | 23 | 26 | $57 |

Newton | 1293 Washington St. (Waltham St.) | 617-244-9199 |
www.lumiererestaurant.com

Demonstrating "what can be done with a few exceptional ingredients",
Michael Leviton's West Newton "destination restaurant" offers an
"ever-changing" menu of "consistently superb" New French dishes
with an "emphasis on local produce" (you can "feel the love with
each bite"); the "classy white", "modernist" setting, "impeccable"

service and "quiet" sophistication make it a natural for "special-occasion" dining, and even though it's "a little dear" pricewise, it "never fails to please."

Lyceum, The *Eclectic*
23 | 21 | 21 | $39

Salem | 43 Church St. (Washington St.) | 978-745-7665 | www.thelyceum.com

Housed in the "historic", circa-1843 building from which Alexander Graham Bell made the first telephone call, this Salem "classic" keeps the trade brisk thanks to "first-rate" cooking and a particularly "great brunch"; "wonderful" staffers, "well-spaced tables" and a "welcoming atmosphere" have made it a "solid" destination for over 20 years; N.B. post-Survey, it changed its menu from American to Eclectic bistro and underwent a plush renovation that includes a fireplace and a bar extension, outdating the Food and Decor scores.

Machu Picchu *Peruvian*
19 | 13 | 15 | $24

Somerville | 25 Union Sq. (Stone Ave.) | 617-623-7972
Somerville | 307 Somerville Ave. (bet. Hawkins St. & Warren Ave.) | 617-628-7070
www.machupicchuboston.com

Transporting you from Somerville to "Lima", these "garlicky" "gems" are celebrated for their "terrific" Peruvian dishes, most notably "amazing" rotisserie chickens; ok, their interiors are "not the prettiest" things around, but "fun atmospheres" and "affordable" tabs serve as distractions.

Maddie's Sail Loft ❶ *New England/Seafood*
▽ 18 | 18 | 18 | $25

Marblehead | 15 State St. (bet. Front & Washington Sts.) | 781-631-9824

This "classic sailing bar" – a "Marblehead staple" since 1942 – is a "spirited" "holdout" from the town's "pre-boutique" era, populated by "locals" who drink and nosh on New England seafood in the downstairs pub and in the upstairs dining room; fans say this "unique maritime experience" has benefited from "new ownership", i.e. "better service" and "improvements overall."

Maggiano's Little Italy *Italian*
19 | 18 | 19 | $33

Park Square | 4 Columbus Ave. (bet. Boylston & Stuart Sts.) | 617-542-3456 | www.maggianos.com

You almost "expect to see Sinatra walk in behind you" at this "1940s-esque", checkered-tablecloth chain where "monster portions" of "red-sauce" Italiana are dished out in "enjoyably hectic" Park Square surroundings; some dub it a "mixed bag", citing a "mass-production", "quantity-trumps-quality" approach, but fans tout this "crowd-pleaser" as a "big night out" for "not a lot of money."

Mamma Maria *Italian*
25 | 22 | 23 | $54

North End | 3 North Sq. (Garden Ct.) | 617-523-0077 | www.mammamaria.com

Ignore the "hokey name": this North End Italian is one "classy" joint, an "upscale", "special-occasion" magnet whose "romantic" environs (a series of "small rooms") are spread throughout a "beautiful old townhouse"; it's known for "inventive twists" on classic dishes, "lovely service" and "valet parking", and in spite of some "steep pricing", it's consistently "mobbed on weekends" – "reservations are only estimates" here.

Mantra *French/Indian* | 18 | 21 | 16 | $47 |

Downtown Crossing | 52 Temple Pl. (bet. Tremont & Washington Sts.) | 617-542-8111 | www.mantrarestaurant.com

Fusing "Indian food with French preparation" techniques, this Downtown Crossing hybrid "tries hard" but unfortunately "doesn't quite meet expectations" – and is "expensive" to boot; still, the atmosphere is "hip", the crowd "young" and the decor "fabulous" (a "clever" reworking of a former bank building), making the sometimes "nonexistent" service more bearable.

Marco Cucina Romana Ⓜ *Italian* | 26 | 21 | 25 | $47 |

North End | 253 Hanover St., 2nd fl. (bet. Cross & Parmenter Sts.) | 617-742-1276 | www.marcoboston.com

"Literally a level above the competition", this "charming" North Ender – "tucked away on the second floor of a building on busy Hanover Street" – is "worth climbing a flight of stairs" for a taste of the "hearty", "real-deal" Northern Italian cooking of chef Marc Orfaly (Pigalle); "informative" service and a "cozy", "intimate" vibe enhance its allure, but the space is "small", so "reservations are essential."

Mare Ⓜ *Italian* | 26 | 21 | 22 | $51 |

North End | 135 Richmond St. (North St.) | 617-723-6273 | www.marenatural.com

A "top-notch" mix of "imaginative seafood" and dishes assembled from mostly "organic" ingredients makes this "modern" Italian rather "unusual for the North End"; "attentive" service, "trendy" atmospherics and an "all-too-cool" setting (including "full-length windows" that open up to the street in the summertime) help justify the rather "expensive" outcome.

Market ●Ⓑ⊠ *American* | ▽ 16 | 16 | 17 | $46 |

Financial District | 21 Broad St. (Water St.) | 617-263-0037 | www.mktboston.com

This "upscale" Financial District venue features a New American menu presented in a four-story space offering everything from a candlelit lounge to a "roof deck"; visitors say it's "still working out the kinks", which helps explain the "quiet" mood and sometimes "lackluster" feel.

NEW Market *American* | - | - | - | M |

Theater District | W Boston | 100 Stuart St. (Tremont St.) | 617-310-6790 | www.marketbyjgboston.com

For this New American in the Theater District's W hotel, renowned chef Jean-Georges Vongerichten has put together a moderately priced menu of 'greatest hits' from his other restaurants, featuring dishes peppered with French, Asian and Italian influences and served in sexy brown, gray and black environs overlooking Tremont Street; N.B. an adjacent lounge serves small plates from the restaurant.

	FOOD	DECOR	SERVICE	COST

Marliave *Continental/Italian*
▽ 22 | 17 | 19 | $39

Downtown Crossing | 10 Bosworth St. (Tremont St.) | 617-422-0004 | www.marliave.com

After a lengthy closure, this "historic" Downtown Crossing duplex originally founded in 1885 was restored in 2008 by a "new owner", who's given the Italian menu a Continental twist; the "classy" upstairs dining room offers a view, while downstairs is "more casual" with an "amazing" bar serving Prohibition-era cocktails.

Martsa's on Elm Ⓜ *Tibetan*
▽ 21 | 16 | 20 | $20

Somerville | 233A Elm St. (Grove St.) | 617-666-0660

"Bargain" tabs draw fans to this Davis Square Tibetan, a "small", "cute" showcase for a "delicious" cuisine that's "in a league all its own"; "nice" staffers keep the mood "lively and fun", while the "ample" lunch buffet is a "fantastic way to sample the range of savory dishes."

Mary Chung ⌿ *Chinese*
21 | 8 | 18 | $20

Central Square | 464 Massachusetts Ave. (Central Sq.) | Cambridge | 617-864-1991

"Like Chinatown in Cambridge", this "cash-only" Central Square "cult" Chinese is an "icon" thanks to a menu that aspires to "spicy greatness" for "unbeatable bargain" tabs; while it's "low on atmosphere" (verging on "dreary"), patrons "keep coming back" for "excellent" weekend dim sum and "house specialties" that you "won't find" elsewhere.

Masa ☻ *Southwestern*
23 | 21 | 20 | $38

South End | 439 Tremont St. (Appleton St.) | 617-338-8884
Woburn | 348A Cambridge Rd. (Rte. 3/3A) | 781-938-8886
www.masarestaurant.com

"Change-of-pace" seekers who "aren't afraid of some kick" tout this "upscale" South Ender purveying Southwestern fare rife with "bold", "exotic" flavors and washed down with "great margaritas of all shapes and sizes" (indeed, the place is a veritable "tequila-lover's dream"); "lively" goings-on at the bar and "reasonable prices" make up for the generally "accommodating" though occasionally "spotty" service; N.B. the Woburn offshoot opened post-Survey.

Masala Art *Indian*
23 | 21 | 20 | $33

Needham | Needham Ctr. | 990 Great Plain Ave. (Chestnut St.) | 781-449-4050 | www.masala-art.com

"Ambitious" is the word for this "classy" Needham Indian, dishing out "flavorful" chow (and a "crowd-pleasing" lunch buffet) in a "funky cool" space that's "more beautiful" than the norm for the genre; a "relaxed atmosphere" and "friendly" service keep the trade brisk, while the Spice Bar, a variation on the "chef's table" concept, offers "interesting" interactive cooking sessions.

Ma Soba *Asian*
20 | 19 | 17 | $31

Beacon Hill | 156 Cambridge St. (Hancock St.) | 617-973-6680 | www.masobaboston.com

"Neighborhood sushi" for the "Beacon Hill crowd" sums up the scene at this Asian, a "standby" offering "good-value" lunch boxes

and "windows that slide open in warmer weather"; though surveyors split on the food quality ("creative" vs. "unremarkable"), there's
general agreement that "service can be slow" when the place is
crowded, especially "before Celtics games."

Masona Grill 🅜 *American/Peruvian*   25 | 18 | 23 | $38

West Roxbury | 4-6 Corey St. (Centre St.) | 617-323-3331 |
www.masonagrill.net
Fairly "exotic" for "white-bread West Roxbury", this "adorable little"
spot features an "imaginative" kitchen that fuses New American
and Peruvian flavors into especially "delicious" dishes; the "homey"
environs and "excellent" service leave fans "never disappointed."

Massimino's Cucina Italia *Italian*   23 | 17 | 21 | $33

North End | 207 Endicott St. (Commercial St.) | 617-523-5959 |
www.massiminosboston.com
A "tiny place with heart", this "unpretentious" red-sauce Italian "off
the main drag in the North End" has "loads of character", starting
with its "talkative" staff; a "feel-like-family" vibe and "delectable"
grub plated in "huge" portions may be reasons why it's becoming increasingly "full of tourists."

Matt Murphy's Pub 🗷 *Pub Food*   22 | 18 | 19 | $26

Brookline | 14 Harvard St. (bet. Kent St. & Webster Pl.) | 617-232-0188 |
www.mattmurphyspub.com
The "staff gets to know the locals" at this "real-deal" Irish pub in
Brookline Village where "hearty" grub (including some "amazing
homemade ketchup") is slung in a "comfortable" setting; it may
be "a little more expensive than the standard" and that
"cash-only" policy is a drag, but for the most part, the "loud"
crowds are content.

Maurizio's *Italian*   25 | 17 | 23 | $42

North End | 364 Hanover St. (Clark St.) | 617-367-1123 |
www.mauriziosboston.com
"Authentic Sardinian" dishes distinguish this Italian "treasure" in
the North End from the pack, while the "well-thought-out" menu,
"reasonable prices" and "helpful" service keep it "popular" (and
"noisy"); despite "not much atmosphere" and "limited seating",
supporters insist this "tiny place" has a "big impact."

Max & Dylans
Kitchen & Bar *American*   - | - | - | M

Charlestown | 1 Chelsea St. (City Sq.) | 617-242-7400
Downtown Crossing | 15 West St. (bet. Tremont & Washington Sts.) |
617-423-3600
www.maxanddylans.com
Downtown Crossing is home to this "awesome little place"
(named after the owners' sons) serving upscale yet moderately
priced American bar food in sleek environs that incorporate two
bars – upstairs and down – many TVs, hardwood floors as well as
glowing faux votives on the tables; the Charlestown sibling is a
similar neighborhood spot.

	FOOD	DECOR	SERVICE	COST

☒ Maxwell's 148 🛇Ⓜ *Asian/Italian* 26 | 24 | 27 | $54

Natick | 148 E. Central St. (Rte. 135) | 508-907-6262 |
www.maxwells148.com

"Attention to detail" is the thing at this "sophisticated" destination in Natick whose "diverse menu" is a blend of "top-notch" Asian and Northern Italian dishes, paired with a "wine list that's the equal of the food"; "extraordinary" service and "high-end pricing" come with the territory, but "don't be deceived" by its "unassuming" strip-mall exterior: this is a "place to dine and to linger."

McCormick & Schmick's *Seafood* 21 | 19 | 20 | $46

Faneuil Hall | Faneuil Hall Mktpl. | N. Market Bldg. (North St.) |
617-720-5522
Park Square | Park Plaza Hotel | 34 Columbus Ave. (Arlington St.) |
617-482-3999
www.mccormickandschmicks.com

An "endless menu" that "changes daily depending on what's freshly caught" reels folks into this seafood chain where the atmosphere is "clubby", both at the Park Square locale, which is well-situated for a "dash to the theater", and the Faneuil Hall outpost, offering a "pleasant" patio; some protest "kind-of-costly" tabs, but so long as you have an "expense account" (or come for the "fantastic happy-hour" deals), the "unsurpassed variety" can't be beat.

Mela *Indian* 24 | 20 | 20 | $29

South End | 578 Tremont St. (bet. Public Alley 701 & Union Park) |
617-859-4805 | www.melarestaurant.com

"Upmarket" Indian grub comes to the South End via this "stylish" eatery that whips up "tasty", "well-prepared" meals in a "modern" setting; those seeking something "quick" for lunch tout the "great deal" buffet, but no matter when you show up, the "attentive" staff "won't let your glass run dry."

Melting Pot *Fondue* 20 | 18 | 19 | $44

Park Square | 76 Arlington St. (Columbus Ave.) | 617-357-7007
Bedford | 213 Burlington Rd. (Network Dr.) | 781-791-0529
Framingham | 92 Worcester Rd. (Under Prince Way) | 508-875-3115
www.meltingpot.com

"Do-it-yourself" types are fond of this "novel" fondue franchise for its "interactive" approach; the "long, slow meals" make it appropriate for "first dates" or "large crowds", and although the morsels are "tasty", you'll "end up spending a lot of money" for them.

Merchants Row *New England* - | - | - | M

Concord | Colonial Inn | 48 Monument Sq. (Rte. 62) | 978-369-2373 |
www.concordscolonialinn.com

"Stick-to-your-ribs Yankee cooking" (think New England favorites like wild game and "classic prime rib") is yours at this "solid" dining room housed in Concord's historic Colonial Inn, a "wonderful place to rest your feet after traveling the revolutionary paths"; it's got special appeal for history-minded "grandmas and grandpas" who enjoy olde-fashioned service by "kind tavern maids."

	FOOD	DECOR	SERVICE	COST

Merengue *Dominican*

| - | - | - | I |

Roxbury | 156 Blue Hill Ave. (Clifford St.) | 617-445-5403 |
www.merenguerestaurant.com

Authentic Dominican comfort fare at "outstanding-value" tabs is
the draw at this longtime Roxbury dining room that's festooned with
colorful native art; even though the staff seems to operate on "island
time", no one minds with food this "amazing."

☒ Meritage ☒ *American*

| 27 | 27 | 26 | $68 |

Waterfront | Boston Harbor Hotel | 70 Rowes Wharf (Atlantic Ave.) |
617-439-3995 | www.meritagetherestaurant.com

"Fabulous harbor views" are only part of the package at this "special" Waterfront "wine-lover's paradise" via chef Daniel Bruce,
whose "innovative" New American dishes are available in "small
and large" portions ("enabling those with smaller appetites to sample more") and designed to be paired with a "perfect" selection of
"terrific" *vini*; true, it's "expensive, but totally worth it" given the
"polished service", "sumptuous surroundings" and overall
"exquisite dining experience."

Met Bar & Grill *Steak*

| 21 | 20 | 19 | $37 |

Dedham | Legacy Pl. | 400 Legacy Pl. (Providence Hwy.) | 781-467-1234
Natick | Natick Collection | 1245 Worcester St. (Speen St.) |
508-651-0003
www.metbarandgrill.com

A "great spin-off" of the Metropolitan Club, this steakhouse in the
"swanky Natick Collection" is "not your standard mall restaurant",
what with its "slick cocktails" and "sleek, dark-wood" setting; sure,
the steaks are "terrific" but the "make-your-own burger bar" verges
on the "life-altering" (the "condiment options" alone are "dizzying"), leaving "small portions" and "high prices" as the only drawbacks; N.B. the Dedham branch premiered post-Survey.

Metropolis Cafe *Eclectic*

| 23 | 19 | 20 | $37 |

South End | 584 Tremont St. (bet. Clarendon & Dartmouth Sts.) |
617-247-2931 | www.metropolisboston.com

"It's a squeeze but worth it" at this "casually bustling" South End
cafe, a "locals' spot" that's "always reliable" for "delicious" Eclectic
eats for "lower-than-expected" dough; the "tightly packed" tables
right out of a "cramped Parisian bistro" are a perfect fit with the
"equally European service" – "just hope your waiter remembers
you"; P.S. "brunch is when it really shines."

Metropolitan Club *Steak*

| 21 | 21 | 20 | $49 |

Chestnut Hill | 1210 Boylston St. (Hammond St.) | 617-731-0600 |
www.metclubandbar.com

Bringing a "cool urban vibe to the suburbs", this "swanky" Chestnut
Hill chop shop offers "terrific" steakhouse standards along with
some "sophisticated" twists on New American classics; while its
"young, professional" crowd and "hopping" bar scene get mixed
marks ("hip" vs. "pretentious"), there's consensus on the "inconsistent" service and "pricey" pricing.

	FOOD	DECOR	SERVICE	COST

Middle East, The ● *Mideastern*
| | 17 | 15 | 17 | $20 |

Central Square | 472-480 Massachusetts Ave. (Brookline St.) |
Cambridge | 617-492-9181 | www.mideastclub.com

"Cheap and tasty" sums up the sustenance at this Central Square
Middle Eastern "landmark", but the mainly Lebanese menu plays
second fiddle to "three music venues" that are part of the "community-
oriented" complex; "fantastic bands", belly dancers, a "young
crowd", "grumpy" service and "funky, down-home" decor are all
part of the package.

Middlesex Lounge ● Ⓩ *Eclectic*
| ▽ 17 | 17 | 16 | $22 |

Central Square | 315 Massachusetts Ave. (Blanche St.) | Cambridge |
617-868-6739 | www.middlesexlounge.com

"Better known as a place to get a groove on", this "popular" nightclub/
eatery in Central Square ("owned by Miracle of Science next door")
attracts party animals more bent on "dancing and drinking" than
dining, even though the Eclectic small plates on offer are "better
than your typical pub food"; the cocktails may be "a step above" the
norm, but the "snarky" service, "knee-high tables" and "limited"
menu are less memorable.

Midwest Grill *Brazilian/Steak*
| 20 | 13 | 18 | $32 |

Inman Square | 1124 Cambridge St. (bet. Elm & Norfolk Sts.) |
Cambridge | 617-354-7536 ●
Saugus | 910 Broadway (Rte. 1) | 781-231-2221
www.midwestgrillrestaurant.com

Brace yourself for a "food coma" after a visit to this "fun" Inman
Square Brazilian rodizio, where the $24.95 "all-you-can-eat-meat"
deal draws gluttons with "bottomless-pit appetites"; an "unlimited
food bar" buffet offsets the "tightly packed tables", but the "endless
skewers" of beef get mixed response: "tender and tasty" vs.
"average – you get what you pay for"; N.B. the Saugus branch
premiered post-Survey.

Miel *French*
| 21 | 22 | 22 | $52 |

Waterfront | InterContinental Boston | 510 Atlantic Ave. (Congress St.) |
617-217-5151 | www.intercontinentalboston.com

This "high-end" Waterfront brasserie in the InterContinental hotel
"pleases the palate" with a "fine" array of "French country" dishes
drawn from the Côte d'Azur region, served in "posh", "power
lunch"–ready environs; nature lovers love its "beautiful" outdoor patio, but even though the "view is priceless", some say the tabs are
"too pricey for what you get."

Mike's City Diner ⊄ *Diner*
| 20 | 13 | 18 | $17 |

South End | 1714 Washington St. (E. Springfield St.) | 617-267-9393
"Good neighborhood energy" abounds at this "quintessential greasy
spoon" in the South End where "substantial" diner classics are
"served fast" in a "small", "hole-in-the-wall" setting brimming with
"tons of character"; "cheap" prices, "heaping" portions and "fun
people-watching" account for the "long lines"; N.B. breakfast
and lunch only.

	FOOD	DECOR	SERVICE	COST

NEW Milestone 🅢🅜 *Mediterranean* | - | - | - | M

Wellesley | 13 Central St. (Abbott St.) | 781-446-6950 |
www.milestoneofwellesley.com

This upscale eatery lures preppy Wellesley families with midpriced,
Mediterranean fare – everything from pasta to a Macedonian-
style pork chop – and a chic setting where natural stone complements the warmth of the red-salmon walls; dim lighting adds
a romantic touch.

Miracle of Science Bar & Grill ❷ *Pub Food* | 19 | 17 | 17 | $19

Central Square | 321 Massachusetts Ave. (State St.) | Cambridge |
617-868-2866 | www.miracleofscience.us

"Geek chic" is alive and well at this "laid-back" Central Square
"techie" magnet near MIT that lures in everyone from "grad students" to "Internet millionaires" with its "unfussy" New American
grub and "to-die-for" burger selection; the "lab stool" seating,
"high-IQ vibe" and "periodic-table-of-the-elements menu" help
take your mind off the "slow service."

Mission Bar & Grill ❷ *Pub Food* | 19 | 18 | 17 | $23

MFA | 724 Huntington Ave. (Tremont St.) | 617-566-1244 |
www.themissionbar.com

"Affordable", "upscale tavern food" that's a "step up from standard
pub grub" is dispensed at this "low-key" Brigham Circle bar and grill
near the MFA; it's catnip for "after-work crowds of doctors and
nurses", so "wear your scrubs to fit in."

Z Mistral *French/Mediterranean* | 27 | 26 | 25 | $65

South End | 223 Columbus Ave. (bet. Berkeley & Clarendon Sts.) |
617-867-9300 | www.mistralbistro.com

Regulars "dress to impress" at this "wow"-inducing South End bastion of "sophistication" that's "still one of the hottest tickets in
town" thanks to chef Jamie Mammano's "delectable" French-Med
menu; given the "stylish", high-ceilinged setting (with "lighting that
makes everyone glow"), "smooth-as-silk" service, "elite", "power-
broker" following and "mortgage payment"–worthy price tags, this
is "fine dining" personified – "noisy" acoustics notwithstanding.

M.J. O'Connor's *Pub Food* | - | - | - | I

Park Square | 27 Columbus Ave. (Arlington St.) | 617-482-2255 |
www.mjoconnorsboston.com 🅢🅜
Seaport District | Westin Boston Waterfront Hotel | 425 Summer St.
(bet. A & D Sts.) | 617-443-0800 | www.mjoconnors.com

A handsome dark-wood bar imported from Ireland provides the central gathering place at this budget-friendly American pub grub spot
that's been a Park Square staple for years, and a second location
now resides in the Westin Boston Waterfront.

Mooo . . . *Steak* | 24 | 24 | 25 | $69

Beacon Hill | XV Beacon Hotel | 15 Beacon St. (bet. Bowdoin &
Somerset Sts.) | 617-670-2515 | www.mooorestaurant.com

Ignore the "ridiculous name": this "popular-as-all-get-out" Beacon Hill
steakhouse draws "politicos" and assorted "chic" types with its "excel-

lent" chops, "spiffy" service and "hip", cow-centric decor (that's a bit "less manly" than the genre norm); it's best enjoyed "on someone else's tab", however, given the "breathlessly expensive" pricing, but overall, mooost rate it a "great dining experience from start to finish."

Morse Fish Seafood   ▽ 21 | 5 | 19 | $16
South End | 1401 Washington St. (Union Park) | 617-262-9375 | www.morsefish.com

"Fresh fish, stale space" sums up the scene at this "simple" South End eatery/market slinging "value-priced" seafood prepared any way you like it – "so long as that's fried or broiled"; Styrofoam dishware and "nil decor" to the contrary, the "unpretentious" joint draws a mixed crowd of "urbanites, hipsters and policemen."

☑ Morton's The Steakhouse Steak   25 | 22 | 24 | $66
Back Bay | Exeter Plaza | 699 Boylston St. (Exeter St.) | 617-266-5858
Seaport District | World Trade Center East | Two Seaport Ln. (bet. Congress St. & Northern Ave.) | 617-526-0410
www.mortons.com

"Consistency abounds" at this "can't-go-wrong" steakhouse chain pairing "well-prepared" chops that "hang off the plate" with "seriously powerful martinis" in a Back Bay "basement" and a "jumping" Seaport District locale; "arm-and-a-leg" pricing comes with the territory, along with a "Saran-wrapped presentation" of raw meats (accompanied by an instructional "recitation" by the waiter) – a "shtick" that many find "tired."

Mother Anna's Italian   21 | 14 | 19 | $30
North End | 211 Hanover St. (Cross St.) | 617-523-8496 | www.motherannas.com

In the North End since 1937, this "locals' spot" vends "solid redsauce" Italian fare in a "relaxing", "not-fancy" milieu; while the "basic" cooking is "not a standout", "excellent" pricing and "great patio seating" help explain why it's "been around forever."

Mr. Bartley's Burger Cottage ☒ ⊨ Burgers   24 | 13 | 15 | $16
Harvard Square | 1246 Massachusetts Ave. (Plympton St.) | Cambridge | 617-354-6559 | www.mrbartley.com

"Doing it right forever" (or at least since 1961), this "perennial" Harvard Square patty palace is renowned for "big, juicy" burgers "named after celebrities and politicians" and washed down with "dreamy shakes"; despite "no bathroom", a "cash-only" policy, "crazy-busy" atmospherics and "rough 'n' ready" decor recalling the "dorm room of a poster-crazed college student", everyone's more than content to "go with the flow" here.

Mr. Crepe French   18 | 12 | 15 | $13
Somerville | 51 Davis Sq. (bet. Elm St. & Highland Ave.) | 617-623-0661 | www.mrcrepe.com

This "relaxed" Davis Square "college hangout" specializes in "massive" French crêpes in sweet and savory iterations that are "tasty" to some, "unimpressive" to others; "cheap" pricing can result in "long waits" and a "zoo"-like "weekend rush."

	FOOD	DECOR	SERVICE	COST

Mr. Sushi *Japanese*

21 | 14 | 19 | $28

Arlington | 693 Massachusetts Ave. (bet. Central & Water Sts.) | 781-643-4175

Brookline | 329 Harvard St. (Babcock St.) | 617-731-1122 | www.mrsushibrookline.com

"Inauspicious name" to the contrary, proponents praise the "reliably fresh" sushi at this "efficient" Japanese duo that manages to get the job done with "no frills" (and "you rarely have to wait"); they may suffer from "no decor" and "dumbed-down" menus, but they're popular for a simple reason: the "price is right."

MuLan
Taiwanese Cuisine Ⓜ *Taiwanese*

23 | 11 | 17 | $19

Kendall Square | 228 Broadway (Clark St.) | Cambridge | 617-441-8813 | www.mulan.4t.com

Popular with "MIT students" and curiosity seekers, this "different" Kendall Square venue specializes in "authentic Taiwanese" fare as well as some "unusual" Chinese dishes; the "typical looking" storefront setting is "not for a romantic meal or special night out", but "cheap" tabs and "friendly" service keep regulars regular.

Muqueca Ⓜ *Brazilian*

24 | 13 | 19 | $21

Inman Square | 1093 Cambridge St. (Elm St.) | Cambridge | 617-354-3296 | www.muquecarestaurant.com

This "ridiculously tasty" Brazilian "foodie dive" near Inman Square is "always crowded" with "adventurous eaters" for a "good reason": instead of the "typical meat-oriented menu" common to the genre, it specializes in seafood and "signature stews big enough to share"; prices are more than "affordable", for both the "flavorful" chow and the beer-and-wine selection; N.B. it's scheduled to move down the block to 1006 Cambridge Street in spring 2010.

Myers + Chang *Asian*

23 | 19 | 20 | $34

South End | 1145 Washington St. (E. Berkeley St.) | 617-542-5200 | www.myersandchang.com

Asian dining goes "trendy" at this "chic diner" in the South End from restaurateur Christopher Myers, where "fashionable" folks dig into chef Joanne Chang's "modern" Chinese, Thai and Vietnamese specialties; sure, it's "loud" and the "family-style small-plates" approach means the "bill can add up quickly", but ultimately most say this eating "adventure" is one "highly entertaining experience."

Naked Fish *Nuevo Latino/Seafood*

19 | 18 | 19 | $34

Waltham | 455 Totten Pond Rd. (3rd Ave.) | 781-684-0500

Billerica | 15 Middlesex Tpke. (Bedford St.) | 978-663-6500

Framingham | 725 Cochituate Rd. (Speen St.) | 508-820-9494
www.nakedfish.com

For an "interesting change from the usual", check out this "unique" suburban mini-chain specializing in "Cuban-inspired seafood" and cocktails, jazzed up by "hopping" after-work bar scenes; although it's "above average" overall for "strip-mall" dining, critics carp that the "workmanlike" food is "inconsistent", the atmosphere "corporate" and the staff "overworked" – nevertheless, the pricing "won't break the bank."

Namaskar *Indian* ▽ 23 | 19 | 22 | $24

Somerville | 234 Elm St. (Chester St.) | 617-623-9955 | www.namaskarcuisine.com

Often "overlooked" despite a location "in the heart of Davis Square" in Somerville, this "reliable" spot turns out "authentic", "unfailingly good" Indian fare – including some "hard-to-find regional dishes" – that may "singe your taste buds and make you sweat" ("be careful how you order"); "friendly service" and moderate pricing complete the "tasty" picture.

Navy Yard Bistro & Wine Bar *American* 23 | 18 | 22 | $35

Charlestown | 6th St. (1st Ave.) | 617-242-0036 | www.navyyardbistro.com

"Neighborhood restaurants" don't get much more "cozy" than this Charlestown bistro that's praised for "well-prepared" New Americana and for tabs that "won't bankrupt you"; though it can be "hard" to locate ("hidden" away in the Navy Yard), this "perfect little find" stands out in an area that "lacks choices."

Nebo ◑🅱 *Pizza* 21 | 19 | 20 | $30

North End | 90 N. Washington St. (Thacher St.) | 617-723-6326 | www.neborestaurant.com

"Close to the Boston Garden", this "hip" North End pizza purveyor is a "great spot to grab a quick bite before or after a game" given its "delish" thin-crust pies and "wonderful" homemade pastas "based on the owners' mothers' recipes"; slick modern looks and a "good selection of wine" add to its upscale feel.

Neighborhood Restaurant & Bakery ⊄ *Portuguese* ▽ 23 | 12 | 15 | $14

Somerville | 25 Bow St. (bet. Somerville Ave. & Summer St.) | 617-623-9710

There's no need to "eat again all day" after hunkering down at this Somerville Portuguese cafe famed for "value" dining, especially its "enormous breakfasts" where the portions are so "plentiful" that the omelets practically "come with a side of eggs"; "spotty service" and "hole-in-the-wall" decor are forgotten in warm weather, when a patio seat under a grape trellis is "pleasant" indeed; N.B. lunch is served also, but not dinner.

🅩 Neptune Oyster *Seafood* 27 | 20 | 22 | $42

North End | 63 Salem St. (Cross St.) | 617-742-3474 | www.neptuneoyster.com

"Escape the typical Italian fare in the North End" at this "sardine"-sized, perennially "packed" seafooder famed for its "magnificent" raw bar selection and "vaunted hot lobster roll", served in a "little-bit-of-Paris" setting; the "cramped conditions" aren't helped by the "no-reservations" policy, so savvy shuckers snag seats by "arriving early" and "checking their bank account" before digging in (it's on the "pricey" side).

NewBridge Cafe ⊉ *American* | 24 | 7 | 16 | $20 |

Chelsea | 650 Washington Ave. (Woodlawn Ave.) | 617-884-0134 | www.newbridgecafe.com

Ok, it's "not fine dining", but this "long-standing" Chelsea "dive", a former barroom turned eatery, offers "basic" American comfort grub at a "basic price" and is renowned for its signature steak tips, "marinated and grilled to perfection"; downsides include so-so service and "fuhgeddaboudit" decor ("don't use the bathroom"), but those "cheap" tabs are fine as is.

New Dong Khanh   ▽ | 22 | 8 | 14 | $15 |
Restaurant ⊉ *Vietnamese*

Chinatown | 81-83 Harrison Ave. (Kneeland St.) | 617-426-9410

"On a cold day when you want a hot bowl of noodle soup" or in summer when a cooling bubble tea or fruit smoothie is in order, join the "often crazy lines" for this Vietnamese in Chinatown; just "don't expect great service", but be happy that the "solid" eats are "fresh, fast" and "cheap"; P.S. aesthetes dised that the decor needed "a major overhaul" – and the owners heard them post-Survey (which outdates the Decor score).

New Ginza *Japanese* | 24 | 18 | 21 | $37 |

Watertown | 63-65 Galen St. (Aldrich Rd.) | 617-923-2100 | www.newginzaboston.com

The sushi is "sublime" at this Watertown Center Japanese, a "reliable" destination for "excellent" raw fish as well as "top-notch" traditional cooked specialties, all ferried by a "gracious", "energetic" crew; the blond wood-lined setting is "pretty", the vibe "pleasant" and the pricing "reasonable (for sushi)" – no wonder it's "always packed."

New Jang Su BBQ Ⓜ *Korean*   ▽ | 23 | 11 | 19 | $26 |

Burlington | 260 Cambridge St. (Arthur Woods Ave.) | 781-272-3787

"Adventuresome" types and do-it-yourselfers tout this "authentic" Burlington Korean where a "wide selection of quality BBQ" is cooked on a table grill (small fries "love the drama"); it "doesn't look like much from the outside" – or inside, for that matter – but "attentive staffers" and "affordable prices" are ample distractions.

New Mother India Ⓜ *Indian* | 22 | 15 | 19 | $30 |

Waltham | 336 Moody St. (Gordon St.) | 781-893-3311 | www.newmotherindia.com

A "great beer selection" distinguishes this "pleasant" Waltham Indian from the rest of the pack, though fans report that its "high-quality" cooking is just as "satisfying"; lunchtime takes an "all-you-can-eat approach" via an "excellent buffet" and prices are "reasonable", leaving only service as a matter of debate: "polite" vs. "incompetent."

New Shanghai *Chinese* | 16 | 10 | 16 | $24 |

Chinatown | 21 Hudson St. (Kneeland St.) | 617-338-6688 | www.newshanghairestaurant.com

Not "your usual Chinese", this Chinatownie offers a "great mix of spicy and mild" fare that's "reliable" and "cheap" – especially the "rocking lunch specials"; N.B. post-Survey, new owners took over and made menu alterations, most likely outdating the Food score.

Nico *Italian*   - | - | - | E

North End | 417 Hanover St. (bet. Harris & Salutation Sts.) | 617-742-0404 | www.nicoboston.com

The owners of Strega Ristorante present this North End sibling where a Sicilian chef offers traditional, uncomplicated yet pricey Italian cuisine in upscale surroundings festooned with chandeliers, silky red curtains and white cloths and roses on the tables; for added visual interest, there are long windows that open to bustling Hanover Street in summer and, at the marble bar up front, flat-screens playing sports and *cinema Italiano*.

9 Tastes *Thai*   20 | 14 | 18 | $19

Harvard Square | 50 JFK St. (Mt. Aubrun St.) | Cambridge | 617-547-6666 | www.9taste.com

"Reliable", "tasty" and "cheap" "Thai standards" "do the trick" for the hungry, "frugal students" who frequent this Harvard Square basement; it's "a bit crowded" and the "decor is unimaginative", but the "friendly" servers do their best to get everyone in and out "fast."

No Name *New England/Seafood*   19 | 10 | 15 | $27

Seaport District | 15 W. Fish Pier St. (Northern Ave.) | 617-338-7539 | www.nonamerestaurant.com

Like the name suggests, this "no-frills" "ramshackle hut" in the Seaport District supplies "no-fuss, no-muss" dining with "no atmosphere" and "no-nonsense" service, just "simply prepared" New England seafood at "true-delight prices"; like everything else here, the "noisy", "touristy" crowd is "casual to the nth degree."

☑ No. 9 Park ☒ *French/Italian*   28 | 24 | 27 | $75

Beacon Hill | 9 Park St. (bet. Beacon & Tremont Sts.) | 617-742-9991 | www.no9park.com

Barbara Lynch still "dazzles" at her "jewel box"-esque Beacon Hill flagship where "movers and shakers" for whom "money is no object" "celebrate in style" with "elegant", "intriguing" French-Italian creations that "marry unexpected tastes and textures" with "decadent, heavenly" results; if the "smaller-than-small portions" are occasional balloon-bursters, the "savvy", "polished" "service team" and "superior" bartenders ("mixology is an art here", as is wine selection) "heighten the experience" – right on up to "cloud 9."

Noodle Street *Asian*   ▽ 19 | 11 | 16 | $15

Boston University | 627 Commonwealth Ave. (bet. Granby & Sherborn Sts.) | 617-536-3100 | www.noodlestreet.com

Those who like it "hot 'n' healthy" tout this "deelish" Asian noodle shop near Boston University for its encyclopedic (verging on "confusing") menu that allows you to "customize" your meal with lots of "flavorful" choices; "students" naturally show up since it's so "inexpensive", and they don't mind "nothing-fancy" decor and middling service.

No. 1 Noodle House *Asian*

| 18 | 7 | 15 | $17 |

Newton | 51 Langley Rd. (bet. Beacon & Union Sts.) | 617-527-8810
This "simple" Asian purveyor in Newton Centre may supply "no frills or thrills" on the menu, but it does provide "decent stir-fry" and "huge bowls of noodle soup" for "cheap" tabs – and the service is "quick"; what with the "hole-in-the-wall" looks, it's probably best for "takeout."

NEW North 26 *New England*

| - | - | - | M |

Faneuil Hall | Millennium Bostonian | 26 North St. (Clinton St.) | 617-557-3640 | www.millenniumhotels.com
Innovative spins on New England classics are served from breakfast to dinner at this moderately priced arrival in the Millennium Bostonian hotel, whose minimalist contemporary ambiance is realized with hardwood floors, wood accents and neutral colors (candlelight warms it up in the evening); it incorporates a patio and front bar, both overlooking Faneuil Hall, an airy main room with vaulted ceilings and a semi-private space with a wine wall.

North Street Grille ⊠ *American*

| ∇ 23 | 11 | 15 | $23 |

North End | 229 North St. (Lewis St.) | 617-720-2010
"Everything you could ever want" in a brunch (except for the weekend "lines") is yours at this North End American offering a "wide variety" of options at the "prices you want to pay"; while dinner is more of a "low-key" event, it's equally "delicious", making the "slow" service and "nothing-to-write-home-about" decor easier to swallow.

⊠ Not Your Average Joe's *American*

| 18 | 16 | 18 | $26 |

Arlington | 645 Massachusetts Ave. (Pleasant St.) | 781-643-1666
Needham | 109 Chapel St. (bet. Great Plain Ave. & May St.) | 781-453-9300
Watertown | 55 Main St. (Church St.) | 617-926-9229
Newburyport | Firehouse Ctr. | 1 Market Sq. (State St.) | 978-462-3808
Beverly | Commodore Plaza | 45 Enon St. (bet. Hoover Ave. & Lincoln St.) | 978-927-8950
Methuen | The Loop | 90 Pleasant Valley St. (Milk St.) | 978-974-0015
Randolph | 16 Mazzeo Dr. (West St.) | 781-961-7200
Dartmouth | 61 State Rd. (bet. Slocom Rd. & Suffolk Ave.) | 508-992-5637
Westborough | 291 Turnpike Rd. (Otis St.) | 508-986-2350
www.notyouraveragejoes.com
Additional locations throughout the Boston area
"Fun for a night away from the stove", this "spirited" local chain and its "down-to-earth" staff serve up "reasonably priced" American comfort chow from an "enormous", "something-for-everyone" menu (be warned: its focaccia and dipping oil starter is "addictive" and "could be an entire meal"); picky eaters find it "a bit out of the corporate playbook", but most label it an "easy" choice for "solid" grazing.

NEW Nourish *American*

| - | - | - | M |

Lexington | 1727 Massachusetts Ave. (Waltham St.) | 781-674-2400 | www.nourishlexington.com
Dishes made from locally sourced ingredients take center stage at this Lexington Center American serving a mix of affordable barbecue and vegetarian fare; the clean, bright dining room features

colorful walls decorated with local artists' works, and there's a full bar offering organic beers and wines.

☑ Oak Room *Steak*

25 | 27 | 26 | $65

Back Bay | Fairmont Copley Plaza | 138 St. James Ave. (bet. Dartmouth & Trinity Sts.) | 617-267-5300 | www.theoakroom.com

"Very old and very Boston", this "elegant" Back Bay "grande dame" is a "throwback to the glory days of formal fine dining", offering "superb" steakhouse fare and "expert traditional service"; cushy "leather chairs" and acres of "wood paneling" embellish its "regal" feel, and though modernists scoff it's "stuffy", proponents say this "classy joint" is more than "worth the impact on your wallet."

Oceana *American/Seafood*

24 | 21 | 20 | $47

Waterfront | Boston Marriott Long Wharf | 296 State St. (Atlantic Ave.) | 617-227-3838 | www.oceanaatlongwharf.com

"Harbor views" and "tasty" food sum up this "pleasurable" Waterfront New American in the Marriott Long Wharf, a nautically themed dining room offering a "complex" menu emphasizing seafood; indeed, it "should be busier" even though it's "not inexpensive" (insiders say the Sunday brunch offers real "bang for the buck").

Oceanaire Seafood Room *Seafood*

24 | 24 | 23 | $57

Financial District | 40 Court St. (Tremont St.) | 617-742-2277 | www.theoceanaire.com

"So good, it's hard to believe it's a chain", this "exceptional" seafood franchise's Financial District outpost features "all the exuberance of a steakhouse in a fish house", starting with its "bountiful menu" and "fine wine list"; the "incredible" setting in a "defunct bank", "happening" bar scene and "big prices" reflect the overall "classy" mood.

Oga's *Japanese*

26 | 20 | 21 | $42

Natick | 915 Worcester St./Rte. 9 (Rte. 27) | 508-653-4338 | www.ogasnatick.com

"Even visitors from Japan are impressed" by the "artfully presented" sushi at this Natick "surprise" incongruously set in a "not particularly scenic" suburban strip mall; given the "sublime" raw fish, "unusual rolls" and "creatively interpreted Japanese dishes", no one is bothered by the "generic decor", while "friendly" service, "easy parking" and a "great sake menu" blunt the rather "pricey" tabs.

☑ Oishii Ⓜ *Japanese*

27 | 17 | 21 | $55

Chestnut Hill | 612 Hammond St. (Boylston St.) | 617-277-7888
Sudbury | Mill Vill. | 365 Boston Post Rd./Rte. 20 (Concord Rd.) | 978-440-8300

☑ Oishii Boston ◑Ⓜ *Japanese*

South End | 1166 Washington St. (E. Berkeley St.) | 617-482-8868 | www.oishiiboston.com

"Pristine" "flavors come shining through" thanks to "chefs who care about the fundamentals" at this "sublime" sushi set that provides "aesthetic" as well as "culinary treats" with "fantastical", "innovative presentations"; the staffers can be "quite helpful" in their "recommendations" at all locations, whether at the original Chestnut

Hill "shoebox" ("always a wait", "expensive"), the more "modern" Sudbury branch (less "frenetic", "expensive") or the "hoity-toity" South End offshoot ("dark, romantic", "insanely expensive").

Z Oleana *Mediterranean*   28 | 23 | 25 | $52

Inman Square | 134 Hampshire St. (bet. Elm & Norfolk Sts.) | Cambridge | 617-661-0505 | www.oleanarestaurant.com

"Attention to detail" is the hallmark of this "compelling" Inman Square "foodie attraction", where a "coveted reservation" allows the opportunity to sample chef-owner Ana Sortun's "unrivaled" Arabic-Mediterranean cooking (and simultaneously get an "education in spices" from the "enthusiastic" staffers); though seating is a little "cramped" and the pricing decidedly "upscale", diehards declare "there's no other restaurant like it"; P.S. a meal on the "first-come, first-served" patio is as "close to heaven" as you'll find in these parts.

Olecito *Mexican*   24 | 21 | 21 | $31

NEW **Kenmore Square** | 700 Commonwealth Ave. (bet. Cummington & Hinsdale Sts.) | 617-353-7257 | www.olecito.net 🅂 🅼
Inman Square | 12 Springfield St. (Cambridge St.) | Cambridge | 617-876-1374 🗗

Olé Mexican Grill *Mexican*

Inman Square | 11 Springfield St. (Cambridge St.) | Cambridge | 617-492-4495 | www.olegrill.com

"Fine Mexican dining" is yours in Inman Square via this "not typical" cantina where the "well-executed classic dishes" (including "addictive guacamole prepared tableside") are *elegante y picante* and served in a "charmingly authentic setting"; for those who think it's a little too "pricey", across-the-street offspring Olecito (there's a new one in Kenmore Square too) offers "great takeout" prepared "in a flash."

Olivadi Restaurant *Italian*   - | - | - | M

Norwood | 32 Guild St. (Central St.) | 781-762-9090 | www.olivadirestaurant.com

Regional Italian classics with contemporary twists make up the mid-priced menu at this "nice spot" in Norwood Center; wood and tile floors, sun-colored walls and exposed brick impart a Tuscan ambiance to the "big seating area", while a granite chef's table overlooks the main draw: a semi-open kitchen with a wood-burning pizza oven.

Z Olives *Mediterranean*   25 | 22 | 23 | $57

Charlestown | 10 City Sq. (Main St.) | 617-242-1999 | www.toddenglish.com

A "long-standing" Charlestown "favorite", this Todd English "flagship" is "still the place to go" for "top-notch" Med meals that are "as magnificent to look at as they are to eat"; a "warm" setting and "congenial" service keep the mood "vibrant", but some sniff it's too "expensive."

Om ⬤ *American*   19 | 23 | 17 | $46

Harvard Square | 92 Winthrop St. (JFK St.) | Cambridge | 617-576-2800 | www.omrestaurant.com

"Style" is the watchword at this "trendier-than-thou" Harvard Square lounge-cum-restaurant offering "classy" New Americana with an "Asian flair" served in a "beautiful" setting with a distinct "nightclub" vibe; though the "exotic" cocktails are "amazing" and the scene "happening", critics cite "pretentious service" and food that's "overpriced and underportioned."

Orinoco: A Latin Kitchen ⓜ *Venezuelan* | 25 | 19 | 21 | $30 |

South End | 477 Shawmut Ave. (W. Concord St.) | 617-369-7075
Brookline | 22 Harvard St. (Webster St.) | 617-232-9505
www.orinocokitchen.com

"Homey" and "unassuming", this "laid-back" South Ender draws "crowds" thanks to its "vibrant", "gently priced" Venezuelan eats (including "mouthwatering" empanadas and "to-die-for" arepas), so be prepared for "long waits" and a "tight squeeze"; fortunately, the Brookline Village location "takes the heat off" with somewhat "bigger" digs, plus a "full bar."

Orleans ❶ *American* | 17 | 17 | 16 | $32 |

Somerville | 65 Holland St. (Wallace St.) | 617-591-2100 |
www.orleansrestaurant.com

More "pickup joint" than fine-dining destination, this Davis Square bar/eatery offers "decent" all-day Americana, augmented by some pizzas at night; the "loud" acoustics, "hit-or-miss" service and "mediocre-to-pretty-good" grub may be a drag, but the "college" crowd is more intent on sucking down "fun cocktails" to care.

Orta ⓜ *Italian* | - | - | - | I |

Hanover | 75 Washington St./Rte. 53 (Columbia Rd.) | 781-826-8883 |
www.ortarestaurant.com

Though named for a lake in Italy's Piedmont region, this trattoria near Hanover in Pembroke from longtime chef and restaurateur Jimmy Burke (ex Tuscan Grill) was inspired by a trip to Naples; the affordable menu specializes in Neapolitan pizza, pasta and entrees, while the setting offers ochre walls, an Italian-tile floor and a brick oven in the dining room.

Osushi *Japanese* | 23 | 21 | 20 | $44 |

Back Bay | Westin Copley Pl. | 10 Huntington Ave. (Dartmouth St.) |
617-266-2788 | www.osushirestaurant.com

"Small" and "sexy", this "luxe" Japanese set in a Back Bay hotel "shopping center" purveys "fresh", "artfully prepared" rolls and other "inventive" plates, supplemented by a "large sake menu"; fashionably "dim lighting" ("bring a flashlight") and "Asia-modern" decor enhance its "trendy" vibe, but don't forget to carry a "fat wallet" – it's on the "expensive" side.

Other Side Cafe ❶ *Sandwiches* | 19 | 15 | 14 | $18 |

Back Bay | 407 Newbury St. (Mass. Ave.) | 617-536-8437

Definitely "not for the afternoon tea set", this "funky, grungy" Back Bay cafe metes out "oversized portions" of "delicious, healthy" and "inexpensive" sandwiches, salads and soups, of which there are "lots of vegan and vegetarian options"; the target market? – "cool indie kids" and bike "couriers" who "don't mind loud music" and "slow service" by "annoyed" "tattooed" people.

Out of the Blue ⓜ *Seafood* 　　22 | 16 | 19 | $31

Somerville | 215 Elm St. (Grove St.) | 617-776-5020 |
www.outofthebluerestaurant.com

For "excellent value, right in Davis Square", Somerville seafood-
cravers come to this "casual and family-friendly" "charmer" offering
"simple, fresh" fish with Italian and New England influences; items
from land "do not disappoint" either, and when one factors in the
"generous portions" and the "nice people" who bring them, it's
understandable why it "gets crowded."

Oxford Spa *Sandwiches* 　　21 | 12 | 15 | $12

Porter Square | 102 Oxford St. (Crescent St.) | Cambridge |
617-661-6988

"Everything you expect from a locally owned, high-end" breakfast
and lunch stop is found at this spot near Porter Square: "excellent
housemade pastries", "fresh", "consistently delicious sandwiches"
and "slight overpricing"; the counter-serve space is "cozy" if heavy
with the "general air of student grubbiness" – or maybe that's just
the "hit-or-miss servers"?

Ⓩ O Ya ⓈⓂ *Japanese* 　　28 | 23 | 26 | $112

Leather District | 9 East St. (South St.) | 617-654-9900 |
www.oyarestaurantboston.com

"Oh yeah", "the accolades are warranted!" – this "tiny" Leather
District firehouse-turned-"sleek" izakaya provides culinary "tran-
scendence" via "wildly creative Japanese-fusion morsels" bursting
with "extraordinary" "flavors not found elsewhere"; "put yourself in
the capable hands" of the "enthusiastic" staff by ordering the
"knockout omakase" – but bear in mind those 15 or so courses yield
about "17 bites of food", which causes the "still hungry" to cry "o ya
gotta be kidding me" when handed the "mortgage payment"–worthy,
"nosebleed"-triggering bill.

Pagliuca's *Italian* 　　22 | 15 | 19 | $35

North End | 14 Parmenter St. (Hanover St.) | 617-367-1504 |
www.pagliucasrestaurant.com

No "modern concoctions" are made at this North Ender, just "straight-
up, authentic" Southern Italian red-sauce classics – and that's just
what its "ton of local regulars" prefer; though "not the place for a romantic dinner" (the "homey", "cozy" setting's "low ceilings" can
make it "feel quite cramped"), it does boast large "windows that
open to the street", plus "value" prices on both food and wine.

🆕 Pairings *American* 　　- | - | - | M

Park Square | Boston Park Plaza Hotel & Towers | 50 Park Plaza
(bet. Arlington & Charles Sts.) | 617-262-3473 | www.pairingsboston.com

Boston Park Plaza's former Bonfire steakhouse has been lightened
up as this New American offering small plates (from the same chef)
accompanied by many wines in 3- or 6-oz. pours; the decor has also
been refreshed with lighter colors, brighter lighting, reupholstered
banquettes and chairs, and all-glass doors that open up to the sidewalk for alfresco dining; N.B. breakfast is also served.

NEW Palio's Italian Grill *Italian*　　　- | - | - | M

Lexington | 94 Hartwell Ave. (bet. Great Rd. & Rte. 128) | 781-402-0033 | www.paliosgrill.com

With expense accounts on the wane, the owners of fancy Lexington steakhouse Max Stein's renamed it and shifted the focus toward midpriced Italian fare, including huge portions of pasta; the white tablecloths are gone, but a new lounge is a welcome attraction.

Palm, The *Steak*　　　23 | 19 | 23 | $63

Back Bay | Westin Copley Pl. | 200 Dartmouth St. (bet. St. James Ave. & Stuart St.) | 617-867-9292 | www.thepalm.com

"Fred Flintstone would love" the "insanely large portions" of "well-prepared meat" and "memorable sides" hauled by "smooth servers" at this Back Bay link of the "reliable" steakhouse chain; however, it's "business" types who keep it "bustling" – at least those who still have "expense accounts"; P.S. quite a few design-mavens declare the "tacky decor" "has got to change."

Palmers *American*　　　- | - | - | M

Andover | 18 Elm St. (bet. High St. & Post Office Ave.) | 978-470-1606 | www.palmers-restaurant.com

A North Shore destination for many years, this classic Andover American offers diners two separate, affordable experiences; in the downstairs tavern, a casual menu is served to the strains of live music (Thursday–Saturday evenings), while upstairs is the home of elegant dining rooms with linens, beamed ceilings and fireplaces.

Panificio *Italian*　　　19 | 15 | 15 | $20

Beacon Hill | 144 Charles St. (bet. Cambridge & Revere Sts.) | 617-227-4340 | www.panificioboston.com

"Home-cooked goodness" comes out of the kitchen of this "rustic", "relaxed" Italian bakery/cafe in Beacon Hill purveying "plentiful breakfast options", "reliable sandwiches", soups, salads and pizzas for lunch and "dinner specials" that are "great for takeout"; whether it's all "reasonable" or "overpriced" is a point of contention, but nearly everyone has issues with the "sourpusses" behind the counter.

Paolo's Trattoria *Italian*　　　∇ 21 | 18 | 19 | $36

Charlestown | 251 Main St. (Lawnwood Ave.) | 617-242-7229 | www.paolosboston.com

"A boon for Charlestown dwellers" not in the mood to "schlep across the bridge" for Italian fare, this "great neighborhood joint" "consistently satisfies" with an "affordable", "diverse menu" and "nice wines"; the "cozy" setting "can get noisy" due to "high ceilings, brick walls" and tightly spaced tables, but when it's quiet, it's the "perfect date spot."

Papa Razzi *Italian*　　　18 | 17 | 19 | $33

Back Bay | 271 Dartmouth St. (bet. Boylston & Newbury Sts.) | 617-536-9200
Chestnut Hill | The Mall at Chestnut Hill | 199 Boylston St. (Hammond Pond Pkwy.) | 617-527-6600

(continued)

(continued)

Papa Razzi

Hanover | Merchants Row | 2087 Washington St./Rte. 53 (Rte. 123) | 781-982-2800
Framingham | 155 Worcester Rd. (bet. Caldor Rd. & Walsh St.) | 508-848-2300
Wellesley | 16 Washington St. (Rte. 128, exit 21) | 781-235-4747
Burlington | 2 Wall St. (Rte. 3A) | 781-229-0100
Concord | 768 Elm St. (Concord Tpke./Rte. 2) | 978-371-0030
www.paparazzitrattoria.com

"Everyone can find something" on the "solid", "reasonably priced" ("for the most part") menu proffered at this "quick and efficient", "kind of slick" and "noisy" Italian chain, which means it "works for a family dinner, a business lunch", a night out with "girlfriends" or as a "fill-in" for the "undecided"; just "don't expect to eat anything that actually tastes like it was cooked in Italy" and you too will "be happy."

Paramount *American*   23 | 16 | 17 | $20

Beacon Hill | 44 Charles St. (Mt. Vernon St.) | 617-720-1152 | www.paramountboston.com

"Even with a hangover", it's worth the additional "pain" of having to "wait" on "huge" though "quickly moving" "lines" to get a "trayful" of "delicious and cheap" American breakfast at this "small", "crazy" cafeteria-cum-diner in Beacon Hill (not to worry, "a table magically opens by the time you need it"); at night, it "transforms" into a candlelit, table-service spot for "inspired dinners" – but it's "not as much fun" as the daytime.

Paris Creperie *French*   22 | 12 | 16 | $12

Brookline | 278 Harvard St. (Beacon St.) | 617-232-1770 | www.paris-creperie.com

"A mind-boggling variety of delicious sweet and savory crêpes" is churned out in this "tiny" Coolidge Corner "hole-in-the-wall"; there's "always a wait" – partially because the "cute hipster" staffers really "take their time" – and the "hodgepodge seating" is "limited", but "if you aren't in a rush" and don't mind "eating while strolling", you're guaranteed a "tasty, cheap" "bite."

Parish Cafe *Sandwiches*   22 | 14 | 18 | $23

Back Bay | 361 Boylston St. (bet. Arlington & Berkeley Sts.) | 617-247-4777 ◐
NEW **South End** | 493 Massachusetts Ave. (Tremont St.) | 617-391-0501
www.parishcafe.com

Boosters of this "interesting concept" in the Back Bay admit to "falling deeper in love" each time they try a new "upscale sandwich" made from "unique" recipes by almost "every famous chef in town", all paired with "specialty cocktails" that "follow the same blueprint"; a "knowledgeable staff" monitors the "hectic" (and "not impressively decorated") interior, while patio-dwellers have "fun people-watching" while debating whether the fare is "inexpensive" or "pricey for what it is"; N.B. the South End offshoot opened post-Survey.

	FOOD	DECOR	SERVICE	COST

Parker's *New England*
22 | 24 | 24 | $49

Downtown Crossing | Omni Parker House | 60 School St. (Tremont St.) |
617-227-8600 | www.omnihotels.com

For a "classy" taste of "classic Boston", hit this "historic spot" in a "beautiful" Downtown Crossing hotel, a "stately", "storied room" where Parker House rolls and Boston cream pies were invented and continue to "live up to their reputations"; though the rest of the New England menu may be merely "ok" (some ingenuity-seekers are flat-out "bored"), "old-world" experiences like this and their accompanying "admirable service" "seem to be disappearing", so enjoy it while it lasts – it's "well worth the money."

NEW Pasha *Turkish*
- | - | - | M

Arlington | 669A Massachusetts Ave. (Water St.) |
781-648-5888

This casual arrival in Arlington Center offers an affordable menu of traditional Turkish fare for lunch and dinner, accompanied by wine, beer or coffee; the quaint setting – with red-and-green fabric on the ceiling, red stars on the off-white walls and a tiny bar – further reflects the Mideast/Med theme, as does the background music.

Passage to India *Indian*
▽ 20 | 15 | 20 | $28

Porter Square | 1900 Massachusetts Ave. (Somerville Ave.) |
Cambridge | 617-497-6113
Salem | 157 Washington St. (Rte. 114) | 978-832-2200
www.passageindia.com

These separately owned Indian eateries provide equally "awesome flavors", "pleasant atmospheres" and "friendly service", with an added "touch of Colonial class" at the Salem spot courtesy of an English co-proprietor; "great lunch buffets" beckon in the daytime, while "nice, quiet" midpriced dinners can be had when they're not "packed."

NEW Pazzo Ⓜ *Italian*
- | - | - | M

Back Bay | 269 Newbury St. (bet. Fairfield & Gloucester Sts.) |
617-267-2996 | www.pazzoboston.com

Although the name means 'crazy' in Italian, this Back Bay arrival from the owners of Bacco and Tapéo is anything but, offering a mid-priced menu in a simple setting with oversized banquettes, subdued earth-toned and brick walls, and black granite tabletops; other assets include two bars and a patio perfect for watching Newbury Street shoppers.

Peach Farm ☽ *Chinese/Seafood*
25 | 7 | 16 | $23

Chinatown | 4 Tyler St. (Beach St.) | 617-482-3332

"Don't be turned off" by the "dingy", "cavelike" setting of this often "noisy" and "packed" Chinatown "cellar" – "your mouth will thank you for every bite" of its "hearty", "authentically prepared" Cantonese fare, "especially the seafood", which is "brought to your table still flapping in a bucket for your inspection" (slightly elevating otherwise "so-so service"); the penny-wise appreciate that the rates are "super-affordable", while post-partyers are grateful that it's open until 3 AM.

	FOOD	DECOR	SERVICE	COST

Peking Cuisine *Chinese*
▽ 21 | 17 | 23 | $25

Newton | 870 Walnut St. (Beacon St.) | 617-969-0888

Newtonites know to hit this "friendly neighborhood Chinese" joint in a "little strip mall" for "consistent", inexpensive fare the whole family can get into; indeed, it's got a slew of "regular customers" who appreciate that the "nice people who work there" always remember them.

Pellana *Steak*
▽ 26 | 21 | 21 | $64

Peabody | 9 Rear Sylvan St. (bet. Andover & Endicott Sts.) | 978-531-4800 | www.pellanasteakhouse.com

A "deceiving location" in a "suburban strip mall" masks the "elegant oak-paneled room within" at this "great steakhouse" in Peabody, where "yummy" beef is served "with all the usual trimmings"; "nice" servers are appropriate guides for "special occasions", but even so, it may be "a little expensive for the neighborhood."

Pellino's *Italian*
- | - | - | M

Marblehead | 261 Washington St. (bet. Atlantic Ave. & Pleasant St.) | 781-631-3344 | www.pellinos.com

Many Marblehead "families" "count on" this "cozy", "quiet spot" for midpriced Italian dinners featuring "perfectly cooked pastas, delicious sauces" and the like, all brought by "personable" staffers.

Penang ● *Malaysian*
22 | 17 | 17 | $24

Chinatown | 685 Washington St. (Kneeland St.) | 617-451-6373 | www.penangusa.com

"Still yummy" "after all these years", this "casual" Chinatown eatery's "addictive Malaysian fare" is an "excellent value" and sometimes "spicier than expected" – when they "warn" you on the menu to "ask the waiter" before ordering, "they're serious!"; the bamboo-heavy environs, which some deem as "interesting" and others "quite odd", can get "loud" and "overcrowded at peak hours", but service is usually "very fast" (bordering on "pushy").

☑ Petit Robert Bistro *French*
24 | 20 | 22 | $39

Kenmore Square | 468 Commonwealth Ave. (W. Charlesgate) | 617-375-0699
South End | 480 Columbus Ave. (Rutland Sq.) | 617-867-0600
Needham | 45 Chapel St. (Highland Ave.) | 781-559-0532
www.petitrobertbistro.com

"Almost perfect replicas of French bistros" can be found at these "unpretentious", "cozy" sibs in Kenmore Square and the South End, where "authentic" "comfort fare for Francophiles" is paired with "suitable wines"; "respectful service" from "accented" staffers earns cheers, but it's the "great bang for the buck" that really gets fans to cry *"c'est magnifique!"*; P.S. suburbanites are "excited for the Needham location", which opened post-Survey.

P.F. Chang's China Bistro *Chinese*
19 | 19 | 18 | $32

Back Bay | Prudential Ctr. | 800 Boylston St. (Fairfield St.) | 617-378-9961
Theater District | Transportation Bldg. | 8 Park Plaza (bet. Boylston & Stuart Sts.) | 617-573-0821

(continued)

P.F. Chang's China Bistro

East Cambridge | Cambridgeside Galleria | 100 Cambridgeside Pl. (bet. 1st & 2nd Sts.) | Cambridge | 617-250-9965
Dedham | 410 Legacy Pl. (Mt. Vernon St.) | 781-461-6060
Peabody | 210 Andover St. (Sylvan St.) | 978-326-2410
Natick | Natick Collection | 1245 Worcester St. (Speen St.) | 508-651-7724
www.pfchangs.com

Expect "major hustle-bustle" at this "noisy" Chinese chain where the "sanitized", "mass-produced" menus "aren't really authentic" yet do "appeal to most palates"; no one minds the "spotty" service and "ersatz" Sino decor since they "have the formula down" – starting with "nothing-fancy" prices and an overall "fun" vibe.

Phoenicia *Lebanese*   ∇ 21 | 13 | 19 | $24

Beacon Hill | 240 Cambridge St. (Blossom St.) | 617-523-4606
"Don't let the bland decor put you off" this family-owned business whose "fabulous" Lebanese comestibles deliver a "delicious" "change of pace" to Beacon Hill for "value" tabs; indeed, it's "not a place to bring a date", so ask the "friendly, helpful" staffers to pack it to go, "then enjoy a picnic along the Charles."

Pho Hoa *Vietnamese*   ∇ 22 | 9 | 15 | $14

Chinatown | 17 Beach St. (Washington St.) | 617-423-3934
Dorchester | 1356 Dorchester Ave. (Kimball St.) | 617-287-9746
North Quincy | 409 Hancock St. (Billings Rd.) | 617-328-9600
www.phohoa.com

"True to the name, the pho is the star" at these separately owned, "family-friendly" eateries, which "hit the spot" for "authentic" Vietnamese served in "generous portions" and at "fantastic prices"; because they're "spacious", they're usually "not nearly as packed" as others of their ilk, allowing for "fast", "easy in and out."

Pho Lemongrass *Vietnamese*   20 | 15 | 18 | $24

Brookline | 239 Harvard St. (Webster St.) | 617-731-8600 | www.pholemongrass.com
"On a cold winter evening", Brookliners "go with the pho" at this "affordable" Coolidge Corner canteen whose "finely flavored and seasoned" Vietnamese eats, "friendly", "quick service" and "pleasant environment" make it "interesting to return to time and time again."

Pho n' Rice *Thai/Vietnamese*   - | - | - | I

Somerville | 289 Beacon St. (Sacramento St.) | 617-864-8888 | www.phonrice.com
This quaint Somerville Thai-Vietnamese cafe serves dozens of soup, noodle and rice dishes at budget-friendly prices; the simple decor (and lack of a liquor license) keeps the pho-cus on the food.

Pho Pasteur *Vietnamese*   23 | 10 | 16 | $18

Chinatown | 682 Washington St. (Beach St.) | 617-482-7467 | www.phopasteurboston.net
Reports that the "spicy, sweet", "amazing pho" ladled out at this Chinatown Vietnamese can "cure the common cold" are unsubstan-

tiated, but "ridiculously cheap" prices for "huge portions" of its "fantastic" fare are guaranteed; just "look past the dingy dining room" and "admire the efficiency" of the staff as it "shuttles people in and out" of the "always bustling" space.

Piattini *Italian* 23 | 18 | 20 | $35

Back Bay | 226 Newbury St. (bet. Exeter & Fairfield Sts.) | 617-536-2020 | www.piattini.com

The "adorable below-street-level" dining room proves a "private", "pleasant" "place" for a quiet, intimate meal, while the patio provides a "beautiful" spot to Back Bay "people-watch" at this "cozy" establishment dishing out nearly "perfect little plates" of Italian victuals paired with "unusual flights of wine at a great price" – which is welcome news considering the nibbles "do add up in terms of cost", especially if you're hungry; N.B. a cafe/gelateria premiered on the second floor post-Survey.

Picante Mexican Grill *Californian/Mexican* 19 | 13 | 18 | $14

Central Square | 735 Massachusetts Ave. (bet. Inman & Prospect Sts.) | Cambridge | 617-576-6394 | www.picantemex.com

Spanning "several degrees of spicy, from mild to super-hot", the "awesome salsa bar" at this "reliable, cheap" Central Square stop really peps up its Californian-influenced Mexican grub; on the other *mano*, "cheesy decorations" bring the already "grubby setting" down, but "if you can ignore" it, you'll "be happy" – especially if you close your eyes and get it to go.

Picco *Dessert/Pizza* 22 | 16 | 18 | $25

South End | 513 Tremont St. (Berkeley St.) | 617-927-0066 | www.piccorestaurant.com

What a "brilliant idea!" – this "cute", "high-end" South End parlor specializes in "crunchy yet melt-in-your-mouth" pizzas "with interesting toppings" and "gourmet ice cream made in-house", plus there's a "fun selection" of beer and wines; the only thing "needing improvement is the service", which can be "slow" and "not always nice", and obviously you should "expect a lot of parents with kids . . . little kids . . . loud little kids."

Piccola Venezia *Italian* 22 | 18 | 20 | $31

North End | 263 Hanover St. (bet. Cross & Richmond Sts.) | 617-523-3888 | www.piccolaveneziaboston.com

Doing the "North End on a budget"? – nourish yourself at this "cozy", "old-school Italian" whose "huge servings" of "tasty", "traditional" victuals help it to "endure" "in a neighborhood with no shortage of good restaurants"; locals find "value" too, testifying it's "a nice place to go for a quick bite before a game" or just "lingering with friends."

Piccolo Nido 🅢 *Italian* ▽ 24 | 19 | 25 | $37

North End | 257 North St. (Lewis St.) | 617-742-4272 | www.piccolonido.com

Slightly separate from "the main action in the North End", this "little nest", as it translates, is owned by a "neighborhood personality" ("gotta love him") who provides "attentive" staffers and "unfailingly reliable", "traditional Italian" fare for "reasonable prices" – all of which, in turn, guarantees "cheerful, pleasant" evenings.

Pie Bakery & Café *American/Dessert* | 18 | 14 | 15 | $14 |

Newton | 796 Beacon St. (Centre St.) | 617-332-8743 |
www.piebakeryandcafe.com

Newtonians have "fun" coming to sample the "sweet and savory" pies, plus other light American fare, baked at this "small" cafe featuring "a counter where you can watch the kitchen in action"; however, some leave "unimpressed" by goods they deem "pricey" for being "ok but not great", while others go away "disappointed" because someone at the counter was "kind of mean" to them.

Pierrot Bistrot Français ⓈDISH *French* | 24 | 19 | 24 | $42 |

Beacon Hill | 272 Cambridge St. (Anderson St.) | 617-725-8855 |
www.pierrotbistrot.com

"Reminding" Beacon Hill folk of "a neighborhood bistro in Paris", this corner establishment supplies "wonderful, authentic", "old-fashioned French cooking" alongside "complementary wines", about which the "friendly owner and staff" make "helpful recommendations"; "decent prices" sweeten the deal, and while there aren't many fans of the "clown pictures everywhere", "exposed brick provides warmth to the intimate room."

Pigalle Ⓜ *French* | 26 | 22 | 24 | $59 |

Theater District | 75 S. Charles St. (bet. Stuart St. & Warrenton Pl.) |
617-423-4944 | www.pigalleboston.com

"Hidden on the quieter side of Charles Street", this "cozy, elegant" Theater District destination touts a "tour de force" in Marc Orfaly's "marvelous" French fare with an "inventive" "edge"; a "romantic ambiance" is abetted by "service that makes you feel wonderfully pampered" (not to mention "terrific wines"), and while dollar-watchers calculate it's "pricey for what you get", their "innovation"-backing counterparts deem it "well worth every cent."

Pizzeria Regina *Pizza* | 24 | 12 | 14 | $17 |

Back Bay | Prudential Ctr. | 800 Boylston St. (Ring Rd.) | 617-424-1115
Leather District | South Station | Grand Concourse (Essex St.) |
617-261-6600
Faneuil Hall | Faneuil Hall Mktpl. | 226 Faneuil Hall Mktpl. (Congress St.) |
617-742-1713
North End | 11½ Thacher St. (Margin St.) | 617-227-0765
Braintree | South Shore Plaza | 250 Granite St. (I-95, exit 6) | 781-848-8700
Medford | 44 Station Landing (Revere Beach Pkwy.) | 781-306-1222
Watertown | Arsenal Mall | 485 Arsenal St., 2 (Elm St.) | 617-926-5300
Peabody | Northshore Mall | 210 Andover St. (Cross St.) | 978-538-9700
Burlington | Burlington Mall | 1131 Middlesex Tpke. (Rte. 128) |
781-270-4212
Auburn | Auburn Mall | 385 Southbridge St. (Auburn St.) | 508-721-0090
www.pizzeriaregina.com
Additional locations throughout the Boston area

"Stick to the original" when craving this familiar name's "real-deal" pizza, because the "humble", "slightly grungy" North End address is where the "ancient wood-burning oven" resides – just look at the "droves" "waiting" on "long lines" for the "amazing", "gooey" goods, which are brought by "waitresses as crusty as the pies"; the other locations, mostly set in "food courts", are "nothing in comparison."

Plaza III – The Kansas City Steakhouse *Steak*

| 21 | 19 | 21 | $53 |

Faneuil Hall | Faneuil Hall Mktpl. | 100 S. Market St. (Merchants Row) | 617-720-5570 | www.plazaiiisteakhouse.com/

"For that manly meat experience" in Faneuil Hall, nearby business folk "take clients" to this "high-end" steakhouse with a somewhat "low-key atmosphere" to wheel and deal over "huge, crusty" cuts they ascertain "stand up to competition well"; nah, counter detractors, "compared to others, this place is nothing special."

Pleasant Cafe ● *American*

| ∇ 18 | 8 | 15 | $21 |

Roslindale | 4515 Washington St. (Beech St.) | 617-323-2111 | www.pleasantcafe.com

While this Roslindale "neighborhood hangout for beer, pizza" and other American grub dates back to the 1940s, it seems like "it's been there since the world was created", with prices and "waitresses that haven't changed since then" either; indeed, it was, is and, hopefully, will be "always fun", whether for eating in the vinyl booths, "taking out" or "sitting in the bar and watching the Sox."

Poe's Kitchen at the Rattlesnake ● *Mexican*
(fka Rattlesnake Bar & Grill)

| - | 15 | 15 | $25 |

Back Bay | 384 Boylston St. (bet. Arlington & Berkeley Sts.) | 617-859-8555 | www.rattlesnakebar.com

Attracting "nearby office workers as well as students", this "popular hang" in the Back Bay aims to ditch its "mediocre at best" reputation with the 2009 appointment of chef Brian Poe, who imbues Mexican fare with South American and Southwest flavors; the interior's been spruced up (possibly outdating the Decor score), the roof deck remains "cool" and only time will tell if the "aloof staff" got it together.

Polcari's *Italian*

| 17 | 16 | 17 | $28 |

Woburn | 309 Montvale Ave. (bet. Central & Washington Sts.) | 781-938-1900
Saugus | 92 Broadway/Rte. 1 (Walnut St.) | 781-233-3765
www.polcaris.com

"Large servings for big families with big appetites" is the stock in trade of this "old reliable" in Saugus and Woburn dishing out "everyday" "red-sauce" Italian "as well as Pizzeria Regina pizza" in "gaudy" checked-tablecloth surroundings; even discerning palates who peg it merely "mediocre" begrudgingly admit "it'll do in a pinch."

Pomodoro ⊄ *Italian*

| 24 | 18 | 21 | $37 |

North End | 319 Hanover St. (bet. Prince & Richmond Sts.) | 617-367-4348 | www.pomodoroboston.com
Brookline | 24 Harvard St. (Washington St.) | 617-566-4455

"Noisy, small and hard to get a seat in", this "rustic" North Ender vends the same "skillfully prepared but simple Italian cooking" with "fresh ingredients" and "red sauce to dream about" as its "sophisticated but homey" Brookline Village offshoot, which diverges with "bigger", hence more "relaxing", digs; service "can vary from perfect to unfriendly", while the cash-only policy always "irritates, considering some entrees are north of $20."

NEW Pomodoro ⓜ *Italian* — | — | — | M

Needham | 1019 Great Plain Ave. (Chapel St.) | 781-444-9200 | www.restaurantpomodoro.com

This dinner-only Italian in Downtown Needham offers a family-friendly menu of classics like spaghetti bolognese and shrimp scampi at prices that won't break the bank; the rustic dining room features maple floors and exposed-brick walls, while the creative martinis dispensed from the bar make it an attractive meeting place for drinks.

Ponzu *Asian* ▽ 23 | 18 | 20 | $32

Waltham | 286 Moody St. (Gordon St.) | 781-736-9188 | www.theponzu.com

"Wow", "what a great surprise" marvel first-timers to Waltham's "best-kept secret", which harbors a "large variety" of "contemporary" Asian fusion small and large plates prepped in "clever", "flavorful" ways by "friendly sushi chefs" and servers; opinions on the decor veer from "nice" to "uninspiring", but since it's "best enjoyed with a group", it's usually "fun" either way.

Pops ❶ *American* 22 | 20 | 19 | $35

South End | 560 Tremont St. (Clarendon St.) | 617-695-1250 | www.popsrestaurant.net

"Fun food with flair" flies out of the kitchen of this "adorable" South End New American whose "sophisticated twists on comfort" fare seem even more "scrumptious" for being "pretty reasonably priced"; the "bold", "classy" yet "quirky" space gets "cramped" but "not uncomfortable", unless you're saddled with one of the "indifferent" members of the otherwise "professional" staff; N.B. post-Survey additions include a luminous new white bar and a small-plates menu.

Porcini's *Mediterranean* 22 | 17 | 22 | $37

Watertown | 68 School St. (Arsenal St.) | 617-924-2221 | www.porcinis.com

At this Watertown haunt, a "nondescript", somewhat "foreboding exterior" sheaths a slightly "dark" dining room that could use "some updating" – but "the real reason you go out to eat" is the food, and surveyors say the Mediterranean meals are not only "terrific" here, but "fair priced" to boot; an "outgoing" staff adds "warmth" to the proceedings, especially at the "friendly bar", which is "worth a stop even if you don't have to wait for a table."

NEW Post 390 *American* — | — | — | M

Back Bay | 406 Stuart St. (Clarendon St.) | 617-399-0015 | www.post390restaurant.com

Executive chef Eric Brennan cranks out moderately priced American comfort food from two shining exposed kitchens at this saucy urban

FOOD · DECOR · SERVICE · COST

Back Bay tavern courtesy of Kenneth A. Himmel, of Grill 23 & Bar fame; the bi-level space features black glazed columns, wood-slatted walls, a four-sided fireplace, a bar downstairs, private dining and views of bustling Copley Square all around.

NEW Prana Café, The *Vegan*

`-` `-` `-` `M`

Newton | 292 Centre St. (Jefferson St.) | 617-527-7726 | www.thepranacafe.com

This breakfast, lunch and dinner spot in Newton offers a midpriced menu of locally sourced, mostly raw vegan fare, served in a vibrant green-and-chocolate setting with tables, barstools at a window counter and a cozy couch for relaxing, as well as a kids' area.

☑ Prezza *Italian*

`27` `22` `24` `$57`

North End | 24 Fleet St. (Moon St.) | 617-227-1577 | www.prezza.com

"Not your typical North End" eatery, this "classy" spot puts a "unique", even "edgy" spin on Italian with "flavorful" results quite different from "typical red-sauce fare"; a "vast wine list", "helpful, charming" staff and "stylish", "intimate", "quite romantic" setting add to a night out that's a "heavenly" "treat" – "when you can afford it."

Prose ☒ Ⓜ *American*

`▽` `24` `14` `14` `$37`

Arlington | 352A Massachusetts Ave. (Wyman Terrace) | 781-648-2800

A true "labor of love", this "tiny", "nondescript" Arlington eatery is known for a chef-owner "who is also [often] the waitress, quite opinionated" and, truth be told, sometimes "a bit curt" – but any perceived hassles are "worth it" for her "seasonal", "inventive" and "reasonably priced" New American cuisine featuring "lots of locally produced ingredients"; since "everything is cooked from scratch", "service is quite slow" ("she does warn you"), "but if you've got the time", the fare is "sublime."

Publick House, The *Pub Food*

`21` `20` `17` `$28`

Brookline | 1648 Beacon St. (Washington St.) | 617-277-2880 | www.eatgoodfooddrinkbetterbeer.com

"A beer snob's dream", this Brookline tavern serves an "extraordinary selection" of "rare" brews "served in brand-appropriate glasses" alongside "hefty portions" of "awesome" Belgian *cuisine à la bière* (the "standout" being "mind-blowing mac 'n' cheese" "mixed with whatever your little heart desires"); there's a "maddening" "line out the door almost every night", hence the "slow" service, but once you get their attention, the staffers give "excellent recommendations."

Punjab *Indian*

`25` `21` `19` `$27`

Arlington | 485 Massachusetts Ave. (Medford St.) | 781-643-0943 | www.punjabarlington.com

"After being luxuriously renovated" a while back, this Arlingtonian's "classy" space means "even more folks can enjoy" what many consider "the crown jewel of Indian food in the 'burbs", as it brims with "aromatic", "distinctive spices and flavors"; indeed, the cuisine – not to mention the "yummy cocktails" and "reasonable prices" – makes up for service that's sometimes "ok" but often "disjointed."

	FOOD	DECOR	SERVICE	COST

Punjabi Dhaba ●⊕ *Indian* | 24 | 7 | 14 | $12

Inman Square | 225 Hampshire St. (Cambridge St.) | Cambridge |
617-547-8272 | www.royalbharatinc.com

Like a Punjabi "roadside diner" transported to Inman Square, this
"not-very-attractive" "two-story shack" is a "mecca" for "authentic,
tasty" "Indian street food" offered "at its greasy best" for "minus-
cule prices"; it's basically "self-serve" and "by no means fast", but at
least there's a "continuous loop" of "loud" "Bollywood" musicals to
keep you occupied as you "wait" on the "insane lines"; P.S. there is
"limited" seating, but really, "take it home."

Punjab Palace *Indian* | 24 | 15 | 21 | $23

Allston | 109 Brighton Ave. (bet. Harvard & Linden Sts.) | 617-254-1500 |
www.punjabpalace.com

"Bollywood videos playing on large-screen TVs" notwithstanding,
this Allston subcontinental is somewhat "posher" (and larger) than
India Quality, its Kenmore Square sibling; what's similar is the fare:
"flavorful", "wonderful curries" and more sold for a "steal" in "generous portions" whose spiciness the "attentive servers" will "adjust
according to your preferences."

Purple Cactus | ∇ 21 | 14 | 21 | $10
Burrito & Wrap Bar *Eclectic/Mexican*

Jamaica Plain | 674 Centre St. (Seaverns Ave.) | 617-522-7422 |
www.thepurplecactus.com

"Get a fast Mex fix without the guilt" at this Jamaica Plain "weeknight
staple" that puts Eclectic, "healthy" spins on its burritos, wraps, salads
and fresh-fruit smoothies in "small, colorful", counter-serve surroundings "with a few tables"; unfortunately, some spice-aholics
deem the offerings "too bland."

Qingdao Garden *Chinese* | 24 | 5 | 15 | $18

Porter Square | 2382 Massachusetts Ave. (bet. Dudley & Harvey Sts.) |
Cambridge | 617-492-7540

"Skip the Americanized stuff and dive into" the "amazing homemade dumplings", "outstanding Northern Chinese dishes" and all-
day weekend dim sum that "grace the menu" at this "unique in the
best sense" Porter Square eatery; service can either be "ultrahelp-
ful" or "atrocious", and the setting "doesn't look like much" – "but
who cares" with such low prices?

☒ Radius ☒ *French* | 26 | 25 | 25 | $69

Financial District | 8 High St. (bet. Federal & Summer Sts.) |
617-426-1234 | www.radiusrestaurant.com

Michael Schlow's "rarefied" Financial District "masterpiece"
delivers "imaginative, edgy, impeccably prepared" New French fare
and "divine wines" – with the aid of "knowledgeable", "attentive"
servers – to a "debonair clientele" in a "dramatic", "handsome",
"circular" room (the only issue there: "tables are crowded on top of
each other"); the across-the-board "artistry" "helps mitigate the
sticker shock", especially felt by complainers of portions that are "at
times woefully small."

	FOOD	DECOR	SERVICE	COST

Rami's *Mideastern*

23 | 7 | 15 | $13

Brookline | 324 Harvard St. (Babcock St.) | 617-738-3577 |
www.ramisboston.com

"Close your eyes when you bite into" the "far-out falafel" sold at this
"hole-in-the-wall" "Brookline bargain" and "you're transported to
Israel"; the shawarma and other Middle Eastern "fast food" are equally
"lick-your-fingers good" – just don't let the sometimes "grumpy"
service from the "dry-humored staff" and "small, crowded" dining
room get you down; P.S. being a kosher establishment, it's "closed
on the Sabbath."

Rani *Indian*

20 | 19 | 17 | $28

Brookline | 1353 Beacon St. (Harvard St.) | 617-734-0400 |
www.ranibistro.com

With "enough diversity to make it stand out", this Indian serves not
just the "traditional Northern fare", but "interesting and delicious
regional cuisine", of which the Hyderabadi dishes particularly "should
be tried"; "service is spotty", but the vibe is relatively "upscale" –
which is why it's "a little pricier than some" of its competitors.

Redbones BBQ ● *BBQ*

22 | 14 | 18 | $23

Somerville | 55 Chester St. (Elm St.) | 617-628-2200 | www.redbones.com
"Bring your elastic pants" to Davis Square's "reasonably priced"
"hog heaven", because its "addictive", "succulent", "sauce-covered"
BBQ is served in "massive portions" and paired with "tons of beers"
("spin the wheel" "if you can't decide"); the "utilitarian" "roadside-
diner" decor is "funkier" in the basement bar ("decked out voodoo
style"), while staffers are "efficient" in helping the "huge crowds"
"gorge" and "stagger out the door" "satisfied"; P.S. a shout-out to
the "bicycle valet": "sooo cute!"

Red Fez ● *Mideastern*

18 | 18 | 16 | $35

South End | 1222 Washington St. (Perry St.) | 617-338-6060
Though "conventional", the "decent variety" of Middle Eastern fare
offered at this South End haunt is "well priced" and "tasty", and it
adequately soaks up the "yummy drinks" (like a Tang-rimmed martini); the decor – "a mix of bold and muted colors" among Moroccan
accoutrements – abets a "festive" vibe, but it's too bad "marginal
service" can kill the buzz; P.S. a "huge patio", weekend live music
and belly dancing and "free parking" are "pluses."

Red House Ⓜ *Eclectic*

20 | 21 | 20 | $39

Harvard Square | 98 Winthrop St. (bet. Eliot & JFK Sts.) | Cambridge |
617-576-0605 | www.theredhouse.com

Boasting a "cozy fireplace in the bar for cold evenings", a "tiny but
so wonderful patio for the warm months" and a variety of "private",
"romantic" dining rooms, this "charming" Harvard Square Eclectic in
a "cute old house" with "sloped ceilings and winding stairs" "nur-
tures" its supporters whatever the weather; the "genteel" vibe car-
ries over to the fare, much of it offered in half portions (still "quite
plentiful") and all "balancing predictability with innovation"
"without steep pricing."

Redline ☒ *American*   17 | 14 | 15 | $25

Harvard Square | 59 JFK St. (bet. Eliot & Winthrop Sts.) | Cambridge |
617-491-9851 | www.redlinecambridge.com

"Grad students" in particular come to this "clubby", "cozy" Harvard
Square spot for a "one-stop evening" where they fill up on "informal", "right-priced" New American eats and either chill out with
"sporting events on TV" or get down to "live music" and DJs; just
"don't expect much" from the menu and you'll have a better chance
of "leaving with a sense of fulfillment."

Red Rock Bistro *American*   20 | 21 | 18 | $38

Swampscott | 141 Humphrey St./Rte. 129 (Redington St.) |
781-595-1414 | www.redrockbistro.com

When it comes to Swampscott restaurants, "you can't beat the
setting" of this "high-profile location" "overlooking the ocean"
with "beautiful views of the Boston skyline" ("ask for a table outside or by a window"), while the seafood-heavy New American
menu holds its own with many "brilliant" preparations and "large
portions"; the rest of the experience wildly diverges between "moderate" and "rip-off" pricing, "loud" and "quiet" atmospheres, and
"pleasant" and "snooty service."

Red Sky ◑ *American*   ▽ 18 | 22 | 20 | $30

Faneuil Hall | 16 North St. (Congress St.) | 617-742-3333 |
www.redskyboston.com

An "alternative" to the Faneuil Hall usual, this "chic, classy"
hangout offers a "reasonably priced" menu of New American
fare for "elegant" lunches, dinners and "late-night dining" amid
"loud music, hip people" and an "awesome bar atmosphere"; yes,
despite its daytime hours, it really is a "nightclub", but it's "not
stuck-up" in any way.

Rendezvous *Mediterranean*   26 | 19 | 24 | $47

Central Square | 502 Massachusetts Ave. (Brookline St.) | Cambridge |
617-576-1900 | www.rendezvouscentralsquare.com

Central Square suppers "pray to the altar" of "restaurateur par
excellence" Steve Johnson at his "whopper" of a "casual" restaurant, a "jazzed-up" "former Burger King" where he "creatively
combines" "locally sourced ingredients" to yield "glorious, distinctive" Mediterranean fare ("quite well priced", just like the "fantastic
wine list"); "friendly, helpful service" keeps the "comfort level high",
especially during Sunday's prix fixe service, featuring the same
"wonderful food for a little less cash."

Restaurante Cesaria ☒ *Cape Verdean*   - | - | - | I

Dorchester | 266 Bowdoin St. (bet. Hamilton & Quincy Sts.) |
617-282-1998 | www.restaurantecesaria.com

"If you are willing to travel to Dorchester to find it", this colorful cafe
offers the unique tastes of Cape Verdean fare, an exotic mixture of
Portuguese and West African cuisines; inexpensive prices help to
make it "worth the trip", while weekend musicians from the home-
land merit sticking around a while.

☒ Rialto *Italian*

26 | 25 | 25 | $63

Harvard Square | Charles Hotel | 1 Bennett St. (Eliot St.) | Cambridge | 617-661-5050 | www.rialto-restaurant.com

At Jody Adams' "beautiful", "modern", "stylish" Harvard Square establishment, the culinary "goddess" works with "creative", "incredible combinations" of "the freshest ingredients" that "layer flavor after flavor" into her "regional Italian specialties"; like the menu, the "impressive wine list" contains several "wallet-busters", so "bring the wealthy in-laws" and succumb to the "savvy suggestions" of the staffers, "exemplars of stellar service" all.

Rincon Limeno *Colombian/Peruvian*

- | - | - | I

East Boston | 409 Chelsea St. (Shelby St.) | 617-569-4942 | www.rinconlimenorestaurant.com

Though the translation of its name would have you believe it's a 'corner of Lima', this casual East Boston eatery augments its "delicious Peruvian food" with authentic Colombian fare, of which "amazing", "fresh ceviche" is the star, all of it served in heaping piles; though the colorful digs are tiny, "great service" and "cheap" bills attract families.

Ristorante Damiano ● *Italian*

- | - | - | M

North End | 307 Hanover St. (bet. Prince & Richmond Sts.) | 617-742-0020 | www.ristorantedamiano.com

Midpriced Italian cuisine is served at this intimate North Ender with exposed brick and gold-tone walls hung with family photos of the Sicilian owner; guests sip wine and unwind while watching the open kitchen, or get a closer view of the action at the chef's table.

Ristorante Fiore *Italian*

21 | 21 | 19 | $40

North End | 250 Hanover St. (bet. Cross & Parmenter Sts.) | 617-371-1176 | www.ristorantefiore.com

"Good luck getting a table" on this North Ender's "rocking roof deck", which along with the "street-level patio" is one of "two outdoor dining options" providing a respite from the often "chaotic", "cozy" interior; "although nothing phenomenal", the "old-time" Italian fare is "consistently good" and "not too pricey", while the "wine selection is quite extensive" and the "chatty" "service is more hit than miss."

Ristorante Marcellino Ⓜ *Italian*

▽ 16 | 15 | 16 | $39

Waltham | 11 Cooper St. (Pine St.) | 781-647-5458 | www.marcellinorist.com

Friends of this "old-school" Waltham "hideaway" tout its "often terrific", "traditional" Southern Italian cuisine, which is brought to table by a "knowledgeable staff"; foes, however, cite occasionally "rude" servers and a "price-to-quality ratio" that "just isn't there" as reasons it should either "lower" the tabs or try out some "fresh ideas."

NEW Ristorante Pavarotti *Italian*

- | - | - | M

Reading | 601 Main St./Rte. 28 (Haven St.) | 781-670-9050 | www.ristorantepavarotti.com

A native Calabrian has opened this newcomer along Reading's main strip, but don't expect just Southern Italian fare – along with pastas and seafood, the midpriced menu includes entrees like a veal chop with shiitake mushrooms; everything's served in a warmly decorated room with a tiled floor, soft sconce lighting and, yes, music sung by Pavarotti.

Ristorante Toscano *Italian*   24 | 23 | 22 | $53
Beacon Hill | 41-47 Charles St. (bet. Chestnut & Mt. Vernon Sts.) | 617-723-4090 | www.toscanoboston.com
"Congratulations" are in order, as the relatively new management of this Beacon Hill Italian spot has "much improved" it with "beautiful" "freshened" wood-and-leather decor and "revitalized" "upmarket" fare featuring "tasty" "tributes to authentic Florentine recipes"; mostly "doting" servers offer "terrific advice" on the "great wines", and although it's "pretty pricey", "the clientele can handle it."

Ristorante Villa Francesca *Italian*   ▽ 19 | 18 | 19 | $41
North End | 150 Richmond St. (Hanover St.) | 617-367-2948 | www.ristorantevillafrancesca.com
An "attractive setting" (tin ceilings, brick archways, "windows open in the summer"), "knowledgeable, attentive" service and red-sauce "classics done well" lure North End sightseers to this caffe "off the hustle and bustle of Hanover Street"; however, some connoisseurs caution that those "passionate" about big Italian flavors may find it too "ordinary" "for the money charged."

Riva *Italian*   ▽ 26 | 19 | 24 | $44
Scituate | 116 Front St. (Otis Pl.) | 781-545-5881 | www.rivarestaurant.net
"Outstanding" sums up this harborside "jewel" in Scituate, whose "small quarters" foodies continue to "jam" for an "extensive menu" of "yummy" Italian cuisine with "pizzazz"; likewise, the "engaging, energetic" staff remains "constantly on alert to answer any questions" that may arise.

NEW Robinwood *American*   - | - | - | I
Jamaica Plain | 536 Centre St. (Robinwood Ave.) | 617-524-7575 | www.robinwoodcafegrille.com
Families flock to this Jamaica Plain American diner for burgers, pizzas, pastas and heartier entrees, plus breakfast served all day, all offered at budget-friendly prices (nothing tops $17); painted in soothing sea-foam green and tan, the dining room is decorated with vintage photos of Italy and Greece, the latter an ode to the owners' heritage.

Rocca *Italian*   24 | 24 | 21 | $48
South End | 500 Harrison Ave. (Perry St.) | 617-451-5151 | www.roccaboston.com
This South Ender "intrigues" as much with its "refreshing approach to Italian cooking" – namely "terrific", "artfully presented" Ligurian specialties – as it does with "interesting cocktail variants", an "impressive wine list" and a "hip" setting comprised of a "swanky lounge", a "soothing dining" room and "über-cool outdoor seating"; though "great for sharing", the "portions are disappointingly modest" for the price – "free parking", on the other hand, is "nirvana."

Rodizio Brazilian Steakhouse *Brazilian* ▽ 22 | 18 | 22 | $43

Somerville | 129 Broadway (bet. Michigan & Wisconsin Aves.) |
617-776-1129

Hard-core carnivores "won't leave hungry" from this Somerville spot
specializing in "succulent, moist" Brazilian barbecue served
tableside and an all-you-can-eat buffet of "tasty" sides; the yellow-
walled, brightly lit room is a bit utilitarian, while the prices veer
toward the expensive.

NEW Ronnarong Thai Tapas Bar ⑤ *Thai* - | - | - | I

Somerville | 255 Washington St. (bet. Bonner Ave. & Sarborn Ct.) |
617-625-9296

This revamp of Union Square's Great Thai Chef is a meditation on
simplicity, from the boxed herb gardens on the windows to the
peaceful green interior with bamboo floors, floral watercolor paintings
and a mahogany-accented bar; chef/co-owner Ronnarong 'Ronnie'
Saksua has added exotic tapas and creative sake and wine cocktails
to the still-inexpensive menu.

Roobar Ⓜ *American* 21 | 20 | 21 | $37

Plymouth | Cordage Park | 10 Cordage Park Circle (Court St.) |
508-746-4300 | www.theroobar.com
See review in Cape Cod Directory.

Rosebud Diner *Diner* 16 | 18 | 18 | $16

Somerville | 381 Summer St. (bet. Cutter Ave. & Grove St.) |
617-666-6015 | www.rosebuddiner.com

"Have your eggs" with a side of "sass" at this "tiny" Davis Square
diner housed in a "real-deal" dining car from 1941, where "wise-
cracking waitresses" dish out "jet fuel coffee" and "filling", "bad-for-
you food served just right" and for cheap; in short, it makes for a
"fun and funky" experience that "remains true to its beginnings."

NEW Rowes Wharf Sea Grille *Seafood* - | - | - | M

Waterfront | Boston Harbor Hotel | 70 Rowes Wharf (Atlantic Ave.) |
617-856-7744 | www.roweswharfseagrille.com

A picturesque harbor view and fresh, innovative seafood define this
Boston Harbor Hotel arrival serving breakfast, lunch and dinner in a
classy nautical-themed setting – rich blues, hardwood floors – that
feels more yacht than restaurant (though prices are easier on the wallet than at Meritage upstairs); in summer, diners can enjoy meals on
the terrace, getting glimpses of concerts and outdoor film series.

Royal East *Chinese* 20 | 14 | 21 | $24

Central Square | 782-792 Main St. (Windsor St.) | Cambridge |
617-661-1660 | www.royaleast.com

"Low prices do not mean low quality" at this Central Square
"banquet restaurant" where "meals can soar" – just "let the owner
guide you" to the "fresh" Cantonese seafood and other "authentic"
specialties; however, if you fail to "ignore the Americanized"
options, you'll join in the chorus of critics who bemoan it "never
truly distinguishes" itself.

	FOOD	DECOR	SERVICE	COST

Rubin's *Deli* | 19 | 9 | 14 | $22 |

Brookline | 500 Harvard St. (Kenwood St.) | 617-731-8787 |
www.rubinskosher.com

An "endearingly gruff appeal" draws Brookliners to this "popular kosher establishment" where "dependable" deli fare and "Jewish soul
food" made with "care and attention to authenticity" are served up
in "reasonably sized and -priced portions" by occasionally "surly"
staffers; while the kitchen is making strides to somewhat "modern-
ize the menu", "nostalgics" urge it to "stick to corned beef."

Rudi's Resto-Café & Bar *American* | - | - | - | I |

Roxbury | Hampton Inn Crosstown Ctr. | 811 Massachusetts Ave.
(Melnea Cass Blvd.) | 617-345-5432 | www.rudisrestocafe.com

With a sleek industrial look and tall glass walls that overlook the
Hampton Inn's courtyard, this affordable New American serves as a
cosmopolitan beacon in Roxbury's gritty Newmarket Square area on
the cusp of the South End; it's a two-for-one venue with a lounge for
night owls and a dining room for business and pleasure.

Rustic Kitchen *Italian* | 20 | 20 | 20 | $38 |

Theater District | Radisson Hotel Boston | 210 Stuart St. (bet. Church St. &
Park Pl.) | 617-423-5700

Hingham | The Derby Street Shoppes | 94 Derby St. (Cushing St.) |
781-749-2700
www.rustickitchen.biz

"Fresh, comforting" menus of "basic Italian with a little flair" plus
"cool", "modern" atmospheres make for "great scenes" at these
"casual" Hingham and Theater District sibs that up their ante with
"knowledgeable waiters" and "bartenders that rock"; but the fare's
more pleasing "to the eye than to the palate" judge gourmands who
"expect more for the price."

☑ Ruth's Chris Steak House *Steak* | 24 | 23 | 23 | $64 |

Downtown Crossing | Old City Hall | 45 School St. (Province St.) |
617-742-8401 | www.ruthschris.com

"Nothing beats a steak sizzling in butter" at this New Orleans–based
chain where the "melt-in-your-mouth" chops are "cooked to perfection" and delivered on "hot plates" by "attentive" servers; "nestled
in Old City Hall" near Downtown Crossing, the "fantastic setting"
makes it a "must for special occasions", and while some find it "too
expensive", the "off-the-charts" prices are manageable "so long as
your boss doesn't care how much you spend."

Sabur *Mediterranean*   ▽ | 22 | 21 | 22 | $35 |

Somerville | 212 Holland St. (bet. Claremon & Moore Sts.) |
617-776-7890 | www.saburrestaurant.com

Many who've "stumbled onto" this "cozy" place with "copper-
topped tables" and an open hearth in Somerville's Teele Square have
become "addicted" to its "unusual, delicious" fare encompassing
"many regions" of the Eastern Mediterranean, the Balkans, Greece
and North Africa among them; "knowledgeable" staffers help to
navigate the menu, helping to make for a "memorable" experience.

Sagra *Italian*

| 16 | 16 | 15 | $31 |

Somerville | 400 Highland Ave. (Clarendon St.) | 617-625-4200 | www.sagrarestaurant.com

"You get a lot for the price" at this "pretty standard Italian" eatery in Davis Square – and while a few folks admit their "delight" at the dishes, just as many cop to feeling "underwhelmed"; reports of service "slow" and "attitude"-filled crop up more often than not, leaving some Somervilleans wondering if the space, which has changed hands "a number of times over the years", is "cursed."

Sakurabana ⊠ *Japanese*

| 25 | 12 | 19 | $31 |

Financial District | 57 Broad St. (Milk St.) | 617-542-4311 | www.sakurabanaonline.com

"A must for lunchers in the Financial District", this Japanese "staple" is "always jammed" ("get there early to snag a table") with "suits" digging into an "extensive selection" of "fresh sushi" served in "abundant amounts" and at "reasonable prices"; fare this "fabulous" "needs a more upscale facility", but "fast service" gets everyone in, out and back to work right quick; P.S. dinners are not as "crazy."

Salts ⊠Ⓜ *American/French*

| 26 | 22 | 26 | $61 |

Central Square | 798 Main St. (bet. Cherry & Windsor Sts.) | Cambridge | 617-876-8444 | www.saltsrestaurant.com

Although "not an informal" experience, the "friendly" yet "refined" staff at this "quaint" Central Square spot done up in "elegant burgundy, black" and tan decor "makes you feel right at home" as it ferries "impeccably crafted" French–New American fare filled with "creative" yet "accessible" "twists" that render it "simultaneously gourmet and comforting"; indeed, it's "exactly what fine dining should be", right up to the "pricey" ("but worth it") tabs.

Salvatore's ● *Italian*

| 20 | 18 | 17 | $33 |

Seaport District | 225 Northern Ave. (D St.) | 617-737-5454 | www.salvatoresboston.com

"Big portions" of "well-prepared" classic Italian fare come for "wonderful prices" at this Seaport venue; the "bright", modern decor leaves a few tradition-seekers "cold" (the patio's "nice"), and some of the "friendly" staffers can't mask their "inexperience", but optimists encourage "with a little work", it's "potentially a great spot."

Sanctuary ⊠Ⓜ *Eclectic*

| ▽ 19 | 20 | 18 | $26 |

Financial District | 189 State St. (Atlantic Ave.) | 617-573-9333 | www.sanctuaryboston.com

Large Buddhas and "clean lines" create the "cool atmosphere" at this tri-level Financial District club, which plies after-workers with "great martinis" and "tasty", "quality" Eclectic "morsels" priced right.

Sandrine's *French*

| 24 | 22 | 23 | $48 |

Harvard Square | 8 Holyoke St. (bet. Mass. Ave. & Mt. Auburn St.) | Cambridge | 617-497-5300 | www.sandrines.com

Both "traditional and innovative" French fare, with many Alsatian influences, fill the "astounding" *carte* at this "tasteful" Harvard Square bistro boasting "old-world elegance" in its "comfortable, inviting" setting; though generally "unobtrusive", the "serious, professional" servers can "match entrees" to selections from the "first-class wine and beer list", helping to make the entire "delectable experience" "worth the price."

S&S *Deli*

18 | 13 | 16 | $21

Inman Square | 1334 Cambridge St. (bet. Hampshire & Prospect Sts.) | Cambridge | 617-354-0777 | www.sandsrestaurant.com

A "no-frills, solid performer" since 1919, this Inman Square "staple" attracts "endless lines" for its "massive weekend brunches", though its "huge menu" of "homey", "real deli" fare gets doled out by the "surly", "efficient" staff every other day of the week too; a contingency of foes fume it's too "pricey" for being "consistently mediocre", but let's face it, it must be "doing something right."

Santarpio's Pizza ●≠ *Pizza*

25 | 8 | 13 | $17

East Boston | 111 Chelsea St. (bet. Paris Pl. & Porter St.) | 617-567-9871 | www.santarpiospizza.com

"Pizza aficionados" "brave the lines" and the "sketchy" "dump" setting of this East Boston "landmark" where "surly", "crusty" servers "yell at nonregulars" as they dole out "superb thin-crust" pies as well as "inexpensive", "succulent homemade sausages and tasty lamb kebabs"; yes, with the exception of the fare, the experience has "many flaws", but "everyone needs to go" "at least once."

Saporito's Ⓜ *Italian*

∇ 26 | 15 | 24 | $50

Hull | 11 Rockland Circle (George Washington Blvd.) | 781-925-3023 | www.saporitoscafe.com

Urbanites aplenty "schlep" to this "old cottage" in a "remote neighborhood" in Hull where "passionate", "gracious owners" offer up a "beautiful bounty" of "fresh, unique" Northern Italian fare; the dining room is "intimate but not stunning" (the wooden booths in particular are "uncomfortable"), and the prices are a smidge "high", but obviously none of that matters, as it's "always packed."

Sapporo *Japanese/Korean*

∇ 21 | 15 | 20 | $33

Newton | 81 Union St., downstairs (Beacon St.) | 617-964-8044

"Locals love" this family-owned neighborhood spot in Newton Centre where the Japanese-Korean cooking is the "real thing" and the staff is "friendly"; the "small" subterranean setting includes a nine-seat sushi bar and is also renowned for some mighty "great box lunches."

Saraceno *Italian*

∇ 23 | 21 | 22 | $39

North End | 286 Hanover St. (bet. Parmenter & Prince Sts.) | 617-227-5353 | www.saracenos.com

"Step back in time" at this "classic Italian" in the North End where a "red-gravy" menu straight out of the "Sinatra era" has stayed "consistent" for the last 25 years; the triple-decker layout lures tourists to the ground floor and "regulars upstairs", while the over-the-top, "fresco"-festooned basement is an "excellent date spot"; no matter where you wind up, service is "attentive" and the mood "old school."

Scampo ● *Italian*

22 | 24 | 22 | $55

Beacon Hill | Liberty Hotel | 215 Charles St. (Cambridge St.) | 617-536-2100 | www.scampoboston.com

The "old Charles Street Jail", now the "hot" Liberty Hotel, is home to this "excellent" Beacon Hill "place to be seen", where star chef Lydia Shire showcases a "truly interesting" Italian menu ("prison food it's not"); the "cosmopolitan", brick-walled setting is comprised of "various seating areas" – bar, counters, tables, an alfresco patio – but no matter where you sit, you'll find "polished service", "rapacious pricing" and a noise level somewhere between "vibrant" and "deafening."

Scarlet Oak Tavern *Steak*

20 | 24 | 20 | $45

Hingham | 1217 Main St. (Whiting St.) | 781-749-8200 | www.scarletoaktavern.com

This "old inn turned restaurant" in Hingham gives the "quiet South Shore" a jolt with "spacious", "beautifully redone" digs oozing "farmhouse chic" as well as a "vibrant bar" area with a fireplace; the "well-prepared" steaks and American comfort items are debatable, however: "better than average" vs. "doesn't knock your socks off."

Scollay Square *American*

19 | 19 | 20 | $37

Beacon Hill | 21 Beacon St. (Bowdoin St.) | 617-742-4900 | www.scollaysquare.com

A "solid" choice for Beacon Hill "power-lunching" and eavesdropping on local "politicos and wannabes", this retro-minded American manages to "channel the spirit of the old red-light district of the same name" in a "lofty-ceilinged" space decorated with "photos of Boston in earlier eras"; look for a "midrange" menu of classic comfort "standards", "friendly" staffers and an overall "fun vibe."

Scoozi *Italian*

18 | 14 | 15 | $26

Back Bay | 235 Newbury St. (Fairfield St.) | 617-247-8847 | www.scooziboston.com

Maybe the staff's "clueless", but the "location's plum" at this "hip" Back Bay Italian where the "fun Euro atmosphere" and "amazing patio" outshine the merely "standard Italian" grub; still, the pizzas are "yummy" and the prices "cheap", though many say "what you're really paying for is an outdoor seat on Newbury Street."

Scutra 🅱 *Eclectic*

23 | 20 | 22 | $45

Arlington | 92 Summer St. (Mill St.) | 781-316-1816 | www.scutra.com

"Unexpected" for Arlington, this "out-of-the-way" "suburban sleeper" run by a husband-and-wife team offers "beautifully prepared" Eclectic dishes for "reasonable" dough; though nitpickers say it "tries too hard to be interesting", most find it "memorable", with special kudos for its "cozy" setting and "pleasant", "professional" service.

Seiyo *Japanese*

∇ 25 | 24 | 22 | $35

South End | 1721C Washington St. (Mass. Ave.) | 617-447-2183 | www.seiyoboston.com

This "great little" South End sushi bar renowned for its "extensive" menu of "high-quality" fish satisfies both "novices and more adventurous" types; "fast" service and "simple", "chic" decor add to its allure, and there's an attached "wine store" with a "good selection" of labels.

☑ Sel de la Terre *French*

23 | 21 | 22 | $46

Back Bay | Mandarin Oriental | 774 Boylston St. (Fairfield St.) | 617-266-8800 ●

Waterfront | 255 State St. (Atlantic Ave.) | 617-720-1300 ●

Natick | Natick Collection | 1245 Worcester St. (Speen St.) | 508-650-1800

www.seldelaterre.com

Originally opened on the Waterfront, with spin-offs in the Natick Collection and the Back Bay, this "notable" French chainlet (itself a more casual spin-off of L'Espalier) offers "high-quality" Provençal cuisine in "stylish" but "rustic" settings; the "skilled" cooking is paired with a "wine list to suit all pocketbooks" served by a "quick", "down-to-earth" team, while "phenomenal" breads from on-site bakeries ice the cake; the only quibble: there's "nothing country about the prices."

Sensing *French*

- | - | - | E

Waterfront | Fairmont Battery Wharf | 3 Battery Wharf (Commercial St.) | 617-994-9000 | www.sensingrestaurant.com

Chef Guy Martin has exported his upscale Paris restaurant of the same name to the Waterfront's Fairmount Battery Wharf, where he's serving an internationally influenced contemporary French menu that makes use of local ingredients; a chef's table made with tiger-eye marble overlooks the open kitchen, adding a sexy counterpoint to the silk curtains and sycamore tabletops.

Seoul Food *Korean*

∇ 22 | 8 | 17 | $19

Porter Square | 1759 Massachusetts Ave. (bet. Forest & Prentiss Sts.) | Cambridge | 617-864-6299

"Really authentic Korean home cooking" ("like eating at a street food stall in Asia") is yours at this "tiny" Porter Square "hole-in-the-wall" where the "mom-and-pop" owners are so hands-on they'll "tell you off if you don't stir your bibimbop properly"; penny-pinchers praise the "cheap" tabs, but given its "nothing-to-look-at" looks, it "does mostly take-out business."

Serafina Ristorante *Italian*

∇ 20 | 19 | 19 | $48

Concord | 195 Sudbury Rd. (Thoreau St.) | 978-371-9050 | www.serafinaristorante.com

"Slightly different preparations of common dishes" are the calling cards of this Concord Northern Italian "staple" boasting an encyclopedic menu that offers "plenty of choices for even the fussiest of diners"; frequented by "authors" (yoo-hoo, "Doris Kearns Goodwin"), "not-so-famous locals" and random "mature" types, it also enjoys quite the "lively" bar scene.

75 Chestnut *American*

21 | 21 | 21 | $38

Beacon Hill | 75 Chestnut St. (bet. Brimmer & River Sts.) | 617-227-2175 | www.75chestnut.com

"Like putting on a comfy cardigan", this American feels "welcoming" to all "even though it's in posh Beacon Hill"; many regulars "flock to the bar" for "free cheese and crackers" and the "fantastic wines and drinks", while families are "never let down" by the "solid" comfort food (at "price points to match all budgets") and "congenial" service in the "cozy" dining room, especially on "wintry nights."

Shabu-Zen *Japanese*   22 | 16 | 17 | $25

Allston | 80 Brighton Ave. (Reedsdale St.) | 617-782-8888
Chinatown | 16 Tyler St. (bet. Beach & Kneeland Sts.) | 617-292-8828 ●
www.shabuzen.com

"Really get to know your friends" as you "dip your food in the same broth" at these "interactive" shabu-shabu specialists in Allston and Chinatown, where "cook-it-yourself" types have "fun" making their own Japanese hot pot meals; first-timers applaud the "novelty" aspect of these "unique experiences", and even though there's "not much service" by definition, they're "affordable" and "perfect first date spots."

Shanghai Gate *Chinese*   ▽ 24 | 16 | 15 | $21

Allston | 204 Harvard Ave. (Commonwealth Ave.) |
617-566-7344

"In case you thought all Chinese food tastes the same", this "refreshingly original" Allston storefront whips up "truly authentic" Shanghainese dishes with "strong flavors" that just might "knock your socks off"; the "off-the-beaten-path" address, "sketchy" decor and "lousy" service are all forgotten when the "great-deal" bill appears.

Shangri-La Ⓜ *Taiwanese*   23 | 9 | 15 | $18

Belmont | 149 Belmont St. (School St.) | 617-489-1488
"Weekend dim sum" brings "long queues" to this "small" Belmont spot offering "unusual", "authentic Taiwanese" cooking for an "affordable" price; despite "sparse decor" and "rude" servers more "interested in turning tables" than waiting on you, diehards insist the "excellent" chow keeps them "coming back."

Shanti: Taste of India *Indian*   - | - | - | M

Dorchester | 1111 Dorchester Ave. (Savin Hill Ave.) | 617-929-3900 |
www.shantiboston.com

An "undiscovered gem" in Dorchester, this "solid" Indian purveys an "authentic", "carefully seasoned" menu that also throws regional dishes from Bangladesh and Pakistan into the mix; "attentive" service, "good-deal" lunch buffets and a "comfortable" interior (including surprisingly "lush bathrooms") are all part of the package.

Shawarma King *Lebanese*   22 | 7 | 15 | $13

Brookline | 1383 Beacon St. (Harvard St.) | 617-731-6035 |
www.thebestshawarmaking.com

For a taste of "Lebanon in Brookline", check out this "tiny", "crowded" spot offering the namesake dish and other standards rendered with a "delicious tang"; "large servings" and "inexpensive" tabs trump the "noisy" acoustics, "oblivious" staffers and the inevitable "garlic breath", but insiders agree "takeout is the thing" what with the "not-elegant" setting.

	FOOD	DECOR	SERVICE	COST

Sherborn Inn, The *New England*   19 | 20 | 18 | $38

Sherborn | The Sherborn Inn | 33 N. Main St./Rte. 16 (Rte. 27) |
508-655-9521 | www.sherborninn.com

Set in a "Colonial-era" inn, this "charming" eatery located in
Sherborn offers New England "comfort food at a comfort price"
either in a "fireplace"-equipped tavern or a more-formal dining
room; although "nothing to write home about" generally, it's "good
for the 'burbs."

Shogun Ⓜ *Japanese*   ▽ 23 | 16 | 21 | $30

Newton | 1385 Washington St. (Elm St.) | 617-965-6699 |
www.shogunwestnewton.com

They're "always happy to see you" at this West Newton "local
favorite" that has employed the same sushi chef for 20-plus years;
regulars relish the "inexpensive" pricing and "small", homey
environs, and though the Japanese dishes lean toward the "predictable", ultimately it's a "good neighborhood restaurant" that
"doesn't feel overdone."

Sibling Rivalry *American*   24 | 22 | 23 | $54

South End | 525 Tremont St. (Berkeley St.) | 617-338-5338 |
www.siblingrivalryboston.com

At this "hip" South End "gimmick that works", diners choose from
two "inventive" New American menus conceived by "dueling brothers" Bob and David Kinkead "using the same main ingredients"; the
"interesting theme" continues in the dining rooms (one "reasonably
elegant", the other "fun and lighthearted"), which, along with the
"cool patio", get "crazy" "noisy"; as for the battles of value and service, they're still being waged, with "overpriced" leading "worth it"
and "solicitous" ahead of "disinterested."

Sichuan Garden *Chinese*   22 | 15 | 17 | $25

Brookline | 295 Washington St. (Harvard St.) | 617-734-1870
Woburn | 2 Alfred St. (Rte. 95) | 781-935-8488
www.sichuangarden2.com

There's "no need to go to Chinatown" for "spicy" chow thanks to
these "wow"-inducing Brookline/Woburn alternatives that "don't
turn down the heat for the New England palate"; insiders stick to the
"authentic Sichuan" offerings (the "generic Chinese food is just
ok"), but no matter what you order, prices are "decent" and commu-
nication with the staff "difficult."

🗹 Sichuan Gourmet *Chinese*   27 | 16 | 21 | $24

Framingham | 271 Worcester Rd./Rte. 9 (bet. Ordway & Pierce Sts.) |
508-626-0248 | www.laosichuan.com

"When they say spicy, they mean it" at this Chinese "find in
Framingham", where the "outstanding" Sichuan cooking can "make
your eyeballs sweat" and leave you "breathing fire" (though
"wimps" report that it can "tone down the heat if requested"); given
all the fireworks on the plate, the atmosphere is "irrelevant", though
some manage to remember the "cheap" pricing, "busy" pace and
"somewhat harried" service.

Sidney's Grille   *American*

▽ 21 | 19 | 20 | $33

Central Square | Le Meridien Hotel | 20 Sidney St. (Green St.) | Cambridge | 617-577-0200 | www.sidneysgrille.com

A "refuge from the bustle of Cambridge", this "quiet" Central Square New American in the Le Meridien offers just "what you'd expect from a hotel restaurant", including a "great weekend brunch"; an "excellent location", spacious layout and "reasonable price-to-quality" ratio make up for the fact that there's "no ambiance."

Silvertone Bar & Grill ⊠ *American*

21 | 16 | 19 | $25

Downtown Crossing | 69 Bromfield St. (Tremont St.) | 617-338-7887 | www.silvertonedowntown.com

"Rock-solid" American comfort food and "potent cocktails" collide at this "hidden" Downtown Crossing underground lair that lures "young professionals" seeking "after-work" thrills in a "retro", "speakeasy"-esque setting; sure, it can be "too damn noisy" and "crowded", but that's to be expected given the "honest" pricing, "sassy service" and that "to-die-for mac 'n' cheese."

NEW Singh's Café   *Indian*

- | - | - | I

Wellesley Hills | 312 Washington St. (Maugus Ave.) | 781-235-1666 | www.singhscafe.com

Along busy Route 16 in Wellesley Hills, tucked away on a subterranean level, this budget-friendly Indian arrival specializes in cuisine from the Northern region of the country – lamb, kebabs, lentils and roti (though there are some Southern options as well); the cheery, yellow-walled environs include a full bar, and there's a buffet offered for weekday lunch and weekend brunch.

Siros   *Italian*

▽ 19 | 20 | 20 | $42

North Quincy | Marina Bay | 307 Victory Rd. (Marina Dr.) | 617-472-4500 | www.sirosrestaurants.com

It's "all about being outside" at this longtime Italian overlooking Quincy's Marina Bay, where the "cool" waterfront location (and boat-docking facilities) trumps the "decent" albeit "solid" Italian grub; service is "good" and the ambiance "pleasant", but economists figure it's "a bit expensive" for the area.

NEW Six Burner ⊠ Ⓜ *American*

- | - | - | I

Back Bay | 130 Dartmouth St. (bet. Columbus Ave. & Stuart St.) | 617-262-4393 | www.sixburnerboston.com

Across the street from the Back Bay commuter-rail station, this American features an inexpensive menu focusing on comfort foods; there's a patio for warm-weather dining, and the interior is adorned with earthy tans, browns, a touch of dark red and candles on the tables.

606 Congress   *American*

21 | 23 | 22 | $42

Seaport District | Renaissance Boston Waterfront Hotel | 606 Congress St. (D St.) | 617-476-5606 | www.606congress.com

Post-Survey, a new chef scrapped this "big, open, sleek" Seaport District hotel eatery's small-plates concept for a more straightfor-

	FOOD	DECOR	SERVICE	COST

ward New American menu, leaving the Food score in doubt; "yummy" cocktails remain, and most likely, the "smooth service" too.

Sixty2 on Wharf Ⓜ *Italian* ▽ 24 | 21 | 21 | $44

Salem | 62 Wharf St. (Derby St.) | 978-744-0062 | www.sixty2onwharf.com

Bringing a "breath of fresh air" to Salem's Pickering Wharf district, this "upscale" Italian offers a "modern", "carefully prepared" menu via an "ambitious young chef", along with a well-parsed wine list; "uneven service" (sometimes "friendly", sometimes "over-rehearsed") seems to be its only shortcoming.

Skipjack's *Seafood* 20 | 17 | 19 | $37

Back Bay | 199 Clarendon St. (bet. Boylston St. & St. James Ave.) | 617-536-3500
Newton | 55 Needham St. (Rte. 128) | 617-964-4244
Foxboro | Patriots Place | 226 Patriot Pl. (Washington St.) | 508-543-2200
Natick | 1400 Worcester Rd./Rte. 9 (Speen St.) | 508-628-9900
www.skipjacks.com

Afishionados assert this "'other' Boston seafood chain" holds its own with "excellent value and freshness"; critics counter it "doesn't hold a candle" to its rival, specifying "mediocre" quality and an "unimaginative" menu, but an "eager-to-please staff" and "relaxed, comfortable" setting help make it, at the least, a "good alternative."

Sky ◑ *American* 19 | 19 | 19 | $38

Norwood | 1369 Providence Hwy. (Sumner St.) | 781-255-8888
Sudbury | 120 Boston Post Rd./Rte. 20 (Old Country Rd.) | 978-440-8855
www.sky-restaurant.com

"Popular" with "large groups" and "young families", these Norwood and Sudbury New Americans serve "solid", "interesting" fare in a "comfortable" setting decked out in "funky decor"; while naysayers feel "no urge to return" to the "noisy and crowded" environs for dishes they consider "too pricey" and "average at best", partyers "go for the bar scene."

Smith & Wollensky *Steak* 23 | 23 | 22 | $63

Back Bay | The Castle at Park Sq. | 101 Arlington St. (Columbus Ave.) | 617-423-1112 | www.smithandwollensky.com

The Back Bay's "lovely" old Armory ("unique" in its "faux-medieval" architecture) is the "treasured setting" of this homage to dry-aged prime, in which "energetic", "knowledgeable" staffers serve a "testosterone"-filled clientele "big steaks, big drinks and big bills"; it doesn't stray too far from its "chain formula", leading originality-seekers to opine "you won't leave disappointed, but you won't remember it either."

🆕 Sofia *Italian/Steak* - | - | - | M
(fka Vintage)

West Roxbury | 1430 VFW Pkwy. (Spring St.) | 617-469-2600 | www.sofiaboston.com

The owners of Vintage steakhouse, set on the busy VFW Parkway in West Roxbury, have changed the name and upped the ante on the old-world Italian favorites, so there's more 'sauce' with the beef; the swanky, clubby decor with hardwood floors and dark-brown tones remains the same.

Sofra Bakery & Café *Mideastern* 26 | 19 | 17 | $14
Huron Village | 1 Belmont St. (Mt. Auburn St.) | Cambridge | 617-661-3161 | www.sofrabakery.com
At Survey time, it hadn't "ironed out the wrinkles yet", but the "early read" was "promising" on this "quaint, different" Middle Easterner near Huron Village, which "feeds cravings" for chef Ana Sortun's "Oleana without the reservations or cost"; "out-of-this-world pastries" and savories won raves, though it's "a bit cramped" amid the kilim rugs and could use "more seating."

Sol Azteca *Mexican* 20 | 19 | 19 | $28
Fenway | 914A Beacon St. (bet. Park Dr. & St. Marys St.) | 617-262-0909
Newton | 75 Union St. (Beacon St.) | 617-964-0920
www.solaztecarestaurants.com
Fans of the "reliable", "authentic Mexican" fare served by these separately owned Fenway and Newton cantinas proclaim "the *sol* shines bright here", citing "reasonable prices" and "pleasant" "outdoor seating" that's "perfect" for enjoying "amazing sangria" and "potent margaritas"; inside, the "friendly and helpful" servers navigate a "somewhat cramped", "cozy" setup featuring tiled tabletops.

Solea Restaurant & 23 | 21 | 21 | $36
Tapas Bar ◑ *Spanish*
Waltham | 388 Moody St. (Cushing St.) | 781-894-1805 |
www.solearestaurant.com
"Dalí's less self-conscious, easier-to-get-into younger sibling" provides Waltham diners with a "festive" "Spanish atmosphere" that's "perfect" for a midpriced "romantic dinner" or just nibbling on a "great selection of tapas"; diners have a choice between a "fun and social" bar that's "crowded after work with young professionals" and a "quieter" dining area, both of which are patrolled by "helpful" servers.

Soma ☒ *American* ▽ 22 | 21 | 18 | $43
Beverly | 256 Cabot St. (bet. Dane & Hale Sts.) | 978-524-0033 |
www.somabeverly.com
A "great place before the North Shore Music Theater", this Beverly hipster attracts with an "extraordinary martini bar" and "wonderful cocktails" served in a modern yet "warm atmosphere" featuring exotic woods; while "fun", the Mediterranean-influenced New American fare is "inconsistent", plus ticket-holders often have to "wait for it."

Sonsie ◑ *Eclectic* 20 | 21 | 18 | $40
Back Bay | 327 Newbury St. (bet. Hereford St. & Mass. Ave.) |
617-351-2500 | www.sonsieboston.com
"Still the place to see and be seen", this Back Bay Eclectic draws "a trendy, sexy crowd" and is "great for celebrity sightings" at its mahogany bar, "intimate" "downstairs wine room" and "front cafe tables" providing "views of the Newbury Street scene"; while fans

cheer the "interesting" midpriced menu, "hangover-curing brunch" and "pizza to die for", foes snipe it's "average with big attitude."

Sophia's Grotto *Mediterranean*
23 | 22 | 24 | $32

Roslindale | 22R Birch St. (bet. Belgrade Ave. & Corinth St.) | 617-323-4595 | www.sophiasgrotto.com

Lots of "surprises" await at this "cute nook" in Roslindale that serves a "varied and well-executed menu" of Mediterranean fare including "wood-fired pizza" in a "lovely, cozy, festive" space with a "wonderful patio"; "friendly service" and "reasonable prices" further enchant.

Sorella's ∅ *American*
▽ 26 | 18 | 21 | $27

Jamaica Plain | 386-388 Centre St. (Sheridan St.) | 617-524-2016

A Jamaica Plain "tradition", this "real neighborhood joint" serves "astoundingly varied" American breakfasts starring "more omelets and waffles than you can shake a stick at" that are "so darn good, they might be illegal"; "a down-home atmosphere" permeates the "funky surroundings", and a "friendly staff" strives to accommodate "brutally" "long lines on weekends."

Sorelle *Coffeehouse*
▽ 23 | 19 | 21 | $14

Charlestown | 1 Monument Ave. (Main St.) | 617-242-2125 ∅
Charlestown | 100 City Sq. (Chelsea St.) | 617-242-5980
www.sorellecafe.com

This duo of Charlestown coffeehouses-cum-cafes provides locals with a "bright, cheerful" spot in which to "read, work or study" while enjoying "addictive coffee", "fresh, high-quality" "bakery items" and "top-notch sandwiches"; the "roomy, contemporary" City Square location "has WiFi" and a wine bar, while the "tiny but nicely located" Monument Avenue branch is "more intimate."

⚡ Sorellina *Italian*
27 | 28 | 26 | $65

Back Bay | 1 Huntington Ave. (Dartmouth St.) | 617-412-4600 | www.sorellinaboston.com

"Luxurious", "modern", "perfectly lit" and "visually stunning" are some of the accolades bestowed upon the highly rated black-and-white decor at this "awesome experience" in the Back Bay – while just as "wow"-worthy is Jamie Mammano's Italian fare filled with "contemporary" "twists" and "sumptuous combinations of fresh ingredients"; "caring, professional service" helps to create a "terrific ambiance" overall that leaves admirers "wishing" they "could afford to go more often."

Sorento's Ⓜ *Italian/Persian*
18 | 13 | 17 | $29

Marlborough | 128 Main St. (bet. Court & Florence Sts.) | 508-486-0090 | www.sorentos.com

"Quick, basic Italian" fare of the "pasta, pizza and salad" variety is served (slightly incongruously) alongside a menu of Persian specialties at this "dependable", "easy and familiar" Marlborough haunt; true, the offerings are "average", but they're "big enough to share" and "affordable."

	FOOD	DECOR	SERVICE	COST

Sorriso ⊠ *Italian*

20 | 19 | 19 | $35

Leather District | 107 South St. (bet. Beach & Essex Sts.) | 617-259-1560 | www.sorrisoboston.com

Serving "reasonably priced rustic Italian dishes" and "great pizzas", this Leather District trattoria "draws a professional crowd" for "value" lunches, while at night it's a "quieter, cozier scene"; service is "efficient and quick", and there's a "mellow, romantic feel" in the "deceptively big", "high-ceilinged" space that's also a "nice place for a drink after work."

Soul Fire *BBQ*

21 | 17 | 19 | $20

Allston | 182 Harvard Ave. (Commonwealth Ave.) | 617-787-3003 | www.soulfirebbq.com

Some aficionados "swear by" the "tremendous barbecue" dished out at this "often overlooked" "neighborhood gem" "in the middle of Allston" – while others call it "nothing special"; but the "well-organized" space with its "cool ambiance" and "soul music in the background", plus a "friendly" staff and "great prices", have fans hailing the package as "perfect in so many ways."

Sound Bites *American/Mideastern*

22 | 14 | 16 | $15

Somerville | 704 Broadway (Boston Ave.) | 617-623-8338
Somerville | Ball Sq. | 711 Broadway (bet. Josephine & Willow Aves.) | 617-623-9464
www.soundbitesrestaurant.com

Since relocating to "larger quarters", "the inevitable lines" for this Somerville American's "unbelievable breakfasts" "now move quicker" and "service isn't as rushed"; so while the "wait is shorter", there still is one, but it's "worth it" for such "huge portions for your buck"; Mideastern plates join the menu lineup at lunch and dinner and at the sibling BBQ & Grill.

South End Buttery *American/Bakery*

21 | 18 | 19 | $18

South End | 314 Shawmut Ave. (Union Park St.) | 617-482-1015 | www.southendbuttery.com

Fans of this "charming" bakery – a "favorite breakfast/brunch spot" "in a gorgeous part of the South End" – are "so glad it expanded" to include an "adorable" bistro (which the scores may not reflect) serving "innovative" New American lunch and dinner fare to add to the "fantastic cupcakes"; detractors call it "overrated", but pets-lovers like that "a portion of the proceeds are donated" to local animal rescue causes – and you can "bring your dog if sitting outside."

South Street Diner ◗ *Diner*

16 | 12 | 16 | $17

Leather District | 178 Kneeland St. (South St.) | 617-350-0028 | www.southstreetdiner.com

In a "city that shuts down early", this "always packed" Leather District "institution" is "one of only" a handful of places "open all night", meaning you can "get your grease on" "in the wee hours of the morning" via budget-boosting "old-time diner" fare; while the whole experience may be "ok" at best, with the help of the "friendly, quirky staff", it "serves its purpose."

	FOOD	DECOR	SERVICE	COST

Spice Thai Cuisine *Thai*
▽ 21 | 15 | 14 | $20

Harvard Square | 24 Holyoke St. (Mt. Auburn St.) | Cambridge | 617-868-9560 | www.spicethaicuisine.com

With its "convenient Harvard Square location", this "small" eatery where "the prices are right" is a "regular haunt" for lovers of "reliable", "tasty Thai food"; while "service is generally efficient and fast", customers "disappointed by the no-alcohol" policy can opt for takeout; P.S. "'spicy' means it", but "you can ask for a milder version."

Spiga Trattoria Italiana 🗷 *Italian*
- | - | - | M

Needham | 18 Highland Circle (bet. Highland Ave. & Needham St.) | 781-449-5600 | www.spigaitaliana.com

Marisa Iocco (ex Bricco, Mare, Umbria) is now at the helm of this Needham trattoria, an intimate haven that's been renovated to include a patio, a mirrored bar (serving wine and beer only) and a wood-fired oven dispensing the chef's famous thin-crust pizzas along with other midpriced Italian fare; N.B. cafeteria-style prevails at lunch while full-service and white tablecloths define dinner.

Sportello *Italian*
- | - | - | M

Seaport District | 348 Congress St. (Farnsworth St.) | 617-737-1234 | www.sportelloboston.com

Homemade pastas, soups and salads take center stage at this upscale take on a funky, affordable Italian trattoria courtesy of chef Barbara Lynch (No. 9 Park); done up in brushed chrome and white-and-brown tones, its coffee shop–like setting includes wraparound counter seating and a take-out area serving sweet and savory snacks.

🇿 Square Café *American*
26 | 26 | 23 | $45

Hingham | 150 North St. (bet. Central & Main Sts.) | 781-740-4060 | www.thesquarecafe.com

"Obviously popular" with a "local crowd", this "South Shore treasure" "in the heart of Hingham" serves a "small but interesting menu" of "consistently high-quality" New American comfort food; devotees appreciate "friendly service" and "cozy" environs, "stunningly decorated and lively with people", while bestowing extra kudos on the "well-priced and smartly chosen wine list."

St. Alphonzo's Kitchen Ⓜ *American*
▽ 22 | 12 | 23 | $22

South Boston | 87 A St. (W. 3rd St.) | 617-269-2233 | www.stalphonzoskitchen.com

Though its fans feel like they're "the only ones who know about it", they're enthusiastically spreading the word about this "hidden" Southie "gem", a "tiny" "gourmet diner" whipping up New American cooking that "makes both bellies and wallets happy."

Stanhope Grille *American*
▽ 23 | 20 | 23 | $43

Back Bay | The Back Bay Hotel | 350 Stuart St. (Berkeley St.) | 617-532-3827 | www.thedoylecollection.com

Discoverers of this "modern restaurant" decorated in earth tones and "hidden" inside the "vibrant" Back Bay Hotel judge it a "gem" for New American fare that offers "something for everyone"; "impeccable service" extends to the sunken "outdoor patio", "a wonderful place to dine during warm weather"; N.B. a new chef and menu instituted post-Survey outdate the Food score.

Stars on Hingham Harbor *Diner*   16 | 12 | 15 | $24

Hingham | 3 Otis St./Rte. 3A (North St.) | 781-749-3200 | www.starshingham.com

"A cut above a diner", this "popular spot" is a "fun place for the family" to command a booth and chow down on "wonderful breakfasts" and well-priced "classic" American "staples" (including "burgers to kill for") in a "relaxed" – and "quite noisy" – setting "across from Hingham Harbor"; "spotty service" irks, but it's nothing that can't be washed away by "amazing beers", plus "sports on plasma TVs", at the bar.

Stella ● *Italian*   24 | 22 | 21 | $44

South End | 1525 Washington St. (W. Brookline St.) | 617-247-7747 | www.bostonstella.com

There's "always a buzz" at this "hip and chic" Italian South Ender "out of South Beach"; "trendy" crowds brave the "noisy" setting because "it's the place" "to see and be seen" "along bustling Washington Street", and though some cry "overhyped", the converted contend "service is just right" and the menu's "takes on pasta and pizza" are "inventive."

Stellina *Italian*   22 | 18 | 21 | $40

Watertown | 47 Main St./Rte. 20 (Rte. 16) | 617-924-9475 | www.stellinarestaurant.com

This "longtimer" in Watertown Square provides "a treat that won't break the bank" with its "seasonal Italian fare from different regions"; the setting includes an interior trattoria that exudes "cozy" "warmth", a "beautiful patio" "with a fountain" that "transports you to another world" and a bar where chatty Cathys enjoy "dining and schmoozing."

Stephanie's on Newbury *American*   20 | 19 | 18 | $37

Back Bay | 190 Newbury St. (Exeter St.) | 617-236-0990 | www.stephaniesonnewbury.com

Stephi's on Tremont *American*

NEW **South End** | 571 Tremont St. (Union Park St.) | 617-236-2063 | www.stephisontremont.com

A "Back Bay staple" for its "prime" "sidewalk patio" that's "a people-watching haven", this midpriced New American's "stylish home cooking" "hits the spot" for those "craving comfort food"; "service can be spotty" in the "warm" clubby space, though the biggest complaint is that it can be "noisy" and is "so popular you typically have to wait"; N.B. the Tremont location opened post-Survey.

Steve's Greek Restaurant *Greek*   20 | 10 | 17 | $20

Back Bay | 316 Newbury St. (Hereford St.) | 617-267-1817 | www.stevesgreek.com

Faneuil Hall | Faneuil Hall Mktpl. | 1 Faneuil Hall Sq. (Congress St.) | 617-263-1166

This "reliable neighborhood institution" – "an informal haven among Newbury Street's countless upscale restaurants" – offers "straightforward", "quick and tasty", "classic Greek" fare; with "inexpensive" prices", a "small", plain dining area and "fast service", it's the "closest thing to a diner in the Back Bay"; N.B. the Faneuil Hall food-court take-out stall offers a similar menu and value.

Stix Restaurant & Lounge ● ⊠ Ⓜ *Eclectic* 17 | 17 | 18 | $36

Back Bay | 35 Stanhope St. (bet. Berkeley & Clarendon Sts.) | 617-456-7849 | www.stixboston.com

For a meal with an "interesting twist", diners detour to this "hip" Back Bay sibling of 33 Restaurant for its "innovative" "food on skewers" with "tremendous dipping sauces"; the "funky decor" ("the bar lights up in colors"), "friendly staff" and "innovative" drinks make for a "fun atmosphere", though some snap it "can get expensive" for "meat lollipops" that are "better in concept than practice."

Stockyard *Steak* 15 | 13 | 16 | $33

Brighton | 135 Market St. (N. Beacon St.) | 617-782-4700 | www.stockyardrestaurant.com

"A neighborhood standby for decades", this "huge" Brighton steakhouse's "many rooms" are packed with "families and locals" chowing down on "substantial fare without the frills"; the "decor and staff are pretty old-school" (there's "lots of dark wood"), and while herds herald the "solid" fare as a "good value", crossed carnivores beef it's "lost its mojo."

Stone Soup Cafe 🍴 *Eclectic* ▽ 25 | 17 | 21 | $37

Ipswich | 141 High St. (bet. Currier Park & Mitchell Rd.) | 978-356-4222

Fans of this "satisfying stop" in quiet Ipswich praise its "fresh", sometimes "unusual" Eclectic fare focusing on soup "ingredients available for the season", "monster sandwiches" and Thursday–Sunday–only dinners; "low" prices make the wait "worth it", especially for the "top-notch brunch"; N.B. post-Survey, it moved from Central Street about a mile north to High Street, outdating the Decor score.

NEW Stork Club Boston ● *American* - | - | - | M

South End | 604 Columbus Ave. (Northampton St.) | 617-391-0256 | www.storkclubboston.com

Live music sets the scene at this snazzy South End nightspot where midpriced Southern-accented American fare is served in a space done up with cool browns, hardwood floors and brick walls; blues, jazz and Afro-Cuban bands play nightly while guests sup in the lounge or adjacent dining room.

Strega Restaurant & Lounge Ⓜ *Italian* ▽ 21 | 19 | 18 | $38

Salem | 94 Lafayette St. (Peabody St.) | 978-741-0004 | www.stregasalem.com

"Glitzophiles" and lovers of "authentic Italian" fare "wait in line" for seats at this Salem trattoria's "lovely" dining area; detractors who determine the "service could be better" and the moderately priced food is "spotty" suggest "sticking to" the "big, inviting bar" for some "great atmosphere."

	FOOD	DECOR	SERVICE	COST

Strega Ristorante *Italian*
21 | 18 | 19 | $45

North End | 379 Hanover St. (bet. Clark & Fleet Sts.) | 617-523-8481 |
www.stregaristorante.com

Cheerleaders of this "noisy" North End Italian with "mobster movies
playing" on "a bank of TVs" and "service that's a little in your face"
contend that the "super-modern" decor and "fun atmosphere" – plus a
"pretty good chance of running into a celeb" – enhance "authentic"
dishes that "you can tell a lot of love goes into"; "disappointed" dons
differ, calling it a "Hollywood caricature" with "way more hype
than it's worth."

Strip-T's ⊠ *American*
∇ 22 | 12 | 18 | $19

Watertown | 95 School St. (Arsenal St.) | 617-923-4330 |
www.stripts.com

"Long live this little neighborhood" "gem" that's "worth the trip" to
"the backstreets of Watertown" root supporters of the "funky",
"family-run" venue's "offbeat menu" of "healthy, fresh and yummy"
"comfort food" (e.g. "amazing" "homemade soups"); the "homey"
"quarters are a little cramped", so some say it's "mostly a take-out
spot", but the "friendly" service, "hearty portions" and "bargain"
prices can "soothe the soul."

Studio 3 *American*
- | - | - | M

NEW Dedham | Showcase Cinema de Lux Legacy Pl. | 670 Legacy Pl.
(Rte. 128) | 781-326-2100

Foxboro | Showcase Cinema de Lux Patriot Pl. | 24 Patriot Pl.
(Washington St./Rte. 1) | 800-315-4000
www.nationalamusements.com

Dinner-and-a-movie gets a chic upgrade at this full-service American
duo tucked inside the Showcase Cinema de Lux in Dedham's Legacy
Place and Foxboro's Patriot Place; dark woods and purple distinguish Foxboro, Dedham is done up in white and both feature an
upbeat vibe and full bar, offering a convenient meeting place for a
pre-flick lunch or dinner or a post-credits cocktail.

NEW Suffolk Grille ◐ *American*
- | - | - | M

Canton | 2790 Washington St./Rte. 138 (Blue Hill River Rd.) |
339-237-4700 | www.suffolkgrille.com

Its location near Route 93 in Canton makes this moderately priced
American arrival a convenient spot for classy business lunches, and
it also hosts a lively after-work-drinks crowd at its horseshoe-
shaped granite bar; a mural depicting a Colonial scene lends extra
character to the sleek, modern interior.

Sugar & Spice *Thai*
20 | 16 | 17 | $19

Porter Square | 1933 Massachusetts Ave. (Davenport St.) | Cambridge |
617-868-4200 | www.sugarspices.com

A "friendly", "quick" staff serves "delicious and affordable" Thai
fare in a "pleasant, modern room" with "eclectic, funky" decor at
this Porter Square spot; while it "won't make you think you're in
Bangkok", the "fresh ingredients" and "decent-sized portions"
should at least "hold you over until your next trip."

	FOOD	DECOR	SERVICE	COST

Suishaya ● *Japanese/Korean* ▽ 21 | 14 | 14 | $30

Chinatown | 2 Tyler St. (Beach St.) | 617-423-3848
This small Chinatown Korean also serves an assortment of Japanese fare and stays open until 2 AM nightly, attracting night owls with its affordable prices and "ginormous Japanese beer cans"; but sushi lovers are forewarned – you could wind up "waiting forever" due to uneven service.

Sultan's Kitchen ⧄ *Turkish* 24 | 8 | 13 | $17

Financial District | 116 State St. (Broad St.) | 617-570-9009 | www.sultans-kitchen.com
"Long lines" of Financial District workers ignore the "gruff service" and lack of atmosphere at this "crazy popular change from the usual sandwich place" and focus on the "fresh, flavorful" doner kebab and other Turkish fare that's "inexpensive" and "prepared to order"; the interior is "not much to look at" and the "tables are cramped", so most admirers simply "get takeout."

Summer Winter ⧄ *American* 24 | 22 | 20 | $54

Burlington | Boston Marriott Burlington | 1 Mall Rd. (I-95, exit 33B) | 781-221-6643 | www.markandclarkrestaurants.com
"Fans of Arrows" in Ogunquit, Maine, are "not disappointed" by this "fantastic" venue from owners Mark Gaier and Clark Frasier in the Burlington Marriott, an "incredible" "suburban" "surprise" that offers "beautifully presented" New American fare spotlighting local ingredients including "produce from an on-premises greenhouse"; the "casual yet refined" atmosphere gets kudos, so occasionally "below-par" service has diners concluding "once the kinks are worked out" it should be across-the-board "excellent."

Sunset Cafe *American/Portuguese* ▽ 19 | 14 | 15 | $23

Inman Square | 851 Cambridge St. (bet. Harding & Hunting Sts.) | Cambridge | 617-547-2938 | www.thesunsetcafe.net
Despite a "convenient location" in Inman Square and "good" "Portuguese dishes at low prices", the big attraction of this American-Iberian is live "fado music on the weekends"; while some sit on their hands for "neglectful service", admirers applaud the "wine selection" while deeming it a wholly "underappreciated gem."

Sunset Cantina ● *Mexican/Pub Food* 20 | 17 | 19 | $22

Boston University | 916 Commonwealth Ave. (bet. Pleasant & St. Paul Sts.) | 617-731-8646

Sunset Grill & Tap ● *Mexican/Pub Food*

Allston | 130 Brighton Ave. (Harvard Ave.) | 617-254-1331
www.allstonsfinest.com
"Beer connoisseurs" "always have a good time" pouring over the "enormous global beer list" ("over 100 on tap", seemingly "countless by the bottle") at this "designed-for-fun" Allston grill, which augments its "stars" with a "huge menu" featuring "every type" of American pub fare "imaginable"; the BU cantina concentrates on an "extensive tequila selection" (with a Mexican focus on the grub), while both are "loud, crowded" and "well priced."

	FOOD	DECOR	SERVICE	COST

Super Fusion Cuisine *Asian* ▽ 27 | 8 | 20 | $28

Brookline | 690A Washington St. (Beacon St.) | 617-277-8221

A "secret for outstanding sushi", this "unique" Washington Square "hole-in-the-wall" is a "real find" with "value" prices on "wonderfully fresh" rolls and Asian fusion fare boasting "striking taste combinations"; "what it lacks in space and decor" (the "cramped quarters" have "limited seating"), "it easily makes up for in taste, price and innovation", plus "takeout is always an option."

Sweet Basil Ⓜ⌿ *Italian* 25 | 16 | 22 | $33

Needham | 942 Great Plain Ave. (Highland Ave.) | 781-444-9600 | www.sweetbasilneedham.com

"Thank goodness" for this "crazy busy" "bargain" cheer Needhamites who shower a "chorus of kudos" upon its "ridiculously big portions" of "loaded-with-garlic", "delicious traditional Italian dishes"; though it's "tight and noisy, who cares", shrug fans, when there's also BYO and "friendly service" – now "if they only took reservations and credit cards."

ⅡⅢⅢ Symphony 8 ⓈⓂ *American* – | – | – | M

Fenway | 8 Westland Ave. (St. Stephen St.) | 617-267-1200 | www.symphony8boston.com

Just a stone's throw from Symphony Hall, this multilevel, moderately priced Fenway American combines three spaces under one roof: a main room with red walls and a black bar, an adjoining Kelly-green pub called Siansa 8 and a downstairs speakeasy called Prohibited; two menus, one offering bistro fare and the other late-night pub grub (plus all-day Irish breakfast), are available throughout.

Taberna de Haro Ⓢ *Spanish* 23 | 18 | 20 | $37

Brookline | 999 Beacon St. (St. Marys St.) | 617-277-8272 | www.tabernaboston.com

A "fantastic wine list" complements the "authentic and uncompromising" selection of "wonderfully savory" tapas that flows from this Brookline Spaniard's "open kitchen" to the "charming", "cozy" dining room where "happy people eating well" sit "elbow to elbow"; though it can be "a little pricey" and "slow", the "delicious" fare and "neighborhood feel" leave most shouting "*olé!*"

Tacos El Charro *Mexican* ▽ 23 | 10 | 19 | $19

Jamaica Plain | 349 Centre St. (Hyde Sq.) | 617-522-2578

"Tucked away" in a corner of Jamaica Plain, this "true Mexican" "hole-in-the-wall" may "look a bit rough around the edges", but its amigos applaud the "authentic", "outstanding tacos and enchiladas"; "good prices" and "sweet employees" make it all the more "worth finding"; P.S. only beer and wine are served, so there's sangria, but "no margaritas."

Tacos Lupita *Mexican/Salvadoran* 25 | 6 | 14 | $11

Revere | 107 Shirley Ave. (Walnut Ave.) | 781-284-2430 Ⓜ⌿
Somerville | 13 Elm St. (Porter St.) | 617-666-0677 ⌿
Lynn | 129 Munroe St. (Washington St.) | 781-593-6437

(continued)

Tacos Lupita
Lawrence | 505 Broadway (Manchester St.) |
978-681-4517 M◿

This quartet's lack of decor may "make you wince", but its Mexican-Salvadoran fare "will make you swoon", from the "mouthwatering pork" and "mean burritos" to "perfect guacamole" and "homemade tortillas"; since it's staffed by "unhurried ladies whose respect you gotta earn", the service is "hit-or-miss", but economical "eat-and-runners" agree it delivers plenty of "bang for your buck."

Taiwan Cafe ◐◿ *Taiwanese*

| 23 | 8 | 15 | $19 |

Chinatown | 34 Oxford St. (Beach St.) | 617-426-8181

Adventurers seeking "lunch specials" and "late-night" fixes "jam pack" this "no-frills" "storefront" in Chinatown that serves up "amazing" Taiwanese fare; cognoscenti coax "don't be scared" off by "authentic" dishes that spotlight the likes of "intestines" and "fermented tofu", as there are also offerings "for the faint of heart" – all delivered "fresh", "cheap" and "fast."

NEW Tajine ◿ *Moroccan*

| - | - | - | M |

Harvard Square | 1105 Massachusetts Ave. (bet. Remington & Trowbridge Sts.) | Cambridge | 617-520-2080

Welcoming staffers guide guests through a midpriced menu of North African dishes prepared in a clay pot at this Harvard Square arrival; despite the strip-mall setting, the interior is a romantic oasis with red walls, dark wood tables, mirrors and Moroccan decorations; N.B. no alcohol.

Tamarind Bay Bistro & Bar *Indian*

| 24 | 15 | 18 | $30 |

Harvard Square | 75 Winthrop St. (JFK St.) | Cambridge |
617-491-4552

Tamarind Bay Coastal
Indian Kitchen *Indian*
Brookline | 1665 Beacon St. (Winthrop Rd.) | 617-277-1752
www.tamarind-bay.com

This "cheerful", "unconventional Indian" in Harvard Square (with a seafood-centric Brookline sib) features "subtle" "sauces made from scratch" in "refined" and "innovative" dishes that "trump the minimalist service and decor"; though some grouse it's "expensive" for having "subterranean" digs, optimists opine it's "a welcome change."

☑ Tangierino ◐ *Moroccan*

| 24 | 26 | 21 | $45 |

Charlestown | 83 Main St. (Pleasant St.) | 617-242-6009 |
www.tangierino.com

With its "delicious" French-inspired Moroccan menu, "belly dancers" and a subterranean cigar and hookah lounge "draped with silk and velvet", this "swank, sexy" and "seductive spot" in Charlestown offers an "exotic" experience that's "almost as good" as being in Tangiers; despite the "unpolished" service and "cramped" seating, most say a night here is "as cool as it gets" and "easily worth the inflated prices."

Tango *Argentinean/Steak* | 21 | 20 | 22 | $31 |

Arlington | 464 Massachusetts Ave. (Swan Pl.) | 781-443-9000 |
www.tangoarlington.com

"Carnivores cry no more over the price of steak" since this Arlington Argentinean offers "meat, meat and more meat" – plus "tasty side dishes" – at a "great value"; while some beef that it's merely "trying hard and getting close" to true authenticity, they're stampeded by cheerers of the "scrumptious" selection and staff that "treats you like family", plus it "really classes up" the neighborhood.

Tanjore *Indian* | 22 | 14 | 17 | $24 |

Harvard Square | 18 Eliot St. (Bennett St.) | Cambridge | 617-868-1900 |
www.tanjoreharvardsq.com

When habitués of Harvard Square "have a hankering", they head to this "small and friendly" Indian for "interesting regional dishes" that are "well made" and employ "just the right spice"; the "comprehensive menu" features dishes that "other places don't", and the "good value" is a bonus for diners "on a budget."

Tantric *Indian* | 20 | 18 | 20 | $29 |

Theater District | 123 Stuart St. (Tremont St.) | 617-367-8742 |
www.tantricbistro.com

This "hip" Theater District spot features a "lovely" yet "funky setting" for dining on "delicately spiced", "upscale" Indian that "won't break the budget"; though purists pout it has "more style than substance", fans say the "presentation", "creative" "specialty drinks", summer "sidewalk scene" and staff that "understands curtain times while making you feel welcome" all add up to a "reliable go-to."

Tapéo *Spanish* | 22 | 20 | 19 | $37 |

Back Bay | 266 Newbury St. (bet. Fairfield & Gloucester Sts.) |
617-267-4799 | www.tapeo.com

Tapas lovers congregate at this "cozy" Back Bay "charmer", but the "rich, exotic fare" also includes a few Spanish entrees; foes suspect some servers "couldn't care less" while lamenting prices that get you "a little for a lot", but "after all, it is Newbury Street" – thankfully, there's a sidewalk patio to take the "great people-watching" scene in.

Taqueria Mexico *Mexican* | 22 | 10 | 19 | $16 |

Waltham | 24 Charles St. (bet. Moody & Prospect Sts.) | 781-647-0166 |
www.taqueramexico.com

"As close as you can come to the real thing" in Waltham, this taqueria doles out "killer" "homestyle Mexican cooking" priced for "solid values"; the setting, festooned with "slightly dingy" "hats and blankets", "lacks", while the "service is sometimes painfully slow" (although certainly "friendly").

☒ Taranta *Italian/Peruvian* | 27 | 21 | 23 | $44 |

North End | 210 Hanover St. (Cross St.) | 617-720-0052 |
www.tarantarist.com

A "breath of fresh air" blows through the North End courtesy of chef-owner José Duarte's "creative" "fusion" of Peruvian and Southern

	FOOD	DECOR	SERVICE	COST

Italian cuisines (gourmands report that the "surprising mix of flavors works incredibly well") at this "charming" spot with three "lovely", "traditional" levels and a "lively", "knowledgeable" staff; it's "a little expensive, but worth it", especially to environmentalists who award it bonus points for having "gone completely green."

Tartufo *Italian*   22 | 17 | 20 | $43

Newton | 22 Union St. (bet. Beacon St. & Langley Rd.) | 617-244-8833 | www.tartuforestaurant.com

"Reasonably varied, well-executed Italian" fare "appropriate for a neighborhood restaurant" is what's on offer at this "tasteful" Newtonian; when it fills, the "noise level can be monstrous" because with "wood floors and tables [so] close together", there's "no place for the sound to go", but the staff is so "nice", it's "a pleasure anyway."

Tasca *Spanish*   23 | 20 | 22 | $28

Brighton | 1612 Commonwealth Ave. (Washington St.) | 617-730-8002 | www.tascarestaurant.com

"Bring your friends and bring your appetite" to this "quaint", "festive" Brighton Spaniard, because not only is there a "great variety" of "wonderfully crafted", "tasty tapas", but it's "reasonably priced"; "frequent special events include musical performances", "flamenco dancers" and "multicourse dinners" paired with wine or "sublime sangria", while "friendly" service is a constant.

Tashi Delek 🗷 *Tibetan*   - | - | - | M

Brookline | 236 Washington St. (bet. Davis Ave. & Davis Ct.) | 617-232-4200 | www.tashidelekboston.com

Named for a Tibetan greeting, this Brookline Villager offers momos, noodle soups and other authentic, midpriced fare, washed down by selections from a full bar; a likeness of the Dalai Lama looks over the small dining room, where both the color scheme (burgundy and yellow) and background music reflect the motif.

Tavern in the Square *American*   17 | 16 | 15 | $24

Central Square | 730 Massachusetts Ave. (bet. Inman & Prospect Sts.) | Cambridge | 617-868-8800
Porter Square | Porter Exchange Mall | 1815 Massachusetts Ave. (Roseland St.) | Cambridge | 617-354-7766
NEW **Salem** | 189 Washington St. (New Derby St.) | 978-740-2337
www.taverninthesquare.com

"College crowds" frequent these "deafening" sports pubs in Central and Porter squares and Salem to "cheer" the goings-on on the "tons" of "big TVs"; the "simple" American grub that's "slowly" served to them may not get as much applause, but most say it's sufficiently "solid" – "affordable"-tab seekers, on the other hand, admit to "usually eating here out of necessity rather than choice."

Tavern on the Water *American*   13 | 16 | 14 | $26

Charlestown | Charlestown Navy Yard | 1 Pier 6 8th St. (1st Ave.) | 617-242-8040 | www.tavernonthewater.com

Since all you're getting is "marginal" American pub grub and merely "ok service", "you don't want to be stuck inside" this "kind of dumpy" "dive" tavern in the Charlestown Navy Yard; you do, however, need to check out the "divine view of the city skyline" from its "fantastic waterfront" patio, best enjoyed "post-work" with "a bottle of beer."

NEW Tavolino *Italian*　　　　　　- | - | - | M

Foxboro | Gillette Stadium | 274 Patriot Pl. (Washington St./Rte. 2) | 508-543-6543
Westborough | 33 E. Main St. (bet. Prospect & Willow Sts.) | 508-366-8600
www.tavolinorestaurant.us

'Less red-sauce American-Italian and more Italian-Italian' is how owner Graham Silliman describes the pizza, pasta and steaks served at these casual arrivals in Gillette Stadium's Patriot Place and Westborough; the expansive settings feature cushy barstools overlooking the stone pizza ovens, booths and sports-fan amenities such as many strategically placed TVs.

Tavolo *Italian*　　　　　　- | - | - | I

Dorchester | The Carruth | 1918 Dorchester Ave. (Ashmont St.) | 617-822-1918 | www.tavoloristorante.com

The "kid brother" of chef-owner Chris Douglass' "Ashmont Grill up the street", this "small" Dorchester Italian displays colorful decor (aqua floors, artful designs on a chalkboard wall) that feels funky and upscale, "homey and urban all at once"; while some samplers report it's "still working out the kinks", the fare "packs a punch", and for puny tabs no less.

Teatro Ⓜ *Italian*　　　　　24 | 21 | 21 | $44

Theater District | 177 Tremont St. (bet. Avery & West Sts.) | 617-542-6418 | www.teatroboston.com

A Theater District "hit", this renovated synagogue-cum-"urban trattoria" presents a "scrumptious", "fresh approach to Italian food with a wonderfully light touch" (and "the price is right" too); "crowded tables", "a narrow room" and "unique arched" ceilings instigate "impossible noise levels" (it's "too loud to converse"), but if you "go after" curtain time, you may discover the more "comfortable setting" the "subdued" lighting and "courteous", "attentive" staff intended.

NEW Technique Ⓢ *New England*　　　- | - | - | M

East Cambridge | Athenaeum Bldg. | 215 First St. (bet. Athenaeum St. & Linskey Way) | Cambridge | 617-218-8088 | www.bostonculinaryarts.com

Tucked inside one of the world's most famous culinary institutes, Le Cordon Bleu in Cambridge, this teaching restaurant offers moderately priced New England cuisine prepared by students in an open kitchen and served in a brick-walled, fine-dining setting; N.B. it's closed during school vacations, plus every Saturday, Sunday and third Monday, when a new group of students is trained to take over.

NEW Teele Square Cafe *American*　　- | - | - | I

Somerville | 1153 Broadway St. (Curtis St.) | 617-625-0082 | www.teelesqcafe.com

It feels like a crime to pay single-digit prices for freshly made American classics, but guilt fades quickly at this colorful Somerville cafe from longtime restaurateur Jonathan Adelson; creative breakfast, lunch and dinner fare, plus Sunday brunch, is ordered at a counter in a family-friendly setting with bright red-and-yellow walls.

Temple Bar ● *American*   20 | 21 | 18 | $33

Porter Square | 1688 Massachusetts Ave. (Sacramento St.) | Cambridge | 617-547-5055 | www.templebarcambridge.com

"Dark, sultry" and "trendy", this Porter Square resto-lounge draws an "attractive crowd" for "creative drinks" tempered by a "wide selection" of "dependable" New American fare with "often interesting twists" and "decent prices"; if the "energetic scene" gets "too noisy", just sink into an "enormous round booth" or snag a spot on the "nice" patio (a must for a "fantastic brunch") and enjoy the "great people-watching."

Tempo 🅂 *American*   21 | 20 | 22 | $38

Waltham | 474 Moody St. (Maple St.) | 781-891-9000 | www.tempobistro.com

"Newbury Street meets Waltham" at this "lively", "trendy" New American whose "cool atmosphere" and decor is of the "type one would find in Boston" – "just more reasonably priced"; the "extensive menu includes everything" ("comfort", "innovation", "great wines"), and the "friendly" staffers can point you away from what's "unexceptional" and toward what's "great."

ⓩ Ten Tables *American/European*   27 | 20 | 25 | $43

Jamaica Plain | 597 Centre St. (Pond St.) | 617-524-8810
Harvard Square | 5 Craigie St. (Berkeley St.) | Cambridge | 617-576-5444
www.tentables.net

"Locals are lucky" to have this "homey" spot in Jamaica Plain, as its European–New American fare is "prepared with love", served with "gusto" by a "knowledgeable" staff and loaded with "spectacular", "surprising tastes and textures"; those "loathe to give it a good review" because, "true" to its name, there are just 10 tables – and it's "10 times as good as" many more expensive competitors – now send their friends to Harvard Square, where a slightly larger offshoot opened post-Survey.

NEW Teranga *Senegalese*   - | - | - | M

South End | 1746 Washington St. (Mass. Ave.) | 617-266-0003 | www.terangaboston.com

Boston's abuzz over this South End Senegalese, the city's first, serving authentic midpriced cuisine such as *dibi* (grilled marinated lamb chops with onion and mustard sauce) in a cozy setting outfitted with African artwork, large drumlike pendant lights, decorative gourds on the tables and a sapele-and-zebrawood bar dispensing beer and wine.

Terramia Ristorante *Italian*   26 | 19 | 24 | $48

North End | 98 Salem St. (Parmenter St.) | 617-523-3112 | www.terramiaristorante.com

"In the North End's highly competitive Italian" scene, this "brilliant" "gem" "wins hearts" with a "heavenly" selection of "upscale", "creatively interpreted" fare that's "beautifully presented and equally delicious" (and includes "no chicken Parmesan or cheese ravioli"); "there's no room to move" in the "tiny" environs and "no coffee means it's not a place to linger", even though the "efficient", "personable" servers may make you want to.

Thai Basil *Thai*   23 | 16 | 17 | $25

Back Bay | 132 Newbury St. (bet. Clarendon & Dartmouth Sts.) | 617-578-0089

To "revive yourself after a day of shopping on Newbury Street", this "casual", "unpretentious" Back Bay Thai – "a little hard to spot" due to its "lower-level" setting – provides "tasty" "staples" that "fulfill every craving"; you don't need a lot of cash, but "patience" is required, especially at lunchtime when the "service could be more attentive."

Thaitation *Thai*   - | - | - | I

Fenway | 129 Jersey St. (bet. Park Dr. & Queensberry St.) | 617-585-9909 | www.thaitation.com

Fenway folks can Thai one on for cheap at this cozy, inexpensive cafe; the yellow walls inside are hung with artwork and set against tiled floors, while outside there's warm-weather seating.

1369 Coffeehouse ⊅ *Coffeehouse*   20 | 17 | 19 | $9

Central Square | 757 Massachusetts Ave. (Pleasant St.) | Cambridge | 617-576-4600

Inman Square | 1369 Cambridge St. (Springfield St.) | Cambridge | 617-576-1369

www.1369coffeehouse.com

A steady stream of "quirky" "characters" files into these "indie coffee shops" for "fantastic" java, teas and "tasty treats" ("sweets, soups, salads, sandwiches") whose "inexpensive" tabs earn Boston's No. 1 Bang for the Buck rating; the "friendly" "hipster" staff facilitates a "community vibe", making them "nice places to read a book" and "relax" – "if you can find a seat" (beware "squatters with laptops"); P.S. "Central Square features outdoor seating", while Inman Square's got a stack of games, "nice perks" both.

33 Restaurant & Lounge 🚫Ⓜ *American*   20 | 22 | 19 | $46

Back Bay | 33 Stanhope St. (bet. Berkeley & Clarendon Sts.) | 617-572-3311 | www.33restaurant.com

"Stylish, sleek" and "Euro-chic", this "vibrant" Back Bay venue's "techno" decor (a bar with a "funky" "light show", exposed-brick walls) attracts a "best-dressed crowd" for "pricey" New American meals that, while offering "no fireworks", "never disappoint" either; "it morphs into a nightclub after hours" when everyone "moseys downstairs for dancing" – of course, if you're looking for a "relaxing experience", it could all prove to be "a little too much."

Tomasso Trattoria & Enoteca 🚫 *Italian*   24 | 20 | 22 | $48

Southborough | 154 Turnpike Rd./Rte. 9 (Breakneck Hill Rd.) | 508-481-8484 | www.tomassotrattoria.com

"A little bit of Italy in, believe it or not, Southborough", this venue offers "well-thought-out" large and "tapas-style" plates imbued with "unexpected twists" in an "elegant" yet "casual" setting where an "open kitchen adds to the excitement"; "in spite of criticism of its prices" (and there's lots of it), there are values found in the "thoughtful wine" program, about which the "friendly" staff offers "excellent advice."

Tom Shea's *New England* ▽ 20 | 15 | 19 | $38

Essex | 122 Main St./Rte. 133 (Rte. 22) | 978-768-6931 | www.tomsheas.com

This "quiet" New Englander is known more for its "fabulous views" of the Essex River ("go early to get an outside table") and "graceful" staff than for its "standard" (but "pleasant enough") fare or "fatigued" interior; however, "new owners" have gone to work, starting with a major post-Survey menu redo and renovation, most likely outdating the Food and Decor scores; N.B. look for a name change by June 2010.

Z Top of the Hub ● *American* 20 | 26 | 21 | $56

Back Bay | Prudential Ctr. | 800 Boylston St., 52nd fl. (Ring Rd.) | 617-536-1775 | www.topofthehub.net

"If you want to impress a date, clients" or "out-of-towners", "natives" "recommend" this "glam" New American atop the Prudential Center, which boasts "amazing" "360-degree views" "you will never forget"; if the fare "can't match" the setting, it is "better" than many "expect", while the "winning wine list", nightly live jazz and mostly "professional" staff serve to sweeten the "expensive" deal.

Z Toro *Spanish* 26 | 21 | 20 | $43

South End | 1704 Washington St. (Mass. Ave.) | 617-536-4300 | www.toro-restaurant.com

"Bullfight-level noise" emanates from this "rustic", "tiny" South End Spaniard, giving the "droves of people clamoring for a cramped table" an accurate idea of the "wild" time "famed chef Ken Oringer" has in store for them via his "mouthwateringly delicious" tapas, which "range from authentic to trendy" ("you have to try" the "decadent" grilled corn specialty); "no reservations" mean "excruciating" lines, and "all those small plates" lead to "big bills", but is it "worth it? - absolutely."

NEW Tory Row *American* - | - | - | M

Harvard Square | 3 Brattle St. (Mass. Ave.) | Cambridge | 617-876-8769 | www.toryrow.us

From the London Underground logo to the soccer games on TV to draft beers displayed on a chalkboard and duck confit on the New American menu, this Harvard Square entry from the owners of Audubon Circle and Cambridge 1 is more gastropub than bar; the cheery staff attends to patrons seated at high-top communal tables, prints on the wall are by Shepard Fairey and wood walls and flooring add coziness to its sparse industrial setting.

Tosca Ⓜ *Italian* 25 | 24 | 23 | $52

Hingham | 14 North St. (Mill St.) | 781-740-0080 | www.toscahingham.com

"Capturing the essence of each season", the Northern Italian cuisine whipped up at this "vibrant" venture "impresses" Hingham diners with "not fussy, just terrific" preparations – especially "awesome wood-fired grill" items – "time after time"; it's "expensive but worth it" when one factors in the "attentive servers" and forgives that the "brick, wood" and other "hard surfaces" make the room often "quite noisy."

Townsend's ● American | ▽ 19 | 23 | 21 | $34 |

Hyde Park | 81 Fairmount Ave. (Truman Pkwy.) | 617-333-0306 | www.townsendsrestaurant.com

Hyde Park "couples and families" applaud this "terrific" spot because its "quite tasty", "upscale" New American gastropub fare is offered for "down-to-earth prices"; additionally, the "service is terrific", the "wine list is extensive" and the space is filled with "charm and warmth" despite being somewhat "cavernous"; a few "inconsistencies" have been detected, but fans are sticking around while it "gets the kinks out", as it "fills a real need."

Trata American | - | - | - | I |

Harvard Square | 49 Mt. Auburn St. (Plympton St.) | Cambridge | 617-349-1650 | www.trataharvardsquare.com

Lots of hearty Americana plus brick-oven thin-crust pizzas are the draws at this airy Harvard Square sophomore; hardwood floors, warmly colored walls hung with original artwork and seating alongside windows (which open onto the street in summer) bring a refreshing, slightly upscale feel to the space.

Ⓩ Trattoria di Monica Italian | 26 | 20 | 22 | $45 |

North End | 67 Prince St. (Salem St.) | 617-720-5472

Ⓩ Vinoteca di Monica Italian

North End | 143 Richmond St. (bet. Hanover & North Sts.) | 617-227-0311 www.monicasboston.com

"Out-of-this-world pastas" with "inventive sauces" "entice" North Enders to this "cozy" trattoria whose "sleek" yet "warm" vinoteca sibling "enhances" an already "outstanding" Italian menu with "amazing specials"; but "caveat emptor": many of said specials are "shockingly priced" compared to their "counterparts", and the otherwise "professional" staffers "don't tell you" the costs when they "recite the long list" – so "make sure to ask!"

Trattoria Il Panino Italian | 23 | 16 | 20 | $34 |

North End | 11 Parmenter St. (Hanover St.) | 617-720-1336 | www.trattoriailpanino.com

"Old-world pasta" preparations and other "high-quality" Italian "home cooking" make for "special" meals at this "low-key", moderately priced North End trattoria where "cheerful servers" maneuver among tightly "packed wooden tables" in a "tiny" interior with "windows on one side, a minute open kitchen on the other"; in lovely weather, "sit on the patio" for an even more "beautiful evening."

Trattoria Pulcinella Italian | ▽ 20 | 18 | 19 | $45 |

Huron Village | 147 Huron Ave. (Concord Ave.) | Cambridge | 617-491-6336 | www.trattoriapulcinella.net

Huron Village's "unpretentious" yet "fine neighborhood trattoria" offers a "varied menu" of "simple Italian fare done well"; the "homey

	FOOD	DECOR	SERVICE	COST

atmosphere" is "enhanced by personal service", making it feel like dining in a sometimes "crowded", sometimes "quiet" "friend's home" – until the "top-shelf" tabs are delivered, that is.

☑ Trattoria Toscana ☒ *Italian* 26 | 20 | 27 | $35

Fenway | 130 Jersey St. (Park Dr.) | 617-247-9508

"A corner of Tuscany" "hidden away" "on a quiet side street off the Fenway", this "quaint", "lovely place" "delights" its fans with "charismatic", "funny" servers and "delicious", "memorable" Italian preparations "priced reasonably"; but it "frustrates" them too with a "no-reservations" policy that sometimes leads to "long waits" – which are, ultimately, "well worth it."

Tremont 647/Sister Sorel *American* 21 | 18 | 21 | $38

South End | 647 Tremont St. (W. Brookline St.) | 617-266-4600 | www.tremont647.com

"There's always a party" at this "funky", "hip South End eatery" where chef-owner Andy Husbands' New American comfort food exhibits a "surprising" amount of "inventive", "tasty" "twists" for being so "reasonably priced"; the revelry spills over to next door's "exotic-drinks" retreat, Sister Sorel, and extends to the "great patio", especially during "fabulous", "fun" weekend brunch service when the "warm" "servers dress in their PJs."

Tresca *Italian* 23 | 22 | 21 | $51

North End | 233 Hanover St. (Cross St.) | 617-742-8240 | www.trescanorthend.com

Italophiles aver this North Ender's "fine cuisine" with "some interesting twists" "gets it right", as does the "great wine list" and "Tuscan Villa ambiance", comprised of a "loud, busy" upstairs dining room and a "happening downstairs bar" with large windows that provide "an interesting perspective of the Hanover Street bustle"; as for the tabs, they're "a little pricey", but warranted.

Trident Booksellers & Cafe ◑ *Eclectic* 19 | 15 | 16 | $18

Back Bay | 338 Newbury St. (Mass. Ave.) | 617-267-8688 | www.tridentbookscafe.com

If the idea of "eating a homestyle breakfast in a bookstore" is "cool" to you, then this Back Bay "brainiac" bastion "is your place" – and the "granola"-noshing atmosphere is also available for "lunch/coffee/snack/whatever", as the Eclectic eats (think "quick bites, smoothies") are served until midnight daily; it's "probably more expensive than it's worth" (often "slow service" doesn't help), but the "WiFi is free."

NEW Trina's Starlite Lounge ◑ *American* – | – | – | M

Inman Square | 3 Beacon St. (Cambridge St.) | 617-576-0006 | www.trinastarlitelounge.com

This Inman Square haunt from the owner of Silvertone is a prime destination for those seeking inventive cocktails, but it's also drawing attention for its midpriced Traditional American dinners; the inviting setting features dark woods, candlelight and two bars – one in the dining room and one in back.

	FOOD	DECOR	SERVICE	COST

⚡ Troquet 🅱🅼 *American/French* | 27 | 22 | 25 | $63 |

Theater District | 140 Boylston St. (bet. Charles & Tremont Sts.) | 617-695-9463 | www.troquetboston.com

"Amazing by-the-glass pairings" in either "2- or 4-oz. servings" from a "deep wine list" that's "priced to enjoy" make this "classy" Theater District haunt "an oenophile's delight" – and the French–New American cuisine, featuring "incredible cheeses", "rises to the occasion" with "fantastic, creative" preparations (this is where the "expense" comes in); while the bi-level space gets "noisy" "when full", "great views of the Common" appeal to "romantics", as do staffers who "anticipate every need without being obtrusive."

Tryst *American* | 22 | 22 | 22 | $42 |

Arlington | 689 Massachusetts Ave. (Rte. 60) | 781-641-2227 | www.trystrestaurant.com

With its "lovely", "modern decor", "warm, informative staff" and "accessible menu" of "finely crafted" New American fare running the gamut from "reasonably priced to expensive", this Arlington eatery is a true "oasis" in the 'burbs; "families are welcome" at the "excellent" Sunday jazz brunch, while trysters deem the bar a "classy place to meet" for "amazing" cocktails, "delicious wines" and "great nibbles."

NEW Tupelo 🅼 *Southern* | – | – | – | M |

Inman Square | 1193 Cambridge St. (Tremont St.) | Cambridge | 617-868-0004 | www.tupelo02139.com

Simplicity and affordability define this Inman Square haunt where Southern comfort food is dished out for moderate prices; a mural of a rowdy New Orleans scene inspires good times in the dining room, which is beset with upholstered chairs, red wainscoting, a tile floor and floral-stenciled mirrors.

Turner Fisheries 🅱 *Seafood* | 21 | 20 | 20 | $49 |

Back Bay | Westin Copley Pl. | 10 Huntington Ave. (Dartmouth St.) | 617-424-7425 | www.turnersboston.com

Back Bay guests expecting a "typical" hotel restaurant are "pleasantly surprised" by this "big fish house" with "high-end" (if "generic") decor in the Westin Copley Place, because though its "seafood is not imaginative", it is "fresh and well made" (the "rich" clam chowder is a "superb" standout); however, a contingency "disappointed" by "inconsistent quality" in both the fare and service says, in the long run, it's "not worth the price."

Tuscan Grill *Italian* | 24 | 18 | 20 | $45 |

Waltham | 361 Moody St. (bet. Spruce & Walnut Sts.) | 781-891-5486 | www.tuscangrillwaltham.com

Waltham's "old reliable" Tuscan "chugs along" in fine form, as the "wood-grilled meats, homemade pastas" and "classics with a little extra flair" continue to be "delicious" and "well worth the price"; the "cozy setting" – a "convincing version of an Italian country inn" with only "slightly cheesy murals" – still gets "crowded" and "noisy", but thankfully, the service is as "warm and friendly" as it ever was.

	FOOD	DECOR	SERVICE	COST

Tu y Yo *Mexican*
24 | 16 | 21 | $29

Somerville | 858 Broadway (Powderhouse Circle) | 617-623-5411
NEW **Needham** | 66 Chestnut St. (School St.) | 781-453-1000 |
www.tuyyo2.com

"Adventurers" "looking to expand their repertoire" find plenty that's
"different" at this "truly remarkable" Somerville Mexican prized for
its "real-deal" dishes ("no burritos") made using "recipes handed
down from generation to generation"; the fare (which the "friendly"
servers "know very well") is just as "colorful and exotic" as the
decor – and a "shade pricey", truth be told; N.B. the Needham offshoot opened post-Survey.

28 Degrees Ⓜ *American*
20 | 25 | 20 | $42

South End | 1 Appleton St. (Tremont St.) | 617-728-0728 |
www.28degrees-boston.com

The "NYC" "party vibe" at this "trendy" South End lounge attracts
"glam" "under-40s" seeking the *Sex and the City* experience" of
"swanky sofas", "trippy projections", "cool bathrooms" and sometimes "chilly" receptions from the "hot help"; "dynamite martinis" at
"tony" prices are the drinks of choice, while an "interesting menu"
of "delicious" New American "little dishes" provides sustenance;
P.S. if "loud DJs" irk you, try the "fantastic" patio.

NEW Twenty8 Food & Spirits *American*
– | – | – | M

Foxboro | Renaissance Boston Hotel & Spa at Patriot Place | 28 Patriot Pl.
(Washington St./Rte. 1) | 508-543-5500 | www.twenty8restaurant.com

At this swanky New American tucked inside the lobby of Foxboro's
Renaissance at Patriot Place, a stone hearth oven dispenses midpriced flatbreads and innovative small plates using sustainable, regional ingredients; hanging lights, glass and mirror accents add
dramatic flair to the surroundings, while a long granite bar lures
sports fans and hotel guests.

21st Amendment *Pub Food*
17 | 16 | 18 | $22

Beacon Hill | 150 Bowdoin St. (bet. Beacon & Mt. Vernon Sts.) |
617-227-7100 | www.21stboston.com

"Mingle with lobbyists", "politicos" and "State House staffers" at
this "old-school" "after-work hangout" in Beacon Hill offering a
"dark" yet "cheerful atmosphere" and "dependable" pub fare ("outstanding sliders", "great nachos") that soaks up the booze at "an appropriate price"; "familiar songs" and "unpretentious" service also
make it "easy" for "casual" dinners and "satisfying" lunches.

29 Newbury *American*
20 | 18 | 19 | $39

Back Bay | 29 Newbury St. (bet. Arlington & Berkeley Sts.) |
617-536-0290 | www.29newbury.com

"Typically hopping with alfresco diners", this "cozy", "sophisticated" Newbury Street New American is a "still-trendy" "staple" for
"super people-watching" over generally "tasty" fare and "strong
drinks"; though most Back Bay shoppers give it props for "reasonable prices" and "accommodating" service, dissenters dis it's "too
expensive for what you get": "small portions" and "attitude."

	FOOD	DECOR	SERVICE	COST

T.W. Food *American/French* | 26 | 20 | 25 | $64 |

Huron Village | 377 Walden St. (Concord Ave.) | Cambridge | 617-864-4745 | www.twfoodrestaurant.com

This "lovely, sedate spot tucked away" in Huron Village "features fabulous farm-to-table" New American–New French cuisine in a "creative menu" that "changes depending on what is fresh"; the "intimate" quarters and "friendly yet professional service" keep the focus on the "thoughtful" fare – however, though it "tries hard", some find it a bit "precious" and "expensive."

224 Boston Street *American* | 22 | 20 | 21 | $36 |

Dorchester | 224 Boston St. (Mass. Ave.) | 617-265-1217 | www.224bostonstreet.com

With a "trendy", "snug" interior, a "funky bar" and a "classy garden", this New American "oasis" in an "offbeat" Dorchester location is "right for every season" and occasion; indeed, the "reasonably priced" "comfort food taken up a couple notches" and "friendly, fun staff" have pleased an "eclectic clientele" "for decades", while leaving newcomers "delightfully surprised."

UBurger *Burgers* | 23 | 12 | 16 | $11 |

Boston University | 1022 Commonwealth Ave. (bet. Babcock St. & Winslow Rd.) | 617-487-4855 ●
Kenmore Square | 636 Beacon St. (Kenmore St.) | 617-536-0448 www.uburgerboston.com

"An exemplary tribute to ground cow", this "Kenmore Square burger 'n' shake shack" flips "seriously delicious", "juicy patties" that are "reasonably priced to start" – that is, before you start "customizing" them with a "most creative mixture of things" and pairing them with "fries hand-cut right in front of you" and "to-die-for frappes"; the "aluminum-", TV- and "student-laden" digs are "a little strange", but "you're not going for the decor, are you?"; N.B. the BU branch opened post-Survey.

UFood Grill *Health Food* | 18 | 11 | 17 | $12 |

Downtown Crossing | 530 Washington St. (DeLafayette Ave.) | 617-451-0043
Fenway | LandMark Ctr. | 201 Brookline Ave. (Park Dr.) | 857-254-0082
Watertown | 222 Arsenal St. (bet. Beechwood Ave. & Louise St.) | 617-923-7676
www.ufoodgrill.com

This chain serves "fairly nutritious" fast food ("bison burgers", "fries baked rather than fried") at "inexpensive prices" in "cafeterialike" settings; "you feel good about yourself afterwards" because it's "healthier" than the competition – but that's not enough to entice piners of the "real thing", who think the fare here "tastes a little off."

Umbria Prime ☒ *Italian/Steak* | 23 | 21 | 21 | $45 |

Financial District | 295 Franklin St. (Broad St.) | 617-338-1000 | www.umbriaprime.com

For a "romantic" meal in a neighborhood not known for it – the Financial District – this "super-cute" Italian-style steakhouse delivers thanks to "dim lighting", exposed brick and "intimate" seating; while it's "a little expensive", the "friendly staff" can offer "advice" about "great values" on the "exceptional wine list"; N.B. the multi-level venue also includes a bar, lounge, nightclub and party space.

Union Bar & Grille *American* | 24 | 23 | 24 | $47 |

South End | 1357 Washington St. (bet. Union Park & Waltham Sts.) | 617-423-0555 | www.unionrestaurant.com

"Serving many functions" – from "a dusky date" to dinner with a "group of people that can't agree on anything" to "a post-hangover Sunday brunch" – this "gorgeous" "pillar of the South End scene" plies "carefully executed", "interesting" New American fare that's "not inexpensive", but "more affordable than others of a similar caliber"; "a quiet night is not the norm here", what with the "conducive-to-conversation" "round leather booths" and "vibrant" service.

⊠ Union Oyster | 20 | 19 | 18 | $39 |
House *New England/Seafood*

Faneuil Hall | 41 Union St. (bet. Hanover & North Sts.) | 617-227-2750 | www.unionoysterhouse.com

"An experience not to be missed", this "historic landmark" near Faneuil Hall – dating back to 1826, it's "the oldest restaurant in continuous service in the entire United States" – "deserves its great reputation for oysters, clams" and other "reliable New England" seafood "classics" prepared by "fun" and "friendly shuckers"; with a location on the Freedom Trail, its "atmospheric" "warren of nooks" unsurprisingly "caters to tourists", but it's a "destination for locals" too – "at least once."

Upper Crust *Pizza* | 23 | 11 | 16 | $16 |

Back Bay | 222 Newbury St. (Fairfield St.) | 617-262-0090
Beacon Hill | 20 Charles St. (Beacon St.) | 617-723-9600
NEW **Fenway** | 1330 Boylston St. (bet. Jersey & Kilmamock Sts.) | 617-266-9210
NEW **Jamaica Plain** | 1727 Centre St. (bet. Esther & Manthorne Rds.) | 617-323-6400
South End | 683 Tremont St. (W. Newton St.) | 617-927-0090
Harvard Square | 49 Brattle St. (Church St.) | Cambridge | 617-497-4111
Brookline | 286 Harvard St. (Beacon St.) | 617-734-4900
Lexington | 41 Waltham St. (Mass. Ave.) | 781-274-0089
Waltham | 435 Moody St. (Chestnut St.) | 781-736-0044
Watertown | 94 Main St. (Cross St.) | 617-923-6060
www.theuppercrustpizzeria.com
Additional locations throughout the Boston area

When devotees "debate the defining Boston pie", this local chain places in the upper ranks for "slices the size of your head" and whole pizzas with "chewy"/"crispy" thin crusts available with "myriad fresh toppings" and "awesome whole-wheat" dough; "some locations are obviously better than others" – both decor- and servicewise – and a contingency of crusty connoisseurs calls the 'za "vastly overrated" and "overpriced", but since a new store seemingly "pops up every few months", it's clearly "doing something right."

⬚ Upstairs on the Square *American*
24 | 24 | 22 | $49

Harvard Square | 91 Winthrop St. (JFK St.) | Cambridge | 617-864-1933 |
www.upstairsonthesquare.com

"Really two restaurants in one", this "zany" yet "fine" New American
"overlooking a bustling park" in Harvard Square offers a "less-
expensive" dining area, dubbed the Monday Club Bar, that's "like
stepping into a page" of *Through the Looking-Glass*", while the upstairs Soirée Room provides "the full upscale treatment" amid "gold
chairs, playful sconces and jewel-toned walls" (mostly in shades of
pink); "rivaling" the "quirky" decor are "lovingly prepared",
"professionally served" victuals that are just as "bright", "fun",
"innovative" and "fantastic."

Veggie Planet *Pizza/Vegetarian*
23 | 10 | 13 | $14

Harvard Square | Club Passim | 47 Palmer St. (Church St.) | Cambridge |
617-661-1513 | www.veggieplanet.net

"Carnivores" "dragged kicking and screaming" to this "inspired",
"inexpensive" Harvard Square vegetarian soon exclaim "who knew
meatless could be painless?" – indeed, foodstuffs like "stellar pizzas",
"awesome" salads and "amazing vegan" options "wow" them while
nourishing their "social conscience"; the "pierced and tattooed"
make it an evening by catching an act at "renowned folk" venue Club
Passim, which is attached, but people persnickety about "cavelike"
"basement locations" and "surly service" only come when they can
"muster the patience."

Via Lago ⬚ *American*
▽ 20 | 13 | 18 | $23

Lexington | 1845 Massachusetts Ave. (Bedford St./Rte. 225) |
781-861-6174 | www.vialagocatering.com

"If you're in Lexington", this "friendly" "storefront" works for "easy
take-out" breakfasts and lunches – and quite well, in fact, as the
American fare is "fresh, creative and affordable"; in the evening, it
"turns into" a "table-service" spot, with "home cooking" that's of
equally "remarkable quality" for being so "reasonably priced."

Via Matta ◐⬚ *Italian*
25 | 23 | 22 | $55

Park Square | 79 Park Plaza (Arlington St.) | 617-422-0008 |
www.viamattarestaurant.com

Another "heavenly" "Michael Schlow production", this "spiffy, modern
trattoria" in Park Square is known for its "sophisticated power-scene
vibe" ("celebrity sightings are the norm"), but the real "star" is "pre-
cisely crafted", "high-end Italian" fare that's "traditional" and "creative
at the same time", "seasonal" and served alongside "some killer staples"; the "professionally run" environs include a "cool bar" and a
"lovely" patio that proves to be a "romantic" respite in the summer.

Vicki Lee's Ⓜ *Bakery*
▽ 25 | 18 | 19 | $14

Belmont | 105 Trapelo Rd. (Common St.) | 617-489-5007 |
www.vickilees.com

From its "sunny" corner perch in Belmont's Cushing Square, this
"bright, cheery" breakfast and lunch spot provides an "interesting
gourmet menu" of sandwiches and soups followed by "other-worldly

pastries"; the "friendly, helpful" staff sways folks who can't help grousing that it's "wickedly overpriced", even as they lament that it's "not open for dinner."

Victoria's Diner *Diner* ∇ 20 | 13 | 18 | $21

Roxbury | 1024 Massachusetts Ave. (New Market Sq.) | 617-442-5965 | www.victoriasdiner.com

At this "comfortable", "cute little diner" in Roxbury, the "large", "not-expensive" menu is just as much of "a big hit with the after-church crowd" as it is with "midnight-breakfast" cravers (it's open 24 hours Thursday–Saturday); the staff is "nice" and "you'll always see someone you know" – two more reasons why, to some, it feels like "home."

Village Fish *Italian/Seafood* 20 | 14 | 17 | $34

Needham | 970 Great Plain Ave. (bet. Chapel St. & Dedham Ave.) | 781-449-0544 | www.thevillagefish.com

This Needham nook offers "plentiful portions" of "solid, dependable", "fresh fish" "with an Italian slant" (often "served in the pan"); both the "simple setting" and the "service could use some sprucing up", but "reasonable prices" help to keep it often "packed" – and sometimes "noisy."

Village Smokehouse Ⓜ *BBQ* 19 | 16 | 18 | $27

Brookline | 1 Harvard St. (Washington St.) | 617-566-3782 | www.villagesmokehouse.com

"Get your hands dirty" plowing through "mountains of saucy, perfectly cooked meat" at this "Texas BBQ" pit in Brookline Village that blessedly "puts rolls of paper towels on every table" – and if the kids start "fighting and screaming", don't worry about reproach from the staffers, they "don't bat an eye at anything"; yup, it's "noisy", "festive" and you'll "leave smelling smoky" – but you'll "smack your lips all the way home."

Village Sushi & Grill *Japanese/Korean* ∇ 23 | 18 | 22 | $33

Roslindale | 14 Corinth St. (Birch St.) | 617-363-7874 | www.villagesushiandgrill.com

Sushi mavens find it "hard to believe everyone doesn't know about" this "hidden gem in Roslindale Village", a "wonderful" midpriced joint that serves "incredibly fresh" fin fare in addition to a varied Japanese and Korean menu; whether seated in the "comfortable" modern dining room or "cute outdoor courtyard in the summer.", those satisfying "cravings" appreciate "quick service" from an "enthusiastic staff."

Vinalia Ⓢ *American* 17 | 18 | 17 | $35

Downtown Crossing | Summer Exchange Bldg. | 34 Summer St. (Arch St.) | 617-737-1777 | www.vinaliaboston.com

"One of the more popular business-lunch destinations in the city", this Downtown Crossing New American also draws "strong crowds after work" thanks to its "fantastic wine list" ("definitely go for the pairings"), "rowdy bar" and "relaxing", "upscale dining room"; alas, the midpriced menu "disappoints" detractors who dub it "ordinary", while also grousing about "inattentive" service.

	FOOD	DECOR	SERVICE	COST

Vin & Eddie's Ⓜ *Italian* | ▽ 17 | 16 | 20 | $43

Abington | 1400 Bedford St./Rte. 18 (bet. Rtes. 58 & 139) | 781-871-1469 | www.vin-eddies.com

In quiet Abington, this "down-home" haunt pleases with its "great wine list" and menu that has "more variety and sophistication than the usual Italian"; "attentive, helpful" servers navigate the "busy" room where a wall-sized mural depicting a courtyard scene has served as the backdrop for many first-dates and family dinners over the years.

Vinny's at Night *Italian* | 23 | 13 | 19 | $29

Somerville | 76 Broadway (Hathorn St.) | 617-628-1921 | www.vinnysonbroadway.com

"It's definitely an experience" at this "quirky" yet "fascinating" Italian "tucked away" in back of a "tiny" "convenience store" that dishes out "phenomenal" "red sauce" and "generous servings" of "outrageously delicious" "homemade pasta, sausage" and other moderately priced Sicilian fare; yes, there's "no atmosphere" in the "packed" dining room, but fans swear "dealing with the crowds and noise" "is half the fun."

Vlora ● *Mediterranean* | 22 | 21 | 20 | $40

Back Bay | 545 Boylston St. (bet. Clarendon & Dartmouth Sts.) | 617-638-9699 | www.vloraboston.com

"Quite literally" a "hidden gem", this sophomore situated "on the basement level" of its Back Bay building may be "hard to find", but it's "worth" the "challenge" for "interesting", midpriced "Pan-Med cuisine" that gets "a breath of fresh air" from "Albanian touches"; though the "odd location", "unpredictable bar crowd" and "service kinks" "can make the experience less appealing", enamored eaters find the "clean, modern decor" "satisfying."

Volle Nolle Ⓩ⇄ *Sandwiches* | ▽ 26 | 18 | 25 | $13

North End | 351 Hanover St. (Fleet St.) | 617-523-0003

Devotees of this casual North End sandwich shop done up in tin ceilings and stainless-steel chairs declare that its takes on the subject are "creative", as are the "great" sides; the "personable staff" makes up for the "small dining area", but it really is "better for takeout."

Vox Populi *American* | 16 | 17 | 16 | $35

Back Bay | 755 Boylston St. (bet. Exeter & Fairfield Sts.) | 617-424-8300 | www.voxboston.com

"Trendy and fun", this Back Bay "nightspot" is often "full of pretty" "young professionals" tossing back "wonderful cocktails" (e.g. "fabulous martinis") while soaking up the "sexy" "singles scene" and "cool decor"; "sidewalk tables" enable "great people-watching", but "disappointed" diners find the New American menu "quite pricey for what it is", so many just stick to "finger food."

Wagamama *Noodle Shop* | 18 | 15 | 17 | $20

NEW **Back Bay** | Prudential Ctr. | 800 Boylston St. (Fairfield St.) | 617-778-2344

Faneuil Hall | Faneuil Hall Mktpl. | Quincy Mkt. (Congress St.) | 617-742-9242

(continued)

Wagamama

Harvard Square | 57 JFK St. (Winthrop St.) | Cambridge | 617-499-0930
www.wagamama.us

This "wildly popular" "British import" ladles "noodles galore" in "fun
and hip" environs; the "tremendous selection" of "fresh and creative" ramen, soups and stir-fries is "good, cheap and satisfying",
and the "cafeterialike atmosphere" can be "comfortable if you don't
mind" "shared seating" at "long communal tables"; while some
slurpers "feel rushed", clock-watchers appreciate the "quick service."

Walden Grille *American*

15 | 13 | 14 | $36

Concord | 24 Walden St. (Main St.) | 978-371-2233 |
www.waldengrille.com

Set in a former fire station, this "narrow" "little spot just off the main
square" "in adorable, historic Concord" serves a "comprehensive
menu" of New American fare that locals recommend "for lunch
while shopping"; since it's "not too exciting for dinner", some suggest it's "best to eat at the bar" where the "upbeat atmosphere"
trumps the "mediocre food" and "spotty service."

Warren Tavern *American*

16 | 20 | 16 | $24

Charlestown | 2 Pleasant St. (Main St.) | 617-241-8142 |
www.warrentavern.com

This "authentic tavern from Colonial times" (circa 1780) offers
visitors a "nice bit of history" – "with the low ceilings to prove
it" – as a backdrop for "solid" American pub grub and "a pint",
"just the way our forefathers liked it"; though "lively" groups of
"locals" leave some claiming it's "too crowded", while others gripe
service "needs improving", it's "cool" to "have a burger" "where Paul
Revere hung out."

Washington Square Tavern *American*

22 | 19 | 19 | $32

Brookline | 714 Washington St. (Beacon St.) | 617-232-8989 |
www.washingtonsquaretavern.com

"Word has gotten out", but Brookliners brave "long waits" "again
and again" at this "cozy" "neighborhood hangout" offering "heart-
warming" American gastropub fare "kicked up many notches" along
with "a great beer selection" and a "reasonably priced" "wonder" of
a wine list; some say the "intimate", "publike" setting is "a bit
noisy", and service varies from "attentive" to "dismal", but "regulars" insist it's "a real treat."

West End Johnnie's *Eclectic*

▽ 17 | 18 | 19 | $32

West End | 138 Portland St. (Causeway St.) | 617-227-1588 |
www.westendjohnnies.com

A "fun place to meet a bunch of friends" "near the Boston Garden",
this West End hangout – a high-ceilinged, "open" room filled with
sports-and-movie memorabilia – gets "extremely loud" on event
nights; the "wide variety" of moderately priced Eclectic fare is
"nothing special", but the fact that it exhibits some "fancy" aspira-
tions leaves critics wondering "what this place is trying to be."

West on Centre *American*

18 | 18 | 19 | $33

West Roxbury | 1732 Centre St. (Belgrade Ave.) | 617-323-4199 | www.westoncentreboston.com

"Families and first dates" mix in the "cozy" environs of this "casual", "reasonably priced" "neighborhood place" in West Roxbury serving "middle-of-the-road" American fare with "interesting twists"; though it's sometimes "noisy" when a "big bar crowd" is on hand "to watch a game", most locals still find it something to "boast about."

West Side Lounge ● *American*

22 | 19 | 21 | $33

Porter Square | 1680 Massachusetts Ave. (bet. Shepard & Wendell Sts.) | Cambridge | 617-441-5566 | www.westsidelounge.com

"Dark lighting" doesn't dim the "friendly vibe" of this "hip but laid-back" lounge in Porter Square, where "classy" American bar food at "a fair price" complements "creative drinks" (e.g. "over-the-top martinis"), making an ideal perch "for a casual dinner-date" or just "lingering"; a "helpful staff" adds to the lure for loyal "locals" and "Harvard law kids."

Wine Cellar Ⓜ *Continental/Fondue*

20 | 18 | 18 | $44

Back Bay | 30 Massachusetts Ave. (bet. Beacon & Marlborough Sts.) | 617-236-0080 | www.bostoncellar.com

An "encyclopedic" wine list "lives up to the name" of this "cozy" "little place" in the Back Bay that's "hard to find" but "worth checking out" for its fondue-focused Continental menu and "romantic" surroundings; the "not-so-fond" warn that it's "pricey" and has occasional lapses in service, but big dippers say if you want "the real thing" beyond just "cheese and chocolate", "go here."

Wonder Spice Cafe *Cambodian/Thai*

21 | 14 | 19 | $22

Jamaica Plain | 697 Centre St. (Burroughs St.) | 617-522-0200

With so much variety of "fresh" Cambodian and Thai fare, "you can go again and again" to this Jamaica Plain "hot spot" and find new "delights" every time; a "simple setting", patio and "nice staff" all help to make it a "pleasant" place for "affordable" meals.

Woodman's *New England/Seafood*

23 | 10 | 13 | $28

Essex | 121 Main St./Rte. 133 (Rte. 128) | 978-768-6057 | www.woodmans.com

"Allegedly the place where fried clams were invented", this "authentic seafood dive" in Essex has become an "ultimate tourist destination" and a "quintessential" New England "summer ritual" that involves "huge portions" of "crunchy, fresh" battered seafood plus "long waits" at a "self-service" counter; foes rue the "inflated" prices, saying this "tourist trap" is "more flash than substance", while friends call it "absolutely worth the trip."

NEW Woodward *American*

- | - | - | M

Financial District | Ames Hotel | 1 Court St. (State St.) | 617-979-8200 | www.woodwardatames.com

Tucked off the Ames Hotel lobby in the Financial District, this two-story tavern conceived by Seth Greenberg (Mistral) offers seasonal, locally sourced American fare at affordable prices; the classy, rustic setting features white Windsor chairs and 'cabinets of interest' containing historical knickknacks, and also includes a gas-burning fireplace and alfresco seating.

Woody's Grill & Tap *American*

22 | 16 | 20 | $21

Fenway | 58 Hemenway St. (Westland Ave.) | 617-375-9663
Both a "student hot spot" and a "casual" "neighborhood place", this "cozy" Fenway "find" where "friendly service reigns" has "come a long way" with its "wood-fired pizza pies" and affordable American standards; a "surprisingly good selection of craft beers" fuels the "informal" atmosphere that's a "comfortable" spot to "meet" for a meal or "to watch sports."

Wu Chon House *Japanese/Korean*

22 | 14 | 18 | $23

Somerville | 290 Somerville Ave. (Union Sq.) | 617-623-3313 | www.wuchonhouse.com
Somervilleans in search of "adventure" seek out this Union Square eatery's "good portions" of "delicious", budget-friendly Korean cuisine featuring a "fabulous selection of side dishes", plus some Japanese fare; the decor may be a bit "bland" and the service just "average", but "plenty of choices" help make it a "solid" choice.

Xinh Xinh *Vietnamese*

∇ 25 | 9 | 22 | $15

Chinatown | 7 Beach St. (Washington St.) | 617-422-0501
You can "smell the lemongrass down the street" from this Chinatown "standout" featuring an "expansive menu" of "fresh" Vietnamese fare that includes "exceptional grilled dishes" and "tasty" fruit shakes, plus a couple of Chinese items; the "hole-in-the-wall" "decor leaves something to be desired", but the "helpful" service and "inexpensive" tabs help make it a "find."

Yama *Japanese*

22 | 15 | 18 | $33

Andover | 63 Park St. (bet. Florence & Whittier Sts.) | 978-749-9777 | www.yamaandover.com Ⓜ
Wellesley | 245 Washington St. (Rte. 9) | 781-431-8886 | www.yamawellesley.com
"Good suburban sushi" and other "fresh", "standard" Japanese fare take the spotlight at these midpriced sibs in Andover and Wellesley, where "minimal" decor and "variable" service are overlooked because "it's really all about" the "fun", varied menu; "wonderful portions" and lack of "pretense" make it "great for families" or a "casual night out", but "be sure to bring your own sake" to the Washington Street location, which is liquor-free.

Yangtze River *Chinese*

17 | 13 | 16 | $23

Lexington | 21-25 Depot Sq. (Mass. Ave.) | 781-861-6030 | www.yangtzelexington.com
"Popular with students" as well as "families", this Lexington "stalwart" is known for Mandarin specialties and a buffet that's "a great deal all around"; service can be "mediocre" and the selection seems "sparse" to some surveyors, but it's "dependable" for "more than reasonable prices."

Za *Pizza* — 25 | 19 | 23 | $22
Arlington | 138 Massachusetts Ave. (Milton St.) | 781-316-2334 |
www.zarestaurant.com
"Truly inventive pizzas" and "terrific salads" with "delicious twists
on old favorites" all feature "fresh, local ingredients" at this "bare-
bones" yet "comfortable" Arlington joint that's "run by the same
folks who do EVOO so well"; "capable", "attitude"-free service
makes for a "kid-friendly" atmosphere too.

Zabaglione *Italian* — ∇ 22 | 17 | 20 | $42
Ipswich | 10 Central St. (Market St.) | 978-356-5466
Café Zabaglione *Italian*
Ipswich | 1 Market St. (Central St.) | 978-356-6484
www.zabaglioneristorante.com
For a "quiet dinner" of "traditional Italian cuisine", this Ipswich
eatery fits the bill with "intimate" digs, "pleasant" service and "well-
prepared" fare paired with "decent wines" and followed by "special-
treat" desserts; penny-pinchers who find the tabs "generally pretty
pricey" for the area head to "the more informal cafe" around the corner, where lunch is also offered.

Zaftigs Delicatessen *Deli* — 21 | 16 | 18 | $22
Brookline | 335 Harvard St. (bet. Babcock & Stedman Sts.) |
617-975-0075 | www.zaftigs.com
Brookline's "nonkosher Jewish"-style "staple" is often "mobbed" by
hearty eaters drawn to its "heaping amounts of brunch food" (including "to-die-for banana-stuffed French toast"), "otherworldly"
"overstuffed" sandwiches and other "traditional deli favorites" that
leave patrons "pleasantly plump"; sticklers snipe that despite the
"fun factor" and the "friendly" staff's "cute T-shirts", such "ho-hum"
fare "wouldn't last a week in NYC."

Zebra's Bistro and Wine Bar *American* — 24 | 24 | 24 | $46
Medfield | 21 North St. (Rte. 109) | 508-359-4100 |
www.zebrasbistro.com
Medfield's "oasis in the suburbs" is "a favorite for date night" with
its "cozy lounge" and "romantic" dining room perfect for a "leisurely
dinner" of "inventive", "memorable" fare from an "ever-changing"
New American menu that includes "quality sushi"; "constantly improving" service is "great", but skeptics say the experience is "not
quite close enough" to the city's to "justify Boston prices."

Zen *Japanese* — ∇ 24 | 18 | 21 | $30
Beacon Hill | 21A Beacon St. (bet. Park & Tremont Sts.) | 617-371-1230 |
www.zensushibar.com
Sushi savorers decree the "fresh, tasty" and "inventive rolls" at this
Japanese "jewel" on Beacon Hill "will lead you to enlightenment"; a
fittingly "quiet" upstairs dining room is a "peaceful" setting for med-
itating on "flavorful" dishes and "a decent sake selection"; add in
moderate prices that "can't be beat", and a coterie of locals admits
it's "hard to go elsewhere."

	FOOD	DECOR	SERVICE	COST

Zócalo Cocina Mexicana *Mexican* | 22 | 19 | 21 | $26 |

Brighton | 1414 Commonwealth Ave. (Kelton St.) | 617-277-5700 |
www.zocalobrighton.com
Arlington | 203A Broadway (bet. Adams & Foster Sts.) |
781-643-2299 | www.zocaloarlington.com 🖂

With its "colorful", "festive interior", it "feels as if you're actually in
Mexico" at this Arlington and Brighton duo where the "quality" fare
includes "ceviche made fresh", guacamole prepared "tableside",
"out-of-this-world chiles rellenos" and "imaginative sangrias"; despite "cramped" surroundings and occasional "waits", "reasonable
prices" and "service with a smile" make it "welcoming."

Zoe's ◑ *Chinese* | 19 | 12 | 17 | $20 |

Somerville | 296 Beacon St. (Eustis St.) | 617-864-6265

"Strongly flavored", "truly authentic" Sichuan is the specialty of this
Somerville spot where menu offerings that go "above and beyond
the usual choices" are "so-so on some nights" but mostly "good" –
and "for the price", it's worth "taking a chance"; post-Survey, it
moved into more open, sunnier digs, outdating the Decor score.

Zuzu! *Eclectic/Mideastern* | 20 | 17 | 17 | $27 |

Central Square | The Middle East | 474 Massachusetts Ave.
(Brookline St.) | Cambridge | 617-864-3278 | www.zuzubar.com

"Funky" red, gold and bronze decor, a "young, loud" clientele and a
"generally indifferent" staff give this "hip" Central Square spot that
shares space with The Middle East a particularly "Cambridge-quirky"
vibe; the Eclectic fare is "quite tasty", making it a "unique" meal option in a place that "doesn't take itself too seriously"; N.B. there's
live music on Mondays and a DJ after dinner every other night.

Cape Cod

TOP FOOD

27 Inaho | *Japanese*
Front St. | *Continental/Italian*
Pisces | *Med./Seafood*
Red Pheasant | *Amer./French*
Bramble Inn | *Amer.*

TOP DECOR

29 28 Atlantic | *American*
26 Chatham Bars Inn | *American*
Belfry Inne | *American*
Chillingsworth | *French*
Red Inn | *New England*

⧈ Abba *Mediterranean/Thai* | 27 | 21 | 24 | $54 |

Orleans | 89 Old Colony Way (bet. Old Tote & West Rds.) |
508-255-8144 | www.abbarestaurant.com

For "scrumptious" flavors you "won't come across anywhere else",
hit this "old house" in Orleans where chef Erez Pinhas creates an
"imaginative culinary fusion" of Med and Thai cuisines, which is
"beautifully presented" (along with a "superb wine list") by "knowledgeable" servers; insiders warn that "long waits, even with reservations", and "high prices" are unavoidable, but the "cramped"
interior can be skipped for the "quieter, more spacious" deck.

Academy Ocean Grille *Eclectic/Seafood* | 22 | 19 | 20 | $45 |

Orleans | 2 Academy Pl. (Orleans Rd.) | 508-240-1585 |
www.academyoceangrille.com

This "small", "relaxed" Eclectic seafooder in Orleans with an "enlarged
bar" is a "charming spot for an intimate dinner" (the patio is especially
"great in summer", while a fireplace keeps it "cozy" in winter); better
still, the "competently served", "fresh" fare comes at "a decent price."

Adrian's *American/Italian* | ▽ 16 | 13 | 17 | $34 |

North Truro | Outer Reach Resort | 535 Rte. 6 (Pilgrim Heights Rd.) |
508-487-4360 | www.adriansrestaurant.com

"Great views" of the bay are the real draw at this "casual", "family-
friendly" North Truro eatery doling out American breakfasts and
Italian dinners – which may be "ordinary" at best, but at least feature "fine pizzas"; the interior "lacks charm", but the deck is "nice"
(at "sunset" in particular) "if it's not too buggy."

Alberto's Ristorante *Italian* | 20 | 19 | 20 | $41 |

Hyannis | 360 Main St. (Barnstable Rd.) | 508-778-1770 |
www.albertos.net

Tourists and locals alike "count on" – and get – "satisfaction" from
everything they order off the "wide-ranging menu" at this longtime
Hyannis Northern Italian boasting a "romantic", "elegant" interior
and sidewalk cafe; whippersnappers protest it "needs a youth move-
ment", but "early birds" are too busy digging into their "bargain"
"sunset dinners" to pay them any mind.

Amari Bar & Ristorante *Italian* | 22 | 21 | 21 | $34 |

East Sandwich | 674 Rte. 6A, Old King's Hwy. (Jones Ln.) | 508-375-0011 |
www.amarirestaurant.com

"Generous portions" of "hearty red-sauce Italian" "like grammie
used to make" (at prices she would love) "draw quite a crowd" to

this "rustic" East Sandwich eatery, "even during the long winter"; fans forgive that the "huge", fireplace-blessed setting can get "way too noisy", instead letting themselves be soothed by live music Friday and Saturday; P.S. "you don't want to forget that reservation."

Anthony's Cummaquid Inn Ⓜ *Continental* | 18 | 18 | 18 | $41 |

Yarmouth Port | 2 Main St./Rte. 6A (Willow St.) | 508-362-4501 | www.pier4.com

The location makes this "large" Yarmouth Port Continental a "tourist haven", as the "views of the bay" are "second to none", especially if you "get there before sunset"; though many find everything "enjoyable", old-timers who "remember what the name used to mean" deem it a "shame" that the decor's so "dated" and the fare "mediocre."

Aqua Grille *American/Seafood* | 19 | 19 | 20 | $36 |

Sandwich | 14 Gallo Rd. (Town Neck Rd.) | 508-888-8889 | www.aquagrille.com

A "favorite" for "sunny lunches", this Sandwich "standby" proffers "reliable, tasty", midpriced New American seafood in "nonstressful" surroundings featuring a "great bar" and "interesting views of the Cape Cod Canal"; dinners are also "pleasant", especially with the increased likelihood that the "friendly service" won't be "slow."

Ardeo Grille at Kings Way *Mediterranean* | 20 | 17 | 20 | $28 |

Yarmouth Port | 81 Kings Circuit (Oak Glen, Rte. 6A) | 508-362-7730

Ardeo Mediterranean Taverna *Mediterranean*

South Yarmouth | Union Plaza | 23 Whites Path (Station Ave.) | 508-760-1500

Ardeo on Main *Mediterranean*

Hyannis | 644 Main St. (Sea St.) | 508-790-1115

Ardeo Tuscan Tavern *Mediterranean*

Brewster | 280 Underpass Rd. (Independence Way) | 508-896-4200 www.ardeocapecod.com

"Reasonable prices" for "well-flavored" Mediterranean dishes with "Middle Eastern accents" – "innovative pizzas" being the highlight – keep this "unpretentious" Cape mini-chain "busy" with "families and large groups"; "efficient", "friendly staffs" help to make everyone feel "welcome" when they arrive and "delighted" when they leave.

Arnold's Lobster & Clam Bar ⍅ *Seafood* | 23 | 14 | 14 | $28 |

Eastham | 3580 Rte. 6 (Old Orchard Rd.) | 508-255-2575 | www.arnoldsrestaurant.com

"Be prepared to wait in line" for the "ultimate fried seafood experience" at this "no-frills", cash-only "clam shack" in Eastham, also known for a "super-fresh raw bar" and "awesome hot lobster rolls"; with ice cream, alcohol and miniature golf also on-site, it's easy to see how the annual "must-do" "family" "tradition" can get so "expensive."

Barley Neck Inn *American* | 20 | 20 | 18 | $40 |

East Orleans | Barley Neck Inn | 5 Beach Rd. (bet. Barley Neck Rd. & Main St.) | 508-255-0212 | www.barleyneck.com

Housed in a former sea captain's manor, this "reliable" New American offers a "fresh"-seafood-focused menu in three "elegant", "romantic" rooms with fireplaces for winter dining; adjoining is Joe's Beach Road Bar & Grill, a more "casual" "place for a quick bite to eat", drinks and weekend live music.

Baxter's Boathouse New England/Seafood | 18 | 16 | 15 | $28 |

Hyannis | 177 Pleasant St. (South St.) | 508-775-4490 | www.baxterscapecod.com

"You can't beat the views" at this seasonal "old-school" New England "boaters' hangout" on Hyannis Harbor, the site of "tourists" "rubbing elbows with salty" locals inside (home of a Thursday–Saturday night piano bar) or on the deck, where plates of "greasy"-"great" fried seafood must often be shielded from "pesky gulls"; though dollar-watchers calculate it's "overpriced" for what it is, even they make the "annual visit."

Bayside Betsy's American | 15 | 15 | 17 | $31 |

Provincetown | 177 Commercial St. (Winthrop St.) | 508-487-6566 | www.baysidebetsys.com

"Lovely" harbor views are "the best part" of this "campy, cute" "P-town fixture" offering a "scene-y bar" and "good enough" all-day New American fare at "reasonable prices"; "it's jammed in the summer with tourists", so the "wait for a table can be long" and "Greenland might melt before you're served", but "Betsy herself is charming", and a little of that goes a long way.

Bee-Hive Tavern American | 19 | 20 | 20 | $30 |

East Sandwich | 406 Rte. 6A (bet. Atkins Rd. & Jacobs Meadow) | 508-833-1184 | www.thebeehivetavern.com

Valued by visitors as a convenient "stop for lunch when driving home from the Cape" and by locals as an "efficient" "alternative" year-round, this "bee-themed" American cottage in East Sandwich emits "country charm" thanks in part to a "friendly staff"; the "relaxed" mood is bolstered by fare that, while vacillating between "average" and "very good", does the trick for reasonably priced "comfort."

Belfry Inne & Bistro Ⓜ American | 25 | 26 | 22 | $50 |

Sandwich | Belfry Inne | 8 Jarves St. (bet. Main St. & Rte. 6A) | 508-888-8550 | www.belfryinn.com

Adorned with stained-glass windows and other "elegant" "remnants" from its past as a church, this "enchanting" Sandwich bistro is a "real find" for "clever", "divine" New American dishes; "saintly service" and live weekend jazz piano are two more blessings – just be prepared to dig deep when the basket is passed; N.B. more casual lunches and dinners are available in the adjoining Painted Lady cafe.

Betsy's Diner Diner | 18 | 19 | 18 | $19 |

Falmouth | 457 Main St. (bet. King St. & Nye Rd.) | 508-540-0060

"If you're nostalgic for the '50s", this Falmouth diner is "the place to go" for American comfort food served by a "chatty staff" in "authentic" retro environs; "tourists line up for the dynamite breakfast", but lunch and dinner are equally "fun" – albeit possibly "not so good for the arteries" ("the 'eat heavy' sign outside says it all").

	FOOD	DECOR	SERVICE	COST

Bistro at Crowne Pointe *American*   22 | 21 | 22 | $50

Provincetown | Crowne Pointe Historic Inn & Spa | 82 Bradford St.
(Prince St.) | 508-487-6767 | www.crownepointe.com

"Quiet, romantic" dinners are the stock in trade of this "intimate"
Provincetown bistro boasting "charming" High Victorian decor and
"amazing views", not to mention "inventive, attractively presented"
New American fare; "polite, skillful service" and an "impressive
wine list" complete the "memorable" (and somewhat pricey) picture; N.B. breakfast available for guests of the Crowne Pointe
Historic Inn & Spa only.

Blackfish ☒ *American*   24 | 23 | 21 | $49

Truro | 17 Truro Center Rd. (Castle Rd.) | 508-349-3399

"Bravo" to this "classy" Truro haunt proffering a "creative" "combination of rich, gourmet" New American fare and "knockout" "fresh"
seafood in a space decked out with brick walls, copper-top tables
and a concrete bar; while many feel the service "could be more attentive" for such "upscale" pricing, that doesn't stop it from being
"packed with tourists" (those in-the-know say "go on a weeknight"
for less "noise").

Bleu *French*   25 | 21 | 21 | $43

Mashpee | Mashpee Commons | 10 Market St. (North St.) |
508-539-7907 | www.bleurestaurant.com

Though "set in a Mashpee Commons storefront", Francophiles
deem dining at this "lively" "change of pace for Cape Cod" is "almost
like being in France", as it offers "authentic bistro" fare (alongside
some "novel" yet equally "satisfying" "seasonal" preparations) and
"a bit of attitude"; the "cozy" setting – swathed in multiple shades of
blue – has an "urbane" feel that matches the slightly "pricey" dinner
tabs (lunch is a relative "bargain").

Blue Moon Bistro *Mediterranean*   24 | 20 | 22 | $40

Dennis | 605 Main St./6A (Old Bass River Rd.) | 508-385-7100 |
www.bluemoonbistro.net

Despite its "small, simple" setting, this "real gem" in historic
Dennis shines with "superb" Mediterranean meals that are only
"a little expensive"; the "nice people" who operate it make
"whole families" feel welcome, and they in turn "love it year-round",
especially before performances at the nearby Cape Cod Center
for the Arts.

Bookstore & Restaurant *Seafood*   19 | 15 | 16 | $34

Wellfleet | 50 Kendrick Ave. (Commercial St.) | 508-349-3154 |
www.wellfleetoyster.com

"Talk about fresh and sweet!" – the oysters are just-harvested at
this "reliable standby" for "value" seafood in Wellfleet (the
menu's broad, but your best bet is to "stick to the basics"); if
"long waits", "old-time-everything" decor and service that can
seem "uncaring" rankle, hit the patio or second-floor deck and get
lost in the "wonderful" harbor views or a volume from the
attached tome-seller.

	FOOD	DECOR	SERVICE	COST

☑ Bramble Inn Ⓜ *American* | 27 | 25 | 27 | $65 |

Brewster | Bramble Inn | 2019 Main St./Rte. 6A (bet. Breakwater Rd. & Crocker Ln.) | 508-896-7644 | www.brambleinn.com

"An amazing experience" awaits in this "charming" 1861 Brewster farmhouse where "absolutely fabulous, innovative but not precious" New American "works of art" are ferried by "outstanding" servers in four "elegant" Victorian dining rooms "enhanced" by a "beautiful bar"; "superb wines" can turn "pricey" tabs into "wallet-busters", but they're "worth it" for such a "special night out."

Brazilian Grill *Brazilian* | 21 | 16 | 19 | $37 |

Hyannis | 680 Main St. (bet. Sea & Stevens Sts.) | 508-771-0109 | www.braziliangrillcapecod.com

"Vegans beware!" – though there's a "fine salad bar" at this "upbeat", reasonably priced Brazilian rodizio in Hyannis, it's hard to escape "solicitous" staffers who are so "efficient in their singular task: bringing you piles" of "succulent" grilled meats in many "fantastic choices"; indeed, you'll have to "beg them to stop" – and "you'll be disappointed" when they do (for best results, "don't eat for a week" beforehand).

☑ Brewster Fish House *Seafood* | 26 | 18 | 23 | $47 |

Brewster | 2208 Main St./Rte. 6A (Stonehenge Dr.) | 508-896-7867 | www.brewsterfish.com

An "annoying no-reservations policy" that leads to nearly "intolerable waits" makes getting into this "tiny" Brewster venue a "pain in the neck", but "it's all worth it in the end" for "perfectly prepared" seafood sprinkled with "mouthwatering" "nouvelle twists" and complemented by a "strong wine list"; it may "look like nothing" from the outside, but "unfailingly polite" staffers (not to mention "somewhat pricey" checks) help give it that fine-dining air.

Bubala's by the Bay *Eclectic/Seafood* | 16 | 14 | 16 | $32 |

Provincetown | 183-85 Commercial St. (bet. Court & Winthrop Sts.) | 508-487-0773 | www.bubalas.com

Watching the "parade of beautiful men and their dogs down Commercial Street" from the "see-and-be-seen patio" is "the main event" at this P-town "standby" that also exhibits "great views of the bay" from the "air-conditioned interior"; indeed, the "vast", seafood-heavy Eclectic menu seems "marginal" (and often "a bit pricey") to the "busy" scene, which also trumps "uninspired" decor and servers who swing from "humorous" to "torturous."

Buca's Tuscan Roadhouse *Italian* | 23 | 21 | 22 | $47 |

Harwich | 4 Depot Rd. (Rte. 28) | 508-432-6900 | www.bucasroadhouse.com

You're in Harwich, but you "might as well be in Tuscany" when you sup at this "charming" "gem" serving Northern Italian cuisine that's sometimes "traditional", sometimes "innovative" and always "superb"; the "romantic" setting – marked by beamed ceilings, red-and-white-checked tablecloths and a fireplace – feels even warmer thanks to a "gracious", "knowledgeable" staff, and while it's a tad expensive, the "excellent wine list" displays "fair prices."

	FOOD	DECOR	SERVICE	COST

Cafe Edwige/
Edwige at Night *American*

26 | 17 | 21 | $48

Provincetown | 333 Commercial St. (bet. Freeman & Standish Sts.) | 508-487-2008 | www.edwigeatnight.com

"Wonderful breakfasts", "amazing brunches" and "creative", "carefully constructed" dinners complemented by "imaginative drinks" command somewhat elevated prices at this "bustling" second-floor Provincetown New American employing an "accommodating" staff; the "snug", "funky" setting offers "no ocean view or special atmosphere", but the wooden "booths by the window are great for people-watching – if not a little hard on the backside."

Cape Sea Grille *American*

26 | 24 | 23 | $50

Harwich Port | 31 Sea St. (Rte. 28) | 508-432-4745 | www.capeseagrille.com

At this "elegant" Harwich Port seasider, the "superb attention to detail" extends from the "sophisticated" New American cuisine (starring "refreshing takes on Cape Cod favorites", "perfectly paired" with a "superb wine list") to the "idyllic setting" in an "old sea captain's house" and the "winning", "well-paced" service; for the "perfect special occasion", insiders say "ask for the porch" – and bring a mass of moolah.

Captain Frosty's *New England/Seafood*

21 | 10 | 16 | $18

Dennis | 219 Main St./Rte. 6A (S. Yarmouth Rd.) | 508-385-8548 | www.captainfrosty.com

"A Cape Cod vacation isn't complete without a drive" to this Dennis "throwback" clam shack where fried New England seafood "cravings" (there are also "great lobster rolls", burgers, etc.) are sated with "overflowing" portions and for "reasonable prices"; it's what "memories are made of", especially if you "save room" for "soft-swirl ice cream."

Captain Kidd, The *Pub Food*

18 | 20 | 20 | $28

Woods Hole | 77 Water St. (Luscombe Ave.) | 508-548-8563 | www.thecaptainkidd.com

"Beautiful views of quaint Eel Pond", "friendly service" and moderate prices make this nautically themed Woods Hole "charmer" a "nice" choice "while waiting for the ferry to Martha's Vineyard"; the pub food is "tasty" enough, if "nothing fancy", while the deck's "great in summer", the interior's "cozy in winter" and the whole enterprise is "fun for kids" always.

Captain Linnell House Ⓜ *American*

22 | 25 | 23 | $53

Orleans | 137 Skaket Beach Rd. (West Rd.) | 508-255-3400 | www.linnell.com

"Dress up" without feeling "out of place" at this "elegant" "old sea captain's" "mansion" in Orleans, where "experienced servers" present a "varied menu" of Traditional American fare "with flair" in "classy" French neo-classic dining rooms that overlook sprawling lawns; since this is the kind of "costly" "evening you save for", "romance"-seekers urge you come "without the kids" – "please!"

	FOOD	DECOR	SERVICE	COST

Captain Parker's Pub *New England* | 18 | 14 | 18 | $26 |

West Yarmouth | 668 Rte. 28 (W. Yarmouth Rd.) | 508-771-4266 |
www.captainparkers.com

Connoisseurs "put up with" often long "waits" for the "exceptional",
"thick and creamy" clam chowder for which this "homey", "rustic"
(and possibly "long in the tooth") West Yarmouth "destination" is
"famous"; many feel the rest of the New England fare is purely
"passable", though on the upside, it's "moderately priced."

Casino Wharf *Italian/Seafood* | ▽ 20 | 21 | 21 | $48 |

Falmouth | 286 Grand Ave. (bet. Falmouth Heights Rd. & Worcester Ct.) |
508-540-6160 | www.casinowharffx.com

"Spectacular views of Vineyard Sound", especially "on the deck
overlooking the beach", create a "lovely" backdrop at this Falmouth
Heights venture offering "solid" Northern Italian seafood and pasta; it
can get "noisy" with chatter and live entertainment (nightly in-season,
Friday and Saturday off), but the "elegant" environs abet romance.

Catch of the Day *Seafood* | 25 | 13 | 22 | $29 |

Wellfleet | 975 Rte. 6 (Marconi Beach Rd.) | 508-349-9090 |
www.wellfleetcatch.com

Wellfleet day-trippers expecting "standard clam-shack" fare at this
"unpretentious" market discover "quite a find" in seafood that's not
only "fresh, fresh, fresh" but "perfectly prepared" and "value"
priced; a "pleasant staff", wine and beer make it "great for a nice
lunch" on premises, but "don't overlook takeout" for a picnic at
a nearby beach.

Chapin's Fish 'n Chips & Beach Bar *Seafood* | - | - | - | M |

Dennisport | 228 Lower County Rd. (Shad Hole Rd.) | 508-394-6900 |
www.chapinsbeachbar.com

Formerly the beach bar offshoot of Clancy's, this seasonal
Dennisport seafooder provides similar value as its predecessor in its
classic Cape Cod menu; it's conveniently located along the route to
Chapin's Beach, making it a perfect pit stop for a pre- or post-
sun lobster roll.

Chapoquoit Grill *American* | 22 | 15 | 20 | $34 |

West Falmouth | 410 W. Falmouth Hwy./Rte. 28A (Brick Kiln Rd.) |
508-540-7794 | www.chapoquoitgrill.com

"Don't be fooled" by the "ordinary" setting of this West Falmouth
"mainstay" – the wood-fired brick-oven pizzas are "spectacular"
and the rest of the "creative" New American dinners are what "you
would expect at a more upscale restaurant" (and an "excellent
value" too); "throngs of people, especially in summer", keep it per-
petually "lively" – and make waits for tables often "lengthy."

Chart Room *New England/Seafood* | 20 | 18 | 18 | $36 |

Cataumet | 1 Shipyard Ln. (Shore Rd.) | 508-563-5350

Many Cataumet summerers make this "old-timer" a "weekly" "ritual", creating "a mob scene" where the waits for tables and for the

"predictable" but "tasty" New England seafood take "forever"; no matter, they just cool their heels with "deadly but delicious mud-slides" while listening to the "lively entertainment" and taking in the "beautiful sunset" and "magical" harbor views; P.S. the "to-die-for lobster sandwich" is "not on the menu", but "everyone orders it."

Chatham Bars Inn *American*   22 | 26 | 23 | $55

Chatham | Chatham Bars Inn | 297 Shore Rd. (bet. Chatham Bars Ave. & Seaview St.) | 508-945-0096 | www.chathambarsinn.com

You half "expect to bump into Gatsby" at this "absolutely elegant" oceanside Chatham "luxury hotel" with "several great" eateries, starting with an "airy" main room filled with "old-world charm" and a "dressy crowd" supping on "imaginative" New American fare "well prepared and presented" by "attentive" servers; "less fancy" but still generally "splendid" are the tavern (which underwent a post-Survey renovation) and the beach grill, the latter boasting "amazing views"; all venues, meanwhile, command "premium prices."

Chatham Squire *Eclectic*   18 | 14 | 18 | $29

Chatham | 487 Main St. (bet. Chatham Bars Ave. & Seaview St.) | 508-945-0945 | www.thesquire.com

"Townies and tourists" "mingle easily" at this "informal" "Chatham institution" with a "family-friendly" "restaurant side" doling out "basic pub fare" and Eclectic entrees "at decent prices" and a "terrific" "tavern side" "bustling" with "overwhelming crowds" (expect "huge waits" in season); the setting – festooned with a "colorful" collection of license plates – is "outdated on purpose", but thankfully, "cool and shady in the summer and warm and cozy in the winter."

☑ Chillingsworth Ⓜ *French*   27 | 26 | 26 | $73

Brewster | 2449 Main St./Rte. 6A (Foster Rd.) | 508-896-3640 | www.chillingsworth.com

For "grand events", Brewster bigwigs choose this "formal" "heaven" set on a "charming" over-300-year-old estate where the "sensational" chef-owner "injects New England flair" into "glorious" New French prix fixes, which are then conveyed by "graceful" servers in "romantic rooms"; though said splurgers say it's "worth every penny", the hoi polloi would rather hit the "more laid-back" adjacent bistro for the same "excellence" offered à la carte at "a fraction of the price."

Ciro & Sal's *Italian*   20 | 18 | 16 | $41

Provincetown | 4 Kiley Ct. (Commercial St.) | 508-487-6444 | www.ciroandsals.com

"Part of the fabric of the Cape" for 60 years, this "P-town perennial" still delivers "reliable", "no-nonsense" Northern Italian fare in a "cutesy" yet "cramped" dining room with hanging Chianti bottles; it can be "romantic" ("if there aren't too many loud parties"), "especially next to the fireplace in winter", but during the high season, when service becomes "erratic", many locals would just as soon leave it to the "tourists."

	FOOD	DECOR	SERVICE	COST

Clancy's of Dennisport *American* | 22 | 18 | 21 | $30 |

Dennisport | 8 Upper County Rd. (bet. Rtes. 134 & 28) | 508-394-6661 | www.clancysrestaurant.com

"Be prepared to wait" for "hours" "during the summer" for this Dennisport spot "popular" with "locals" and "knowledgeable tourists" requiring a "typical Cape Cod menu" with "value" (the American "burgers, sandwiches and seafood" are sold in "portions big enough to share"); there's a "great view of the river" and "outdoor dining" too, not to mention "friendly" staffers.

Cobie's Clam Shack ⊅ *Seafood* | 19 | 7 | 12 | $18 |

Brewster | 3260 Main St. (Linnell Landing Rd.) | 508-896-7021 | www.cobies.com

Folks with a "hankering for seafood" wax "nostalgic" when they pedal up to this "self-serve" stand "on the bike trail near Nickerson State Park" in Brewster, a "summer stop" since 1948 for fried clams, lobster rolls, chowder, ice cream and more, all served in "good portion sizes for the money"; it may be "no better or worse than similar joints", but for an "in-the-rough" experience, it "hits the spot."

Cooke's Seafood *Seafood* | - | - | - | I |

Orleans | 1 S. Orleans Rd./Rte. 28 (Rte. 6A) | 508-255-5518
Hyannis | 1120 Iyannough Rd./Rte. 132 (Bearses Way) | 508-775-0450
Mashpee | 7 Ryans Way (Great Neck Rd.) | 508-477-9595
www.cookesseafood.com

For more than 30 years, this Orleans landmark – which has spun off separately owned locales in Hyannis and Mashpee – has stood as an inexpensive yellow beacon to seafoodies craving whole-belly fried clams, lobster rolls and other fish fixes; after getting their fare from the counter, guests either settle into the dining room, which is festooned with Cape-themed paintings, eat under an awning on the patio or take it to the beach.

Coonamessett Inn *New England* | 18 | 20 | 20 | $37 |

Falmouth | Coonamessett Inn | 311 Gifford St. (Jones Rd.) | 508-548-2300 | www.capecodrestaurants.org

"An older crowd tends" to spend "nicer occasions" at this "charming" Falmouth "institution" offering "old-school" New England fare that, while "not very inspiring", is "well prepared" and conveyed by an "attentive, experienced staff" (Sunday brunch in particular is "great"); their grandkids, though, regard it as a bit of a "stuffy" "function farm", marveling "it's not 1959 anymore, but you'd never know it" were it not "for the prices."

Dan'l Webster Inn *American* | 20 | 22 | 21 | $44 |

Sandwich | Dan'l Webster Inn | 149 Main St. (Rte. 130) | 508-888-3622 | www.danlwebsterinn.com

Whether in the "expensive, elegant" main room, the "less-expensive", "warm and cozy tavern" or the "light and airy" botanical conservatory, patrons enjoy the "old Colonial charm" of this Sandwich "institution" – serving "modestly ambitious, well-executed" New

American fare – just as they have for "over 30 years"; but since it's almost "exactly the same" as it ever was, modish types would rather "leave it to the blue hairs."

Devon's *American/French* | 24 | 20 | 22 | $50 |

Provincetown | 401½ Commercial St. (Washington Ave.) | 508-487-4773 | www.devons.org

"Organic and seasonal" ingredients pepper the "inventive", "refined" New American–French menu proffered at this "charming" all-day "Cape Cod beach cottage" in Provincetown, where "Devon himself" ensures that the service stays "warm" and "attentive"; "prices are high", but they're "worth every penny" assure admirers who also appreciate that the "wine list complements the food so well."

Dolphin *Seafood* | 21 | 17 | 21 | $46 |

Barnstable | 3250 Main St./Rte. 6A (Hyannis Rd.) | 508-362-6610 | www.thedolphinrestaurant.com

This Barnstable "townie bar" adequately sates "families", "judges and lawyers" who desire "nothing fancy" in their "fresh seafood" and Traditional American dishes, but do require "reliability" and "friendly" service; the decor may be somewhat "tired", but sitting "by the fire on a chilly night" is as "cozy as can be."

Dunbar Tea Room *British/Tearoom* | 22 | 22 | 20 | $26 |

Sandwich | Dunbar Tea Shop | 1 Water St. (Main St.) | 508-833-2485 | www.dunbarteashop.com

"You swear you're in the English countryside" when you come upon this "wonderful" carriage house in old Sandwich Village vending "high-tea lunch choices" ("satisfying" sandwiches, "baked goods to die for") amid "elegant", "pristine" and, natch, "feminine decor"; just "come at an off-hour if you don't want a long wait" and "slow" service.

Enzo *French*   ▽ | 24 | 20 | 23 | $53 |

Provincetown | Enzo Guest House | 186 Commercial St. (Court St.) | 508-487-7555 | www.enzolives.com

This "charming" Victorian guest-house restaurant in Provincetown features "varied, interesting" and ultimately "fabulous" French Provençal dishes, about which the "friendly", "knowledgeable" servers advise; the "lovely, intimate" rooms and "street-level terrace" offer "great" views of the "flamboyant traffic passing by."

Fairway | 18 | 14 | 19 | $26 |
Restaurant & Pizzeria *American/Italian*

North Eastham | 4295 State Hwy./Rte. 6 (Brackett Rd.) | 508-255-3893 | www.fairwaycapecod.com

In the morning, "great breakfasts" are served alongside "the best gossip" in town to "North Eastham's finest" at this "friendly, family-run" "coffee shop"; in the evenings, its bar is a "fun place" to "watch the Sox", while the booths host groups chowing down on American and Italian grub – it may be "so-so", but there's "loads of it", providing "top value for your buck"; N.B. no lunch.

	FOOD	DECOR	SERVICE	COST

Fanizzi's by the Sea *American/Italian* | 20 | 21 | 21 | $32 |

Provincetown | 539 Commercial St. (Kendall Ln.) | 508-487-1964 | www.fanizzisrestaurant.com

Like "being in a houseboat at high tide" with "water lapping at the window", this "casual" Provincetown East Ender that "juts out into the bay" is "popular with locals" who find its "reasonable" American-Italian seafood "dependably good" ("just not distinctive") and the staff "always nice"; "one of the few places" "open year-round", it's even more appreciated as a "cozy" "off-season resource."

Fazio's Trattoria *Italian* | 20 | 15 | 15 | $36 |

Hyannis | 294 Main St. (Center St.) | 508-775-9400 | www.fazio.net

Fans feel this "cozy" Hyannis Italian "doesn't get the attention it deserves" for its "homemade pastas", "fantastic pizzas" and "great breads", all of which are "not too expensive"; but perhaps that's because some customers only "used to recommend it" – currently, they can't stop "fuming" over the "indifferent service" and "terrible acoustics"; N.B. post-Survey, the interior was renovated and an outdoor dining space was created, probably outdating the Decor score.

Finely JP's *American* | 21 | 18 | 20 | $40 |

Wellfleet | 554 Rte. 6 (Castanga Dr.) | 508-349-7500

Whether they find the New American cuisine created at this Wellfleet year-rounder "super" or "marginal", or the service "personable" or "not worth mentioning", "customers always seem happy" that "the price is right"; thankfully, the "modern, open room", "relaxing deck" and "ample parking" bear "no hassles."

Firefly Woodfire Grill & Bar *Eclectic* | 20 | 17 | 16 | $36 |

Falmouth | 271 Main St. (Rte. 28) | 508-548-7953 | www.fireflywoodfiregrill.com

Large, "nice crowds" fill this Falmouth "fun spot" for "good people-watching" from the "cute tables on the sidewalk" and the "chic bar" scene; as for sustenance, some just come for "pizza and drinks" because the rest of the "extensive variety" of "adequate" Eclectic fare may be "too expensive for what you get"; peace-seekers, meanwhile, "avoid it" altogether due to the "excessive noise."

Fishmonger's Cafe *American/Seafood* | 18 | 19 | 18 | $35 |

Woods Hole | 56 Water St. (Luscombe Ave.) | 508-540-5376

"Its days as a hippie enclave are a distant memory" applaud supporters of this all-day New American in "quaint Woods Hole", where the "creative" seafood with Mediterranean accents sports "less sprouts" than it once did; unfortunately, foes are "disappointed" that the "unexciting" fare doesn't fully complement the "friendly service" and "terrific water views."

Five Bays Bistro *American* | 25 | 20 | 22 | $50 |

Osterville | 825 Main St. (Wianno Ave.) | 508-420-5559 | www.fivebaysbistro.com

"Stylish", "upscale" Ostervilleans "meet and greet" at the "active bar" of this "dynamite" New American with a "warm, contemporary setting" and "friendly" service; if the dining area is on your agenda ("reservations are necessary"), be prepared to "yell across the table to converse" – or just "wear earplugs", focus your attention on the "plate-licking good" victuals and be proud that you can "afford it."

Friendly Fisherman's *Seafood*   ∇ 24 | 12 | 16 | $21

North Eastham | 4580 Rte. 6 (Oak Rd.) | 508-255-6770

"Be careful" or "you'll drive by this little fish market" in North Eastham, a mecca for "large", "wonderful lobster rolls" and "ultrafresh" fried seafood, also doled out in "huge portions"; so what if there's "no atmosphere"? – it's "convenient" for "trips to the National Seashore", "less touristy than others" and quite a BYO "deal."

🅩 Front Street *Continental/Italian*   27 | 20 | 24 | $49

Provincetown | 230 Commercial St. (Masonic Pl.) | 508-487-9715 | www.frontstreetrestaurant.com

"You can't go wrong" with anything off the "delicious, gourmet" Continental *carte,* the "extensive" Italian menu (starring "expertly made favorites") or the "awesome wine list" at this "expensive" Provincetown two-for-one with "faultless service" and a "cavelike" yet "romantic" "windowless" setting in a Victorian house; "be sure to make advance reservations", because space is tight and it's "always packed."

Gina's by the Sea 🅜 *Italian*   21 | 16 | 21 | $39

Dennis | 134 Taunton Ave. (Chapin Beach Rd.) | 508-385-3213 | www.ginasbythesea.com

Dennis locals think "tourists are usually unable to find this" "fun, funky" "hole-in-the-wall Italian" – but it's "worth trying", if not for a "taste of Old Cape Cod" ("average" though it may be), then at least "for its character and for the characters who work there"; just "get there early, as it's already jammed by 6 PM."

Hemisphere *New England*   ∇ 17 | 19 | 19 | $33

Sandwich | 98 Town Neck Rd. (Freeman Ave.) | 508-888-6166 | www.hemispherecapecod.com

"Awe-inspiring views" of "Cape Cod Bay and the canal" create re-turnees to this beach-themed Sandwich New Englander, especially since they feel just as "comfortable dressing up [to dine] inside" as they do "sitting on the deck in shorts sipping a cocktail"; indeed, the atmosphere "more than makes up for" times when the "standard fish-house fare" dips from "solid" to "unfortunate."

Impudent Oyster *Seafood*   23 | 18 | 21 | $42

Chatham | 15 Chatham Bars Ave. (Main St.) | 508-945-3545

Whether you opt for the "sunny upstairs room" or the "noisy", "cozy bar" with "mussels and a glass of wine" at this "fun", "friendly" "fix-ture" in "charming Chatham", you're guaranteed "high-quality" sea-food in "fantastic combinations"; dinner prices are geared to the "affluent", while "lunch is a better deal", and it's especially "great off season", since you have to make a reservation well in advance to get in during the summer."

	FOOD	DECOR	SERVICE	COST

Ⓩ Inaho Ⓢ *Japanese* 　　27 | 20 | 20 | $42

Yarmouth Port | 157 Main St./Rte. 6A (Old King's Hwy.) | 508-362-5522 | www.inahocapecod.com

"Right on target" cheer maki mavens of this Yarmouth Port Japanese and its "perfectly prepared", "totally terrific" sushi and "innovative, delicious specials", all of which easily "surpass the decor", as there's "a tight fit between tables" that necessitates "pulling in every time" a staffer passes (some of them are "slow" and "sullen"); meals here can be "expensive", but they're "worth it" – and "cheaper than flying to Tokyo."

Island Merchant *American/Caribbean* 　　- | - | - | M

Hyannis | 302 Main St. (bet. Barnstable Rd. & Center St.) | 508-771-1337 | www.theislandmerchant.com

Have a "fun" island experience right in Hyannis at this "tiny place" displaying an "interesting", moderately priced Caribbean-flecked New American menu, fake palm trees and warm colors; "music lovers" dig the live acts on most evenings, budget-minders come after 10 PM for $2 burgers every night, while everyone raises their glasses to the "great rum punch and other drinks" served at all times.

JT's Seafood *Seafood* 　　17 | 13 | 15 | $29

Brewster | 2689 Main St./Rte. 6A (Winslow Landing Rd.) | 508-896-3355 | www.jt-seafood.com

The promise of "right-off-the-boat" seafood followed by ice cream incites "huge lines" of "families" at "all times of the day" at this "cafeteria-style" clam shack in Brewster; the window workers do their best to be "quick and efficient", and while some numbers-crunchers calculate it's a "good value for the money", others deem it too "expensive" for such "ordinary" eats.

Karoo Kafe *S African* 　　▽ 24 | 18 | 19 | $18

Provincetown | 338 Commercial St. (Center St.) | 508-487-6630 | www.karookafe.com

Ready to try "wild boar sausage, ostrich burgers or snail rangoon"? – then slide into this eatery where the "different-for-the-area" South African fare is "well prepared" and "inexpensive", the latter another "rarity in P-town"; adventurers say the "small indoor/outdoor" digs' bold colors and art lend it an exotic feel, and the "friendly" staff helps to render it "always a good choice", particularly for "quick", "casual lunches."

Kate's Seafood Ⓢ Ⓜ *Seafood* 　　▽ 20 | 9 | 16 | $19

Brewster | 285 Paines Creek Rd. (bet. Lower Rd. & Main St./Rte. 6A) | 508-896-9517

"The sign saying 'fried seafood, ice cream' tells all you need to know" about this inexpensive "roadside clam shack" in Brewster, which dispenses its "great" 'n' "greasy" goods (featuring "iconic onion blossoms") via "window service" to "families" at "picnic tables"; some sweet-toothed surveyors "only go" for the "many flavors" of cold cones, which they take "to the beach at Paine's Creek to watch the sunset."

	FOOD	DECOR	SERVICE	COST

La Cucina Sul Mare *Italian*

25 | 18 | 22 | $40

Falmouth | 237 Main St. (Walker St.) | 508-548-5600 |
www.lacucinasulmare.com

"Roll up your sleeves" before digging into the "huge portions" of
"traditional Italian" fare "beautifully prepared" at this year-round
Falmouth "jewel" where a "husband-and-wife team (he's in the
kitchen)" directs a "strong staff"; the "small" interior and "great patio" get quite "crowded", leading to "long waits on summer weekends", but if you can "be patient", perhaps with "a drink at the bar",
"you won't be let down."

L'Alouette *French*

26 | 20 | 25 | $49

Harwich Port | 787 Main St./Rte. 28 (Julien Rd.) | 508-430-0405 |
www.lalouettebistro.com

"Don't expect to diet" at this year-round Harwich Port "gem", as its
"superb French" fare is classically "rich – but worth the calorie
splurge" (and the "Cape prices"); excitement-seekers are "put off"
by the "standard white-tablecloth" decor ("designed for an older
crowd" *peut-être?*), but even they appreciate that the "tables are not
on top of each other", the "lovely service" and "top-notch wine list."

Landfall *Seafood*

18 | 21 | 19 | $36

Woods Hole | 2 Luscombe Ave. (Water St.) | 508-548-1758 |
www.woodshole.com/landfall

"Watching the Martha's Vineyard ferries" while dining on "simply
grilled" (some say "predictable") seafood has been a "family tradition" since 1946 at this "lively" Woods Hole seafood "standby" with
a somewhat "kitschy" "nautical"-themed dining room, a dock and a
deck "overlooking the harbor"; but tipplers who only come to "relax
with a beer" think it's now "better known for its bar scene."

Laura & Tony's Kitchen *American*

- | - | - | I

North Eastham | Blue Dolphin Inn | 5950 Rte. 6 (Nauset Rd.) |
508-240-6096 | www.lauraandtonyskitchen.com

North Easthamers "really can't beat" the "all-you-can-eat" breakfasts
laid out at this funky, "relaxing" American, "especially at the price":
under $10; the "gracious owners" also operate a catering service.

Laureen's *American*

∇ 23 | 19 | 19 | $29

Falmouth | 170 Main St. (Townhall Sq.) | 508-540-9104 |
www.laureensfalmouth.com

"Falmouth's version of a chick flick" could be filmed at this "charming,
bistro-style" cafe with an airy, arty atmosphere and an "interesting"
New American menu that stars "wonderful" pastries for breakfast,
"gourmet sandwiches" for lunch and "creative" fare for dinner;
"friendly service" lets diners relax in the "quaint" room or "people-
watch" from the "cute outdoor tables."

Liam's at Nauset Beach *Seafood*

20 | 9 | 13 | $19

East Orleans | 239 Beach Rd. (Surf Path) | 508-255-3474

"Onion ring heaven" ("possibly the best" ever) can be found at this
"ramshackle shed" on an East Orleans sand dune, also serving "fried

fish and ice cream" that can be taken to "funky" "picnic tables" or back to your blanket; critics carp about paying relatively "costly" tabs and "waiting in long lines for ordinary takeout", but "when you're at Nauset Beach, there's no better place – in fact, there's no other place."

Lobster Pot *Eclectic/Seafood*   22 | 17 | 20 | $38

Provincetown | 321 Commercial St. (Standish St.) | 508-487-0842 | www.ptownlobsterpot.com

The "slightly downtrodden exterior" (look for the "neon sign") "be-lies" the "delicious lobsters" that "just come so easily out of their shells", plus Eclectic "takes on traditional seafood dishes" (all only "slightly above market prices") at this P-town "tourist landmark"; the bi-level space is a real "madhouse in summer", so "prepare to wait", hope to "get a window" for "amazing views" and "pray for nice people to be seated around you", as "they will be really close."

Lorraine's *Mexican*   ▽ 20 | 16 | 15 | $38

Provincetown | 133 Commercial St. (Pleasant St.) | 508-487-6074 | www.lorrainesrestaurant.vpweb.com

Everyone agrees this "small, dark, no-frills" Provincetown Mexican set in a teak-and-mahogany edifice boasts an "amazing tequila se-lection", from which "margaritas that don't skimp" are made; while surveyors split on the suppers ("superb" vs. "lacking distinct fla-vors") and service ("friendly" vs. "dreadful"), they concur once more about the question of reservations: make them or risk an "interminable wait."

NEW Lyric *American*   - | - | - | E

Yarmouth Port | 43 Main St./Rte. 6A (Willow St.) | 774-330-0000 | www.lyriccapecod.com

Housed in the quaint yellow Cape that was at one time Abbicci, this Yarmouth Port New American has kept the former tenant's gorgeous, cottage-gone-contemporary upgrades, including sleek accoutrements and a stone floor in the intimate bar area and romantic, modern lighting in the quartet of dining rooms; the somewhat pricey menu highlights local, seasonal ingredients and seafood, and for harmonious accompaniment, there's an interesting wine list.

Mac's Seafood Market & Grill *Seafood*   24 | 15 | 17 | $30

Wellfleet | 265 Commercial St. (Kendrick Ave.) | 508-349-0404

Mac's Shack *Seafood*

Wellfleet | 91 Commercial St. (Railroad Ave.) | 508-349-6333 www.macsseafood.com

Proof that "you can't judge a book by it's cover", these "plain" Wellfleet fisheries "expertly prepare" "just-out-of-the-ocean" seafood ("not all fried!") and "generous ice cream scoops", plus "unusual selections" like "wonderful sushi" and burritos; at the beachside grill, "you stand in line, order, they call your number and you eat at picnic ta-bles in the sand" (ideally during an "astounding sunset"), while the roadside-shack sibling offers interior dining as well as a patio.

	FOOD	DECOR	SERVICE	COST

Marshside, The *Seafood*

| | 15 | 25 | 17 | $33 |

Dennis | 28 Bridge St. (bet. Rte. 6A & Rte. 134) | 508-385-4010 |
www.themarshside.com

"Bright, cheerful", "spacious" and "spectacular" are some of the accolades raining down on this longtime seafood purveyor's "great new building", which still boasts "gorgeous views" of the East Dennis marsh; now, patrons suggest, "rebuild the menu" of "nondescript" fare (it's "rather pricey" too), train the "inexperienced" members of the staff and "take reservations" (as it stands, you can "expect long waits at the bar or on the porch outside").

NEW Messina *Italian*

| | - | - | - | M |

Eastham | 4100 State Hwy. (Rte. 6) | 508-247-0360 |
www.messinaofeastham.com

Yellow and cream walls and glass-topped tables impart a light, airy feel to this Eastham Italian newcomer, while the glow of votives and black-and-white photos of the owner's Sicilian ancestors provide atmosphere; a mix of couples, families and groups can usually be found digging into the classic fare, which, like the wine selection, is affordably priced.

Mews *American*

| | 27 | 25 | 25 | $54 |

Provincetown | 429 Commercial St. (Lovetts Ct.) | 508-487-1500 |
www.mews.com

"Life doesn't get any better" than at this year-rounder in P-town's East End, where "upbeat", "refined" staffers make "right-on recommendations" about the "divine" New American fare (the "chef does wonderful things with fresh, local ingredients"); the "more elegant", "romantic" downstairs dining room boasts "million-dollar views" of the bay, while the "lively" upstairs cafe is a place to enjoy "cheaper choices" and an "out-of-this-world vodka selection" with "a group of friends"; P.S. "make reservations way in advance."

Misaki ☒ *Japanese*

| | ▽ 24 | 14 | 16 | $31 |

Hyannis | 379 W. Main St. (Pitchers Way) | 508-771-3771 |
www.misakisushi.com

"While it doesn't look like much", this Japanese in Hyannis employs "skilled sushi chefs" whose "top-notch" creations exhibit pure "artistry", and at "reasonable prices" no less; though complaints about "off-putting" staffers abound, there are reports that the relatively new owners have introduced "friendlier", more "efficient" service.

Moby Dick's *New England/Seafood*

| | 23 | 14 | 17 | $27 |

Wellfleet | 3225 Rte. 6 (Gull Pond Rd.) | 508-349-9795 |
www.mobydicksrestaurant.com

It "looks like a tourist trap", but this "high-quality", "nautical"-themed Wellfleet "institution" turns out "gigantic portions" of "all the usual" seafood suspects at "moderate prices" (BYO makes it even "easier on the wallet"); the lines that lead to its "odd but effective hybrid" of counter and (picnic) table service are "beyond ridiculous", but it's "worth every minute" – and "you'll think about it all winter."

Naked Oyster Bistro & Raw Bar *Seafood* 25 | 19 | 22 | $47
Hyannis | 20 Independence Dr. (Rte. 132) | 508-778-6500 |
www.nakedoyster.com
"If you're looking for 'typical Cape', go someplace else", since this
"upscale" Hyannis "gem" maintains a "happening", "modern setting" (mahogany accents, handcrafted, shell-shaped light fixtures)
to present its "sophisticated menu" of "exquisite" seafood, which is
"served up by a courteous staff"; "don't expect bargains", but do
count on "a wait in season" if you didn't "call for reservations" first.

Napi's *Eclectic* 19 | 20 | 18 | $38
Provincetown | 7 Freeman St. (Bradford St.) | 508-487-1145 |
www.napis-restaurant.com
This "funky institution on a backstreet in Provincetown" is "where
locals go off-season" to get a little bit of "everything, from Greek to
Italian to Brazilian" ("great vegetarian choices" and "Portuguese
specialties" too); "matching" the Eclectic menu is the "quirky", art-
strewn decor – it may be "over the top", but it's got real "character";
P.S. there's "free parking", "no small benefit" in these parts.

Nauset Beach Club *Italian* 25 | 21 | 22 | $52
East Orleans | 222 Main St. (Beach Rd.) | 508-255-8547 |
www.nausetbeachclub.com
A "temple to Northern Italian cooking", this "high-end" East Orleans
year-rounder offers an "exciting menu" "prepared with imagination
and flair", complemented by an "extensive wine list" and presented by
"sincere, gracious" staffers; though its evokes its name with "earth
tones" and wicker (it's "not a beach club"), some feel the setting's
"marred by being noisy", "dark" and "cramped" – but they're in the
minority, as most attest to "top-notch experiences" all around.

Z Not Your Average Joe's *American* 18 | 16 | 18 | $26
Hyannis | Cape Cod Mall | 793 Iyannough Rd. (Airport Rd.) |
508-778-1424 | www.notyouraveragejoes.com
See review in Boston Directory.

Ocean House **M** *American* 25 | 25 | 24 | $48
Dennisport | 425 Old Wharf Rd. (Depot St.) | 508-394-0700 |
www.oceanhouserestaurant.com
"Artfully prepared" New American cuisine with a "heavy Pan-Asian influence" served by a "professional, friendly" staff "always matches
and usually exceeds" the "picture-perfect postcard view" of Nantucket
Sound at this Dennisport "gem"; "even if you only go for appetizers"
and "fantastic drinks" at the "happening bar", "it's worth the visit" –
just try to arrive before sunset, "bring someone you want to impress"
(and plenty of cash) and "program the GPS so you don't get lost."

Optimist Café, The *American/British* ∇ 21 | 21 | 22 | $22
Yarmouth Port | 134 Rte. 6A (Willow St.) | 508-362-1024 |
www.optimistcafe.com
"What a delightful spot!" – this inexpensive American-British cafe
set in an 1849 captain's residence in Yarmouth Port "lives up to its

CAPE COD

FOOD DECOR SERVICE COST

name" with gingerbread trim outside, "funky"/cheery interiors featuring works by local artists and "fun service"; "tasty" lunches and
high teas offer a "nice break from typical Cape fare", while "little
girls" swoon over "wonderful breakfast" fare like heart-shaped waffles.

Orleans Inn *American*

17 | 17 | 19 | $38

Orleans | Orleans Inn | 21 Rte. 6A (Orleans Rotary) | 508-255-2222 |
www.orleansinn.com

When dining at this renovated Victorian–cum–American inn eatery,
the "porch in summer", with its "nice view of Orleans Town Cove",
is "the place to be" (the interior's a bit "fuddy-duddy"); the eats are
"pedestrian", but they're not too highly priced, so one "can see why
families like it."

Osteria La Civetta *Italian*

- | - | - | M

Falmouth | 133 Main St. (Post Office Rd.) | 508-540-1616 |
www.osterialacivetta.com

From the "rustic" setting to the "woman from Bologna" who owns it
to the "handmade pastas" and other "simple, exquisite" Northern
Italian dishes, this year-round, recently expanded Falmouth storefront "feels and tastes authentic"; the portions are "not big" and
prices run at a "slight premium", but it's "worth visiting" – and bringing
home some imported meats and cheeses from the retail section too.

Oyster Company Raw Bar & Grill *Seafood*

23 | 17 | 21 | $35

Dennisport | 202 Depot St. (Rte. 28) | 508-398-4600 |
www.theoystercompany.com

"As one would expect from the name", the "raw bar is exceptional"
("the owners farm their own Quivet Neck oysters") at this "Cape
Cod-casual", year-round Dennisport "gem", while the rest of the
seafood menu is "creatively prepared" and "scrumptious", as are
other items "for the burgers-and-beer crowd"; it's a "tourist favorite", but factor in "neighborly" service and "reasonable prices", and
it's "clear" to see why "locals like it too."

Paddock *American*

20 | 19 | 20 | $40

Hyannis | West End Rotary | 20 Scudder Ave. (Main St.) |
508-775-7677 | www.paddockcapecod.com

"Pleasant" and "reliable", this "family-run" Hyannis haunt serves
"tasty", slightly "pricey" New American fare in "several different"
"old-world" "fine-dining" rooms (young 'uns peg them as "time
warps"); its convenient location next to the Melody Tent makes it a
"great stop before or after a concert", and while service might be a
little "slow" at peak times, the "experienced" staff works to make
"you feel like a VIP at all times."

Pain D'Avignon *Bakery/French*

- | - | - | M

Hyannis | 15 Hinckley Rd. (Iyannough Rd.) | 508-778-8588 |
www.paindavignon.com

Step into this black-and-white Hyannis bakery and be transported to
a Parisian patisserie overflowing with croissants, tarts, cakes,
breads and other temptations, as well as soups, sandwiches and salads; within the space resides Café Boulangerie, a full-service eatery

offering moderate-to-pricey French bistro fare, beer and wine inside and, weather permitting, out.

☑ Pisces *Mediterranean/Seafood* | 27 | 19 | 23 | $51 |

Chatham | 2653 Main St. (Forest Beach Rd.) | 508-432-4600 | www.piscesofchatham.com

"Just-caught seafood" with "imaginative", "flavorful" Mediterranean preparations is ferried by "friendly, knowledgeable" servers at this "charming" Chatham "diamond"; the "intimate" "beach-chic", artwork-festooned setting gets "loud" and "crowded" (it "definitely requires reservations") and "prices are high", but for diehards, "weekends on the Cape aren't great" without an evening here.

Port, The *American/Seafood* | 23 | 23 | 21 | $40 |

Harwich Port | 541 Main St./Rte. 28 (Sea St.) | 508-430-5410 | www.theportrestaurant.com

Though a "first-class" raw bar and "creative", "sparkling" New American seafood are draws at this "modern, trendy restaurant in traditional Harwich Port", the "young crowd" may be even more attracted to the "buzzy", "big-city" scene, not to mention the "attractive", "efficient" staffers (even when some toss "a bit of 'tude").

Post Office Café *American* | 16 | 12 | 14 | $27 |

Provincetown | 303 Commercial St. (Standish St.) | 508-487-3892

The "ordinary" American "diner fare" at this "bland" box is "priced at the lower end" for P-town, but it's "nothing to write home about"; "all dishes" are delivered "with a side of staff attitude" (sometimes it's flat-out "disdainful"), but that and the "crowded, loud" and "chaotic" atmosphere are "just part of the experience."

Red Inn *New England* | 24 | 26 | 23 | $60 |

Provincetown | Red Inn | 15 Commercial St. (W. Vine St.) | 508-487-7334 | www.theredinn.com

"Enter through a delightful garden", start off with a "huge, delicious cocktail" "on the deck" while "looking out at the bay at sunset" ("breathtaking"), then settle in for "expertly prepared" (and "expensive") New England fare featuring "wonderful" local fish at this "class act" in an "incredible old hotel" nearly "on the tip of Provincetown"; "knowledgeable", "hospitable" service furthers its deserved reputation as a "sublime", "romantic getaway."

☑ Red Pheasant *American/French* | 27 | 24 | 25 | $53 |

Dennis | 905 Main St./Rte. 6A (Elm St.) | 508-385-2133 | www.redpheasantinn.com

Whether in summer when the "luscious gardens" "bloom" or "in the dead of winter" "when the big fireplace is roaring", this "lovely antique" barn in Dennis provides a "special", "formal" setting for "gourmet" New American cuisine that "emphasizes seasonal" ingredients ("high-end seafood", "exceptionally prepared game") and "complex" French twists; "pleasant, efficient" staffers and an "incredible wine list" are two more reasons why enthusiasts save up their dough to "go back over and over again."

	FOOD	DECOR	SERVICE	COST

Regatta of Cotuit
at the Crocker House *American*

| 25 | 23 | 24 | $57 |

Cotuit | 4631 Falmouth Rd./Rte. 28 (Rte. 130) | 508-428-5715 |
www.regattarestaurant.com

"Anyone who considers themselves a foodie will have an enjoyable evening" at this historic Federal mansion in Cotuit, as the New American fare is "interesting" and wholly "memorable" (those who query some of the more "oddball combinations" depend on the "impeccable" servers – they really "know the menu"); "special-occasion" celebrators and "couples" laud it too, especially the seven "serene", "cozy" dining rooms.

Roadhouse Cafe *Seafood/Steak*

| 20 | 19 | 19 | $43 |

Hyannis | 488 South St. (Sea St.) | 508-775-2386 |
www.roadhousecafe.com

"Escape" from "busy Hyannis" to this "convivial" year-round hangout offering "lots of choices in terms of both" environments – which include "somewhat upscale" dining rooms, a "lighter-fare" bistro and a bar, all featuring wood paneling and nautical antiques – and "terrific" seafood and steaks served in "nice portions"; jazz on Mondays, a pianist on weekends and valet parking are "added bonuses."

Roobar *American*

| 21 | 20 | 21 | $37 |

Falmouth | 285 Main St. (Cahoon Ct.) | 508-548-8600 |
www.theroobar.com

"Trendy comes to Cape Cod" in the form of this "terribly chic, hopelessly noisy" Falmouth "crowd-pleaser" with a New American menu that offers "something to tickle anyone's taste" – and with everything from "$12 pizzas to $25 entrees", every budget to boot; expect "hopping bars" too; N.B. the separately owned Plymouth location exhibits a slightly more upscale feel.

Ross' Grill *American*

| 22 | 22 | 21 | $44 |

Provincetown | 237 Commercial St. (bet. Gosnold St. & Masonic Pl.) |
508-487-8878 | www.rossgrillptown.com

"Comfortably chic" environs with "gorgeous views" of Provincetown Harbor create a "memorable" setting for "smart", "reliable" New American fare paired with "terrific" *vins* at this only "slightly higher priced" eatery/wine bar; repeat customers cheer the mostly "friendly" service and the fact that it "takes reservations" – "a major plus for a place with an inevitable line and so few tables."

Scargo Café *American*

| 20 | 18 | 21 | $35 |

Dennis | 799 Main St./Rte. 6A (bet. Corporation Rd. & Hope Ln.) |
508-385-8200 | www.scargocafe.com

"Catch dinner before the theater" or yuck it up with the "locals" over "a nightcap afterward" at this year-rounder "across from the Cape Playhouse" in Dennis serving "solid", "reasonably priced" ("albeit not particularly inventive") New American vittles; the "comfortable", woody space (dating from 1865) is "well run" by two brothers who ensure the staff provides a "friendly" greeting upon arrival, "a kind thank you when leaving" and "attentive" service in between.

	FOOD	DECOR	SERVICE	COST

Siena *Italian*
21 | 20 | 19 | $38

Mashpee | Mashpee Commons | 38 Nathan Ellis Hwy. (Rte. 28) | 508-477-5929 | www.siena.us

Sating both the "spaghetti-and-meatballs crowd" and osso buco-cravers is never easy, but this "big, noisy" Mashpee Commons Italian "deserves an A for effort": "if you want something, it's somewhere on the menu", and brought in "huge portions" for moderate prices; indeed, "just about everyone" leaves "satisfied" – unless they're trying to catch a movie next door and they're stuck with a "spotty" server.

Sir Cricket's Fish & Chips 🥡 *Seafood*
24 | 8 | 19 | $18

Orleans | 38 Rt. 6A (Orleans Rd.) | 508-255-4453

There's "nothing fancy" at this "busy" Orleans spot – just "fabulous" "English-style fish 'n' chips" and other inexpensive, "excellent seafood from the store next door"; there's also "not much in terms of seating" (what there is resembles a "high-school cafeteria"), so get it to go.

Stir Crazy Ⓜ *Cambodian*
23 | 16 | 20 | $28

Pocasset | 570 MacArthur Blvd., Rte. 28 (Portside Dr.) | 508-564-6464 | www.stircrazyrestaurant.com

"Gifted" chef-owner Bopha Samms serves up a "welcome change" – namely "delectable", "affordable" Cambodian cuisine with "fresh ingredients" and a "local twist" – just as she has for the past 20 years at her place in Pocasset; "generous but not overwhelming portions" are brought by "friendly" staffers in the pleasant digs.

Terra Luna *American*
24 | 18 | 20 | $46

North Truro | 104 Shore Rd. (Windigo Ln.) | 508-487-1019 | www.theterraluna.com

This "noteworthy" North Truro New American "feels like a neighborhood" "standard" thanks to a "casual", "rustic", "low-key setting" (the former site of a stagecoach stop) and an "interesting" "combo of seasonal specials and reliable" classics; it's "quite popular", so be sure to ask the "friendly" staffers for "a table with elbow room."

Trevi Café & Wine Bar *Mediterranean*
- | - | - | M

Mashpee | Mashpee Commons | 25 Market St. (Fountain St.) | 508-477-0055 | www.trevicafe.com

From the fountain at the front entrance to the awning-topped patio, this Mashpee venue exhibits European flair that extends to its mid-priced Mediterranean menu of tapas, pastas, panini and more; with hardwood floors and candlelight, the casual dining room is a romantic escape, while the granite bar is a place to get lost in television.

🛡 Twenty-Eight Atlantic *American*
26 | 29 | 25 | $65

Chatham | Wequassett Resort and Golf Club | 2173 Orleans Rd./Rte. 28 (Pleasant Bay Rd.) | 508-430-3000 | www.wequassett.com

You "must see" the "beautiful" decor and "phenomenal" view of Pleasant Bay at this all-day dining room in a "fancy" Chatham resort, but you also have to sample the New American cuisine, which often travels "beyond creative and delicious", all the way to "rapturous"; with "top-notch service" added to the mix, it's unsurprisingly "over-the-top expensive", but if you come "knowing what you're getting into", you'll "leave feeling elated."

Vining's Bistro *Eclectic*
▽ 24 | 17 | 24 | $44

Chatham | Gallery Bldg. | 595 Main St. (Seaview St.) | 508-945-5033 | www.viningsbistro.net

Though "hard-to-find", it's worth seeking out this second-floor bistro "overlooking Main Street" in Chatham, where the "casual" setting's as "understated" as the "sophisticated" Eclectic "menu offering a wealth of perfectly [wood-] grilled meats and seafood" is "adventurous"; the "friendly" staff also has an "excellent wine selection" on hand, adding to experiences that "never disappoint."

Whitman House Restaurant, The *American*
▽ 21 | 23 | 21 | $36

Truro | 7 Great Hollow Rd. (Rte. 6) | 508-487-1740 | www.whitmanhouse.com

"Take your favorite aunt" for a "fantastic" meal at this "classy", "cozy" American set in an 1894 inn on four acres of landscaped grounds in Truro; run by the same family for almost five decades, the delightfully "old-fashioned" setting includes four Early American dining rooms as well as the more casual Bass Tavern.

Wicked Oyster *American/Seafood*
24 | 19 | 22 | $43

Wellfleet | 50 Main St. (Rte. 6) | 508-349-3455 | www.thewickedo.com

"If it swims around the Cape, it's likely on the menu" at this "lively" New American in a "charming" early-1700s Wellfleet home providing "prompt service" and "dazzlingly prepared", "deliciously wonderful" seafood-centric breakfasts, lunches and dinners (they're "great bangs for the buck" too); the "casual", "charming" room is "large", but so popular, "reservations are absolutely necessary in season."

Wild Goose Tavern *American*
▽ 21 | 21 | 21 | $35

Chatham | Chatham Wayside Inn | 512 Main St. (bet. Chatham Bars Ave. & Library Ln.) | 508-945-5590 | www.wildgoosetavern.com

A "great menu variety", featuring plenty of "pub-style" American fare, and "chipper service" draw "families" to this Chatham tavern, which pleasantly surprises moms and dads "expecting a hard hit to the wallet" with moderate prices; the "spacious" dining room "can be noisy" (good for when you want to "talk without being overheard"), while the bar is a "fun place" "to meet locals."

Winslow's Tavern *American*
20 | 21 | 18 | $38

Wellfleet | 316 Main St. (bet. Bank St. & Holbrook Ave.) | 508-349-6450 | www.winslowstavern.com

Wellfleet families find the "wonderful" New American fare, "affordable prices" and mostly "friendly service" "more than enough to warrant a return trip" to this "great old building", while oenophiles toast the "unique wine list", which they explore over "more casual meals" at the "upstairs bar"; "tables by the window overlooking the patio" are prized in the "white-all-over" main room, but "eating outside" may be best, since the "noise level" inside is "unbelievable."

Martha's Vineyard

TOP FOOD		TOP DECOR	
27	Détente	American	26	Outermost Inn	American
	Larsen's Fish Mkt.	Seafood		Lambert's Cove	American
26	Bite	Seafood		L'Étoile	French
	L'Étoile	French		Beach Plum	American
25	Atria	American	25	Atria	American

Alchemy American
22 | 23 | 20 | $49

Edgartown | 71 Main St. (bet. School & Summer Sts.) | 508-627-9999
"Cosmopolitan ambiance" materializes at this "expensive" New American where "trendy pretty people" come "to be seen" in the "handsome" lounge upstairs (the milieu of "value bar snacks") and "lively bistro" downstairs, which features outdoor seating "overlooking the always interesting Edgartown streetscape"; the "solid, tasty" dishes and "great wines" keep it a "perennial favorite" for locals, except in January, when it's closed.

Art Cliff Diner Diner
24 | 17 | 21 | $18

Vineyard Haven | 39 Beach Rd. (Five Corners) | 508-693-1224
Some "island secret" – "impossibly long waits" prove the "dreamy crêpes", waffles and omelets are all-too-common knowledge at this "kitschy" "longtime tradition"; so drag yourself to Vineyard Haven "at the crack of dawn" and "bring the paper" and a "bottle of champagne for mimosas", because "a trip to the Vineyard is not complete without breakfast" here; P.S. lunches are equally "fabulous" – and popular.

Atlantic Fish & Chop House Seafood/Steak
- | - | - | M

Edgartown | 2 Main St. (Water St.) | 508-627-7001 | www.atlanticmv.com
"Young" cooks "turn out some fine fare" at this casual Edgartonian, which focuses on steaks and midpriced seafood; owned by the same folks as the exclusive Boathouse Club upstairs, the space feels like an upscale watering hole with white wainscoting and a marble bar, while exhibiting TV sports and harbor views.

Atria American
25 | 25 | 24 | $60

Edgartown | 137 Main St. (bet. Green & Pine Sts.) | 508-627-5850 | www.atriamv.com
"Clever combinations result in truly delicious dishes" at this "refreshingly different" Edgartown New American committed to "local, organic" ingredients, "impeccable service" and "expensive" tabs; a "Hollywood crowd" likes to be seen in the "exquisite", "sophisticated dining room", "romantic" types choose the "elegant", "candle-filled garden", while a nightcap in the "chic yet casual" cellar lounge is "highly recommended" to all.

Beach Plum Inn American
25 | 26 | 26 | $61

Menemsha | Beach Plum Inn | 50 Beach Plum Ln. (North Rd.) | 508-645-9454 | www.beachpluminn.com
"Timed right, you'll see a beautiful sunset while eating expertly prepared", "inspired" New American cuisine plated like "mini architec-

tural wonders" at this "secluded, serene" and "romantic retreat" with "gorgeous views" of Menemsha Harbor; "impeccable service" bolsters the feeling that you've been "invited to an elite dinner party" – although this one ends with a "pricey" bill (it's "worth it"); N.B. BYOB.

Bite, The ⊉ *Seafood*

26 | 11 | 17 | $20

Menemsha | 29 Basin Rd. (North Rd.) | 508-645-9239 | www.thebitemenemsha.com

"It's fried seafood nirvana" at this cash-only take-out "shack with picnic tables crammed by the roadside" in Menemsha; though the "prices clearly reflect its status as a landmark", that doesn't stop clam-diggers from joining the "long lines" ("nothing to be intimidated by"), then taking the short walk to the beach for a "beautiful" "sunset picnic."

☒ Black Dog Tavern *American*

19 | 18 | 18 | $33

Vineyard Haven | 20 Beach St. Ext. (Water St.) | 508-693-9223 | www.theblackdog.com

"Crowds still line up" for "great breakfasts" and "worthy lunches" at this "casual" American "icon" "overlooking the gorgeous harbor" in Vineyard Haven; some say that "dinner is good too", just as many counter it's "unexciting", but either way, it's "not overly expensive", "fine for kids" and "you can advertise that you've eaten here" with "all manner of clothing and accessories with its ubiquitous" logo; N.B. BYOB.

NEW Blue Canoe *Seafood*

- | - | - | M

Vineyard Haven | 52 Beach Rd. (Lagoon Pond Rd.) | 508-693-3332 | www.bluecanoegrill.com

The antique canoe outside this seasonal waterfront cafe is a beacon for yachters to dock and Vineyard Havenites to park for fresh, local seafood accompanied by pleasant harbor views; the classy interior sports tables handcrafted by a local artist plus a small, dark-wood dining bar, and BYOB helps to keep it affordable.

Chesca's *Eclectic/Italian*

23 | 22 | 23 | $52

Edgartown | 38 N. Water St. (Winter St.) | 508-627-1234 | www.chescasmv.com

Edgartonians find it "hard to choose" from the selection of "well-prepared", "delicious" Italian-inspired Eclectic fare proffered at this "noisy" yet "fun night out", and though it's pricey, they deem it "reasonable for the quality and location"; "no reservations" for parties under six mean there's "always a wait", but it's easily dealt with by "sitting on the porch" with an "inventive cocktail" and "watching the crowds go by."

NEW Chilmark Tavern Ⓜ *American*

- | - | - | M

Chilmark | 9 State Rd. (bet. Lagemann Ln. & South Rd.) | 508-645-9400 | www.chilmarktavern.com

Simplicity, seasonality and innovation reign at this New American at Beetlebung Corner on Martha's Vineyard, which offers locally sourced, midpriced fare in a casual setting with an open kitchen,

FOOD DECOR SERVICE COST

hardwood floors, skylights and Alfred Eisenstaedt photos; N.B. Chilmark is a dry town, but the restaurant stocks plenty of fresh juices for DIY mixology.

Cottage City Tavern *American* (fka Park Corner Bistro)

▽ 22 | 20 | 20 | $47

Oak Bluffs | 20H Kennebec Ave. (Circuit Ave.) | 508-696-9922 | www.parkcornerbistro.com

Post-survey, this American "on a busy corner in Oak Bluffs" was re-conceived: the name was changed, the space was renovated, the bar (from where "great cocktails" come) was enlarged and the higher-priced entrees were jettisoned; indeed, the Food and Decor scores are most likely out of date (the Cost estimate too), but hopefully the "sweet and attentive" staff and "terrific brunch" have stayed put.

NEW Danny Quinn's Pub *American*

- | - | - | M

Oak Bluffs | 9 Oak Bluffs Ave. (Circuit Ave. Ext.) | 508-338-4760 | www.dannyquinns.com

If Irish-American folk singer Danny Quinn isn't on stage at his name-sake pub in Oak Bluffs, there's another act livening up the place, which exudes a warm locals' vibe with a wooden bar, dim lighting and carpeted dining room (it helps with the acoustics); the mid-priced American menu is orchestrated by a chef who cooked at The Modern in NYC.

David Ryan's *American*

15 | 16 | 16 | $36

Edgartown | 11 N. Water St. (Main St.) | 508-627-4100 | www.davidryans.com

"Edgartown singles" advise "stick to the cocktails" and microbrews at this bi-level "prototypical tourist trap", because it's "much better for nightlife" than dining; that said, when you're "walking around town and in need of a comfortable" meal, the location is "convenient", while the American fare is "acceptable" and moderately priced.

Z Détente *American*

27 | 22 | 24 | $69

Edgartown | 3 Nevin Sq. | Winter St. (Water St.) | 508-627-8810 | www.detentemv.com

It may just be wishful thinking when some surveyors opine that "not everyone knows about" this "terrific", "tucked away" Edgartonian, since you need to "make a reservation early" if you want to experience chef Kevin Crowell's "adventurous", "awesome" New American creations and his wife Suzanna's "charming" hostessing skills; "service is helpful without being obsequious", so whether you eat in the "pleasant" interior or the "small", "beautiful garden", you can expect a "lovely meal" – and a "pricey" check; N.B. an expansion/renovation is scheduled to be completed in time for summer 2010.

Home Port *New England/Seafood*

20 | 17 | 18 | $47

Menemsha | 512 North Rd. (Basin Rd.) | 508-645-2679 | www.homeportmv.com

"Thank God" this 80-year-old BYO seafood "legend" in Menemsha was "spared" from closing, and the folks who bought it in early 2009 kept it "chugging along" with the same "simply prepared", "fresh seafood" (it costs "a lot of money", "but at least the portions are large"); there's a "cramped, loud" dining room, but there's also "fabulous takeout" to "eat on picnic tables" or, better still, bring to the beach for a "beautiful sunset" meal.

NEW Il Tesoro at the Terrace 🗷 🅼 Italian — | — | — | M

Edgartown | The Charlotte Inn | 27 S. Summer St. (Main St.) | 508-939-3840 | www.iltesoro.net

Tucked inside the Charlotte Inn in Edgartown, this refined Italian offers three different dining areas – an intimate room with European-style decor and a fireplace, an atriumlike space flush with plants and skylights, and an outdoor terrace; fortunately, the tab for all that fine-dining elegance isn't as high as it could be.

Jimmy Seas Pan Pasta Italian 23 | 13 | 19 | $34

Oak Bluffs | 38 Kennebec Ave. (Post Office Sq.) | 508-696-8550

"They roast garlic like nobody's business" at this Oak Bluffs Italian, so "follow your nose" and "bring a hearty appetite" for "hot, steamy pans" of "fantastic pasta" and "fabulous seafood" served in portions "mammoth" "enough to feed a small army" (expect a surcharge if you "plan to split"); just "get there early" or be prepared for an "awful wait" to be "scrunched" into the "tiny", "noisy" space.

Lambert's Cove Inn American 25 | 26 | 25 | $60

West Tisbury | Lambert's Cove Inn | 90 Manaquayak Rd. (Lambert's Cove Rd.) | 508-693-2298 | www.lambertscoveinn.com

Check into this "lovely", "British-y" dining room in a "charming country inn" "nestled" in West Tisbury, a "romantic" place where "you can have a private conversation" while savoring views of a "slice-of-heaven" garden and "superb" American cuisine made with "excellent ingredients" and "presented in delicate, unique ways"; "impeccable" servers do their part to create the "terrific evening", which is expectedly "expensive", even though you have to "bring your own alcohol."

Larsen's Fish Market Seafood 27 | 10 | 20 | $23

Menemsha | 56 Basin Rd. (North Rd.) | 508-645-2680

"Basically a take-out place within a fish market", this Menemsha counter doles out "cardboard plates of oysters, shucked in front of your eyes", "luscious lobster rolls", "freshly steamed steamers" and other "amazingly fresh", "simple" seafood "right off the boat"; it's "all to be eaten outside" on "wooden crates" or at "the beach watching the sunset" – an "unforgettable meal", and a "reasonable" one at that.

Lattanzi's Italian 21 | 17 | 20 | $48

Edgartown | Old Post Office Sq. (bet. Main & Winter Sts.) | 508-627-8854 | www.lattanzis.com

Go for the "cozy, elegant" "fine-dining option" or the casual "pizza division" with a "nice patio" at this "delightful" Edgartown *duetto* where "innovative" Tuscan touches abound in "great" thin-crust,

	FOOD	DECOR	SERVICE	COST

brick-oven pies, pastas and other "Italian comfort foods", all "solid values" "for the island"; whichever side you choose, the "friendly" staff "cares to have you as a guest."

Le Grenier French

| 23 | 16 | 23 | $51 |

Vineyard Haven | 92 Main St. (bet. Church St. & Colonial Ln.) | 508-693-4906 | www.legrenierrestaurant.com

"As old as the money that makes it successful", this Vineyard Haven BYO with an "awkward" location "up a long flight of stairs" and a rustic setting with exposed beams "perfectly executes" "classical French cuisine", which is brought to table by "positively delightful" staffers; the "stagnant menu" "may run against the tide of modernity", but the "core group of stalwarts" that frequents it declares "it's awfully nice to have the choice available."

L'Étoile French

| 26 | 26 | 23 | $73 |

Edgartown | 22 N. Water St. (Winter St.) | 508-627-5187 | www.letoile.net

"Save up for a special occasion" (like "popping the question"), then make a reservation for this New French "delight" in Edgartown delivering "wonderful everything": "exceptional" cuisine, wines and surroundings, which include a "relaxing bar" with a "lighter menu"; in addition, already "efficient" servers "go the extra mile for you", ensuring a wholly "lovely evening."

Lure American

| ▽ 21 | 21 | 22 | $68 |

Edgartown | Winnetu Oceanside Resort | 31 Dunes Rd. (Katama Rd.) | 508-627-3663 | www.luremv.com

"If weather permits", take the "delightful" complimentary water taxi from Edgartown to this "cavernous" New American at the Winnetu Oceanside Resort for a "grown-up" New American meal in the "civilized dining room" or on the patio; "if you can't find a sitter", you'll be relegated to a separate space, the milieu of toys and "chicken fingers" but "pleasant" nonetheless – just come "before dark", because it's "priced more for the scenery than for the food."

NEW Mediterranean Mediterranean

| - | - | - | E |

Oak Bluffs | 15 Island Inn Rd. (Beach Rd.) | 508-693-1617 | www.med-mv.com

Formerly in Vineyard Haven, this beloved brand owned and operated by a husband-and-wife chef team now vends its upscale Mediterranean fare in larger Oak Bluffs digs; the airy interior – all white and taupe with copper and black accents and works from local artists – is open year-round, while summer offers a bonus bar outside, where tapas and light meals pair with a tight selection of wines.

Net Result Seafood

| 25 | 12 | 19 | $21 |

Vineyard Haven | Tisbury Mktpl. | 79 Beach Rd. (Lagoon Pond Rd.) | 508-693-6071 | www.mvseafood.com

"For a true taste of the sea", join the line for this "often-crowded" "dockside seafood store with a carry-out kitchen" in Vineyard Haven, where "incredibly fresh" fish and "wonderfully prepared sushi" are "cheerfully provided" "at affordable prices"; there are "a few picnic tables available" outside, but they fill up quickly, so you're probably better off heading to the "nearby beach."

Newes from America *Pub Food*

18 | 20 | 19 | $28

Edgartown | Kelley House | 23 Kelley St. (N. Water St.) | 508-627-4397 | www.kelley-house.com

It "feels like a whaling-ship captain may walk in at any moment" to this "cozy", "welcoming" Edgartown "Colonial-era building" that's "everything a New England pub should be": a "laid-back" haunt for "generous servings" of "quality", "reasonably priced" sandwiches, burgers and snacks to soak up "excellent beers"; no wonder "locals congregate year-round" to "catch a ballgame" on TV while chatting with the "nice folks" on staff.

Offshore Ale Co. *American*

20 | 20 | 19 | $27

Oak Bluffs | 30 Kennebec Ave. (Healey Way) | 508-693-2626 | www.offshoreale.com

"Kids of all ages love the free baskets of peanuts (or perhaps they just love throwing the shells on the floor)" at this Oak Bluffs brew-pub, but there's more to adore than that, namely "nonpretentious" American grub ("phenomenal pizzas", "great burgers", etc.) and "incredible homemade beers", all "affordable"; the "occasional live band" keeps it "absolutely fun", even in winter when there's a "fire going."

☑ Outermost Inn Ⓜ *American*

25 | 26 | 23 | $85

Aquinnah | Outermost Inn | 81 Lighthouse Rd. (State Rd.) | 508-645-3511 | www.outermostinn.com

For the ultimate "romantic getaway", "leave the kids with a sitter" (they're not allowed if they're under 12) and head to this "spectacular" New American in a "lovely" ocean-view Aquinnah inn for an "imaginative, well-prepared" and "extremely pricey" prix fixe; a "terrific" staff buoys the "elegant but casual" vibe, which is even more of a "special treat" if you get to "see the sunset."

Saltwater *Eclectic*

- | - | - | M

Vineyard Haven | Tisbury Mktpl. | 79 Beach Rd. (Water St.) | 508-338-4666 | www.saltwaterrestaurant.com

At this "great" Eclectic BYO in Vineyard Haven, there's plenty of room in the "sparse" yet "pleasant" dining room (with vaulted ceilings, many windows and sweeping view of a lagoon) to sample its "enjoyable" all-day wares; there are a few reports of sketchy service, but "maybe it needs time" to find its sea legs.

Sharky's Cantina ⦿ *Mexican*

21 | 20 | 20 | $20

Edgartown | 266 Upper Main St. (Chase Rd.) | 508-627-6565
Oak Bluffs | 31 Circuit Ave. (Narragansett Ave.) | 508-693-7501 | www.sharkyscantina.com

"Don't expect miracles" and you'll have "fun" at these "kitschy" Edgartown and Oak Bluffs Mexican "joints" that are always "loaded with locals and tourists" digging into "big stuffed burritos" and other "standard fare"; "reasonable prices" make it an option "for the whole family", while a heady selection of tequilas and "great margaritas" abet "special times out for grown-ups."

	FOOD	DECOR	SERVICE	COST

Sidecar Café & Bar *New England*

- | - | - | I

Oak Bluffs | 16 Kennebec Ave. (Lake Ave.) | 508-693-6261 | www.sidecarcafeandbar.com

At this Oak Bluffs venue, the New England fare exhibits some "memorable" Italian flair and "beautiful execution" that "speaks of a chef and owner who care about what they are doing", even as they keep prices low; the light, intimate space displays local art, the bar is a "great" place to "meet for drinks" and the sidewalk tables prove to be an entertaining vantage point for "people-watching."

Slice of Life *American*

- | - | - | M

Oak Bluffs | 50 Circuit Ave. (bet. Lake & Samoset Aves.) | 508-693-3838 | www.sliceoflifemv.com

This quaint, all-day, year-round cafe just a stone's throw from the ocean in Oak Bluffs may not have water views or outdoor seating, but it has cultivated a loyal following that starts its day at the espresso bar with a pastry, picks up a specialty sandwich for lunch and then returns for moderately priced New American dinners.

NEW State Road Restaurant *American*

- | - | - | M

West Tisbury | 688 State Rd. (Caldwell Ln.) | 508-693-8582 | www.stateroadmv.com

Veteran MV restaurateurs present this West Tisbury New American BYOB serving midpriced breakfasts, lunches and dinners made with vegetables grown on-site; housed in a recently built vineyard-style farmhouse, its rustic-chic environs include three dining rooms, tile and oak floors, vaulted ceilings and a stone fireplace.

Sweet Life Café *American/French*

25 | 22 | 23 | $62

Oak Bluffs | 63 Circuit Ave. (bet. Narragansett & Pequot Aves.) | 508-696-0200 | www.sweetlifemv.com

Lovers of this "jewel of a find in Oak Bluffs" keep "searching for an excuse" to go back for its "just wonderful" New American–New French "gourmet home cooking"; the restored Victorian setting is "beautiful indoors or out" ("if you can, eat in the garden") and an especially "lovely spot for date night", made even more attractive by "friendly, attentive" staffers (if not the "prices you're paying").

Waterside Market *American*

- | - | - | M

Vineyard Haven | 76 Main St. (Church St.) | 508-693-8899 | www.watersidemarket.com

Not far from the ferry terminal in Vineyard Haven, this homey, moderately priced cafe, coffee bar and specialty-foods market is an "easy stop" for a "wide selection" of American breakfasts and lunches made with "fresh ingredients" by an "enthusiastic staff."

Water St. *New England*

- | - | - | E

Edgartown | Harbor View Hotel & Resort | 131 N. Water St. (Cottage St.) | 508-627-7000 | www.harbor-view.com

"Living up to" its "spectacular" setting in the Harborview Hotel & Resort, this "beautiful room" pairs panoramas of Edgartown Harbor with "delightful", "creative" reinterpretations of New England cui-

	FOOD	DECOR	SERVICE	COST

sine utilizing seasonal ingredients and "cooked to perfection"; "excellent" service is another aspect that elicits a sincere "wow."

Zapotec *Southwestern*   19 | 16 | 21 | $29

Oak Bluffs | 14 Kennebec Ave. (Lake Ave.) | 508-693-6800 | www.zapotecrestaurant.com

Southwestern fare may seem "incongruous on the Vineyard", however, it is what's for dinner at this "old" Oak Bluffs "cottage"; the tabs are "inexpensive", but "you have to put up with" bright, "cheesy decorations" and a "small, overcrowded space" to get them; "be prepared to wait" when its "busy", perhaps at the bar, since the fare's "better" after "a pretty good margarita" or two.

Zephrus *American*   20 | 19 | 20 | $38

Vineyard Haven | Mansion House | 9 Main St. (State Rd.) | 508-693-3416 | www.zephrus.com

This Vineyard Haven hotel BYO blows hot and cold – the "enjoyable" "screened-in porch" trumps the "uninspired" interior, and the New American fare is "somewhat uneven" (the "standards" are "solid", while the "innovations" "could use some attention"), just as the menu "varies wildly in price" (thankfully, it's mostly "reasonable"); one fact, however, is indisputable: the "convenient location" is "hard to beat."

Nantucket

American Seasons *American*   25 | 23 | 22 | $67

Nantucket | 80 Centre St. (Easton St.) | 508-228-7111 |
www.americanseasons.com

"Each visit is a voyage of discovery" at this folksy, "candlelit"
Nantucket "foodies' paradise" where "genius" chef Michael
LaScola turns "cutting-edge ingredients" into "knock-your-
socks-off" New American regional riffs under the headings Down
South, New England and Pacific Coast; some object to "spending
a lot" for sometimes "haughty" (though "knowledgeable") service,
but they're drowned out by groupies clinking glasses of "stellar
all American wines."

Arno's *American*   16 | 15 | 16 | $36

Nantucket | 41 Main St. (bet. Center & Federal Sts.) | 508-228-7001 |
www.arnos.net

"Breakfast is the best bet" at this "cozy" bi-level "original", while,
"depending on the day", the American comfort-food lunches and
dinners swing between "so-so" and "great"; nevertheless, it's a
"standby" for families since it's "reasonably priced" ("hard to
find" on Nantucket).

Black-Eyed Susan's ⊄ *American*   26 | 15 | 21 | $36

Nantucket | 10 India St. (Centre St.) | 508-325-0308 |
www.black-eyedsusans.com

"Everyone raves" about the "fantastic" American breakfasts at this
"funky", "dinerlike" "Nantucket classic", but "dinners are also amazing"; even though BYO "keeps prices down", the cash-only policy is
an "unpleasant surprise" for some – as are the "ridiculously long
waits" and often "loud, hot" digs; escaping the "cramped" tables by
"sitting at the counter and watching the short-order show", meanwhile, often generates happy revelations.

Boarding House *American*   21 | 19 | 20 | $62

Nantucket | 12 Federal St. (India St.) | 508-228-9622 |
www.boardinghousenantucket.com

"Earthy", "inventive" New American fare made with "quality"
market-driven ingredients ("expensive relative to off-island"
but "not the highest on Nantucket") is what's for dinner at this
more "humble" sibling to "flashy" Pearl next door; most opt for the
"unparalleled social scene" and "great people-watching" on the
patio ("worth the wait" for), but there are also admirers of the
"crowded, noisy" bar and "romantically lit" cellar, even though it's
"still a basement."

	FOOD	DECOR	SERVICE	COST

Brant Point Grill *American*

21 | 24 | 21 | $64

Nantucket | White Elephant Hotel | 50 Easton St. (Harbor View Way) | 508-228-2500 | www.whiteelephanthotel.com

"Killer views" of Nantucket Harbor and "convenience" draw guests of the White Elephant Hotel to its all-day eatery for "well-prepared" New American dishes and drinks at the "friendly bar"; locals, on the other hand, peg it as "just a tiny bit boring" for being so "pricey."

Brotherhood of Thieves *American*

18 | 20 | 18 | $33

Nantucket | 23 Broad St. (bet. Centre & Federal Sts.) | 508-228-2551 | www.brotherhoodofthieves.com

Dispelling the notion that "everyone on Nantucket wears Ralph Lauren", this "unpretentious" "tradition" gives "local" "families" "a lot of bang for the buck" with "hearty" pub-leaning American grub; the "modern" upstairs "isn't as cozy" as the "rustic" brick-and-beam "watering-hole"-like space downstairs, but the "best seats in the house" may in fact be outside.

Cambridge Street *Eclectic*

- | - | - | M

Nantucket | 12 Cambridge St. (S. Water St.) | 508-228-7109 | www.cambridgestreetnantucket.com

The local artwork on the walls and "young people" at the bar are "worth watching" at this "funky little bistro", just as the "fun", "inventive" Eclectic eats merit noshing; despite the hip scene up front (featuring live music many nights of the week), a children's menu and "reasonable prices" mean it's family-friendly at the tables.

Centre Street Bistro *American*

▽ 16 | 11 | 12 | $34

Nantucket | Meeting House | 29 Centre St. (bet. Chestnut & India Sts.) | 508-228-8470 | www.nantucketbistro.com

If you're a Nantucket local, you'll end up at this New American Meeting House BYOB with "limited atmosphere" in the off-season because, even though it's a crapshoot whether you'll "leave hungry" or "satisfied", it's "cheap"; likewise, if you're a summer tourist, you'll be "caught" here "when you run out of money – and you will."

Chanticleer Ⓜ *French*

25 | 25 | 24 | $76

Siasconset | 9 New St. (Milestone Rd.) | 508-257-6231 | www.thechanticleer.net

There are "no rivals in Siasconset" fawn fans of this "Nantucket classic" where "languorous lunches" and "romantic dinners" star "excellent wines" and "spectacular" French cuisine created with "local seafood and produce"; dining outside "beneath a canopy of roses" and among "beautiful hydrangeas" is "lovely", while the "elegant" interior "does justice to the historic" cottage – but all that's not enough to impress numbers-crunchers who find it "not worth the exalted prices."

Cinco *Nuevo Latino*

▽ 26 | 24 | 25 | $69

Nantucket | 5 Amelia Dr. (Old South Rd.) | 508-325-5151 | www.cinco5.com

"Islanders would rather you didn't know about" this "comfortable" Nantucket "gem" where "enthusiastic", "helpful servers guide" you in choosing from the "intriguing" variety of "creative" Nuevo Latino tapas and "super" Spanish wines; the "romantic", "candlelit", modern-art-bedecked spot is "a touch out of the way", which means the locals can keep "dancing on the patio" among themselves – at least for the time being.

Club Car *Continental*   20 | 19 | 21 | $64

Nantucket | 1 Main St. (Easy St.) | 508-228-1101 | www.theclubcar.com
Traditionalists get "old-style" Continental "classics" from "fabulous" staffers at this "simple, white-tablecloth" "charmer" "in the heart of town", and afterwards, they join other "rich weekenders and singles over 40" in the "crowded, fun bar" – a "high-style" annex set in a 19th-century railway club car – for "live piano" and "creative drinks"; only modernists can't jump onboard, dissing "so-so", "sauce-on-everything" preparations and "inflated prices."

☑ Company of the Cauldron *American*   28 | 24 | 25 | $71

Nantucket | 5 India St. (bet. Centre & Federal Sts.) | 508-228-4016 | www.companyofthecauldron.com
"Ethereal" meals are conjured nightly at this "cozy", "friendly" "romantic" offering an "ever-changing, ever-inspired" New American prix fixe in "a dinner-party-like environment" with harp music (three nights a week) and candlelight; the set menu can be a "deal breaker for picky eaters" (especially considering it's so costly), but for "true gourmands", it's the "most innovative and rewarding experience" Nantucket has to offer.

NEW Crosswinds *American*   - | - | - | M

Nantucket | Nantucket Memorial Airport | 14 Airport Rd. (Macy's Ln.) | 508-228-6005 | www.crosswindsnantucket.com
Upscale preparations of classic American diner fare elevate this affordable Nantucket Memorial Airport eatery offering breakfast, lunch and dinner, plus full bar service; aviation paraphernalia is the decor highlight in the hardwood-floored space, which also features views of the airfield and, by night, candlelight.

DeMarco *Italian*   22 | 18 | 20 | $67

Nantucket | 9 India St. (bet. Centre & Federal Sts.) | 508-228-1836 | www.demarcorestaurant.com
Over "30 years in the same location" and it's "still got it" applaud acolytes of this venture proffering an "upscale" Northern Italian menu ("somewhat limited" but often "amazing") in a "charming" 19th-century townhouse; it's often packed, so "if you can't get a table" in the "bit-cramped upstairs" dining room, ask the "welcoming, attentive" staff to find you a spot at the "lively, attractive bar."

NEW Dune *American*   - | - | - | M

Nantucket | 20 Broad St. (bet. Centre & Federal Sts.) | 508-228-5550 | www.dunenantucket.com
Chef-owner Michael Getter (ex American Seasons) has transformed the old Nantucket clapboard that formerly housed Cioppino's into this New American serving a midpriced, locally

	FOOD	DECOR	SERVICE	COST

sourced menu year-round (though only for dinner during the winter); the elegant, beachy setting includes three dining rooms decorated in sand and seafoam-green tones, plus an outdoor patio.

Even Keel Cafe *American*

| 19 | 14 | 16 | $31 |

Nantucket | 40 Main St. (Federal St.) | 508-228-1979 | www.evenkeelcafe.com

From sunup to well after sundown, it's "smooth sailing" at this "unassuming little place" with a "beautiful, serene" patio – at least as far as the "bountiful", "reliable", "reasonably priced" New American fare is concerned; when it comes to service, well, when it's "busy", "you might keel over before you even get" a "cup of coffee."

Fifty-Six Union *Eclectic*

| 22 | 21 | 23 | $63 |

Nantucket | 56 Union St. (E. Dover St.) | 508-228-6135 | www.fiftysixunion.com

"Nobody's worried about who's who" at this "year-round gem" "on the edge of town" – what draws "mingling natives" is the "attentive service" and "creative" Eclectic fare ("not an expansive menu, but each item is choice"); yes, this is "serious food", but "you can take the kids", especially if you choose the more "bistro"-like of the two interior rooms (bedecked with local art and sculptures) or the patio.

Figs at 29 Fair by Todd English Ⓜ *Mediterranean*

| - | 23 | 19 | $63 |

(fka 29 Fair Street)

Nantucket | 29 Fair St. (Martins Ln.) | 508-228-7800 | www.thesummerhouse.com

Post-Survey, the owners of Nantucket's "famed Summer House" beseeched celeb chef Todd English to bestow upon this "hideaway" in a 300-year-old building his signature Mediterranean fare, including his renowned flatbread pizzas and pastas; otherwise, not much has changed: diners still "venture back in time" via three candlelit rooms sporting original brick fireplaces, exposed beams and antique sconces, then are brought back to the here-and-now when the pricey bill is presented.

Fog Island Cafe *American*

| 21 | 15 | 19 | $21 |

Nantucket | 7 S. Water St. (India St.) | 508-228-1818 | www.fogisland.com

Not only is this "cozy", basic year-round BYOB a "great spot" for "delicious, hearty, healthy", "quick breakfasts" ("especially for families", because it's cheap), but it also "gets the juices flowing" with New American lunches and, in-season, Southwest-influenced dinners; "friendly", "attentive" servers complete the package.

⛴ Galley Beach *Eclectic*

| 24 | 27 | 23 | $78 |

Nantucket | 54 Jefferson Ave. (N. Beach St.) | 508-228-9641 | www.galleybeach.net

If "spectacular sunsets", a "beautiful beach" setting with "waves crashing in the background" and "fantastic food" are "what you pine for", book this "famously romantic" sand-side spot whose "phenomenal" outdoor "real estate" and "out-of-this-world" Eclectic cuisine are "worth" "paying through the nose for"; also on deck is a "professional staff" trained to anticipate "every need" of its patrons, on whom "blue blazers, stripes and khakis" abound.

Jetties, The *Italian/New England* ▽ 14 | 18 | 11 | $25

Nantucket | 4 Bathing Beach Rd. (Hulbert Ave.) | 508-228-2279 | www.thejetties.com

"For family fun, you can't beat" this "very casual" Italian–New Englander, as the "kids can play on the beach while you have an adult conversation" on the deck or a drink while listening to the occasional "nice live music" at the bar; just make sure you're well into vacation mode, because the "lackluster food" is "lackadaisically served" (it's cheap at least).

Le Languedoc Bistro *French* 26 | 22 | 25 | $63

Nantucket | Le Languedoc Inn | 24 Broad St. (bet. Centre & Federal Sts.) | 508-228-2552 | www.lelanguedoc.com

"All the classics" plus "enough inventiveness to keep you coming back" "year after year" – not to mention "an appealing wine list" – is the "tantalizing" formula at this "lovely" French "gem" with a patio, a more formal dining room and a "cozy" bistro/bar below ("cheaper than upstairs" but still "*très* delicious"); the staff's simultaneous "professional" and "laid-back" tone adds to an experience enthusiasts cheer is "wonderful in every way."

Lo La 41° *Eclectic* 21 | 22 | 20 | $55

Nantucket | 15 S. Beach St. (Broad St.) | 508-325-4001 | www.lola41.net

"High-octane" to the nth degree, this "chicly decorated", "intimate spot" is known more for a "wildly hopping" "bar scene", but its "black Armani"–sporting habitués say the Eclectic victuals (there's a "great sushi" menu as well as a bistro *carte*) are "fantastic" too; however, holdouts warn the "small portions" are "way too expensive, even for Nantucket", and the "noise level is impossible" (next time, they might try the "divine patio").

Nantucket Lobster Trap *Seafood* 19 | 15 | 18 | $46

Nantucket | 23 Washington St. (Coffin St.) | 508-228-4200 | www.nantucketlobstertrap.com

"If you've got a hankering for no-frills lobster", this "institution of shirt-staining" is "the place to go" for "more than ample portions" of "decent seafood" at "low prices" ("for the island"); the servers do their best to be "nice and accommodating" while getting "high volumes" of "tourists" fed and out of the "bland", "noisy" environs, but there's "always a line" of more waiting to get in.

Òran Mór *Eclectic* 24 | 23 | 24 | $75

Nantucket | 2 S. Beach St. (Whalers Ln.) | 508-228-8655 | www.oranmorbistro.com

An "awe-inspiring" "use of seasonal ingredients" is the forte of this "enchanting" Eclectic, as "unforgettable" for its "remarkable" fare as it is for an "elegant", "quaint" setting up a flight of "copper stairs" ("perfect for a romantic rendezvous"); in accord with the "veritable symphony" of tastes are an "excellent wine list" and an "attentive staff", and while it's "not cheap", "if anyplace on this expensive island is worth it", it's this one.

Pearl *Asian*   24 | 25 | 22 | $69

Nantucket | 12 Federal St. (India St.) | 508-228-9701 |
www.thepearlnantucket.com

"Hip and stylish" folks who "want it all" find it at this Asian fusion "party" that entices with a "tremendous bar", "delicious libations", "friendly, helpful servers" and "cool", "unexpected decor" that reminds them of weekends spent in "New York"/"LA"/"Miami"/ "Monte Carlo"; the "innovative" coastal cuisine is "fabulous" too, although belt-tighteners blanch "it's hard to enjoy the fresh fish when you're gagging on the prices."

Pi Pizzeria *Pizza*   ▽ 23 | 12 | 20 | $32

Nantucket | 11 W. Creek Rd. (bet. Orange & Pleasant Sts.) |
508-228-1130 | www.pipizzeria.com

"Escape the buzz of Downtown" Nantucket and get "your pizza fix" all in one fell swoop at this parlor baking wood-fired, thin-crust Neapolitan "lusciousness" and additional moderately priced Italian dishes of "solid quality"; there's "always a line" for a table, but takeout is an option, as is the bar.

Queequeg's *Eclectic*   25 | 20 | 24 | $48

Nantucket | 6 Oak St. (Federal St.) | 508-325-0992 |
www.queequegsnantucket.com

"What a treat!" cheer boosters of this "casual" "little jewel" "in the heart of N'tucket town", where the "nice variety" of Eclectic eats is "delightful and delicious all-around", not to mention "reasonably priced" (in island terms); bonus points are earned because "you can usually get a table" in the "snug", "lovely", whale-art-sporting interior, if not on the "adorable" deck.

Ropewalk, The *Seafood*   - | - | - | M

Nantucket | 1 Straight Wharf (Easy St.) | 508-228-8886 |
www.theropewalk.com

Taking its name from its past as a building where ropes for ships were made, this waterside all-day seafooder boasts a patio, three dining rooms, two drinks bars, a raw bar and views of Nantucket Harbor; it's quite a hip scene, but moderate prices make it smart for families too.

Sconset Café ⊘ *American/Eclectic*   21 | 16 | 19 | $48

Siasconset | 8 Main St. (Post Office Sq.) | 508-257-4008 |
www.sconsetcafe.com

"Run by 'Sconseters for 'Sconseters", this "charming", cash-only American-Eclectic provides "homemade muffins" for breakfast, "great sandwiches after a bike ride" in the afternoon and "fresh, lively" dinners amid candlelight and "exhibits of local artists"; service can be "slow" when "crowded", but you're on "island time", so just "relax" and pour another glass from the stash you picked up at the wine-and-books store next door.

	FOOD	DECOR	SERVICE	COST

Sea Grille *Seafood*   22 | 17 | 21 | $49

Nantucket | 45 Sparks Ave. (bet. Pleasant St. & Sanford Rd.) |
508-325-5700 | www.theseagrille.com

Sure, this "Nantucket tradition" "provides the seafood staples", but
it "can also cut loose" with "marvelous" "daily specials"; the digs
may be slightly "dated", but as long as it remains open (mostly)
year-round, "makes everyone feel welcome" (especially "families"
with "kids") and delivers "value", "locals" will keep recommending
it as a "solid performer."

Sfoglia 🗷 *Italian*   24 | 18 | 21 | $62

Nantucket | 130 Pleasant St. (bet. Chins Way & W. Creek Rd.) |
508-325-4500 | www.sfogliarestaurant.com

"High-quality fresh ingredients" are evident in the "creative" fare
proffered at this Italian, which employs "friendly, attentive"
staffers to "help guide" diners through the "limited, quirky menu"
("pricey", but "worth it for the bread" alone); both private and
"communal tables" fill the "shabby-chic" setting, which some aesthetes "don't really dig."

Ships Inn *American*   24 | 22 | 22 | $68

Nantucket | Ships Inn | 13 Fair St. (Lucretia Mott Ln.) | 508-228-0040 |
www.shipsinnnantucket.com

Only "knowledgeable Nantucketers dine" at this "seasonal" "gem"
serving "superb", "creative" American brasserie fare, since it's
virtually "hidden" in the "basement" of an 18th-century whaling
captain's mansion–turned-lodge; it's off the main drag, so couples can take "a romantic walk" at the end of their "lovely evening" –
but the "friendly staff" and "inviting", "cozy bar" make many
"want to linger."

Slip 14 *American*   18 | 17 | 19 | $48

Nantucket | 14 Old South Wharf (New Whale St.) | 508-228-2033 |
www.slip14.com

"Finish up your Nantucket jaunt" at this "casual" New American
"family" "respite" near the ferries, which offers "wonderful outdoor
seating" on a "fun wharf" (inside's a little "dark"); dollar-watchers
who deem the vittles "overpriced" for being only "ok" stick to "sweet
specialty cocktails" at the "nice bar", which hops with a "twentysomething crowd later in the evening."

Straight Wharf *Seafood*   25 | 25 | 24 | $73

Nantucket | 6 Harbor Sq. (Straight Wharf) | 508-228-4499 |
www.straightwharfrestaurant.com

"On a warm summer night", there may not be a more "gorgeous" or
"romantic" setting than the dining porch "overlooking the harbor" at
this "standout", but the "absolutely beautiful" interior is an equally
"tantalizing" "Nantucket habitat" in which to enjoy "inspiring"
"high-end seafood" that "utilizes local ingredients effectively"; a
"split personality" emerges later in the evening when "jocks" and
their quarry create a "loud", "lively bar scene", which is "thankfully,
separated from the main room."

Summer House *American*

20 | 23 | 19 | $71

Siasconset | Summer House | 17 Ocean Ave. (Magnolia Ave.) | 508-257-9976 | www.thesummerhouse.com

A "pianist plays delightful music to accompany" New American meals in this "very expensive" Siasconset inn's "simple but elegant" main room (off of which sits a "great old porch"), while ocean breezes cool at its "beachside bistro"; yes, its location on the coast is undeniably "beautiful", but with "hit-or-miss" dishes and occasional "attitude" from the staff, some suspect it "coasts on the location."

Sushi by Yoshi *Japanese*

25 | 13 | 19 | $37

Nantucket | 2 E. Chestnut St. (Water St.) | 508-228-1801 | www.sushibyyoshi.com

Nantucketers feel "lucky to have a sushi place" that's as "inventive", "super-fresh" and "affordable" as this "jewel"; some say it's "worth the wait" to eat in the "small" "mob scene" ("BYOB, baby!"), but many feel it's "better to do takeout" – the rolls and sashimi "travel well."

⊠ Topper's *American*

27 | 27 | 26 | $95

Nantucket | Wauwinet Inn | 120 Wauwinet Rd. (2 mi. north of Polpis Rd.) | 508-228-8768 | www.wauwinet.com

"Stuff your wallet" with "big bucks", take the "romantic" "water shuttle" "across the harbor from town" and get to this "special-occasion spot" at the Wauwinet Inn "in time to see the sunset"; next up is the "divine culinary experience" of chef David Daniels' "hand-somely plated", "exquisite" New American cuisine, which is presented by "impeccable" servers alongside a "deftly crafted wine list" in a "beautiful" dining room and "lovely", less-formal patio – just "don't expect large portions" and "you won't be disappointed"; P.S. breakfast, lunch and brunch are just as "memorable."

NEW Town *Eclectic*

– | – | – | M

Nantucket | 4 E. Chestnut St. (bet. Center & Federal Sts.) | 508-325-8696 | www.townnantucket.com

This gently priced year-round Eclectic may display many Asian inspirations on its menu, but the setting – overlooking South Water Street in Nantucket's historic district – is all AUK, particularly the front summertime patio, whose oversized wicker chairs offer prime people-watching perches; the intimate interior, with candlelight and dark-wood floors, is just as inviting, especially for those craving something light at the bar.

⊠ 21 Federal *American*

24 | 23 | 23 | $68

Nantucket | 21 Federal St. (bet. Chestnut & Oak Sts.) | 508-228-2121 | www.21federal.com

"After all these years", this "quintessential" Nantucket American in a "handsome", "romantic" Greek Revival edifice complete with a "charming patio" still "pampers" via "delectable creations" made with "local provender" that virtually "dances on the plate"; though a few critics carp that it's "way too expensive" (and perhaps "pretentious"), Federalists affirm it "should never change."

BOSTON/
CAPE COD & THE ISLANDS
INDEXES

LOCATION MAPS

All places are in Boston area unless otherwise noted (CC=Cape Cod; MV=Martha's Vineyard; Nan=Nantucket).

Cuisines

Includes names, locations and Food ratings.

AFGHAN

🅱 Helmand | **E Cambridge** · 26

AFRICAN

NEW Teranga | **S End** · −

AMERICAN

NEW Abby Park | **Milton** · −
Adrian's | **CC** · 16
Alchemist | **Jamaica Plain** · 17
Alchemy | **MV** · 22
American Seasons | **Nan** · 25
Amrheins | **S Boston** · 18
Aqua Grille | **CC** · 19
Ariadne | **Newton** · 21
Art Cliff | **MV** · 24
Asana | **Back Bay** · −
Ashmont Grill | **Dorchester** · 22
Atria | **MV** · 25
Audubon Circle | **Kenmore Sq** · 21
Aura | **Seaport Dist** · 22
Avenue One | **D'town Cross** · 18
Bakers' Best | **Newton** · 22
Bambara | **E Cambridge** · 20
Barker Tavern | **Scituate** · 23
Barley Neck Inn | **CC** · 20
Bayside Betsy's | **CC** · 15
Beach Plum | **MV** · 25
Beacon St. Tavern | **Brookline** · 20
Beehive | **S End** · 18
Bee-Hive Tavern | **CC** · 19
Belfry Inne | **CC** · 25
Betsy's Diner | **CC** · 18
NEW Big Papi's | **Framingham** · −
Biltmore B&G | **Newton** · 18
Birch St. Bistro | **Roslindale** · 19
Bistro/Crowne Pointe | **CC** · 22
Black Cow | **multi.** · 19
🅱 Black Dog | **MV** · 19
Black-Eyed Susan's | **Nan** · 26
Blackfish | **CC** · 24
Black Sheep | **Kendall Sq** · 21
Blarney Stone | **Dorchester** · 16
Blu | **Theater Dist** · 21
Blue on Highland | **Needham** · 17
Blue22 | **Quincy** · 19
Boarding House | **Nan** · 21
NEW Bobby's | **Wellesley Hills** · −
Boston/Salem Beer | **multi.** · 18
🅱 Bramble Inn | **CC** · 27
Brant Point | **Nan** · 21

Bravo | **MFA** · 21
Brenden Crocker's | **Beverly** · 25
🅱 Bristol Lounge | **Back Bay** · 24
Brotherhood/Thieves | **Nan** · 18
Brownstone | **Back Bay** · 15
Burtons | **multi.** · 21
NEW Cafe 47 | **Back Bay** · −
Cafe Edwige/at Night | **CC** · 26
Cambridge Common | **Harv Sq** · 17
Cape Sea | **CC** · 26
Capt. Kidd | **CC** · 18
Capt. Linnell | **CC** · 22
Capt. Parker's | **CC** · 18
Central Kitchen | **Central Sq** · 24
Centre St. Bistro | **Nan** · 16
Chapoquoit Grill | **CC** · 22
Charley's | **multi.** · 18
Charlie's Kitchen | **Harv Sq** · 17
Charlie's Sandwich | **S End** · 23
Chatham Bars | **CC** · 22
Cheers | **multi.** · 14
🅱 Cheesecake | **multi.** · 18
NEW Chilmark Tavern | **MV** · −
Church | **Fenway** · 20
NEW City Table | **Back Bay** · −
Clancy's | **CC** · 22
Clink | **Beacon Hill** · 19
Club Cafe | **S End** · 18
Coda | **S End** · 22
Comfort | **Watertown** · −
🅱 Company/Cauldron | **Nan** · 28
Coolidge Corner | **Brookline** · 17
NEW Corner Tavern | **Back Bay** · −
Cottage City | **MV** · 22
NEW Courtyard/Boston Library | **Back Bay** · −
NEW Crosswinds | **Nan** · −
Cygnet | **Beverly** · 21
Daedalus | **Harv Sq** · 17
Daily Grill | **Back Bay** · 19
Dalia's Bistro | **Brookline** · 19
Dalya's | **Bedford** · 23
Dan'l Webster | **CC** · 20
NEW Danny Quinn's | **MV** · −
David Ryan's | **MV** · 15
🅱 Détente | **MV** · 27
Devlin's | **Brighton** · 20
Devon's | **CC** · 24
Dillon's | **Back Bay** · 16
District | **Leather Dist** · 17
DJ's | **W End** · −

Menus, photos, voting and more – free at ZAGAT.com

Dog Bar	**Gloucester**	23
Dolphin	**CC**	21
Drink	**Seaport Dist**	-
🏿 Duckworth's	**Gloucester**	29
NEW Dune	**Nan**	-
🏿 Eastern Stand.	**Kenmore Sq**	22
Ecco	**E Boston**	-
NEW 88 Wharf	**Milton**	-
Even Keel	**Nan**	19
Fairway	**CC**	18
Fanizzi's	**CC**	20
NEW Farm Bar	**Essex**	-
51 Lincoln	**Newton**	23
Finely JP's	**CC**	21
Fishmonger's	**CC**	18
Five Bays	**CC**	25
Flash's	**Park Sq**	18
Flat Iron	**W End**	22
Flora	**Arlington**	24
Fog Island	**Nan**	21
NEW Forty Carrots	**Chestnut Hill**	-
Franklin	**multi.**	26
Full Moon	**Huron Vill**	20
Garden at Cellar	**Harv Sq**	25
Gardner Museum	**MFA**	20
Gargoyles	**Somerville**	24
G Bar	**Swampscott**	21
Geoffrey's Cafe	**Roslindale**	19
Glory	**Andover**	21
Good Life	**D'town Cross**	17
Grafton St. Pub	**Harv Sq**	17
Grapevine	**Salem**	25
Greg's	**Watertown**	19
Haley House	**Roxbury**	24
Halfway Cafe	**multi.**	17
Harry's	**Westborough**	20
Harvard Gardens	**Beacon Hill**	17
Harvest	**Harv Sq**	25
Highland Kitchen	**Somerville**	23
Houston's	**Faneuil Hall**	22
🏿 Hungry Mother	**Kendall Sq**	27
Independent, The	**Somerville**	18
Isabella	**Dedham**	24
Island Merchant	**CC**	-
Jacob Wirth	**Theater Dist**	17
James's Gate	**Jamaica Plain**	16
Jer-Ne	**Theater Dist**	20
Joe's American	**multi.**	16
John Harvard's	**multi.**	16
Johnny D's	**Somerville**	19
Johnny's Lunch.	**Newton**	18
🏿 J's Nashoba	**Bolton**	26
Kingston	**D'town Cross**	20
Lambert's Cove	**MV**	25
Landing	**multi.**	16
NEW Lansdowne	**Fenway**	-
Laura & Tony's	**CC**	-
Laureen's	**CC**	23
Laurel	**Back Bay**	20
NEW Ledge	**Dorchester**	-
Left Bank	**Tyngsboro**	21
Lexx	**Lexington**	17
Lineage	**Brookline**	23
Living Room	**Waterfront**	15
Local	**W Newton**	-
Locke-Ober	**D'town Cross**	24
NEW Lord Hobo	**E Cambridge**	-
Lucky's	**Seaport Dist**	18
Lure	**MV**	21
NEW Lyric	**CC**	-
Market	**Financial Dist**	16
NEW Market	**Theater Dist**	-
Marshside	**CC**	15
Masona Grill	**W Roxbury**	25
Max/Dylan	**multi.**	-
🏿 Meritage	**Waterfront**	27
Metropolitan	**Chestnut Hill**	21
Mews	**CC**	27
Mike's	**S End**	20
Miracle of Science	**Central Sq**	19
Mission B&G	**MFA**	19
Mr. Bartley's	**Harv Sq**	24
Navy Yard	**Charlestown**	23
NewBridge	**Chelsea**	24
Newes/America	**MV**	18
North St. Grille	**N End**	23
🏿 Not Average Joe's	**multi.**	18
NEW Nourish	**Lexington**	-
🏿 Oak Room	**Back Bay**	25
Oceana	**Waterfront**	24
Ocean House	**CC**	25
Offshore Ale	**MV**	20
Om	**Harv Sq**	19
Optimist Café	**CC**	21
Orleans	**Somerville**	17
Orleans Inn	**CC**	17
🏿 Outermost Inn	**MV**	25
Paddock	**CC**	20
NEW Pairings	**Park Sq**	-
Palmers	**Andover**	-
Paramount	**Beacon Hill**	23
Pie Bakery	**Newton**	18
Pleasant Cafe	**Roslindale**	18
Pops	**S End**	22
Port	**CC**	23
Post Office	**CC**	16
NEW Post 390	**Back Bay**	-
Prose	**Arlington**	24
Redline	**Harv Sq**	17

☑ Red Pheasant | CC	27	
Red Rock | Swampscott	20	
Red Sky | Faneuil Hall	18	
Regatta/Cotuit | CC	25	
NEW Robinwood | Jamaica Plain	–	
Roobar | multi.	21	
Ross' Grill | CC	22	
Rudi's | Roxbury	–	
Salts | Central Sq	26	
Scargo Café | CC	20	
Scollay Sq. | Beacon Hill	19	
Sconset Café | Nan	21	
75 Chestnut | Beacon Hill	21	
Ships Inn | Nan	24	
Sibling Rivalry | S End	24	
Sidney's | Central Sq	21	
Silvertone B&G | D'town Cross	21	
NEW Six Burner | Back Bay	–	
606 Congress | Seaport Dist	21	
Sky | multi.	19	
Slice of Life | MV	–	
Slip 14 | Nan	18	
Soma | Beverly	22	
Sorella's | Jamaica Plain	26	
Sound Bites | Somerville	22	
South End Buttery | S End	21	
South St. Diner | Leather Dist	16	
☑ Square Café | Hingham	26	
St. Alphonzo's | S Boston	22	
Stanhope Grille | Back Bay	23	
Stars on Hingham | Hingham	16	
NEW State Road | MV	–	
Stephanie's | multi.	20	
NEW Stork Club | S End	–	
Strip-T's | Watertown	22	
Studio 3 | multi.	–	
NEW Suffolk Grille | Canton	–	
Summer House | Nan	20	
Summer Winter | Burlington	24	
Sunset Cafe | Inman Sq	19	
Sweet Life | MV	25	
NEW Symphony 8 | Fenway	–	
Tavern in Sq. | multi.	17	
Tavern/Water | Charlestown	13	
NEW Technique | E Cambridge	–	
NEW Teele Sq. | Somerville	–	
Temple Bar | Porter Sq	20	
Tempo | Waltham	21	
☑ Ten Tables | multi.	27	
Terra Luna | CC	24	
33 Rest. | Back Bay	20	
☑ Top of Hub | Back Bay	20	
☑ Topper's | Nan	27	
NEW Tory Row | Harv Sq	–	
Townsend's | Hyde Park	19	

Trata | Harv Sq	–	
Tremont 647 | S End	21	
NEW Trina's | Inman Sq	–	
☑ Troquet | Theater Dist	27	
Tryst | Arlington	22	
Turner Fish | Back Bay	21	
☑ 28 Atlantic | CC	26	
28 Degrees | S End	20	
NEW Twenty8 Food | Foxboro	–	
21st Amendment | Beacon Hill	17	
29 Newbury | Back Bay	20	
☑ 21 Federal | Nan	24	
T.W. Food | Huron Vill	26	
224 Boston St. | Dorchester	22	
Union B&G | S End	24	
☑ Upstairs/Square | Harv Sq	24	
Via Lago | Lexington	20	
Victoria's | Roxbury	20	
Vinalia | D'town Cross	17	
Vox Populi | Back Bay	16	
Walden Grille | Concord	15	
Warren | Charlestown	16	
Washington Sq. | Brookline	22	
Waterside Mkt. | MV	–	
West/Centre | W Roxbury	18	
West Side | Porter Sq	22	
Whitman Hse. | CC	21	
Wicked Oyster | CC	24	
Wild Goose | CC	21	
Winslow's Tavern | CC	20	
NEW Woodward | Financial Dist	–	
Woody's Grill | Fenway	22	
Zebra's Bistro | Medfield	24	
Zephrus | MV	20	

ARGENTINEAN

Tango | Arlington	21	

ARMENIAN

Karoun | Newton	22	

ASIAN

Asana | Back Bay	–	
Betty's Wok | MFA	19	
Billy Tse | multi.	20	
☑ Blue Ginger | Wellesley	26	
Blue22 | Quincy	19	
☑ Elephant Walk | multi.	23	
Floating Rock | Revere	–	
NEW Ginger Park | S End	–	
Grasshopper | Allston	20	
Island Hopper | Back Bay	19	
Jae's | S End	20	
Kowloon | Saugus	17	
Lavender Asian | Sudbury	–	

Ma Soba	**Beacon Hill**	20
🔲 Maxwell's 148	**Natick**	26
Myers + Chang	**S End**	23
Noodle St.	**Boston U**	19
No. 1 Noodle	**Newton**	18
Pearl	**Nan**	24
Penang	**Chinatown**	22
Ponzu	**Waltham**	23
Stir Crazy	**CC**	23
Super Fusion	**Brookline**	27
Wonder Spice	**Jamaica Plain**	21

BAKERIES

Athan's Café	**multi.**	23
Bakers' Best	**Newton**	22
Flour Bakery	**multi.**	26
Haley House	**Roxbury**	24
Hi-Rise	**multi.**	24
Neighborhood Rest.	**Somerville**	23
Pain D'Avignon	**CC**	-
Panificio	**Beacon Hill**	19
South End Buttery	**S End**	21
Vicki Lee's	**Belmont**	25

BARBECUE

Bison County	**Waltham**	18
Blue Ribbon BBQ	**multi.**	25
🔲 East Coast	**Inman Sq**	25
NEW Farm Bar	**Essex**	-
Firefly's	**multi.**	20
Jake's Dixie	**Waltham**	17
NewBridge	**Chelsea**	24
Redbones	**Somerville**	22
Soul Fire	**Allston**	21
Village Smokehse.	**Brookline**	19

BELGIAN

Publick House	**Brookline**	21

BRAZILIAN

Brazilian Grill	**CC**	21
Café Belô	**multi.**	20
Café Brazil	**Allston**	23
Don Ricardo's	**S End**	23
Midwest	**multi.**	20
Muqueca	**Inman Sq**	24
Rodizio	**Somerville**	22

BRITISH

Cornwall's	**Kenmore Sq**	15
Dunbar Tea	**CC**	22
Optimist Café	**CC**	21

BURGERS

Audubon Circle	**Kenmore Sq**	21
B. Good	**multi.**	19
NEW Boston Burger	**Somerville**	-
Brotherhood/Thieves	**Nan**	18
Cambridge Common	**Harv Sq**	17
Charlie's Kitchen	**Harv Sq**	17
Christopher's	**Porter Sq**	17
Miracle of Science	**Central Sq**	19
Mr. Bartley's	**Harv Sq**	24
UBurger	**multi.**	23

CAJUN

Border Cafe	**multi.**	19

CALIFORNIAN

Caliterra	**Financial Dist**	16
Cottage	**Wellesley**	19
Picante	**Central Sq**	19

CAMBODIAN

🔲 Elephant Walk	**multi.**	23
Floating Rock	**Revere**	-
Stir Crazy	**CC**	23
Wonder Spice	**Jamaica Plain**	21

CAPE VERDEAN

Rest. Cesaria	**Dorchester**	-

CARIBBEAN

Island Merchant	**CC**	-

CHILEAN

Chacarero	**D'town Cross**	-

CHINESE

(* dim sum specialist)

Bernard's	**Chestnut Hill**	24
NEW Bistro Chi	**Quincy**	-
Changsho	**Porter Sq**	20
Chau Chow*	**Chinatown**	21
Chef Chang's	**Brookline**	20
Chef Chow's	**Brookline**	20
China Pearl*	**multi.**	21
China Sky	**Wellesley**	19
CK Shanghai	**Wellesley**	22
NEW East by NE	**Inman Sq**	-
East Ocean	**Chinatown**	24
Emperor's Gdn.*	**Chinatown**	21
Golden Temple	**Brookline**	21
Grand Chinatown	**N Quincy**	-
Jumbo	**multi.**	23
NEW Kama	**Quincy**	-
Lotus Blossom	**Sudbury**	22
Mary Chung	**Central Sq**	21
New Shanghai	**Chinatown**	16
Peach Farm	**Chinatown**	25
Peking Cuisine	**Newton**	21
P.F. Chang's	**multi.**	19

Qingdao Gdn.*	**Porter Sq**	24
Royal East	**Central Sq**	20
Shanghai Gate	**Allston**	24
Sichuan Garden	**multi.**	22
🅩 Sichuan Gourmet	**Framingham**	27
Yangtze River*	**Lexington**	17
Zoe's	**Somerville**	19

COFFEEHOUSES

Café Algiers	**Harv Sq**	18
Caffe Paradiso	**N End**	17
Darwin's	**Harv Sq**	24
Mr. Crepe	**Somerville**	18
Sorelle	**Charlestown**	23
1369 Coffeehouse	**multi.**	20
Trident	**Back Bay**	19

COFFEE SHOPS/ DINERS

Art Cliff	**MV**	24
Betsy's Diner	**CC**	18
Charlie's Kitchen	**Harv Sq**	17
Charlie's Sandwich	**S End**	23
Deluxe Town	**Watertown**	22
Harry's	**Westborough**	20
Johnny's Lunch.	**Newton**	18
Mike's	**S End**	20
🆕 Robinwood	**Jamaica Plain**	-
Rosebud	**Somerville**	16
South St. Diner	**Leather Dist**	16
Stars on Hingham	**Hingham**	16
Victoria's	**Roxbury**	20

COLOMBIAN

Rincon Limeno	**E Boston**	-

CONTINENTAL

Anthony Cummaquid	**CC**	18
Cafe Escadrille	**Burlington**	19
Club Car	**Nan**	20
🅩 Front St.	**CC**	27
Locke-Ober	**D'town Cross**	24
Marliave	**D'town Cross**	22
Wine Cellar	**Back Bay**	20

CUBAN

Chez Henri	**Harv Sq**	24
El Oriental/Cuba	**Jamaica Plain**	24

DELIS

Bottega	**multi.**	24
Darwin's	**Harv Sq**	24
🆕 Federal	**Beacon Hill**	-
Hot Tomatoes	**multi.**	22
Rubin's	**Brookline**	19

S&S	**Inman Sq**	18
Zaftigs	**Brookline**	21

DESSERT

🅩 Bristol Lounge	**Back Bay**	24
Café Fleuri	**Financial Dist**	22
Caffe Paradiso	**N End**	17
🅩 Cheesecake	**multi.**	18
Finale	**multi.**	23
Flour Bakery	**multi.**	26
Hi-Rise	**multi.**	24
Picco	**S End**	22
Pie Bakery	**Newton**	18

DOMINICAN

Merengue	**Roxbury**	-

ECLECTIC

Academy Ocean	**CC**	22
Blue Room	**Kendall Sq**	25
Boloco	**multi.**	18
Bond	**Financial Dist**	-
Bravo	**MFA**	21
Bubala's	**CC**	16
Bullfinch's	**Sudbury**	21
Café at Taj	**Back Bay**	20
Cambridge St.	**Nan**	-
Centre St. Café	**Jamaica Plain**	25
Chatham Squire	**CC**	18
Chesca's	**MV**	23
Christopher's	**Porter Sq**	17
Columbus Café	**S End**	19
🅩 Cuchi Cuchi	**Central Sq**	22
Deep Ellum	**Allston**	18
Delux Cafe	**S End**	21
Equator	**S End**	18
🅩 EVOO	**Kendall Sq**	27
Exchange St. Bistro	**Malden**	20
Fifty-Six Union	**Nan**	22
Fire & Ice	**multi.**	16
Firefly Woodfire	**CC**	20
🅩 Galley Beach	**Nan**	24
Glenn's	**Newburyport**	23
Lobster Pot	**CC**	22
Lo La 41°	**Nan**	21
LTK	**Seaport Dist**	20
Lyceum	**Salem**	23
Metropolis	**S End**	23
Middlesex	**Central Sq**	17
Napi's	**CC**	19
Òran Mór	**Nan**	24
Purple Cactus	**Jamaica Plain**	21
Queequeg's	**Nan**	25
Red House	**Harv Sq**	20
Saltwater	**MV**	-

Sanctuary	**Financial Dist**	19
Sconset Café	**Nan**	21
Scutra	**Arlington**	23
Sonsie	**Back Bay**	20
Stix	**Back Bay**	17
Stone Soup	**Ipswich**	25
🆕 Town	**Nan**	-
Trident	**Back Bay**	19
Vining's	**CC**	24
West End Johnnie's	**W End**	17
Zuzu!	**Central Sq**	20

ERITREAN

Asmara	**Central Sq**	21

ETHIOPIAN

Addis Red Sea	**multi.**	22
Asmara	**Central Sq**	21

EUROPEAN

🆉 Eastern Stand.	**Kenmore Sq**	22
🆉 Ten Tables	**multi.**	27
🆕 Tory Row	**Harv Sq**	-

FONDUE

Melting Pot	**multi.**	20
Wine Cellar	**Back Bay**	20

FRENCH

Bleu	**CC**	25
Bon Savor	**Jamaica Plain**	20
Butcher Shop	**S End**	25
Chanticleer	**Nan**	25
🆉 Chillingsworth	**CC**	27
🆉 Clio/Uni	**Back Bay**	27
Devon's	**CC**	24
🆉 Elephant Walk	**multi.**	23
Enzo	**CC**	24
Hungry I, The	**Beacon Hill**	24
Jasmine	**Brighton**	24
Le Grenier	**MV**	23
Le Languedoc	**Nan**	26
Le Lyonnais	**Acton**	23
🆉 L'Espalier	**Back Bay**	28
L'Étoile	**MV**	26
🆉 Lumière	**Newton**	27
Mantra	**D'town Cross**	18
🆉 Mistral	**S End**	27
Mr. Crepe	**Somerville**	18
🆉 No. 9 Park	**Beacon Hill**	28
Paris Creperie	**Brookline**	22
🆉 Radius	**Financial Dist**	26
🆉 Red Pheasant	**CC**	27
Salts	**Central Sq**	26
Sandrine's	**Harv Sq**	24
🆉 Sel de Terre	**Back Bay**	23

Sensing	**Waterfront**	-
Sweet Life	**MV**	25
T.W. Food	**Huron Vill**	26

FRENCH (BISTRO)

🆉 Aquitaine	**multi.**	23
Aquitaine Bis	**Chestnut Hill**	23
Beacon Hill	**Beacon Hill**	22
Bia Bistro	**Cohasset**	24
🆕 Bistro du Midi	**Back Bay**	-
Bistro 712	**Norwood**	24
Chez Henri	**Harv Sq**	24
🆉 Craigie/Main	**Central Sq**	27
🆉 Hamersley's	**S End**	27
L'Alouette	**CC**	26
Les Zygomates	**Leather Dist**	22
Pain D'Avignon	**CC**	-
🆉 Petit Robert	**multi.**	24
Pierrot Bistrot	**Beacon Hill**	24
Pigalle	**Theater Dist**	26
🆉 Sel de Terre	**multi.**	23
🆉 Troquet	**Theater Dist**	27

FRENCH (BRASSERIE)

Bouchée	**Back Bay**	21
Brasserie Jo	**Back Bay**	20
Gaslight Brasserie	**S End**	21
La Voile	**Back Bay**	23
Miel	**Waterfront**	21

GERMAN

Jacob Wirth	**Theater Dist**	17

GREEK

Aegean	**multi.**	21
Demos	**multi.**	21
🆉 Ithaki Med.	**Ipswich**	26
Kouzina	**Newton**	23
Steve's Greek	**multi.**	20

HEALTH FOOD

(See also Vegetarian)

B. Good	**multi.**	19

HUNGARIAN

Jasmine	**Brighton**	24

INDIAN

Bhindi Bazaar	**Back Bay**	22
Bombay Club	**multi.**	20
Bukhara	**Jamaica Plain**	23
Cafe of India	**Harv Sq**	22
Coriander Bistro	**Sharon**	-
Diva Indian	**Somerville**	22
🆕 Dosa Factory	**Central Sq**	-

Ghazal	**Jamaica Plain**	⌐
Grain & Salt	**Allston**	⌐
Haveli	**Inman Sq**	⌐
Himalayan Bistro	**W Roxbury**	24
India Pavilion	**Central Sq**	20
India Quality	**Kenmore Sq**	24
Kashmir	**Back Bay**	23
Kebab Factory	**Somerville**	24
Mantra	**D'town Cross**	18
Masala Art	**Needham**	23
Mela	**S End**	24
Namaskar	**Somerville**	23
New Mother India	**Waltham**	22
Passage to India	**multi.**	20
Punjab	**Arlington**	25
Punjabi Dhaba	**Inman Sq**	24
Punjab Palace	**Allston**	24
Rani	**Brookline**	20
Shanti India	**Dorchester**	⌐
NEW Singh's	**Wellesley Hills**	⌐
Tamarind Bay	**multi.**	24
Tanjore	**Harv Sq**	22
Tantric	**Theater Dist**	20

IRISH

Burren	**Somerville**	14
Doyle's	**Jamaica Plain**	15
Green Briar	**Brighton**	17
James's Gate	**Jamaica Plain**	16
NEW Lansdowne	**Fenway**	⌐
Matt Murphy's	**Brookline**	22

ISRAELI

Jerusalem Pita	**Brookline**	⌐

ITALIAN

(N=Northern; S=Southern)

Abbondanza	**Everett**	23
Adrian's	**CC**	16
Alberto's	N	**CC**	20
Al Dente	**N End**	22
Alta Strada	**Wellesley**	21
Amari	**CC**	22
Amelia's Kitchen	**Somerville**	22
Amelia's Trattoria	**Kendall Sq**	22
Anchovies	**S End**	20
Angelo's	**Stoneham**	26
Antico Forno	S	**N End**	23
Antonio's Cucina	**Beacon Hill**	22
Appetito	**Newton**	19
Artú	**multi.**	21
Assaggio	**N End**	24
Bacco	**N End**	21
Basta Pasta	**Central Sq**	24
Bella Luna/Milky Way	**Jamaica Plain**	⌐

Bella's	**Rockland**	19
Bertucci's	**multi.**	17
Bia Bistro	**Cohasset**	24
Bina Osteria	**D'town Cross**	⌐
Bin 26	**Beacon Hill**	21
Z Bistro 5	N	**W Medford**	27
Bon Caldo	**Norwood**	22
Bottega	N	**multi.**	24
Bricco	**N End**	25
Bridgeman's	N	**Hull**	26
Buca's Tuscan	N	**CC**	23
Butcher Shop	**S End**	25
Caffe Tosca	**Hingham**	24
Caliterra	**Financial Dist**	16
Canestaro	**Fenway**	19
Cantina Italiana	S	**N End**	22
Carlo's Cucina	**Allston**	25
Z Carmen	**N End**	26
Casino Wharf	N	**CC**	20
Chesca's	**MV**	23
Ciao Bella	**Back Bay**	19
Ciro & Sal's	N	**CC**	20
NEW Coppa	**S End**	⌐
Daily Catch	S	**multi.**	24
Dante	**E Cambridge**	24
Davide Rist.	N	**N End**	24
Da Vinci	**Park Sq**	22
Z Davio's	N	**multi.**	25
Z Delfino	**Roslindale**	27
DeMarco	N	**Nan**	22
Donatello	**Saugus**	24
NEW Ducali	**N End**	⌐
Erbaluce	**Park Sq**	⌐
Euno	S	**N End**	24
Fairway	**CC**	18
Fanizzi's	**CC**	20
Fazio's	**CC**	20
Figs	**multi.**	23
Filippo	**N End**	21
Florentine Cafe	**N End**	21
Z Front St.	**CC**	27
Z Galleria Umberto	**N End**	26
Gennaro's Five N.	**N End**	⌐
Z Giacomo's	**multi.**	25
Gina's	**CC**	21
Grapevine	**Salem**	25
Greg's	**Watertown**	19
Grotto	N	**Beacon Hill**	25
Z Il Capriccio	N	**Waltham**	27
NEW Il Casale	**Belmont**	⌐
Il Panino	**N End**	23
NEW Il Tesoro/Terrace	**MV**	⌐
Incontro	**Franklin**	22
Ivy Rest.	**D'town Cross**	20
Jetties	**Nan**	14

Jimmy Seas | MV	23
Joe Tecce's | S | N End	19
🆉 La Campania | Waltham	28
La Cantina | Framingham	20
La Cucina/Mare | CC	25
La Fam. Giorgio | N End	23
La Galleria 33 | N End	26
La Morra | N | Brookline	24
L'Andana | N | Burlington	25
La Summa | S | N End	22
Lattanzi's | N | MV	21
Lil Vinny's | S | Somerville	20
Limoncello | N End	22
L'Osteria | N End	23
Lucca | N | N End	25
Lucca Back Bay | Back Bay	21
Lucia | S | multi.	21
Maggiano's | Park Sq	19
Mamma Maria | N End	25
Marco Romana | N End	26
Mare | N End	26
Marliave | D'town Cross	22
Massimino's Cucina | N End	23
Maurizio's | N End	25
🆉 Maxwell's 148 | Natick	26
🆕 Messina | CC	-
Mother Anna's | N End	21
Nauset Beach | N | CC	25
Nebo | N End	21
Nico | N End	-
🆉 No. 9 Park | Beacon Hill	28
Olivadi | Norwood	-
Orta | Hanover	-
Osteria/Civetta | N | CC	-
Out of/Blue | Somerville	22
Pagliuca's | S | N End	22
🆕 Palio's | Lexington	-
Panificio | Beacon Hill	19
Paolo's Trattoria | Charlestown	21
Papa Razzi | multi.	18
🆕 Pazzo | Back Bay	-
Pellino's | N | Marblehead	-
Piattini | Back Bay	23
Piccola Venezia | N End	22
Piccolo Nido | N End	24
Pi Pizzeria | S | Nan	23
Pizzeria Regina | Medford	24
Polcari's | multi.	17
Pomodoro | multi.	24
🆕 Pomodoro | Needham	-
🆉 Prezza | N End	27
🆉 Rialto | Harv Sq	26
Rist. Damiano | N End	-
Rist. Fiore | N End	21
Rist. Marcellino | S | Waltham	16

🆕 Rist. Pavarotti | Reading	-
Rist. Toscano | N | Beacon Hill	24
Rist. Villa Francesca | N End	19
Riva | Scituate	26
Rocca | S End	24
Rustic Kitchen | multi.	20
Sagra | Somerville	16
Salvatore's | Seaport Dist	20
Saporito's | N | Hull	26
Saraceno | N End	23
Scampo | Beacon Hill	22
Scoozi | Back Bay	18
Serafina | N | Concord	20
Sfoglia | Nan	24
Siena | CC	21
Siros | N Quincy	19
62 on Wharf | Salem	24
🆕 Sofia | W Roxbury	-
🆉 Sorellina | Back Bay	27
Sorento's | N | Marlborough	18
Sorriso | Leather Dist	20
Spiga Trattoria | Needham	-
Sportello | Seaport Dist	-
Stella | S End	24
Stellina | Watertown	22
Strega Rest. | Salem	21
Strega Rist. | N End	21
Sweet Basil | Needham	25
🆉 Taranta | S | N End	27
Tartufo | S | Newton	22
🆕 Tavolino | multi.	-
Tavolo | Dorchester	-
Teatro | Theater Dist	24
Terramia | N End	26
Tomasso | Southborough	24
Tosca | N | Hingham	25
Tratt. Il Panino | N End	23
🆉 Tratt. di Monica/Vinoteca | N End	26
🆉 Tratt. Toscana | N | Fenway	26
Tratt. Pulcinella | Huron Vill	20
Tresca | N End	23
Tuscan Grill | N | Waltham	24
Umbria Prime | Financial Dist	23
Via Matta | Park Sq	25
Village Fish | Needham	20
Vin & Eddie's | N | Abington	17
Vinny's/Night | S | Somerville	23
Zabaglione | Ipswich	22

JAPANESE

(* sushi specialist)

Apollo Grill* | Chinatown	17
Blue Fin* | multi.	22
Cafe Sushi* | Harv Sq	17

China Sky* | **Wellesley** — 19
Douzo* | **Back Bay** — 24
Z Fugakyu* | **multi.** — 25
NEW Ginger Ex.* | **Inman Sq** — -
Ginza* | **multi.** — 23
Haru* | **Back Bay** — 20
Z Inaho* | **CC** — 27
JP Seafood* | **Jamaica Plain** — 23
Kayuga | **multi.** — 24
Kaze | **Chinatown** — 23
Koreana* | **Central Sq** — 21
Lotus Blossom* | **Sudbury** — 22
Misaki* | **CC** — 24
Mr. Sushi* | **multi.** — 21
Net Result* | **MV** — 25
New Ginza* | **Watertown** — 24
Oga's* | **Natick** — 26
Z Oishii* | **multi.** — 27
Osushi* | **Back Bay** — 23
Z O Ya* | **Leather Dist** — 28
Sakurabana* | **Financial Dist** — 25
Sapporo* | **Newton** — 21
Seiyo* | **S End** — 25
Shabu-Zen | **multi.** — 22
Shogun* | **Newton** — 23
Suishaya* | **Chinatown** — 21
Sushi by Yoshi* | **Nan** — 25
Village Sushi* | **Roslindale** — 23
Wagamama | **multi.** — 18
Wu Chon | **Somerville** — 22
Yama* | **multi.** — 22
Zen* | **Beacon Hill** — 24

JEWISH

Zaftigs | **Brookline** — 21

KOREAN

(* barbecue specialist)
Apollo Grill* | **Chinatown** — 17
JP Seafood | **Jamaica Plain** — 23
Kayuga | **multi.** — 24
Koreana* | **Central Sq** — 21
New Jang Su* | **Burlington** — 23
Sapporo | **Newton** — 21
Seoul Food | **Porter Sq** — 22
Suishaya | **Chinatown** — 21
Village Sushi | **Roslindale** — 23
Wu Chon | **Somerville** — 22

KOSHER/
KOSHER-STYLE

Rami's | **Brookline** — 23
Rubin's | **Brookline** — 19

LEBANESE

Byblos | **Norwood** — 24
Cafe Barada | **Porter Sq** — 23

Phoenicia | **Beacon Hill** — 21
Shawarma King | **Brookline** — 22

MALAYSIAN

Penang | **Chinatown** — 22

MEDITERRANEAN

Z Abba | **CC** — 27
Ardeo | **CC** — 20
Athan's Café | **multi.** — 23
Avila | **Theater Dist** — 24
Bar 10 | **Back Bay** — 17
Blue Moon | **CC** — 24
Café Fleuri | **Financial Dist** — 22
Café Mangal | **Wellesley** — 25
Cafeteria | **Back Bay** — 17
Z Caffe Bella | **Randolph** — 26
Casablanca | **Harv Sq** — 22
Chiara | **Westwood** — 26
Figs at 29 Fair | **Nan** — -
Z Ithaki Med. | **Ipswich** — 26
Kouzina | **Newton** — 23
La Voile | **Back Bay** — 23
Les Zygomates | **Leather Dist** — 22
NEW Mediterranean | **MV** — -
NEW Milestone | **Wellesley** — -
Z Mistral | **S End** — 27
Z Oleana | **Inman Sq** — 28
Z Olives | **Charlestown** — 25
Z Pisces | **CC** — 27
Porcini's | **Watertown** — 22
Rendezvous | **Central Sq** — 26
Sabur | **Somerville** — 22
Sophia's | **Roslindale** — 23
Trevi Café | **CC** — -
Vlora | **Back Bay** — 22

MEXICAN

Angela's Café | **E Boston** — -
Baja Betty's | **Brookline** — 20
Cantina la Mexicana | **Somerville** — 24
Casa Romero | **Back Bay** — 23
Cilantro | **Salem** — 18
NEW Dorado | **Brookline** — -
El Sarape | **Braintree** — 25
Forest Café | **Porter Sq** — 20
José's | **Huron Vill** — 19
La Paloma | **Quincy** — 21
La Verdad | **Fenway** — 22
Lorraine's | **CC** — 20
Olé/Olecito | **multi.** — 24
Picante | **Central Sq** — 19
Poe's/Rattlesnake | **Back Bay** — -
Purple Cactus | **Jamaica Plain** — 21
Sharky's | **MV** — 21

Sol Azteca	**multi.**	20
Sunset Grill/Cantina	**Boston U**	20
Tacos El Charro	**Jamaica Plain**	23
Tacos Lupita	**multi.**	25
Taqueria Mexico	**Waltham**	22
Tu y Yo	**multi.**	24
Zócalo Cocina	**multi.**	22

MIDDLE EASTERN

Café Algiers	**Harv Sq**	18
Cafe Jaffa	**Back Bay**	22
Middle East	**Central Sq**	17
Rami's	**Brookline**	23
Red Fez	**S End**	18
Sofra Bakery	**Huron Vill**	26
Sound Bites	**Somerville**	22
Zuzu!	**Central Sq**	20

MOROCCAN

NEW Tajine	**Harv Sq**	-
Z Tangierino	**Charlestown**	24

NEPALESE

Coriander Bistro	**Sharon**	-
Himalayan Bistro	**W Roxbury**	24
Kathmandu Spice	**Arlington**	22

NEW ENGLAND

Arno's	**Nan**	16
Baxter's	**CC**	18
Capt. Frosty's	**CC**	21
Capt. Parker's	**CC**	18
Chart Room	**CC**	20
Coonamessett	**CC**	18
Durgin-Park	**Faneuil Hall**	17
Fireplace	**Brookline**	21
Z Gibbet Hill	**Groton**	24
Green St.	**Central Sq**	24
Hemisphere	**CC**	17
Henrietta's	**Harv Sq**	23
Home Port	**MV**	20
Jasper White's	**multi.**	21
Jetties	**Nan**	14
Landfall	**CC**	18
Longfellow's	**Sudbury**	18
Maddie's Sail	**Marblehead**	-
Merchants Row	**Concord**	23
Moby Dick's	**CC**	19
No Name	**Seaport Dist**	-
NEW North 26	**Faneuil Hall**	-
Out of/Blue	**Somerville**	22
Parker's	**D'town Cross**	22
Red Inn	**CC**	24
Sherborn Inn	**Sherborn**	19
Sidecar Café	**MV**	-

NEW Technique	**E Cambridge**	-
Tom Shea's	**Essex**	20
Z Union Oyster	**Faneuil Hall**	20
Water St.	**MV**	-
Woodman's	**Essex**	23

NOODLE SHOPS

New Dong Khanh	**Chinatown**	22
Wagamama	**multi.**	18

NORTH AFRICAN

Baraka Cafe	**Central Sq**	26

NUEVO LATINO

Betty's Wok	**MFA**	19
Cinco	**Nan**	26
Naked Fish	**multi.**	19

PAKISTANI

Ghazal	**Jamaica Plain**	-
Grain & Salt	**Allston**	-

PERSIAN

Lala Rokh	**Beacon Hill**	23
Sorento's	**Marlborough**	18

PERUVIAN

Don Ricardo's	**S End**	23
Machu Picchu	**Somerville**	19
Masona Grill	**W Roxbury**	25
Rincon Limeno	**E Boston**	-
Z Taranta	**N End**	27

PIZZA

Antico Forno	**N End**	23
Bertucci's	**multi.**	17
Bluestone Bistro	**Brighton**	17
Cambridge 1	**multi.**	22
NEW Ducali	**N End**	-
Emma's	**Kendall Sq**	24
Fairway	**CC**	18
NEW Federal	**Beacon Hill**	-
Figs	**multi.**	23
Z Galleria Umberto	**N End**	26
Hot Tomatoes	**multi.**	22
Lattanzi's	**MV**	21
Nebo	**N End**	21
Picco	**S End**	22
Pi Pizzeria	**Nan**	23
Pizzeria Regina	**multi.**	24
Pleasant Cafe	**Roslindale**	18
Polcari's	**multi.**	17
Santarpio's Pizza	**E Boston**	25
Scoozi	**Back Bay**	18
Sophia's	**Roslindale**	23
Tavolo	**Dorchester**	-

Upper Crust	**multi.**	23
Veggie Planet	**Harv Sq**	23
Woody's Grill	**Fenway**	22
Za	**Arlington**	25

POLISH

| Café Polonia | **S Boston** | 24 |

POLYNESIAN

| Kowloon | **Saugus** | 17 |

PORTUGUESE

Atasca	**Kendall Sq**	23
Casa Portugal	**Inman Sq**	21
Neighborhood Rest.	**Somerville**	23
Sunset Cafe	**Inman Sq**	19

PUB FOOD

Audubon Circle	**Kenmore Sq**	21
Black Cow	**multi.**	19
Blarney Stone	**Dorchester**	16
Boston/Salem Beer	**multi.**	18
Brighton Beer	**Brighton**	-
Bukowski	**multi.**	17
Burren	**Somerville**	14
Cambridge Common	**Harv Sq**	17
Capt. Kidd	**CC**	18
Cheers	**multi.**	14
Coolidge Corner	**Brookline**	17
Cornwall's	**Kenmore Sq**	15
Doyle's	**Jamaica Plain**	15
Green Briar	**Brighton**	17
Halfway Cafe	**multi.**	17
John Harvard's	**multi.**	16
Johnny D's	**Somerville**	19
Joshua Tree	**multi.**	15
NEW Lansdowne	**Fenway**	-
Littlest	**Financial Dist**	-
Matt Murphy's	**Brookline**	22
Mission B&G	**MFA**	19
M.J. O'Connor's	**multi.**	-
Newes/America	**MV**	18
Publick House	**Brookline**	21
Sunset Grill/Cantina	**multi.**	20
21st Amendment	**Beacon Hill**	17
Warren	**Charlestown**	16

RUSSIAN

| Café St. Petersburg | **Newton** | 19 |

SALVADORAN

| Tacos Lupita | **multi.** | 25 |

SANDWICHES

All Star	**Inman Sq**	23
Angelo's	**Stoneham**	26
Boloco	**multi.**	18
Cafe Podima	**Beacon Hill**	19
Flour Bakery	**multi.**	26
Haley House	**Roxbury**	24
Hi-Rise	**multi.**	24
Other Side	**Back Bay**	19
Oxford Spa	**Porter Sq**	21
Parish Cafe	**multi.**	22
Sorelle	**Charlestown**	23
Stone Soup	**Ipswich**	25
Strip-T's	**Watertown**	22
Vicki Lee's	**Belmont**	25
Volle Nolle	**N End**	26

SEAFOOD

Academy Ocean	**CC**	22
Anthony's	**Seaport Dist**	18
Aqua Grille	**CC**	19
Arnold's Lobster	**CC**	23
Atlantica	**Cohasset**	15
Atlantic Fish/Chop	**MV**	-
Atlantic Fish	**Back Bay**	23
Back Eddy	**Westport**	22
Z B&G Oysters	**S End**	26
Barking Crab	**Seaport Dist**	16
Barley Neck Inn	**CC**	20
Baxter's	**CC**	18
Bayside	**Westport**	-
Bite	**MV**	26
NEW Blue Canoe	**MV**	-
Bookstore & Rest.	**CC**	19
Boston Sail	**Waterfront**	15
Z Brewster Fish	**CC**	26
Bubala's	**CC**	16
Capt. Frosty's	**CC**	21
Captain's Table	**Wellesley**	-
Casino Wharf	**CC**	20
Catch of the Day	**CC**	25
Chapin's Fish/Beach Bar	**CC**	-
Chart House	**Waterfront**	21
Chart Room	**CC**	20
Z Clam Box	**Ipswich**	26
Cobie's Clam	**CC**	19
Cooke's	**CC**	-
Courthouse	**E Cambridge**	22
Daily Catch	**multi.**	24
Dolphin	**CC**	21
Dolphin Seafood	**multi.**	18
Z East Coast	**Inman Sq**	25
East Ocean	**Chinatown**	24
Fanizzi's	**CC**	20
Finz	**multi.**	20
Fishmonger's	**CC**	18
Friendly Fisherman	**CC**	24
Z Giacomo's	**multi.**	25

Home Port | **MV**	20
Impudent Oyster | **CC**	23
Jasper White's | **Hingham**	21
JT's Seafood | **CC**	17
Jumbo | **multi.**	23
Kate's Seafood | **CC**	20
KingFish Hall | **Faneuil Hall**	22
Landfall | **CC**	18
Larsen's Fish | **MV**	27
Z Legal Sea | **multi.**	22
Liam's | **CC**	20
Lobster Pot | **CC**	22
Mac's | **CC**	24
Maddie's Sail | **Marblehead**	18
Marshside | **CC**	15
McCormick/Schmick | **multi.**	21
Moby Dick's | **CC**	23
Morse Fish | **S End**	21
Naked Fish | **multi.**	19
Naked Oyster | **CC**	25
Nantucket Lobster | **Nan**	19
Z Neptune Oyster | **N End**	27
Net Result | **MV**	25
No Name | **Seaport Dist**	19
Oceana | **Waterfront**	24
Oceanaire | **Financial Dist**	24
Out of/Blue | **Somerville**	22
Oyster Co. | **CC**	23
Peach Farm | **Chinatown**	25
Z Pisces | **CC**	27
Port | **CC**	23
Roadhouse | **CC**	20
Ropewalk | **Nan**	-
NEW Rowes Wharf | **Waterfront**	-
Sea Grille | **Nan**	22
Sir Cricket's | **CC**	24
Skipjack's | **multi.**	20
Smith/Wollensky | **Back Bay**	23
Straight Wharf | **Nan**	25
Tamarind Bay | **Brookline**	24
Turner Fish | **Back Bay**	21
Z Union Oyster | **Faneuil Hall**	20
Village Fish | **Needham**	20
Wicked Oyster | **CC**	24
Woodman's | **Essex**	23

SMALL PLATES

(See also Spanish tapas specialist)

Bar 10 | Med. | **Back Bay**	17
Bond | Eclectic | **Financial Dist**	-
Clink | Amer. | **Beacon Hill**	19
NEW Coppa | Italian | **S End**	-
Z Cuchi Cuchi | Eclectic | **Central Sq**	22
District | Amer. | **Leather Dist**	17

Drink | Amer. | **Seaport Dist**	-
Flat Iron | Amer. | **W End**	22
Ivy Rest. | Italian | **D'town Cross**	20
La Morra | Italian | **Brookline**	24
Masa | SW | **S End**	23
Z Meritage | Amer. | **Waterfront**	27
Middlesex | Eclectic | **Central Sq**	17
NEW Pairings | Amer. | **Park Sq**	-
Piattini | Italian | **Back Bay**	23
Rist. Damiano | Italian | **N End**	-
Sanctuary | Eclectic | **Financial Dist**	19
606 Congress | Amer. | **Seaport Dist**	21
Sophia's | Med. | **Roslindale**	23
Trevi Café | Med. | **CC**	-

SOUTH AFRICAN

Karoo Kafe | **CC**	24

SOUTH AMERICAN

Bon Savor | **Jamaica Plain**	20

SOUTHERN

Z Hungry Mother | **Kendall Sq**	27
NEW Tupelo | **Inman Sq**	-

SOUTHWESTERN

Cottonwood | **Back Bay**	18
Masa | **multi.**	23
Zapotec | **MV**	19

SPANISH

(* tapas specialist)

BarLola* | **Back Bay**	18
Cinco* | **Nan**	26
Dalí* | **Somerville**	25
Estragon* | **S End**	-
NEW Kama* | **Quincy**	-
Solea* | **Waltham**	23
Taberna/Haro* | **Brookline**	23
Tapéo* | **Back Bay**	22
Tasca* | **Brighton**	23
Z Toro* | **S End**	26

STEAKHOUSES

Z Abe & Louie's | **Back Bay**	26
Atlantic Fish/Chop | **MV**	-
Bokx | **Newton Lower Falls**	23
Z Capital Grille | **multi.**	26
Z Davio's | **multi.**	25
Fleming's Prime | **Park Sq**	24
Frank's Steak | **Porter Sq**	18
Z Grill 23 | **Back Bay**	25
Hilltop Steak | **Saugus**	16
Jimmy's Steer | **multi.**	20
KO Prime | **D'town Cross**	24

Met B&G | **multi.** — 21

Metropolitan | **Chestnut Hill** — 21

Midwest | **multi.** — 20

Mooo... | **Beacon Hill** — 24

🔼 Morton's | **multi.** — 25

🔼 Oak Room | **Back Bay** — 25

Palm | **Back Bay** — 23

Pellana | **Peabody** — 26

Plaza III | **Faneuil Hall** — 21

Roadhouse | **CC** — 20

🔼 Ruth's Chris | **D'town Cross** — 24

Scarlet Oak | **Hingham** — 20

Smith/Wollensky | **Back Bay** — 23

NEW Sofia | **W Roxbury** — -

Stockyard | **Brighton** — 15

Tango | **Arlington** — 21

Umbria Prime | **Financial Dist** — 23

TAIWANESE

MuLan Taiwanese | **Kendall Sq** — 23

Shangri-La | **Belmont** — 23

Taiwan Cafe | **Chinatown** — 23

TEAROOMS

Dunbar Tea | **CC** — 22

Optimist Café | **CC** — 21

TEX-MEX

🔼 Anna's | **multi.** — 22

Boca Grande | **multi.** — 19

Boloco | **multi.** — 18

Border Cafe | **multi.** — 19

Cactus Club | **Back Bay** — 16

Fajitas/'Ritas | **D'town Cross** — 16

THAI

🔼 Abba | **CC** — 27

Amarin Thailand | **multi.** — 22

Bamboo | **Brighton** — 23

Bangkok Bistro | **Brighton** — 22

Bangkok Blue | **Back Bay** — 21

Bangkok City | **Back Bay** — 20

Brown Sugar/Similans | **multi.** — 25

Chilli Duck | **Back Bay** — 21

Dok Bua | **Brookline** — 24

Equator | **S End** — 18

Erawan/Siam | **Waltham** — 22

Green Papaya | **Waltham** — 20

House of Siam | **S End** — 24

Jamjuli | **Newton** — 19

Khao Sarn | **Brookline** — 24

King & I | **Beacon Hill** — 22

Lam's | **Newtonville** — 21

9 Tastes | **Harv Sq** — 20

Penang | **Chinatown** — 22

Pho n' Rice | **Somerville** — -

NEW Ronnarong | **Somerville** — -

Spice Thai | **Harv Sq** — 21

Sugar & Spice | **Porter Sq** — 20

Thai Basil | **Back Bay** — 23

Thaitation | **Fenway** — -

Wonder Spice | **Jamaica Plain** — 21

TIBETAN

House of Tibet | **Somerville** — -

Martsa's/Elm | **Somerville** — 21

Tashi Delek | **Brookline** — -

TURKISH

Brookline Family | **Brookline** — 21

Café Mangal | **Wellesley** — 25

NEW Pasha | **Arlington** — -

Sultan's Kitchen | **Financial Dist** — 24

VEGETARIAN

(* vegan)

Grasshopper* | **Allston** — 20

Grezzo* | **multi.** — 23

NEW Prana Café* | **Newton** — -

UFood | **multi.** — 18

Veggie Planet | **Harv Sq** — 23

VENEZUELAN

La Casa/Pedro | **Watertown** — 21

Orinoco | **multi.** — 25

VIETNAMESE

Lam's | **Newtonville** — 21

Le's | **multi.** — 21

New Dong Khanh | **Chinatown** — 22

Pho Hoa | **multi.** — 22

Pho Lemongrass | **Brookline** — 20

Pho n' Rice | **Somerville** — -

Pho Pasteur | **Chinatown** — 23

Xinh Xinh | **Chinatown** — 25

Locations

Includes names, cuisines, Food ratings and, for locations that are mapped, top list with map coordinates.

Boston

ALLSTON/BOSTON U./BRIGHTON

Athan's Café	Med./Bakery	23
Bamboo	Thai	23
Bangkok Bistro	Thai	22
Bluestone Bistro	Pizza	17
Brighton Beer	Pub	-
Brown Sugar/Similans	Thai	25
Café Belô	Brazilian	20
Café Brazil	Brazilian	23
Carlo's Cucina	Italian	25
Deep Ellum	Eclectic	18
Devlin's	Amer.	20
Grain & Salt	Indian/Pakistani	-
Grasshopper	Asian/Vegan	20
Green Briar	Pub	17
Jasmine	French/Hungarian	24
Joshua Tree	Pub	15
Le's	Viet.	21
Noodle St.	Asian	19
Punjab Palace	Indian	24
Shabu-Zen	Japanese	22
Shanghai Gate	Chinese	24
Soul Fire	BBQ	21
Stockyard	Steak	15
Sunset Grill/Cantina	Mex./Pub	20
Tasca	Spanish	23
UBurger	Burgers	23
Zócalo Cocina	Mex.	22

BACK BAY

(See map on page 246)

TOP FOOD

L'Espalier	French	**D3**	28
Clio/Uni	French	**D1**	27
Sorellina	Italian	**D5**	27
Capital Grille	Steak	**E1**	26
Abe & Louie's	Steak	**D4**	26

LISTING

☑ Abe & Louie's	Steak	26
Asana	Amer./Asian	-
Atlantic Fish	Seafood	23
Bangkok Blue	Thai	21
Bangkok City	Thai	20
BarLola	Spanish	18
Bar 10	Med.	17
B. Good	Health	19

Bhindi Bazaar	Indian	22
NEW Bistro du Midi	French	-
Boloco	Eclectic	18
Bottega	Italian	24
Bouchée	French	21
Brasserie Jo	French	20
☑ Bristol Lounge	Amer.	24
Brownstone	Amer.	15
Bukowski	Pub	17
Cactus Club	Tex-Mex	16
NEW Cafe 47	Amer.	-
Café at Taj	Eclectic	20
Cafe Jaffa	Mideast.	22
Cafeteria	Med.	17
☑ Capital Grille	Steak	26
Casa Romero	Mex.	23
Charley's	Amer.	18
☑ Cheesecake	Amer.	18
Chilli Duck	Thai	21
Ciao Bella	Italian	19
NEW City Table	Amer.	-
☑ Clio/Uni	French	27
NEW Corner Tavern	Amer.	-
Cottonwood	SW	18
NEW Courtyard/Boston Library	Amer.	-
Daily Grill	Amer.	19
Dillon's	Amer.	16
Douzo	Japanese	24
Fire & Ice	Eclectic	16
☑ Grill 23	Steak	25
Haru	Japanese	20
Island Hopper	Asian	19
Jasper White's	New Eng.	21
Kashmir	Indian	23
Laurel	Amer.	20
La Voile	French/Med.	23
☑ Legal Sea	Seafood	22
☑ L'Espalier	French	28
Lucca Back Bay	Italian	21
☑ Morton's	Steak	25
☑ Oak Room	Steak	25
Osushi	Japanese	23
Other Side	Sandwiches	19
Palm	Steak	23
Papa Razzi	Italian	18
Parish Cafe	Sandwiches	22
NEW Pazzo	Italian	-
P.F. Chang's	Chinese	19
Piattini	Italian	23

Pizzeria Regina	*Pizza*	24
Poe's/Rattlesnake	*Mex.*	-
NEW Post 390	*Amer.*	-
Scoozi	*Italian*	18
🏷 Sel de Terre	*French*	23
NEW Six Burner	*Amer.*	-
Skipjack's	*Seafood*	20
Smith/Wollensky	*Steak*	23
Sonsie	*Eclectic*	20
🏷 Sorellina	*Italian*	27
Stanhope Grille	*Amer.*	23
Stephanie's	*Amer.*	20
Steve's Greek	*Greek*	20
Stix	*Eclectic*	17
Tapéo	*Spanish*	22
Thai Basil	*Thai*	23
33 Rest.	*Amer.*	20
🏷 Top of Hub	*Amer.*	20
Trident	*Eclectic*	19
Turner Fish	*Seafood*	21
29 Newbury	*Amer.*	20
Upper Crust	*Pizza*	23
Vlora	*Med.*	22
Vox Populi	*Amer.*	16
Wagamama	*Noodles*	18
Wine Cellar	*Continental/Fondue*	20

BEACON HILL

(See map on page 244)

TOP FOOD

No. 9 Park	*French/Italian*	**D6**	28
Grotto	*Italian*	**A6**	25
Pierrot Bistrot	*French*	**A3**	24
Rist. Toscano	*Italian*	**D2**	24
Mooo...	*Steak*	**C6**	24

LISTING

🏷 Anna's	*Tex-Mex*	22
Antonio's Cucina	*Italian*	22
Artú	*Italian*	21
Beacon Hill	*French*	22
Bin 26	*Italian*	21
Cafe Podima	*Sandwiches*	19
Cheers	*Pub*	14
Clink	*Amer.*	19
NEW Federal	*Pizza/Sandwiches*	-
Figs	*Italian*	23
Grotto	*Italian*	25
Harvard Gardens	*Amer.*	17
Hungry I, The	*French*	24
King & I	*Thai*	22
Lala Rokh	*Persian*	23
Ma Soba	*Asian*	20
Mooo...	*Steak*	24
🏷 No. 9 Park	*French/Italian*	28

Panificio	*Italian*	19
Paramount	*Amer.*	23
Phoenicia	*Lebanese*	21
Pierrot Bistrot	*French*	24
Rist. Toscano	*Italian*	24
Scampo	*Italian*	22
Scollay Sq.	*Amer.*	19
75 Chestnut	*Amer.*	21
21st Amendment	*Pub*	17
Upper Crust	*Pizza*	23
Zen	*Japanese*	24

CHARLESTOWN

Figs	*Italian*	23
Max/Dylan	*Amer.*	-
Navy Yard	*Amer.*	23
🏷 Olives	*Med.*	25
Paolo's Trattoria	*Italian*	21
Sorelle	*Coffee*	23
🏷 Tangierino	*Moroccan*	24
Tavern/Water	*Amer.*	13
Warren	*Amer.*	16

CHELSEA/ EAST BOSTON/ REVERE

Angela's Café	*Mex.*	-
Billy Tse	*Asian*	20
Ecco	*Amer.*	-
Floating Rock	*Cambodian*	-
NewBridge	*Amer.*	24
Rincon Limeno	*Colombian/Peruvian*	-
Santarpio's Pizza	*Pizza*	25
Tacos Lupita	*Mex./Salvadoran*	25

CHINATOWN/ LEATHER DIST.

(See map on page 244)

TOP FOOD

O Ya	*Japanese*	**H9**	28
Pizzeria Regina	*Pizza*	**H10**	24
Kaze	*Japanese*	**G7**	23
Taiwan Cafe	*Taiwanese*	**H7**	23
Jumbo	*Chinese/Seafood*	**H8**	23

LISTING

Apollo Grill	*Japanese/Korean*	17
Chau Chow	*Chinese*	21
China Pearl	*Chinese*	21
District	*Amer.*	17
East Ocean	*Chinese/Seafood*	24
Emperor's Gdn.	*Chinese*	21
Ginza	*Japanese*	23
Jumbo	*Chinese/Seafood*	23
Kaze	*Japanese*	23

Menus, photos, voting and more – free at ZAGAT.com

Les Zygomates	*French/Med.*	22
New Dong Khanh	*Viet.*	22
New Shanghai	*Chinese*	16
☑ O Ya	*Japanese*	28
Peach Farm	*Chinese/Seafood*	25
Penang	*Malaysian*	22
Pho Hoa	*Viet.*	22
Pho Pasteur	*Viet.*	23
Pizzeria Regina	*Pizza*	24
Shabu-Zen	*Japanese*	22
Sorriso	*Italian*	20
South St. Diner	*Diner*	16
Suishaya	*Japanese/Korean*	21
Taiwan Cafe	*Taiwanese*	23
Xinh Xinh	*Viet.*	25

DORCHESTER/ MATTAPAN/ ROXBURY/ WEST ROXBURY

Ashmont Grill	*Amer.*	22
Blarney Stone	*Pub*	16
Haley House	*Amer.*	24
Himalayan Bistro	*Indian/Nepalese*	24
NEW Ledge	*Amer.*	-
Masona Grill	*Amer./Peruvian*	25
Merengue	*Dominican*	-
Pho Hoa	*Viet.*	22
Rest. Cesaria	*Cape Verd.*	-
Rudi's	*Amer.*	-
Shanti India	*Indian*	-
NEW Sofia	*Italian/Steak*	-
Tavolo	*Italian*	-
224 Boston St.	*Amer.*	22
Victoria's	*Diner*	20
West/Centre	*Amer.*	18

DOWNTOWN CROSSING

(See map on page 244)

TOP FOOD

Ruth's Chris	*Steak*	**C8**	24
Locke-Ober	*Amer./Continental*	**E7**	24
KO Prime	*Steak*	**D7**	24
Parker's	*New Eng.*	**C8**	22
Silvertone B&G	*Amer.*	**D7**	21

LISTING

Avenue One	*Amer.*	18
Bina Osteria	*Italian*	-
Boloco	*Eclectic*	18
Chacarero	*Chilean*	-
Fajitas/'Ritas	*Tex-Mex*	16
Good Life	*Amer.*	17

Hot Tomatoes	*Pizza*	22
Ivy Rest.	*Italian*	20
Kingston	*Amer.*	20
KO Prime	*Steak*	24
Locke-Ober	*Amer./Continental*	24
Mantra	*French/Indian*	18
Marliave	*Continental/Italian*	22
Max/Dylan	*Amer.*	-
Parker's	*New Eng.*	22
☑ Ruth's Chris	*Steak*	24
Silvertone B&G	*Amer.*	21
UFood	*Health*	18
Vinalia	*Amer.*	17

FANEUIL HALL

(See map on page 242)

TOP FOOD

Pizzeria Regina	*Pizza*	**F6**	24
Houston's	*Amer.*	**G5**	22
KingFish Hall	*Seafood*	**G6**	22
McCormick/Schmick	*Seafood*	**F6**	21
Plaza III	*Steak*	**F6**	21

LISTING

Bertucci's	*Italian*	17
Bombay Club	*Indian*	20
Cheers	*Pub*	14
Durgin-Park	*New Eng.*	17
Houston's	*Amer.*	22
KingFish Hall	*Seafood*	22
McCormick/Schmick	*Seafood*	21
NEW North 26	*New Eng.*	-
Pizzeria Regina	*Pizza*	24
Plaza III	*Steak*	21
Red Sky	*Amer.*	18
Steve's Greek	*Greek*	20
☑ Union Oyster	*New Eng./Seafood*	20
Wagamama	*Noodles*	18

FENWAY/ KENMORE SQUARE/ MFA

(See map on page 248)

TOP FOOD

Tratt. Toscana	*Italian*	**E6**	26
India Quality	*Indian*	**B7**	24
Petit Robert	*French*	**B7**	24
Elephant Walk	*Cambodian/French*	**C2**	23
UBurger	*Burgers*	**A7**	23

LISTING

| Audubon Circle | *Pub* | 21 |
| Bertucci's | *Italian* | 17 |

Betty's Wok | *Asian/Nuevo Latino* — 19
Boca Grande | *Tex-Mex* — 19
Boloco | *Eclectic* — 18
Boston/Salem Beer | *Pub* — 18
Bravo | *Eclectic* — 21
Burtons | *Amer.* — 21
Cambridge 1 | *Pizza* — 22
Canestaro | *Italian* — 19
Church | *Amer.* — 20
Cornwall's | *Pub* — 15
🗹 Eastern Stand. | *Amer./Euro.* — 22
🗹 Elephant Walk | *Cambodian/French* — 23
Gardner Museum | *Amer.* — 20
India Quality | *Indian* — 24
NEW Lansdowne | *Amer./Irish* — -
La Verdad | *Mex.* — 22
Mission B&G | *Pub* — 19
Olé/Olecito | *Mex.* — 24
🗹 Petit Robert | *French* — 24
Sol Azteca | *Mex.* — 20
NEW Symphony 8 | *Amer.* — -
Thaitation | *Thai* — -
🗹 Tratt. Toscana | *Italian* — 26
UBurger | *Burgers* — 23
UFood | *Health* — 18
Upper Crust | *Pizza* — 23
Woody's Grill | *Amer.* — 22

FINANCIAL DISTRICT

(See map on page 242)

TOP FOOD

Radius | *French* | **K5** — 26
Sakurabana | *Japanese* | **H6** — 25
Sultan's Kitchen | *Turkish* | **G6** — 24
Oceanaire | *Seafood* | **G3** — 24
Umbria Prime | *Italian/Steak* | **I7** — 23

LISTING

Boloco | *Eclectic* — 18
Bond | *Eclectic* — -
Café Fleuri | *Med.* — 22
Caliterra | *Calif./Italian* — 16
Littlest | *Pub* — -
Market | *Amer.* — 16
Oceanaire | *Seafood* — 24
🗹 Radius | *French* — 26
Sakurabana | *Japanese* — 25
Sanctuary | *Eclectic* — 19
Sultan's Kitchen | *Turkish* — 24
Umbria Prime | *Italian/Steak* — 23
NEW Woodward | *Amer.* — -

JAMAICA PLAIN

Alchemist | *Amer.* — 17
Bella Luna/Milky Way | *Italian* — -

Bon Savor | *French/South Amer.* — 20
Bukhara | *Indian* — 23
Centre St. Café | *Eclectic* — 25
Doyle's | *Pub* — 15
El Oriental/Cuba | *Cuban* — 24
Ghazal | *Indian* — -
James's Gate | *Amer./Irish* — 16
JP Seafood | *Japanese/Korean* — 23
Purple Cactus | *Eclectic/Mex.* — 21
NEW Robinwood | *Amer.* — -
Sorella's | *Amer.* — 26
Tacos El Charro | *Mex.* — 23
🗹 Ten Tables | *Amer./Euro.* — 27
Upper Crust | *Pizza* — 23
Wonder Spice | *Cambodian/Thai* — 21

NORTH END

(See map on page 242)

TOP FOOD

Neptune Oyster | *Seafood* | **D5** — 27
Taranta | *Italian/Peruvian* | **D5** — 27
Prezza | *Italian* | **C7** — 27
Carmen | *Italian* | **D6** — 26
Tratt. di Monica/Vinoteca | *Italian* | **C6** | **D6** — 26

LISTING

Al Dente | *Italian* — 22
Antico Forno | *Italian* — 23
Artú | *Italian* — 21
Assaggio | *Italian* — 24
Bacco | *Italian* — 21
Billy Tse | *Asian* — 20
Bricco | *Italian* — 25
Caffe Paradiso | *Coffee* — 17
Cantina Italiana | *Italian* — 22
🗹 Carmen | *Italian* — 26
Daily Catch | *Italian/Seafood* — 24
Davide Rist. | *Italian* — 24
NEW Ducali | *Italian* — -
Euno | *Italian* — 24
Filippo | *Italian* — 21
Florentine Cafe | *Italian* — 21
🗹 Galleria Umberto | *Italian* — 26
Gennaro's Five N. | *Italian* — -
🗹 Giacomo's | *Italian* — 25
Grezzo | *Vegan* — 23
Hot Tomatoes | *Pizza* — 22
Il Panino | *Italian* — 23
Joe's American | *Amer.* — 16
Joe Tecce's | *Italian* — 19
La Fam. Giorgio | *Italian* — 23
La Galleria 33 | *Italian* — 26
La Summa | *Italian* — 22
Limoncello | *Italian* — 22

L'Osteria | *Italian*	23
Lucca | *Italian*	25
Lucia | *Italian*	21
Mamma Maria | *Italian*	25
Marco Romana | *Italian*	26
Mare | *Italian*	26
Massimino's Cucina | *Italian*	23
Maurizio's | *Italian*	25
Mother Anna's | *Italian*	21
Nebo | *Pizza*	21
Z Neptune Oyster | *Seafood*	27
Nico | *Italian*	-
North St. Grille | *Amer.*	23
Pagliuca's | *Italian*	22
Piccola Venezia | *Italian*	22
Piccolo Nido | *Italian*	24
Pizzeria Regina | *Pizza*	24
Pomodoro | *Italian*	24
Z Prezza | *Italian*	27
Rist. Damiano | *Italian*	-
Rist. Fiore | *Italian*	21
Rist. Villa Francesca | *Italian*	19
Saraceno | *Italian*	23
Strega Rist. | *Italian*	21
Z Taranta | *Italian/Peruvian*	27
Terramia | *Italian*	26
Tratt. Il Panino | *Italian*	23
Z Tratt. di Monica/Vinoteca | *Italian*	26
Tresca | *Italian*	23
Volle Nolle | *Sandwiches*	26

PARK SQUARE

(See map on page 246)

TOP FOOD

Via Matta | *Italian* | **C8**	25
Davio's | *Italian/Steak* | **D8**	25
Fleming's Prime | *Steak* | **D8**	24
Finale | *Dessert* | **C8**	23
Da Vinci | *Italian* | **D7**	22

LISTING

Da Vinci | *Italian*	22
Z Davio's | *Italian/Steak*	25
Erbaluce | *Italian*	-
Finale | *Dessert*	23
Flash's | *Amer.*	18
Fleming's Prime | *Steak*	24
Z Legal Sea | *Seafood*	22
Maggiano's | *Italian*	19
McCormick/Schmick | *Seafood*	21
Melting Pot | *Fondue*	20
M.J. O'Connor's | *Pub*	-
NEW Pairings | *Amer.*	-
Via Matta | *Italian*	25

SEAPORT DISTRICT

Anthony's | *Seafood*	18
Aura | *Amer.*	22
Barking Crab | *Seafood*	16
Daily Catch | *Italian/Seafood*	24
Drink | *Amer.*	-
Flour Bakery | *Bakery*	26
LTK | *Eclectic*	20
Lucky's | *Amer.*	18
M.J. O'Connor's | *Pub*	-
Z Morton's | *Steak*	25
No Name | *New Eng./Seafood*	19
Salvatore's | *Italian*	20
606 Congress | *Amer.*	21
Sportello | *Italian*	-

SOUTH BOSTON

Amrheins | *Amer.*	18
Café Polonia | *Polish*	24
Franklin | *Amer.*	26
St. Alphonzo's | *Amer.*	22

SOUTH END

(See map on page 246)

TOP FOOD

Oishii | *Japanese* | **G9**	27
Hamersley's | *French* | **G7**	27
Mistral | *French/Med.* | **E7**	27
Toro | *Spanish* | **J6**	26
Flour Bakery | *Bakery* | **I6**	26

LISTING

Addis Red Sea | *Ethiopian*	22
Anchovies | *Italian*	20
Z Aquitaine | *French*	23
Z B&G Oysters | *Seafood*	26
Beehive | *Amer.*	18
Bombay Club | *Indian*	20
Butcher Shop | *French/Italian*	25
Charlie's Sandwich | *Diner*	23
Club Cafe | *Amer.*	18
Coda | *Amer.*	22
Columbus Café | *Eclectic*	19
NEW Coppa | *Italian*	-
Delux Cafe | *Eclectic*	21
Don Ricardo's | *Brazilian/Peruvian*	23
Equator | *Eclectic/Thai*	18
Estragon | *Spanish*	-
Flour Bakery | *Bakery*	26
Franklin | *Amer.*	26
Gaslight Brasserie | *French*	21
Z Giacomo's | *Italian*	25
NEW Ginger Park | *Asian*	-
Z Hamersley's | *French*	27
House of Siam | *Thai*	24
Jae's | *Asian*	20

Masa	*SW*	23
Mela	*Indian*	24
Metropolis	*Eclectic*	23
Mike's	*Diner*	20
🗹 Mistral	*French/Med.*	27
Morse Fish	*Seafood*	21
Myers + Chang	*Asian*	23
🗹 Oishii	*Japanese*	27
Orinoco	*Venez.*	25
Parish Cafe	*Sandwiches*	22
🗹 Petit Robert	*French*	24
Picco	*Dessert/Pizza*	22
Pops	*Amer.*	22
Red Fez	*Mideast.*	18
Rocca	*Italian*	24
Seiyo	*Japanese*	25
Sibling Rivalry	*Amer.*	24
South End Buttery	*Amer./Bakery*	21
Stella	*Italian*	24
Stephanie's	*Amer.*	20
NEW Stork Club	*Amer.*	–
NEW Teranga	*Senegalese*	–
🗹 Toro	*Spanish*	26
Tremont 647	*Amer.*	21
28 Degrees	*Amer.*	20
Union B&G	*Amer.*	24
Upper Crust	*Pizza*	23

THEATER DISTRICT

(See map on page 244)

TOP FOOD

Troquet	*Amer./French*	**G4**	27
Pigalle	*French*	**H4**	26
Avila	*Med.*	**G4**	24
Teatro	*Italian*	**G5**	24
Blu	*Amer.*	**G6**	21

LISTING

Avila	*Med.*	24
Blu	*Amer.*	21
Boloco	*Eclectic*	18
Jacob Wirth	*Amer./German*	17
Jer-Ne	*Amer.*	20
NEW Market	*Amer.*	–
P.F. Chang's	*Chinese*	19
Pigalle	*French*	26
Rustic Kitchen	*Italian*	20
Tantric	*Indian*	20
Teatro	*Italian*	24
🗹 Troquet	*Amer./French*	27

WATERFRONT

(See map on page 242)

TOP FOOD

Meritage	*Amer.*	**I8**	27
Oceana	*Amer./Seafood*	**G8**	24

Sel de Terre	*French*	**G8**	23
Legal Sea	*Seafood*	**G8**	22
Miel	*French*	**K7**	21

LISTING

Boston Sail	*Seafood*	15
Chart House	*Seafood*	21
🗹 Legal Sea	*Seafood*	22
Living Room	*Amer.*	15
🗹 Meritage	*Amer.*	27
Miel	*French*	21
Oceana	*Amer./Seafood*	24
NEW Rowes Wharf	*Seafood*	–
🗹 Sel de Terre	*French*	23
Sensing	*French*	–

WEST END

Boston/Salem Beer	*Pub*	18
DJ's	*Amer.*	–
Flat Iron	*Amer.*	22
West End Johnnie's	*Eclectic*	17

Cambridge

CAMBRIDGEPORT/ EAST CAMBRIDGE

🗹 Anna's	*Tex-Mex*	22
Bambara	*Amer.*	20
Boca Grande	*Tex-Mex*	19
🗹 Cheesecake	*Amer.*	18
Courthouse	*Seafood*	22
Dante	*Italian*	24
🗹 Helmand	*Afghan*	26
NEW Lord Hobo	*Amer.*	–
P.F. Chang's	*Chinese*	19
Brown Sugar/Similans	*Thai*	25
NEW Technique	*New Eng.*	–

CENTRAL SQUARE

(See map on page 250)

TOP FOOD

Craigie/Main	*French*	**B1**	27
Baraka Cafe	*African*	**H8**	26
Salts	*Amer./French*	**H10**	26
Rendezvous	*Med.*	**H8**	26
Central Kitchen	*Amer.*	**H9**	24

LISTING

Asmara	*Eritrean/Ethiopian*	21
Baraka Cafe	*African*	26
Basta Pasta	*Italian*	24
Bertucci's	*Italian*	17
Central Kitchen	*Amer.*	24
🗹 Craigie/Main	*French*	27
🗹 Cuchi Cuchi	*Eclectic*	22
NEW Dosa Factory	*Indian*	–

Green St. | *New Eng.* 24
India Pavilion | *Indian* 20
Koreana | *Japanese/Korean* 21
Mary Chung | *Chinese* 21
Middle East | *Mideast.* 17
Middlesex | *Eclectic* 17
Miracle of Science | *Pub* 19
Picante | *Calif./Mex.* 19
Rendezvous | *Med.* 26
Royal East | *Chinese* 20
Salts | *Amer./French* 26
Sidney's | *Amer.* 21
Tavern in Sq. | *Amer.* 17
1369 Coffeehouse | *Coffee* 20
Zuzu! | *Eclectic/Mideast.* 20

HARVARD SQUARE

(See map on page 250)

TOP FOOD

Ten Tables | *Amer./Euro.* | **B2** 27
Rialto | *Italian* | **E3** 26
Garden at Cellar | *Amer.* | **F6** 25
Harvest | *Amer.* | **D3** 25
Darwin's | *Coffee/Deli* | **D6** 24

LISTING

Bertucci's | *Italian* 17
B. Good | *Health* 19
Boloco | *Eclectic* 18
Border Cafe | *Cajun/Tex-Mex* 19
Café Algiers | *Mideast.* 18
Cafe of India | *Indian* 22
Cafe Sushi | *Japanese* 17
Cambridge Common | *Pub* 17
Cambridge 1 | *Pizza* 22
Casablanca | *Med.* 22
Charlie's Kitchen | *Diner* 17
Chez Henri | *Cuban/French* 24
Daedalus | *Amer.* 17
Darwin's | *Coffee/Deli* 24
Dolphin Seafood | *Seafood* 18
Finale | *Dessert* 23
Fire & Ice | *Eclectic* 16
Garden at Cellar | *Amer.* 25
Grafton St. Pub | *Amer.* 17
Harvest | *Amer.* 25
Henrietta's | *New Eng.* 23
Hi-Rise | *Bakery/Sandwiches* 24
John Harvard's | *Pub* 16
☒ Legal Sea | *Seafood* 22
Le's | *Viet.* 21
Mr. Bartley's | *Burgers* 24
9 Tastes | *Thai* 20
Om | *Amer.* 19
Red House | *Eclectic* 20
Redline | *Amer.* 17

☒ Rialto | *Italian* 26
Sandrine's | *French* 24
Spice Thai | *Thai* 21
NEW Tajine | *Moroccan* -
Tamarind Bay | *Indian* 24
Tanjore | *Indian* 22
☒ Ten Tables | *Amer./Euro.* 27
NEW Tory Row | *Amer.* -
Trata | *Amer.* -
Upper Crust | *Pizza* 23
☒ Upstairs/Square | *Amer.* 24
Veggie Planet | *Pizza/Veg.* 23
Wagamama | *Noodles* 18

HURON VILLAGE

Bertucci's | *Italian* 17
Full Moon | *Amer.* 20
Hi-Rise | *Bakery/Sandwiches* 24
Jasper White's | *New Eng.* 21
José's | *Mex.* 19
Sofra Bakery | *Mideast.* 26
Tratt. Pulcinella | *Italian* 20
T.W. Food | *Amer./French* 26

INMAN SQUARE

(See map on page 250)

TOP FOOD

Oleana | *Med.* | **E10** 28
East Coast | *BBQ/Seafood* | **D9** 25
Muqueca | *Brazilian* | **D10** 24
Olé/Olecito | *Mex.* | **D9** 24

LISTING

All Star | *Sandwiches* 23
Bukowski | *Pub* 17
Casa Portugal | *Portug.* 21
NEW East by NE | *Chinese* -
☒ East Coast | *BBQ/Seafood* 25
NEW Ginger Ex. | *Asian/Japanese* -
Haveli | *Indian* -
Midwest | *Brazilian/Steak* 20
Muqueca | *Brazilian* 24
☒ Oleana | *Med.* 28
Olé/Olecito | *Mex.* 24
Punjabi Dhaba | *Indian* 24
S&S | *Deli* 18
Sunset Cafe | *Amer./Portug.* 19
1369 Coffeehouse | *Coffee* 20
NEW Trina's | *Amer.* -
NEW Tupelo | *Southern* -

KENDALL SQUARE

Amelia's Trattoria | *Italian* 22
Atasca | *Portug.* 23
Black Sheep | *Amer.* 21
Blue Room | *Eclectic* 25
Emma's | *Pizza* 24

EZ EVOO | *Eclectic* 27
EZ Hungry Mother | *Amer.* 27
EZ Legal Sea | *Seafood* 22
MuLan Taiwanese | *Taiwanese* 23

PORTER SQUARE

Addis Red Sea | *Ethiopian* 22
EZ Anna's | *Tex-Mex* 22
Blue Fin | *Japanese* 22
Boca Grande | *Tex-Mex* 19
Cafe Barada | *Mideast.* 23
Changsho | *Chinese* 20
Christopher's | *Eclectic* 17
EZ Elephant Walk | 23
   Cambodian/French
Forest Café | *Mex.* 20
Frank's Steak | *Steak* 18
Oxford Spa | *Sandwiches* 21
Passage to India | *Indian* 20
Qingdao Gdn. | *Chinese* 24
Seoul Food | *Korean* 22
Sugar & Spice | *Thai* 20
Tavern in Sq. | *Amer.* 17
Temple Bar | *Amer.* 20
West Side | *Amer.* 22

Nearby Suburbs

ARLINGTON/ BELMONT/ WINCHESTER

Blue Ribbon BBQ | *BBQ* 25
Flora | *Amer.* 24
NEW Il Casale | *Italian* -
Jimmy's Steer | *Steak* 20
Kathmandu Spice | *Nepalese* 22
Kayuga | *Japanese/Korean* 24
Lucia | *Italian* 21
Mr. Sushi | *Japanese* 21
EZ Not Average Joe's | *Amer.* 18
NEW Pasha | *Turkish* -
Prose | *Amer.* 24
Punjab | *Indian* 25
Scutra | *Eclectic* 23
Shangri-La | *Taiwanese* 23
Tango | *Argent./Steak* 21
Tryst | *Amer.* 22
Vicki Lee's | *Bakery* 25
Za | *Pizza* 25
Zócalo Cocina | *Mex.* 22

BRAINTREE/MILTON/ QUINCY

NEW Abby Park | *Amer.* -
Bertucci's | *Italian* 17
NEW Bistro Chi | *Chinese* -
Blue22 | *Amer./Asian* 19

EZ Cheesecake | *Amer.* 18
China Pearl | *Chinese* 21
NEW 88 Wharf | *Amer.* -
El Sarape | *Mex.* 25
Firefly's | *BBQ* 20
Grand Chinatown | *Chinese* -
Joe's American | *Amer.* 16
NEW Kama | *Spanish* -
La Paloma | *Mex.* 21
Pho Hoa | *Viet.* 22
Pizzeria Regina | *Pizza* 24
Siros | *Italian* 19

BROOKLINE

EZ Anna's | *Tex-Mex* 22
Athan's Café | *Med./Bakery* 23
Baja Betty's | *Mex.* 20
Beacon St. Tavern | *Amer.* 20
Bertucci's | *Italian* 17
B. Good | *Health* 19
Boca Grande | *Tex-Mex* 19
Bottega | *Italian* 24
Brookline Family | *Turkish* 21
Chef Chang's | *Chinese* 20
Chef Chow's | *Chinese* 20
Coolidge Corner | *Pub* 17
Daily Catch | *Italian/Seafood* 24
Dalia's Bistro | *Amer.* 19
Dok Bua | *Thai* 24
NEW Dorado | *Mex.* -
Finale | *Dessert* 23
Fireplace | *New Eng.* 21
EZ Fugakyu | *Japanese* 25
Ginza | *Japanese* 23
Golden Temple | *Chinese* 21
Jerusalem Pita | *Israeli* -
Kayuga | *Japanese/Korean* 24
Khao Sarn | *Thai* 24
La Morra | *Italian* 24
Lineage | *Amer.* 23
Matt Murphy's | *Pub* 22
Mr. Sushi | *Japanese* 21
Orinoco | *Venezuelan* 25
Paris Creperie | *French* 22
Pho Lemongrass | *Viet.* 20
Pomodoro | *Italian* 24
Publick House | *Pub* 21
Rami's | *Mideast.* 23
Rani | *Indian* 20
Rubin's | *Deli* 19
Shawarma King | *Lebanese* 22
Sichuan Garden | *Chinese* 22
Super Fusion | *Asian* 27
Taberna/Haro | *Spanish* 23
Tamarind Bay | *Indian* 24
Tashi Delek | *Tibetan* -

Upper Crust	*Pizza*	23
Village Smokehse.	*BBQ*	19
Washington Sq.	*Amer.*	22
Zaftigs	*Deli*	21

CHESTNUT HILL

Aquitaine Bis	*French*	23
Bernard's	*Chinese*	24
Bertucci's	*Italian*	17
☎ Capital Grille	*Steak*	26
Charley's	*Amer.*	18
☎ Cheesecake	*Amer.*	18
NEW Forty Carrots	*Amer.*	-
☎ Legal Sea	*Seafood*	22
Le's	*Viet.*	21
Metropolitan	*Steak*	21
☎ Oishii	*Japanese*	27
Papa Razzi	*Italian*	18

DEDHAM/HYDE PARK/ ROSLINDALE

☎ Aquitaine	*French*	23
B. Good	*Health*	19
Birch St. Bistro	*Amer.*	19
☎ Delfino	*Italian*	27
Finz	*Seafood*	20
Geoffrey's Cafe	*Amer.*	19
Halfway Cafe	*Pub*	17
Isabella	*Amer.*	24
Joe's American	*Amer.*	16
Met B&G	*Steak*	21
P.F. Chang's	*Chinese*	19
Pleasant Cafe	*Amer.*	18
Sophia's	*Med.*	23
Studio 3	*Amer.*	-
Townsend's	*Amer.*	19
Village Sushi	*Japanese/Korean*	23

LEXINGTON

Lexx	*Amer.*	17
NEW Nourish	*Amer.*	-
NEW Palio's	*Italian*	-
Upper Crust	*Pizza*	23
Via Lago	*Amer.*	20
Yangtze River	*Chinese*	17

MEDFORD/ SOMERVILLE

Amelia's Kitchen	*Italian*	22
☎ Anna's	*Tex-Mex*	22
☎ Bistro 5	*Italian*	27
Boloco	*Eclectic*	18
NEW Boston Burger	*Burgers*	-
Burren	*Pub*	14
Café Belô	*Brazilian*	20
Cantina la Mexicana	*Mex.*	24
Dalí	*Spanish*	25

Diva Indian	*Indian*	22
Gargoyles	*Amer.*	24
Highland Kitchen	*Amer.*	23
House of Tibet	*Tibetan*	-
Independent, The	*Amer.*	18
Johnny D's	*Amer.*	19
Joshua Tree	*Pub*	15
Kebab Factory	*Indian*	24
Lil Vinny's	*Italian*	20
Machu Picchu	*Peruvian*	19
Martsa's/Elm	*Tibetan*	21
Mr. Crepe	*French*	18
Namaskar	*Indian*	23
Neighborhood Rest.	*Portug.*	23
Orleans	*Amer.*	17
Out of/Blue	*Seafood*	22
Pho n' Rice	*Thai/Vietnamese*	-
Pizzeria Regina	*Pizza*	24
Redbones	*BBQ*	22
Rodizio	*Brazilian*	22
NEW Ronnarong	*Thai*	-
Rosebud	*Diner*	16
Sabur	*Med.*	22
Sagra	*Italian*	16
Sound Bites	*Amer./Mideast.*	22
Tacos Lupita	*Mex./Salvadoran*	25
NEW Teele Sq.	*Amer.*	-
Tu y Yo	*Mex.*	24
Vinny's/Night	*Italian*	23
Wu Chon	*Japanese/Korean*	22
Zoe's	*Chinese*	19

NEEDHAM/NEWTON/ WABAN

Amarin Thailand	*Thai*	22
Appetito	*Italian*	19
Ariadne	*Amer.*	21
Bakers' Best	*Amer.*	22
Bertucci's	*Italian*	17
Biltmore B&G	*Amer.*	18
Blue on Highland	*Amer.*	17
Blue Ribbon BBQ	*BBQ*	25
Bokx	*Steak*	23
Café St. Petersburg	*Russian*	19
51 Lincoln	*Amer.*	23
Jamjuli	*Thai*	19
Johnny's Lunch.	*Diner*	18
Jumbo	*Chinese/Seafood*	23
Karoun	*Armenian/Mideast.*	22
Kouzina	*Greek/Med.*	23
Lam's	*Thai/Viet.*	21
Local	*Amer.*	-
☎ Lumière	*French*	27
Masala Art	*Indian*	23
No. 1 Noodle	*Asian*	18
☎ Not Average Joe's	*Amer.*	18

Peking Cuisine | *Chinese*	21
Z Petit Robert | *French*	24
Pie Bakery | *Amer./Dessert*	18
NEW Pomodoro | *Italian*	-
NEW Prana Café | *Vegan*	-
Sapporo | *Japanese/Korean*	21
Shogun | *Japanese*	23
Skipjack's | *Seafood*	20
Sol Azteca | *Mex.*	20
Spiga Trattoria | *Italian*	-
Sweet Basil | *Italian*	25
Tartufo | *Italian*	22
Tu y Yo | *Mex.*	24
Village Fish | *Italian/Seafood*	20

WALTHAM/ WATERTOWN

Aegean | *Greek*	21
Bison County | *BBQ*	18
Comfort | *Amer.*	-
Deluxe Town | *Diner*	22
Demos | *Greek*	21
Z Elephant Walk | *Cambodian/French*	23
Erawan/Siam | *Thai*	22
Green Papaya | *Thai*	20
Greg's | *Amer./Italian*	19
Halfway Cafe | *Pub*	17
Z Il Capriccio | *Italian*	27
Jake's Dixie | *BBQ*	17
Z La Campania | *Italian*	28
La Casa/Pedro | *Venez.*	21
Naked Fish | *Nuevo Latino/Seafood*	19
New Ginza | *Japanese*	24
New Mother India | *Indian*	22
Z Not Average Joe's | *Amer.*	18
Pizzeria Regina | *Pizza*	24
Ponzu | *Asian*	23
Porcini's | *Med.*	22
Rist. Marcellino | *Italian*	16
Solea | *Spanish*	23
Stellina | *Italian*	22
Strip-T's | *Amer.*	22
Taqueria Mexico | *Mex.*	22
Tempo | *Amer.*	21
Tuscan Grill | *Italian*	24
UFood | *Health*	18
Upper Crust | *Pizza*	23

Outlying Suburbs

NORTH OF BOSTON

Abbondanza | *Italian*	23
Angelo's | *Italian*	26
Black Cow | *Pub*	19
Blue Fin | *Japanese*	22

Border Cafe | *Cajun/Tex-Mex*	19
Brenden Crocker's | *Amer.*	25
Burtons | *Amer.*	21
Café Belô | *Brazilian*	20
Z Cheesecake | *Amer.*	18
China Pearl | *Chinese*	21
Cilantro | *Mex.*	18
Z Clam Box | *Seafood*	26
Cygnet | *Amer.*	21
Dog Bar | *Amer.*	23
Donatello | *Italian*	24
Z Duckworth's | *Amer.*	29
Exchange St. Bistro | *Eclectic*	20
NEW Farm Bar | *Amer./BBQ*	-
Finz | *Seafood*	20
Franklin | *Amer.*	26
G Bar | *Amer.*	21
Glenn's | *Eclectic*	23
Glory | *Amer.*	21
Grapevine | *Amer./Italian*	25
Grezzo | *Vegan*	23
Hilltop Steak | *Steak*	16
Z Ithaki Med. | *Med.*	26
Jimmy's Steer | *Steak*	20
Joe's American | *Amer.*	16
Kowloon | *Asian*	17
Landing | *Amer.*	16
Z Legal Sea | *Seafood*	22
Lyceum | *Eclectic*	23
Maddie's Sail | *New Eng./Seafood*	18
Masa | *SW*	23
Midwest | *Brazilian/Steak*	20
Naked Fish | *Nuevo Latino/Seafood*	19
Z Not Average Joe's | *Amer.*	18
Palmers | *Amer.*	-
Passage to India | *Indian*	20
Pellana | *Steak*	26
Pellino's | *Italian*	-
P.F. Chang's | *Chinese*	19
Pizzeria Regina | *Pizza*	24
Polcari's | *Italian*	17
Red Rock | *Amer.*	20
NEW Rist. Pavarotti | *Italian*	-
Boston/Salem Beer | *Pub*	18
Sichuan Garden | *Chinese*	22
62 on Wharf | *Italian*	24
Soma | *Amer.*	22
Stone Soup | *Eclectic*	25
Strega Rest. | *Italian*	21
Tacos Lupita | *Mex./Salvadoran*	25
Tavern in Sq. | *Amer.*	17
Tom Shea's | *New Eng.*	20
Woodman's | *New Eng./Seafood*	23
Yama | *Japanese*	22
Zabaglione | *Italian*	22

Menus, photos, voting and more – free at ZAGAT.com

SOUTH OF BOSTON

Atlantica | *Seafood*	15
Back Eddy | *Seafood*	22
Barker Tavern | *Amer.*	23
Bayside | *Seafood*	-
Bella's | *Italian*	19
Bia Bistro | *French/Italian*	24
Bistro 712 | *French*	24
Bon Caldo | *Italian*	22
Bridgeman's | *Italian*	26
Burtons | *Amer.*	21
Byblos | *Lebanese*	24
☑ Caffe Bella | *Med.*	26
Caffe Tosca | *Italian*	24
Chiara | *Med.*	26
Coriander Bistro | *Indian/Nepalese*	-
☑ Davio's | *Italian/Steak*	25
Halfway Cafe | *Pub*	17
Incontro | *Italian*	22
Jasper White's | *New Eng.*	21
Joe's American | *Amer.*	16
☑ Not Average Joe's | *Amer.*	18
Olivadi | *Italian*	-
Orta | *Italian*	-
Papa Razzi | *Italian*	18
Riva | *Italian*	26
Roobar | *Amer.*	21
Rustic Kitchen | *Italian*	20
Saporito's | *Italian*	26
Scarlet Oak | *Steak*	20
Skipjack's | *Seafood*	20
Sky | *Amer.*	19
☑ Square Café | *Amer.*	26
Stars on Hingham | *Diner*	16
Studio 3 | *Amer.*	-
NEW Suffolk Grille | *Amer.*	-
NEW Tavolino | *Italian*	-
Tosca | *Italian*	25
NEW Twenty8 Food | *Amer.*	-
Vin & Eddie's | *Italian*	17

WEST OF BOSTON

Aegean | *Greek*	21
Alta Strada | *Italian*	21
Amarin Thailand | *Thai*	22
Bertucci's | *Italian*	17
NEW Big Papi's | *Amer.*	-
☑ Blue Ginger | *Asian*	26
NEW Bobby's | *Amer.*	-
Border Cafe | *Cajun/Tex-Mex*	19
Bullfinch's | *Eclectic*	21
Cafe Escadrille | *Continental*	19
Café Mangal | *Med.*	25
☑ Capital Grille | *Steak*	26
Captain's Table | *Seafood*	-

☑ Cheesecake | *Amer.*	18
China Sky | *Chinese/Japanese*	19
CK Shanghai | *Chinese*	22
Cottage | *Calif.*	19
Dalya's | *Amer.*	23
Dolphin Seafood | *Seafood*	18
Firefly's | *BBQ*	20
☑ Fugakyu | *Japanese*	25
☑ Gibbet Hill | *New Eng./Steak*	24
Halfway Cafe | *Pub*	17
Harry's | *Diner*	20
Joe's American | *Amer.*	16
John Harvard's | *Pub*	16
☑ J's Nashoba | *Amer.*	26
La Cantina | *Italian*	20
L'Andana | *Italian*	25
Lavender Asian | *Asian*	-
Left Bank | *Amer.*	21
☑ Legal Sea | *Seafood*	22
Le Lyonnais | *French*	23
Longfellow's | *New Eng.*	18
Lotus Blossom | *Chinese/Japanese*	22
☑ Maxwell's 148 | *Asian/Italian*	26
Melting Pot | *Fondue*	20
Merchants Row | *New Eng.*	-
Met B&G | *Steak*	21
NEW Milestone | *Med.*	-
Naked Fish | *Nuevo Latino/Seafood*	19
New Jang Su | *Korean*	23
☑ Not Average Joe's | *Amer.*	18
Oga's | *Japanese*	26
☑ Oishii | *Japanese*	27
Papa Razzi | *Italian*	18
P.F. Chang's | *Chinese*	19
Pizzeria Regina | *Pizza*	24
☑ Sel de Terre | *French*	23
Serafina | *Italian*	20
Sherborn Inn | *New Eng.*	19
☑ Sichuan Gourmet | *Chinese*	27
NEW Singh's | *Indian*	-
Skipjack's | *Seafood*	20
Sky | *Amer.*	19
Sorento's | *Italian/Persian*	18
Summer Winter | *Amer.*	24
NEW Tavolino | *Italian*	-
Tomasso | *Italian*	24
Walden Grille | *Amer.*	15
Yama | *Japanese*	22
Zebra's Bistro | *Amer.*	24

Far Outlying Areas

CAPE COD

☑ Abba | *Med./Thai*	27
Academy Ocean | *Eclectic/Seafood*	22

Adrian's | *Amer./Italian*	16
Alberto's | *Italian*	20
Amari | *Italian*	22
Anthony Cummaquid | *Continental*	18
Aqua Grille | *Amer./Seafood*	19
Ardeo | *Med.*	20
Arnold's Lobster | *Seafood*	23
Barley Neck Inn | *Amer.*	20
Baxter's | *New Eng./Seafood*	18
Bayside Betsy's | *Amer.*	15
Bee-Hive Tavern | *Amer.*	19
Belfry Inne | *Amer.*	25
Betsy's Diner | *Diner*	18
Bistro/Crowne Pointe | *Amer.*	22
Blackfish | *Amer.*	24
Bleu | *French*	25
Blue Moon | *Med.*	24
Bookstore & Rest. | *Seafood*	19
Ⓩ Bramble Inn | *Amer.*	27
Brazilian Grill | *Brazilian*	21
Ⓩ Brewster Fish | *Seafood*	26
Bubala's | *Eclectic/Seafood*	16
Buca's Tuscan | *Italian*	23
Cafe Edwige/at Night | *Amer.*	26
Cape Sea | *Amer.*	26
Capt. Frosty's | *New Eng./Seafood*	21
Capt. Kidd | *Pub*	18
Capt. Linnell | *Amer.*	22
Capt. Parker's | *New Eng.*	18
Casino Wharf | *Italian/Seafood*	20
Catch of the Day | *Seafood*	25
Chapin's Fish/Beach Bar | *Seafood*	-
Chapoquoit Grill | *Amer.*	22
Chart Room | *New Eng./Seafood*	20
Chatham Bars | *Amer.*	22
Chatham Squire | *Eclectic*	18
Ⓩ Chillingsworth | *French*	27
Ciro & Sal's | *Italian*	20
Clancy's | *Amer.*	22
Cobie's Clam | *Seafood*	19
Cooke's | *Seafood*	-
Coonamessett | *New Eng.*	18
Dan'l Webster | *Amer.*	20
Devon's | *Amer./French*	24
Dolphin | *Seafood*	21
Dunbar Tea | *British/Tearoom*	22
Enzo | *French*	24
Fairway | *Amer./Italian*	18
Fanizzi's | *Amer./Italian*	20
Fazio's | *Italian*	20
Finely JP's | *Amer.*	21
Firefly Woodfire | *Eclectic*	20
Fishmonger's | *Amer./Seafood*	18
Five Bays | *Amer.*	25
Friendly Fisherman | *Seafood*	24
Ⓩ Front St. | *Continental/Italian*	27
Gina's | *Italian*	21
Hemisphere | *New Eng.*	17
Impudent Oyster | *Seafood*	23
Ⓩ Inaho | *Japanese*	27
Island Merchant | *Amer./Carib.*	-
JT's Seafood | *Seafood*	17
Karoo Kafe | *S African*	24
Kate's Seafood | *Seafood*	20
La Cucina/Mare | *Italian*	25
L'Alouette | *French*	26
Landfall | *Seafood*	18
Laura & Tony's | *Amer.*	-
Laureen's | *Amer.*	23
Liam's | *Seafood*	20
Lobster Pot | *Eclectic/Seafood*	22
Lorraine's | *Mex.*	20
NEW Lyric | *Amer.*	-
Mac's | *Seafood*	24
Marshside | *Seafood*	15
NEW Messina | *Italian*	-
Mews | *Amer.*	27
Misaki | *Japanese*	24
Moby Dick's | *New Eng./Seafood*	23
Naked Oyster | *Seafood*	25
Napi's | *Eclectic*	19
Nauset Beach | *Italian*	25
Ⓩ Not Average Joe's | *Amer.*	18
Ocean House | *Amer.*	25
Optimist Café | *Amer./British*	21
Orleans Inn | *Amer.*	17
Osteria/Civetta | *Italian*	-
Oyster Co. | *Seafood*	23
Paddock | *Amer.*	20
Pain D'Avignon | *Bakery/French*	-
Ⓩ Pisces | *Med./Seafood*	27
Port | *Amer./Seafood*	23
Post Office | *Amer.*	16
Red Inn | *New Eng.*	24
Ⓩ Red Pheasant | *Amer./French*	27
Regatta/Cotuit | *Amer.*	25
Roadhouse | *Seafood/Steak*	20
Roobar | *Amer.*	21
Ross' Grill | *Amer.*	22
Scargo Café | *Amer.*	20
Siena | *Italian*	21
Sir Cricket's | *Seafood*	24
Stir Crazy | *Cambodian*	23
Terra Luna | *Amer.*	24
Trevi Café | *Med.*	-
Ⓩ 28 Atlantic | *Amer.*	26
Vining's | *Eclectic*	24
Whitman Hse. | *Amer.*	21
Wicked Oyster | *Amer./Seafood*	24

Wild Goose | *Amer.* 21
Winslow's Tavern | *Amer.* 20

MARTHA'S VINEYARD

Alchemy | *Amer.* 22
Art Cliff | *Diner* 24
Atlantic Fish/Chop | *Seafood/Steak* -
Atria | *Amer.* 25
Beach Plum | *Amer.* 25
Bite | *Seafood* 26
Z Black Dog | *Amer.* 19
NEW Blue Canoe | *Seafood* -
Chesca's | *Eclectic/Italian* 23
NEW Chilmark Tavern | *Amer.* -
Cottage City | *Amer.* 22
NEW Danny Quinn's | *Amer.* -
David Ryan's | *Amer.* 15
Z Détente | *Amer.* 27
Home Port | *New Eng./Seafood* 20
NEW Il Tesoro/Terrace | *Italian* -
Jimmy Seas | *Italian* 23
Lambert's Cove | *Amer.* 25
Larsen's Fish | *Seafood* 27
Lattanzi's | *Italian* 21
Le Grenier | *French* 23
L'Étoile | *French* 26
Lure | *Amer.* 21
NEW Mediterranean | *Med.* -
Net Result | *Seafood* 25
Newes/America | *Pub* 18
Offshore Ale | *Amer.* 20
Z Outermost Inn | *Amer.* 25
Saltwater | *Eclectic* -
Sharky's | *Mex.* 21
Sidecar Café | *New Eng.* -
Slice of Life | *Amer.* -
NEW State Road | *Amer.* -
Sweet Life | *Amer./French* 25
Waterside Mkt. | *Amer.* -
Water St. | *New Eng.* -
Zapotec | *SW* 19
Zephrus | *Amer.* 20

NANTUCKET

American Seasons | *Amer.* 25
Arno's | *Amer.* 16
Black-Eyed Susan's | *Amer.* 26
Boarding House | *Amer.* 21
Brant Point | *Amer.* 21
Brotherhood/Thieves | *Amer.* 18
Cambridge St. | *Eclectic* -
Centre St. Bistro | *Amer.* 16
Chanticleer | *French* 25
Cinco | *Nuevo Latino* 26
Club Car | *Continental* 20
Z Company/Cauldron | *Amer.* 28
NEW Crosswinds | *Amer.* -
DeMarco | *Italian* 22
NEW Dune | *Amer.* -
Even Keel | *Amer.* 19
Fifty-Six Union | *Eclectic* 22
Figs at 29 Fair | *Med.* -
Fog Island | *Amer.* 21
Z Galley Beach | *Eclectic* 24
Jetties | *Italian/New Eng.* 14
Le Languedoc | *French* 26
Lo La 41° | *Eclectic* 21
Nantucket Lobster | *Seafood* 19
Òran Mór | *Eclectic* 24
Pearl | *Asian* 24
Pi Pizzeria | *Pizza* 23
Queequeg's | *Eclectic* 25
Ropewalk | *Seafood* -
Sconset Café | *Amer./Eclectic* 21
Sea Grille | *Seafood* 22
Sfoglia | *Italian* 24
Ships Inn | *Amer.* 24
Slip 14 | *Amer.* 18
Straight Wharf | *Seafood* 25
Summer House | *Amer.* 20
Sushi by Yoshi | *Japanese* 25
Z Topper's | *Amer.* 27
NEW Town | *Eclectic* -
Z 21 Federal | *Amer.* 24

BOSTON/CAPE COD

LOCATIONS

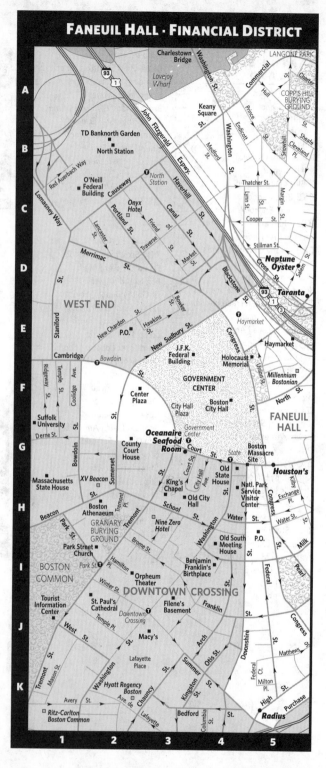

FANEUIL HALL · FINANCIAL DISTRICT

LANGONE PARK

Charlestown Bridge

Washington St.

Lovejoy Wharf

93
1

COPP'S HILL BURYING GROUND

Commercial St.
Hull St.
Charter St.
Sheafe St.
Cleveland Pl.

Keany Square

John Fitzgerald Expwy.

Prince St.
Endicott St.
Salem St.

TD Banknorth Garden

North Station

Washington St.
Medford St.

Red Auerbach Way

O'Neill Federal Building

Causeway St.

North Station T

Haverhill St.

Thatcher St.
Lynn St.
Margin St.
Cooper St.

Lomasney Way

Portland St.
Onyx Hotel

Canal St.

Friend St.
Traverse St.

Stillman St.

Lancaster St.

Merrimac St.

Market St.

Neptune Oyster

WEST END

Staniford St.

New Chardon St.

Hawkins St.

Bowker St.

Blackstone St.

Cross St.
Salem St.

93
1
3

Taranta

P.O.

Haymarket T

New Sudbury St.

Congress St.

Haymarket

Cambridge St.

Bowdoin T

J.F.K. Federal Building

Holocaust Memorial

Millennium Bostonian

Ridgeway St.
Temple St.
Coolidge Ave.

Center Plaza

GOVERNMENT CENTER

City Hall Plaza

Boston City Hall

Union St.
North St.

FANEUIL HALL

Suffolk University

Derne St.

Bowdoin St.

Somerset St.

County Court House

Government Center T

Oceanaire Seafood Room

Court Sq.
Court St.

State St.

Boston Massacre Site

Houston's

Massachusetts State House

XV Beacon

King's Chapel

City Hall Ave.

Old State House T

Natl. Park Service Visitor Center

Killby St.
Exchange Pl.

Beacon St.

Park St.

Boston Athenaeum

Tremont Pl.

Old City Hall

School St.

Water St.

Water St.
Milk St.

Nine Zero Hotel

Washington St.

Old South Meeting House

P.O.

GRANARY BURYING GROUND

Tremont St.

Brome St.

Federal St.

Park Street Church

Hamilton Pl.

Benjamin Franklin's Birthplace

Pearl St.

BOSTON COMMON

Park St. T

Orpheum Theater

DOWNTOWN CROSSING

Winter St.

Franklin St.

Congress St.

Tourist Information Center

St. Paul's Cathedral

Filene's Basement

Franklin St.

Downtown Crossing T

Devonshire St.

Temple Pl.

Macy's

Arch St.

Matthews St.

West St.

Lafayette Place

Summer St.

Otis St.

Federal Ct.
Milton Pl.

Tremont St.
Mason St.

Washington St.

Chauncy St.

Kingston St.

Columbia St.

Bedford St.

High St.

Avery St.

Ave. de Lafayette

Purchase St.

Ritz-Carlton Boston Common

Hyatt Regency Boston

Radius

A B C D E F G H I J K

1 2 3 4 5

242

Menus, photos, voting and more – free at ZAGAT.com

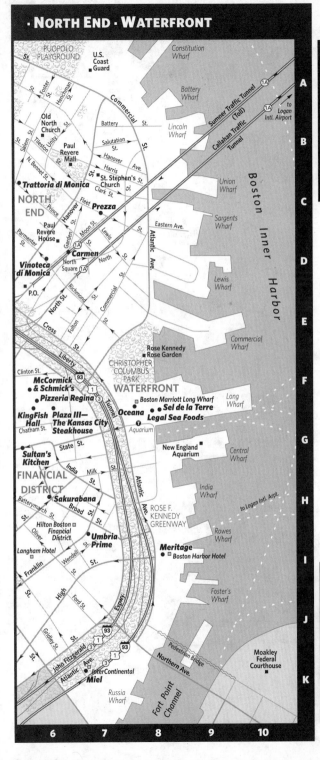

PUOPOLO PLAYGROUND

U.S. Coast Guard

Constitution Wharf

Foster St.

Henchman St.

Commercial St.

Battery Wharf

Sumner Traffic Tunnel (Toll)

to Logan Intl. Airport

Callahan Traffic Tunnel

Lincoln Wharf

Battery St.

Old North Church

Univ.

St.

N. Bennet St.

Tileston St.

Paul Revere Mall

Salutation St.

Hanover Ave.

Union Wharf

Harris St.

Boston Inner Harbor

Trattoria di Monica

St. Stephen's Church

Clark St.

NORTH END

Hanover

Prince St.

Fleet St.

Prezza

Garden

Moon St.

Lewis St.

Eastern Ave.

Sargents Wharf

Paul Revere House

Parmenter St.

Carmen

North

St.

North Square

1A

North St.

Vinoteca di Monica

P.O.

Richmond St.

Atlantic Ave.

Lewis Wharf

North St.

Commercial St.

Cross St.

Fulton St.

Commercial Wharf

Liberty

St.

Rose Kennedy Rose Garden

Clinton St.

CHRISTOPHER COLUMBUS PARK

McCormick & Schmick's

93

1

WATERFRONT

Pizzeria Regina

Tunnel

Boston Marriott Long Wharf

Long Wharf

KingFish Hall

Plaza III— The Kansas City Steakhouse

Chatham St.

Oceana

Sel de la Terre

Legal Sea Foods

Aquarium

State St.

Sultan's Kitchen

India St.

Milk St.

New England Aquarium

Central Wharf

FINANCIAL DISTRICT

Sakurabana

Batterymarch St.

Broad St.

India Wharf

ROSE F. KENNEDY GREENWAY

to Logan Intl. Arpt.

Hilton Boston Financial District

Oliver St.

Umbria Prime

Meritage

Boston Harbor Hotel

Rowes Wharf

Langham Hotel

Wendell St.

Franklin St.

Foster's Wharf

High St.

Ford St.

Espwy.

93

3

Gridley St.

93

John Fitzgerald

Atlantic Ave.

1

Pedestrian Bridge

Moakley Federal Courthouse

InterContinental

Miel

Northern Ave.

Russia Wharf

Fort Point Channel

MAPS

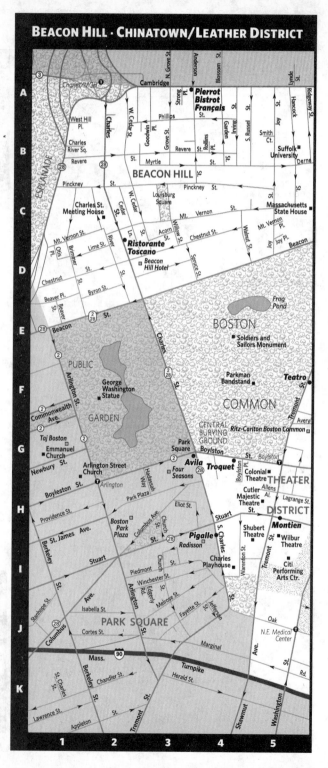

BEACON HILL · CHINATOWN/LEATHER DISTRICT

Menus, photos, voting and more – free at ZAGAT.com

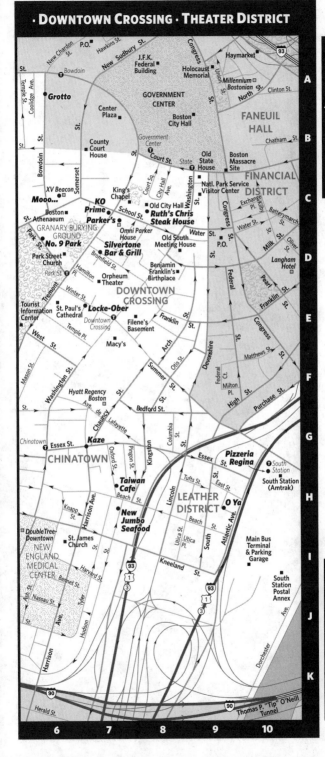

New Chardon St. P.O. Hawkins St.
New Sudbury St.
Bowdoin
Temple St.
Coolidge Ave.
Grotto
St.
J.F.K.
Federal
Building
Holocaust
Memorial
*Millennium
Bostonian
North*
Haymarket
93
Clinton St.
Clinton St.
**GOVERNMENT
CENTER**
Center
Plaza
Boston
City Hall
**FANEUIL
HALL**
Chatham St.
County
Court
House
Somerset
Government
Center
Court St.
State
Old
State
House
Boston
Massacre
Site
**FINANCIAL
DISTRICT**
XV Beacon
Mooo...
Boston
Athenaeum
**KO
Prime**
Parker's
King's
Chapel
City Hall
Ave.
Court Sq.
Washington
Natl. Park Service
Visitor Center
Exchange
Pl.
Batterymarch
St.
**GRANARY BURYING
GROUND**
No. 9 Park
Park St.
Park Street
Church
School St.
**Ruth's Chris
Steak House**
Omni Parker
House
**Silvertone
Bar & Grill**
Old South
Meeting House
Water St.
P.O.
Water St.
Milk St.
Oliver St.
Congress
Tremont
Hamilton
Pl.
Park St.
Bromfield St.
Benjamin
Franklin's
Birthplace
Federal
Pearl
St.
**Langham
Hotel**
**Orpheum
Theater**
**DOWNTOWN
CROSSING**
Franklin
St.
Congress
St.
Tourist
Information
Center
Winter St.
**St. Paul's
Cathedral**
Locke-Ober
Temple Pl.
*Downtown
Crossing*
Filene's
Basement
Franklin
St.
Devonshire
St.
West
St.
Mason St.
Macy's
Arch
St.
Summer
Otis St.
St.
Federal
Ct.
Milton
Pl.
High
Matthews St.
Washington St.
Washington
St.
Hyatt Regency
Boston
Ave. de Lafayette
Chauncy
Bedford St.
Purchase St.
Chinatown
Essex St.
Kaze
CHINATOWN
Oxford St.
Pingon St.
Kingston
Columbia
St.
Essex
St.
East St.
Tufts St.
St.
**Pizzeria
Regina**
**South
Station
(Amtrak)**
South
Station
**Taiwan
Cafe**
Beach
St.
Lincoln
**LEATHER
DISTRICT**
Beach
St.
Atlantic Ave.
O Ya
Knapp
St.
Harrison Ave.
**New
Jumbo
Seafood**
Utica
Utica
Pl.
St.
South
Main Bus
Terminal
& Parking
Garage
**DoubleTree-
Downtown**
St. James
Church
Kneeland
St.
**NEW
ENGLAND
MEDICAL
CENTER**
Bennet St.
Harvard St.
93
1
3
93
1
3
**South
Station
Postal
Annex**
Ash St.
Nassau St.
Tyler
Hudson
Harrison
Ave.
Dorchester
90
Herald St.
90
Thomas P. "Tip" O'Neill
Tunnel

| 6 | 7 | 8 | 9 | 10 |

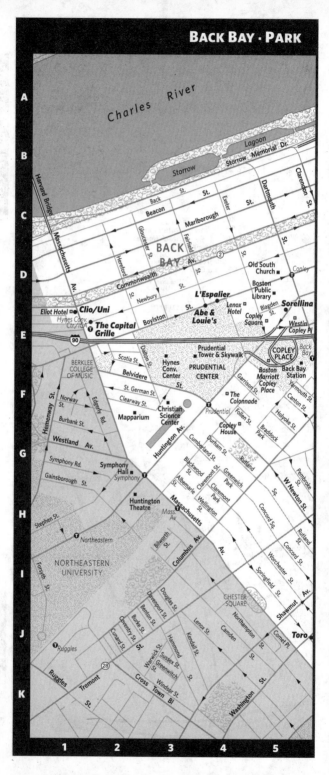

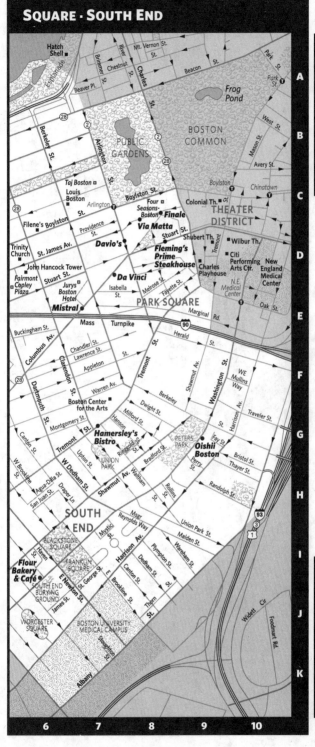

Hatch Shell

Mt. Vernon St.

River St.

Brimmer St.

Chestnut St.

Charles St.

Beacon St.

Park St.

Park St.

Esplanade

Beaver Pl.

Frog Pond

PUBLIC GARDENS

Arlington St.

BOSTON COMMON

West St.

Mason St.

Avery St.

Boylston

Chinatown

Taj Boston

Louis Boston

Four Seasons-Boston

Colonial Th.

THEATER DISTRICT

Filene's Boylston

Boylston St.

Finale

Arlington

Via Matta

Providence St.

Stuart St.

Shubert Th.

Wilbur Th.

Trinity Church

St. James Av.

Davio's

Fleming's Prime Steakhouse

Tremont

Citi Performing Arts Ctr.

New England Medical Center

John Hancock Tower

Da Vinci

Charles Playhouse

Fairmont Copley Plaza

Stuart St.

Isabella St.

Melrose St.

N.E. Medical Center

Jurys Boston Hotel

Fayette St.

Mistral

PARK SQUARE

Marginal Rd.

Oak St.

Buckingham St.

Mass Turnpike

Herald

Columbus Av.

Chandler St.

Tremont St.

Washington St.

Clarendon

Lawrence St.

Appleton

St.

Shawmut Av.

WE Mullins Way

Dartmouth

Warren Av.

Berkeley

Harrison Av.

Traveler St.

Boston Center for the Arts

Dwight St.

St.

Canton St.

Montgomery St.

Tremont St.

Milford St.

Hanson

Hamersley's Bistro

Ringgold St.

Bradford St.

PETERS PARK

Fay St.

Oishii Boston

W Dedham St.

UNION PARK

Waltham

Shawmut Av.

Bristol St.

Thayer St.

W Brookline St.

Agua-Dila St.

San Juan St.

Draper Ln.

Rollins St.

Randolph St.

SOUTH END

Msgr. Reynolds Way

Mystic

Union Park St.

Malden St.

93

Harrison Av.

Wareham St.

BLACKSTONE SQUARE

Plympton St.

Flour Bakery & Café

Haven

FRANKLIN SQUARE

E Newton St.

St. George St.

Brookline St.

Canton St.

Dedham St.

Thorn St.

SOUTH END BURYING GROUND

James St.

WORCESTER SQUARE

BOSTON UNIVERSITY MEDICAL CAMPUS

Stoughton St.

Widett Cir.

Foodmart Rd.

Albany

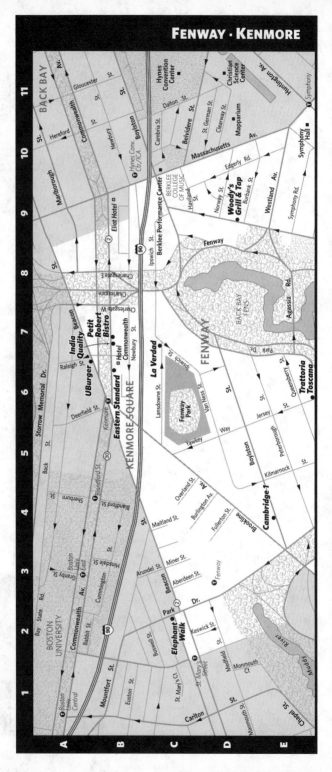

Menus, photos, voting and more - free at ZAGAT.com

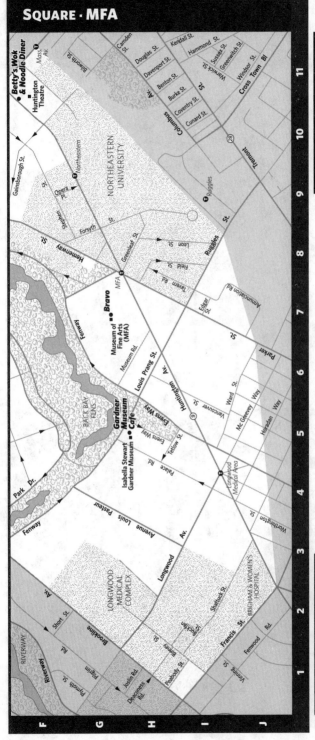

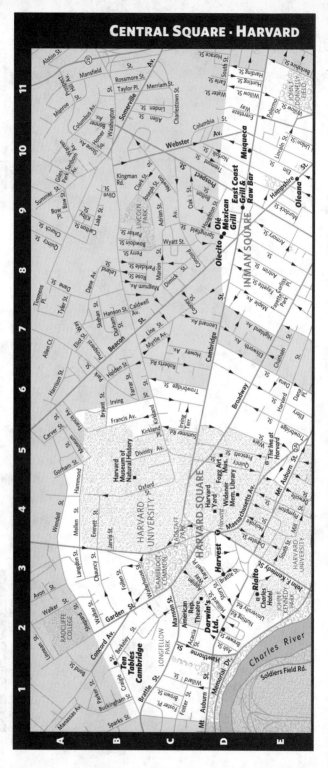

Menus, photos, voting and more – free at ZAGAT.com

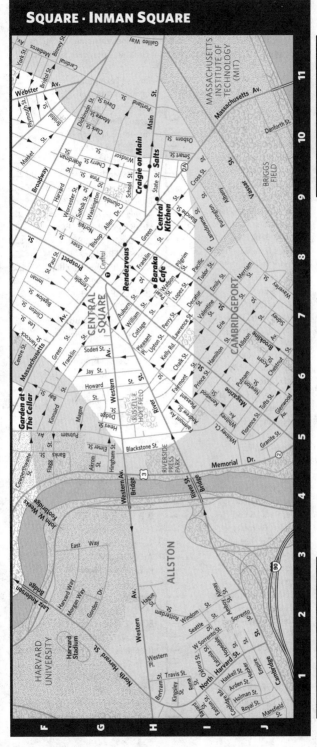

Special Features

Listings cover the best in each category and include names, locations and Food ratings. Multi-location restaurants' features may vary by branch.

ADDITIONS

(Properties added since the last edition of the book)

Abby Park	**Milton**	–
Angela's Café	**E Boston**	–
Bayside	**Westport**	–
Big Papi's	**Framingham**	–
Bistro Chi	**Quincy**	–
Bistro du Midi	**Back Bay**	–
Blue Canoe	**MV**	–
Bobby's	**Wellesley Hills**	–
Boston Burger	**Somerville**	–
Cafe 47	**Back Bay**	–
Chapin's Fish/Beach Bar	**CC**	–
Chilmark Tavern	**MV**	–
City Table	**Back Bay**	–
Coppa	**S End**	–
Coriander Bistro	**Sharon**	–
Corner Tavern	**Back Bay**	–
Courtyard/Boston Library	**Back Bay**	–
Crosswinds	**Nan**	–
Danny Quinn's	**MV**	–
Dorado	**Brookline**	–
Dosa Factory	**Central Sq**	–
Ducali	**N End**	–
Dune	**Nan**	–
East by NE	**Inman Sq**	–
88 Wharf	**Milton**	–
Farm Bar	**Essex**	–
Federal	**Beacon Hill**	–
Forty Carrots	**Chestnut Hill**	–
Ginger Ex.	**Inman Sq**	–
Ginger Park	**S End**	–
Il Casale	**Belmont**	–
Il Tesoro/Terrace	**MV**	–
Kama	**Quincy**	–
Lansdowne	**Fenway**	–
Ledge	**Dorchester**	–
Lord Hobo	**E Cambridge**	–
Lyric	**CC**	–
Market	**Theater Dist**	–
Mediterranean	**MV**	–
Messina	**CC**	–
Milestone	**Wellesley**	–
Nico	**N End**	–
North 26	**Faneuil Hall**	–
Nourish	**Lexington**	–
Pain D'Avignon	**CC**	–
Pairings	**Park Sq**	–

Palio's	**Lexington**	–
Palmers	**Andover**	–
Pasha	**Arlington**	–
Pazzo	**Back Bay**	–
Pomodoro	**Needham**	–
Post 390	**Back Bay**	–
Prana Café	**Newton**	–
Rist. Pavarotti	**Reading**	–
Robinwood	**Jamaica Plain**	–
Ronnarong	**Somerville**	–
Rowes Wharf	**Waterfront**	–
Singh's	**Wellesley Hills**	–
Six Burner	**Back Bay**	–
Sofia	**W Roxbury**	–
Spiga Trattoria	**Needham**	–
State Road	**MV**	–
Stork Club	**S End**	–
Studio 3	**multi.**	–
Suffolk Grille	**Canton**	–
Symphony 8	**Fenway**	–
Tajine	**Harv Sq**	–
Tashi Delek	**Brookline**	–
Tavolino	**multi.**	–
Technique	**E Cambridge**	–
Teele Sq.	**Somerville**	–
Teranga	**S End**	–
Tory Row	**Harv Sq**	–
Town	**Nan**	–
Trina's	**Inman Sq**	–
Tupelo	**Inman Sq**	–
Twenty8 Food	**Foxboro**	–
Woodward	**Financial Dist**	–

BREAKFAST

(See also Hotel Dining)

Arno's	**Nan**	16
Art Cliff	**MV**	24
Bakers' Best	**Newton**	22
Bayside Betsy's	**CC**	15
Betsy's Diner	**CC**	18
☑ Black Dog	**MV**	19
Black-Eyed Susan's	**Nan**	26
Bon Savor	**Jamaica Plain**	20
Brookline Family	**Brookline**	21
Cafe Edwige/at Night	**CC**	26
Centre St. Bistro	**Nan**	16
Chacarero	**D'town Cross**	–
Charlie's Sandwich	**S End**	23
Deluxe Town	**Watertown**	22
Even Keel	**Nan**	19

Fairway | **CC**	18
Flour Bakery | **S End**	26
Fog Island | **Nan**	21
Haley House | **Roxbury**	24
Harry's | **Westborough**	20
Hi-Rise | **multi.**	24
Johnny's Lunch. | **Newton**	18
Laureen's | **CC**	23
Mike's | **S End**	20
Neighborhood Rest. | **Somerville**	23
Optimist Café | **CC**	21
Oxford Spa | **Porter Sq**	21
Panificio | **Beacon Hill**	19
Paramount | **Beacon Hill**	23
Rosebud | **Somerville**	16
Rubin's | **Brookline**	19
S&S | **Inman Sq**	18
Sconset Café | **Nan**	21
Sorella's | **Jamaica Plain**	26
Sorelle | **Charlestown**	23
Sound Bites | **Somerville**	22
South End Buttery | **S End**	21
South St. Diner | **Leather Dist**	16
Stars on Hingham | **Hingham**	16
Trident | **Back Bay**	19
Via Lago | **Lexington**	20
Vicki Lee's | **Belmont**	25
Victoria's | **Roxbury**	20
Waterside Mkt. | **MV**	-
Wicked Oyster | **CC**	24

BRUNCH

🛛 Abe & Louie's | **Back Bay**	26
Alchemist | **Jamaica Plain**	17
🛛 Aquitaine | **S End**	23
Aquitaine Bis | **Chestnut Hill**	23
Ashmont Grill | **Dorchester**	22
Bakers' Best | **Newton**	22
Beacon Hill | **Beacon Hill**	22
Bleu | **CC**	25
Blue Room | **Kendall Sq**	25
Bombay Club | **S End**	20
Bon Savor | **Jamaica Plain**	20
Bullfinch's | **Sudbury**	21
Cafe Edwige/at Night | **CC**	26
Café Fleuri | **Financial Dist**	22
Café Polonia | **S Boston**	24
Centre St. Café | **Jamaica Plain**	25
Charley's | **multi.**	18
Columbus Café | **S End**	19
Coonamessett | **CC**	18
Cottage City | **MV**	22
Dante | **E Cambridge**	24
Delux Cafe | **S End**	21

🛛 East Coast | **Inman Sq**	25
Gargoyles | **Somerville**	24
Haley House | **Roxbury**	24
Harvest | **Harv Sq**	25
Henrietta's | **Harv Sq**	23
Johnny D's | **Somerville**	19
🛛 J's Nashoba | **Bolton**	26
KingFish Hall | **Faneuil Hall**	22
🛛 Legal Sea | **Harv Sq**	22
Lyceum | **Salem**	23
🛛 Meritage | **Waterfront**	27
Metropolis | **S End**	23
Mews | **CC**	27
Middle East | **Central Sq**	17
North St. Grille | **N End**	23
Oceana | **Waterfront**	24
Olé/Olecito | **Inman Sq**	24
Panificio | **Beacon Hill**	19
Sabur | **Somerville**	22
S&S | **Inman Sq**	18
🛛 Sel de Terre | **Waterfront**	23
Sidney's | **Central Sq**	21
Sonsie | **Back Bay**	20
South End Buttery | **S End**	21
Stephanie's | **Back Bay**	20
Stone Soup | **Ipswich**	25
Temple Bar | **Porter Sq**	20
🛛 Topper's | **Nan**	27
Tremont 647 | **S End**	21
Tryst | **Arlington**	22
Union B&G | **S End**	24
🛛 Upstairs/Square | **Harv Sq**	24
West Side | **Porter Sq**	22
Zaftigs | **Brookline**	21

BUFFET

(Check availability)

Amrheins | **S Boston**	18
Aura | **Seaport Dist**	22
Bhindi Bazaar | **Back Bay**	22
Blue Room | **Kendall Sq**	25
Bombay Club | **S End**	20
Brazilian Grill | **CC**	21
🛛 Bristol Lounge | **Back Bay**	24
Bukhara | **Jamaica Plain**	23
Café Belô | **Somerville**	20
Café Fleuri | **Financial Dist**	22
Cafe of India | **Harv Sq**	22
Caliterra | **Financial Dist**	16
Casino Wharf | **CC**	20
Changsho | **Porter Sq**	20
Chatham Bars | **CC**	22
China Pearl | **Woburn**	21
Clink | **Beacon Hill**	19
Coonamessett | **CC**	18

Dan'l Webster | **CC**	20
Diva Indian | **Somerville**	22
Fanizzi's | **CC**	20
Fire & Ice | **multi.**	16
Firefly's | **multi.**	20
Ghazal | **Jamaica Plain**	-
Haveli | **Inman Sq**	-
Henrietta's | **Harv Sq**	23
Himalayan Bistro | **W Roxbury**	24
Hungry I, The | **Beacon Hill**	24
India Pavilion | **Central Sq**	20
Joshua Tree | **Allston**	15
Z J's Nashoba | **Bolton**	26
Kashmir | **Back Bay**	23
Kathmandu Spice | **Arlington**	22
Kebab Factory | **Somerville**	24
Laura & Tony's | **CC**	-
Lotus Blossom | **Sudbury**	22
Mantra | **D'town Cross**	18
Martsa's/Elm | **Somerville**	21
Masala Art | **Needham**	23
Mela | **S End**	24
Merchants Row | **Concord**	-
Midwest | **Inman Sq**	20
Namaskar | **Somerville**	23
Neighborhood Rest. | **Somerville**	23
New Mother India | **Waltham**	22
Oceana | **Waterfront**	24
Parker's | **D'town Cross**	22
Passage to India | **Porter Sq**	20
Plaza III | **Faneuil Hall**	21
Rani | **Brookline**	20
Rodizio | **Somerville**	22
Shanti India | **Dorchester**	-
Sidney's | **Central Sq**	21
NEW Singh's | **Wellesley Hills**	-
606 Congress | **Seaport Dist**	21
Sky | **Norwood**	19
Stanhope Grille | **Back Bay**	23
Sunset Grill/Cantina | **Allston**	20
Tamarind Bay | **Harv Sq**	24
Tanjore | **Harv Sq**	22
Tantric | **Theater Dist**	20
Tavern in Sq. | **multi.**	17
Water St. | **MV**	-
Yangtze River | **Lexington**	17

BUSINESS DINING

Z Aquitaine | **multi.**	23
Asana | **Back Bay**	-
Avenue One | **D'town Cross**	18
Bambara | **E Cambridge**	20
Beacon Hill | **Beacon Hill**	22
Bina Osteria | **D'town Cross**	-
NEW Bistro du Midi | **Back Bay**	-

Blu | **Theater Dist**	21
Z Blue Ginger | **Wellesley**	26
Bokx | **Newton Lower Falls**	23
Bond | **Financial Dist**	-
Z Bristol Lounge | **Back Bay**	24
Café Fleuri | **Financial Dist**	22
Caliterra | **Financial Dist**	16
Z Capital Grille | **multi.**	26
NEW City Table | **Back Bay**	-
Z Clio/Uni | **Back Bay**	27
NEW Courtyard/Boston Library | **Back Bay**	-
Cygnet | **Beverly**	21
Daily Grill | **Back Bay**	19
Z Davio's | **Foxboro**	25
Z Eastern Stand. | **Kenmore Sq**	22
NEW 88 Wharf | **Milton**	-
Fleming's Prime | **Park Sq**	24
Good Life | **D'town Cross**	17
Green Papaya | **Waltham**	20
Z Grill 23 | **Back Bay**	25
Z Hamersley's | **S End**	27
Harvest | **Harv Sq**	25
Henrietta's | **Harv Sq**	23
Z Il Capriccio | **Waltham**	27
Jer-Ne | **Theater Dist**	20
KO Prime | **D'town Cross**	24
Z Legal Sea | **multi.**	22
Z L'Espalier | **Back Bay**	28
Locke-Ober | **D'town Cross**	24
Lucca Back Bay | **Back Bay**	21
Mantra | **D'town Cross**	18
Market | **Financial Dist**	16
NEW Market | **Theater Dist**	-
McCormick/Schmick | **multi.**	21
Z Meritage | **Waterfront**	27
Metropolitan | **Chestnut Hill**	21
Z Mistral | **S End**	27
Mooo... | **Beacon Hill**	24
Z Morton's | **multi.**	25
Z No. 9 Park | **Beacon Hill**	28
NEW North 26 | **Faneuil Hall**	-
Z Oak Room | **Back Bay**	25
Oceanaire | **Financial Dist**	24
Olivadi | **Norwood**	-
Z Olives | **Charlestown**	25
NEW Pairings | **Park Sq**	-
Palm | **Back Bay**	23
Papa Razzi | **multi.**	18
Plaza III | **Faneuil Hall**	21
NEW Post 390 | **Back Bay**	-
Z Radius | **Financial Dist**	26
Z Rialto | **Harv Sq**	26
NEW Rowes Wharf | **Waterfront**	-
Rudi's | **Roxbury**	-

Menus, photos, voting and more - free at ZAGAT.com

☑ Ruth's Chris | **D'town Cross**	24
Sandrine's | **Harv Sq**	24
☑ Sel de Terre | **multi.**	23
Sensing | **Waterfront**	-
Sidney's | **Central Sq**	21
606 Congress | **Seaport Dist**	21
Smith/Wollensky | **Back Bay**	23
Sportello | **Seaport Dist**	-
Stephanie's | **S End**	20
NEW Suffolk Grille | **Canton**	-
Summer Winter | **Burlington**	24
NEW Tavolino | **Foxboro**	-
Turner Fish | **Back Bay**	21
NEW Twenty8 Food | **Foxboro**	-
☑ Upstairs/Square | **Harv Sq**	24
Vinalia | **D'town Cross**	17
NEW Woodward | **Financial Dist**	-

BYO

Art Cliff | **MV**	24
Beach Plum | **MV**	25
☑ Black Dog | **MV**	19
Black-Eyed Susan's | **Nan**	26
NEW Blue Canoe | **MV**	-
Café Mangal | **Wellesley**	25
Captain's Table | **Wellesley**	-
☑ Clam Box | **Ipswich**	26
Fog Island | **Nan**	21
Friendly Fisherman | **CC**	24
Home Port | **MV**	20
Lambert's Cove | **MV**	25
Larsen's Fish | **MV**	27
Le Grenier | **MV**	23
Liam's | **CC**	20
Moby Dick's | **CC**	23
Saltwater | **MV**	-
Sushi by Yoshi | **Nan**	25
Sweet Basil | **Needham**	25
Yama | **Wellesley**	22

CELEBRITY CHEFS

Alta Strada | *Michael Schlow* | **Wellesley**	21
☑ B&G Oysters | *Barbara Lynch* | **S End**	26
☑ Blue Ginger | *Ming Tsai* | **Wellesley**	26
Butcher Shop | *Barbara Lynch* | **S End**	25
NEW Coppa | *Ken Oringer & Jamie Bissonnette* | **S End**	-
☑ Craigie/Main | *Tony Maws* | **Central Sq**	27
Drink | *Barbara Lynch* | **Seaport Dist**	-
NEW Dune | *Michael Getter* | **Nan**	-
Figs | *Todd English* | **multi.**	23
NEW Ginger Park | *Patricia Yeo* | **S End**	-
NEW Il Casale | *Dante de Magistris* | **Belmont**	-
Jasper White's | *Jasper White* | **multi.**	21
KingFish Hall | *Todd English* | **Faneuil Hall**	22
KO Prime | *Ken Oringer* | **D'town Cross**	24
L'Andana | *Jamie Mammano* | **Burlington**	25
La Verdad | *Ken Oringer* | **Fenway**	22
☑ L'Espalier | *Frank McClelland* | **Back Bay**	28
Locke-Ober | *Lydia Shire* | **D'town Cross**	24
☑ Lumière | *Michael Leviton* | **Newton**	27
Market | *Rene Michelena* | **Financial Dist**	16
NEW Market | *Jean-Georges Vongerichten* | **Theater Dist**	-
☑ Mistral | *Jamie Mammano* | **S End**	27
Myers + Chang | *Joanne Chang* | **S End**	23
☑ No. 9 Park | *Barbara Lynch* | **Beacon Hill**	28
☑ Oleana | *Ana Sortun* | **Inman Sq**	28
☑ Olives | *Todd English* | **Charlestown**	25
NEW Post 390 | *Eric Brennan* | **Back Bay**	-
☑ Radius | *Michael Schlow* | **Financial Dist**	26
☑ Rialto | *Jody Adams* | **Harv Sq**	26
Scampo | *Lydia Shire* | **Beacon Hill**	22
Sensing | *Guy Martin* | **Waterfront**	-
Sibling Rivalry | *David/Bob Kinkead* | **S End**	24
Sofra Bakery | *Ana Sortun* | **Huron Vill**	26
☑ Sorellina | *Jamie Mammano* | **Back Bay**	27
Sportello | *Barbara Lynch* | **Seaport Dist**	-
Summer Winter | *Clark Frasier/ Mark Gaier* | **Burlington**	24
☑ Toro | *Ken Oringer* | **S End**	26
Via Matta | *Michael Schlow* | **Park Sq**	25

CHILD-FRIENDLY

(Alternatives to the usual fast-food places; * children's menu available)

Adrian's* | CC	16
Amarin Thailand | multi.	22
☒ Anna's | multi.	22
Ardeo* | CC	20
Arno's* | Nan	16
Art Cliff | MV	24
Artú | multi.	21
Atlantic Fish* | Back Bay	23
Baja Betty's* | Brookline	20
Bakers' Best | Newton	22
Bamboo | Brighton	23
Bangkok Bistro | Brighton	22
Barking Crab* | Seaport Dist	16
Bee-Hive Tavern* | CC	19
Bertucci's* | multi.	17
B. Good | multi.	19
Bison County | Waltham	18
☒ Black Dog* | MV	19
Blue Fin* | multi.	22
Blue Ribbon BBQ | multi.	25
Boca Grande | multi.	19
Boloco | multi.	18
Border Cafe* | Saugus	19
Bottega | Brookline	24
Brazilian Grill | CC	21
Brown Sugar/Similans | Boston U	25
Cafe Barada | Porter Sq	23
Café Belô | Somerville	20
Café Fleuri* | Financial Dist	22
Cambridge St.* | Nan	-
Canestaro | Fenway	19
Cantina la Mexicana | Somerville	24
Capt. Frosty's* | CC	21
Capt. Kidd* | CC	18
Charley's* | multi.	18
Chau Chow | Chinatown	21
Cheers* | multi.	14
Chef Chang's | Brookline	20
Chef Chow's | Brookline	20
China Pearl | multi.	21
☒ Clam Box | Ipswich	26
Coolidge Corner* | Brookline	17
Cottage* | Wellesley	19
Courthouse* | E Cambridge	22
Demos* | multi.	21
Dolphin Seafood* | multi.	18
Donatello | Saugus	24
Durgin-Park* | Faneuil Hall	17
Fifty-Six Union | Nan	22
Fire & Ice | multi.	16
Firefly's* | multi.	20
Flour Bakery | S End	26

Fog Island* | Nan	21
Frank's Steak* | Porter Sq	18
Full Moon* | Huron Vill	20
☒ Galleria Umberto | N End	26
Golden Temple | Brookline	21
Grasshopper | Allston	20
Greg's | Watertown	19
Halfway Cafe* | multi.	17
Hilltop Steak* | Saugus	16
Hi-Rise* | multi.	24
Home Port* | MV	20
Il Panino | N End	23
Island Hopper | Back Bay	19
Jae's* | S End	20
Jasper White's* | multi.	21
Jetties* | Nan	14
Joe's American* | multi.	16
Johnny's Lunch.* | Newton	18
JP Seafood | Jamaica Plain	23
Karoo Kafe | CC	24
Kowloon* | Saugus	17
La Cantina* | Framingham	20
La Fam. Giorgio* | N End	23
Laura & Tony's* | CC	-
☒ Legal Sea* | multi.	22
Le's* | multi.	21
Lobster Pot* | CC	22
Longfellow's* | Sudbury	18
Lure* | MV	21
Maggiano's* | Park Sq	19
Merengue* | Roxbury	-
Midwest | Inman Sq	20
Mike's | S End	20
Moby Dick's* | CC	23
Morse Fish* | S End	21
Mr. Bartley's* | Harv Sq	24
Naked Fish* | multi.	19
Nantucket Lobster* | Nan	19
Neighborhood Rest.* | Somerville	23
New Jang Su | Burlington	23
No Name* | Seaport Dist	19
No. 1 Noodle | Newton	18
☒ Not Average Joe's* | multi.	18
Offshore Ale* | MV	20
Optimist Café* | CC	21
Out of/Blue | Somerville	22
Paddock* | CC	20
Panificio | Beacon Hill	19
Papa Razzi* | multi.	18
Paris Creperie | Brookline	22
Peach Farm | Chinatown	25
Peking Cuisine | Newton	21
Penang | Chinatown	22
P.F. Chang's | Theater Dist	19
Phoenicia | Beacon Hill	21

Menus, photos, voting and more – free at ZAGAT.com

Pho Hoa | multi.	22
Pho Pasteur | Chinatown	23
Picante | Central Sq	19
Picco | S End	22
Pizzeria Regina | multi.	24
Polcari's* | multi.	17
Punjab | Arlington	25
Purple Cactus* | Jamaica Plain	21
Redbones* | Somerville	22
Rubin's* | Brookline	19
S&S | Inman Sq	18
Scargo Café* | CC	20
Sconset Café | Nan	21
Sea Grille* | Nan	22
Sichuan Garden | multi.	22
Siena* | CC	21
Skipjack's* | multi.	20
Sky* | multi.	19
Sorella's* | Jamaica Plain	26
Sorelle | Charlestown	23
Stars on Hingham* | Hingham	16
Stir Crazy* | CC	23
Sunset Cafe* | Inman Sq	19
Tacos El Charro | Jamaica Plain	23
Tacos Lupita | multi.	25
Taqueria Mexico* | Waltham	22
Tom Shea's* | Essex	20
Trident | Back Bay	19
🗹 Union Oyster* | Faneuil Hall	20
Veggie Planet | Harv Sq	23
Via Lago* | Lexington	20
Victoria's* | Roxbury	20
Village Smokehse.* | Brookline	19
Woodman's* | Essex	23
Za | Arlington	25
Zaftigs* | Brookline	21

DELIVERY

Bamboo | Brighton	23
Bangkok Bistro | Brighton	22
Bangkok City | Back Bay	20
Bertucci's | multi.	17
Bluestone Bistro | Brighton	17
Brown Sugar/Similans | Boston U	25
Cafe Podima | Beacon Hill	19
Canestaro | Fenway	19
Changsho | Porter Sq	20
Chef Chang's | Brookline	20
Chef Chow's | Brookline	20
Chilli Duck | Back Bay	21
Golden Temple | Brookline	21
9 Tastes | Harv Sq	20
Redbones | Somerville	22
Sichuan Garden | Woburn	22
Spice Thai | Harv Sq	21

Super Fusion | Brookline	27
Trident | Back Bay	19
Upper Crust | multi.	23
Zen | Beacon Hill	24

ENTERTAINMENT

(Call for days and times of performances)

Alchemist | live music | Jamaica Plain	17
Amari | live music | CC	22
Barley Neck Inn | live music | CC	20
Bee-Hive Tavern | live music | CC	19
Belfry Inne | jazz/piano | CC	25
Bleu | jazz | CC	25
Bravo | jazz/piano | MFA	21
Bullfinch's | jazz | Sudbury	21
Burren | live music | Somerville	14
Byblos | belly dancing | Norwood	24
Café Brazil | guitar/karaoke | Allston	23
Café Fleuri | jazz | Financial Dist	22
Café St. Petersburg | piano | Newton	19
Casino Wharf | live music | CC	20
Chart Room | bass/piano | CC	20
Church | live music | Fenway	20
Club Car | piano | Nan	20
🗹 Company/Cauldron | harpist | Nan	28
DJ's | live music | W End	–
Dog Bar | live music | Gloucester	23
El Sarape | guitarist | Braintree	25
Fireplace | jazz/Latin | Brookline	21
Glenn's | blues/jazz | Newburyport	23
Good Life | DJ | D'town Cross	17
Green Briar | bands/DJ | Brighton	17
Jacob Wirth | singalongs | Theater Dist	17
Jake's Dixie | blues | Waltham	17
Jetties | live music | Nan	14
Johnny D's | live music | Somerville	19
Karoun | belly dancing | Newton	22
Kowloon | varies | Saugus	17
La Casa/Pedro | live music | Watertown	21
Les Zygomates | varies | Leather Dist	22
Lucky's | live music | Seaport Dist	18
Middle East | live music | Central Sq	17
Offshore Ale | bands | MV	20
Orleans | varies | Somerville	17
Red Fez | Middle Eastern | S End	18
Redline | live music | Harv Sq	17

Rest. Cesaria | folk | **Dorchester** -

Roadhouse | jazz/piano | **CC** 20

Sunset Cafe | Brazilian/ 19
Portuguese folk | **Inman Sq**

🅩 Tangierino | belly dancing | 24
Charlestown

Tavern in Sq. | DJ | **Central Sq** 17

🅩 Top of Hub | jazz | **Back Bay** 20

Tryst | jazz | **Arlington** 22

28 Degrees | DJ | **S End** 20

Veggie Planet | folk | **Harv Sq** 23

Warren | varies | **Charlestown** 16

Zuzu! | bands/DJs | **Central Sq** 20

FIREPLACES

🅩 Abe & Louie's | **Back Bay** 26

Academy Ocean | **CC** 22

Aegean | **Watertown** 21

Alberto's | **CC** 20

Amari | **CC** 22

Anthony Cummaquid | **CC** 18

Aqua Grille | **CC** 19

Asana | **Back Bay** -

Atlantica | **Cohasset** 15

Atria | **MV** 25

Back Eddy | **Westport** 22

Barker Tavern | **Scituate** 23

Barking Crab | **Seaport Dist** 16

Barley Neck Inn | **CC** 20

Beacon Hill | **Beacon Hill** 22

Beacon St. Tavern | **Brookline** 20

NEW Big Papi's | **Framingham** -

Bison County | **Waltham** 18

Bistro/Crowne Pointe | **CC** 22

Black Cow | **Newburyport** 19

🅩 Black Dog | **MV** 19

Black Sheep | **Kendall Sq** 21

Bon Caldo | **Norwood** 22

Bookstore & Rest. | **CC** 19

🅩 Bristol Lounge | **Back Bay** 24

Brotherhood/Thieves | **Nan** 18

Buca's Tuscan | **CC** 23

Capt. Linnell | **CC** 22

Chapoquoit Grill | **CC** 22

Chatham Bars | **CC** 22

Chiara | **Westwood** 26

🅩 Chillingsworth | **CC** 27

Christopher's | **Porter Sq** 17

Ciro & Sal's | **CC** 20

Coonamessett | **CC** 18

Cottage | **Wellesley** 19

Dalya's | **Bedford** 23

Dan'l Webster | **CC** 20

DeMarco | **Nan** 22

Dillon's | **Back Bay** 16

Dog Bar | **Gloucester** 23

Dolphin | **CC** 21

Dolphin Seafood | **Natick** 18

Donatello | **Saugus** 24

Dunbar Tea | **CC** 22

Enzo | **CC** 24

Euno | **N End** 24

Figs at 29 Fair | **Nan** -

Finz | **multi.** 20

Fireplace | **Brookline** 21

🅩 Gibbet Hill | **Groton** 24

Gina's | **CC** 21

Glory | **Andover** 21

🅩 Grill 23 | **Back Bay** 25

Harvest | **Harv Sq** 25

🅩 Helmand | **E Cambridge** 26

Hungry I, The | **Beacon Hill** 24

Incontro | **Franklin** 22

James's Gate | **Jamaica Plain** 16

Joe's American | **multi.** 16

Joshua Tree | **Allston** 15

🅩 J's Nashoba | **Bolton** 26

🅩 La Campania | **Waltham** 28

La Fam. Giorgio | **N End** 23

L'Alouette | **CC** 26

L'Andana | **Burlington** 25

Landing | **Manchester/Sea** 16

Lattanzi's | **MV** 21

Left Bank | **Tyngsboro** 21

Le Lyonnais | **Acton** 23

Longfellow's | **Sudbury** 18

Lyceum | **Salem** 23

Marco Romana | **N End** 26

Marshside | **CC** 15

Merchants Row | **Concord** -

Met B&G | **Dedham** 21

Metropolitan | **Chestnut Hill** 21

Mews | **CC** 27

Miel | **Waterfront** 21

🅩 Mistral | **S End** 27

Nauset Beach | **CC** 25

Newes/America | **MV** 18

Ocean House | **CC** 25

Offshore Ale | **MV** 20

🅩 Oleana | **Inman Sq** 28

Olé/Olecito | **Inman Sq** 24

Òran Mór | **Nan** 24

Orleans Inn | **CC** 17

Orta | **Hanover** -

🅩 Outermost Inn | **MV** 25

Palmers | **Andover** -

Porcini's | **Watertown** 22

NEW Post 390 | **Back Bay** -

Publick House | **Brookline** 21

Red House | **Harv Sq** 20

Red Inn | **CC** 24

☑ Red Pheasant | **CC**	27
Rist. Fiore | **N End**	21
Riva | **Scituate**	26
Roadhouse | **CC**	20
Ross' Grill | **CC**	22
Scampo | **Beacon Hill**	22
Scargo Café | **CC**	20
Scarlet Oak | **Hingham**	20
Sherborn Inn | **Sherborn**	19
Ships Inn | **Nan**	24
Sky | **Norwood**	19
Smith/Wollensky | **Back Bay**	23
NEW Sofia | **W Roxbury**	-
South End Buttery | **S End**	21
NEW State Road | **MV**	-
Stephanie's | **Back Bay**	20
Stockyard | **Brighton**	15
Summer House | **Nan**	20
Taberna/Haro | **Brookline**	23
☑ Topper's | **Nan**	27
Townsend's | **Hyde Park**	19
☑ 28 Atlantic | **CC**	26
☑ Upstairs/Square | **Harv Sq**	24
Vining's | **CC**	24
Warren | **Charlestown**	16
West/Centre | **W Roxbury**	18
Wicked Oyster | **CC**	24
Wild Goose | **CC**	21

HISTORIC PLACES

(Year opened; * building)

1700 | 28 Atlantic* | **CC**	26
1700 | Wicked Oyster* | **CC**	24
1707 | Longfellow's* | **Sudbury**	18
1709 | Figs at 29 Fair* | **Nan**	-
1716 | Merchants Row* | **Concord**	-
1720 | Chart House* | **Waterfront**	21
1740 | Dunbar Tea* | **CC**	22
1742 | Union Oyster* | **Faneuil Hall**	20
1745 | Newes/America* | **MV**	18
1750 | Landing* | **Manchester/Sea**	16
1750 | Scarlet Oak* | **Hingham**	20
1778 | Chillingsworth* | **CC**	27
1780 | Warren* | **Charlestown**	16
1786 | Red Pheasant* | **CC**	27
1790 | Lambert's Cove* | **MV**	25
1790 | Regatta/Cotuit* | **CC**	25
1796 | Coonamessett* | **CC**	18
1800 | Alchemy* | **MV**	22
1800 | Bistro/Crowne Pointe* | **CC**	22
1800 | DeMarco* | **Nan**	22
1800 | Durgin-Park* | **Faneuil Hall**	17
1800 | Mantra* | **D'town Cross**	18
1802 | Red House* | **Harv Sq**	20
1805 | Red Inn* | **CC**	24

1805 | Terra Luna* | **CC**	24
1825 | Piccolo Nido* | **N End**	24
1827 | Sherborn Inn* | **Sherborn**	19
1830 | Abba* | **CC**	27
1830 | Anthony Cummaquid* | **CC**	18
1831 | Ships Inn* | **Nan**	24
1835 | Capt. Linnell* | **CC**	22
1840 | Brotherhood/Thieves* | **Nan**	18
1840 | Hungry I, The* | **Beacon Hill**	24
1843 | Lyceum* | **Salem**	23
1847 | 21 Federal* | **Nan**	24
1849 | Optimist Café* | **CC**	21
1850 | Dalya's* | **Bedford**	23
1850 | Dolphin* | **CC**	21
1850 | Le Lyonnais* | **Acton**	23
1850 | Post Office* | **CC**	16
1856 | Parker's* | **D'town Cross**	22
1857 | Living Room* | **Waterfront**	15
1860 | Franklin* | **S End**	26
1860 | Jimmy Seas* | **MV**	23
1860 | Òran Mór* | **Nan**	24
1860 | Pisces* | **CC**	27
1860 | Sweet Life* | **MV**	25
1861 | Bramble Inn* | **CC**	27
1865 | Scargo Café* | **CC**	20
1865 | Wild Goose* | **CC**	21
1868 | Barley Neck Inn* | **CC**	20
1868 | Jacob Wirth | **Theater Dist**	17
1870 | Enzo* | **CC**	24
1875 | Club Car* | **Nan**	20
1875 | Cygnet* | **Beverly**	21
1875 | Locke-Ober | **D'town Cross**	24
1875 | Orleans Inn* | **CC**	17
1876 | Lobster Pot* | **CC**	22
1882 | Doyle's* | **Jamaica Plain**	15
1890 | Amrheins | **S Boston**	18
1890 | Atria* | **MV**	25
1890 | Fireplace* | **Brookline**	21
1890 | Lucia* | **Winchester**	21
1891 | North St. Grille* | **N End**	23
1891 | Smith/Wollensky* | **Back Bay**	23
1894 | Whitman Hse.* | **CC**	21
1896 | Slip 14* | **Nan**	18
1897 | Cape Sea* | **CC**	26
1899 | Rani* | **Brookline**	20
1899 | Scollay Sq.* | **Beacon Hill**	19
1900 | Capt. Kidd* | **CC**	18
1900 | Chatham Squire* | **CC**	18
1900 | Chez Henri* | **Harv Sq**	24
1900 | Club Cafe* | **S End**	18
1900 | Elephant Walk* | **Waltham**	23
1900 | Front St.* | **CC**	27
1900 | Mr. Bartley's* | **Harv Sq**	24

1900	Prose*	**Arlington**	24
1900	Santarpio's Pizza*	**E Boston**	25
1900	Topper's*	**Nan**	27
1901	Morse Fish	**S End**	21
1902	Gardner Museum*	**MFA**	20
1903	Walden Grille*	**Concord**	15
1905	Davide Rist.*	**N End**	24
1906	Upstairs/Square*	**Harv Sq**	24
1907	Mother Anna's*	**N End**	21
1910	Tosca*	**Hingham**	25
1912	Chatham Bars	**CC**	22
1912	Courthouse	**E Cambridge**	22
1912	Oak Room*	**Back Bay**	25
1914	Mr. Crepe*	**Somerville**	18
1914	Woodman's	**Essex**	23
1915	Strega Rest.*	**Salem**	21
1917	No Name	**Seaport Dist**	19
1919	S&S	**Inman Sq**	18
1920	Caliterra*	**Financial Dist**	16
1920	Nauset Beach*	**CC**	25
1920	O Ya*	**Leather Dist**	28
1920	Rubin's*	**Brookline**	19
1923	J's Nashoba*	**Bolton**	26
1926	Pizzeria Regina	**N End**	24
1926	Pleasant Cafe*	**Roslindale**	18
1927	Charlie's Sandwich	**S End**	23
1927	Poe's/Rattlesnake*	**Back Bay**	–
1928	Union B&G*	**S End**	24
1930	Centre St. Bistro*	**Nan**	16
1930	Harvard Gardens	**Beacon Hill**	17
1931	Cantina Italiana	**N End**	22
1931	Home Port	**MV**	20
1933	Forest Café	**Porter Sq**	20
1933	Green St.*	**Central Sq**	24
1933	Greg's	**Watertown**	19
1935	Clam Box*	**Ipswich**	26
1937	Paramount	**Beacon Hill**	23
1938	Frank's Steak	**Porter Sq**	18
1938	Gina's	**CC**	21
1940	Even Keel*	**Nan**	19
1941	Rosebud*	**Somerville**	16
1943	Art Cliff*	**MV**	24
1946	Harry's	**Westborough**	20
1946	Landfall	**CC**	18
1946	Maddie's Sail	**Marblehead**	18
1947	Café at Taj	**Back Bay**	20
1947	Deluxe Town*	**Watertown**	22
1947	South St. Diner*	**Leather Dist**	16
1948	Cobie's Clam	**CC**	19
1948	Joe Tecce's	**N End**	19
1950	Ciro & Sal's	**CC**	20
1950	Fazio's*	**CC**	20
1950	Kowloon	**Saugus**	17
1952	Beach Plum	**MV**	25
1952	Liam's	**CC**	20
1953	La Cantina	**Framingham**	20
1955	Casablanca	**Harv Sq**	22
1955	Charlie's Kitchen	**Harv Sq**	17
1955	Vin & Eddie's	**Abington**	17
1957	Baxter's	**CC**	18
1959	Golden Temple	**Brookline**	21
1960	Caffe Paradiso	**N End**	17

HOTEL DINING

Ames Hotel
🆕 Woodward | **Financial Dist** — –

Back Bay Hotel, The
Stanhope Grille | **Back Bay** — 23

Barley Neck Inn
Barley Neck Inn | **CC** — 20

Beach Plum Inn
Beach Plum | **MV** — 25

Beacon Hill Hotel
Beacon Hill | **Beacon Hill** — 22

Belfry Inne
Belfry Inne | **CC** — 25

Blue Dolphin Inn
Laura & Tony's | **CC** — –

Boston Harbor Hotel
Ⓩ Meritage | **Waterfront** — 27
🆕 Rowes Wharf | **Waterfront** — –

Boston Marriott Burlington
Summer Winter | **Burlington** — 24

Boston Marriott Long Wharf
Oceana | **Waterfront** — 24

Boston Park Plaza Hotel & Towers
🆕 Pairings | **Park Sq** — –

Bramble Inn
Ⓩ Bramble Inn | **CC** — 27

Bulfinch Hotel
Flat Iron | **W End** — 22

Charles Hotel
Henrietta's | **Harv Sq** — 23
Ⓩ Rialto | **Harv Sq** — 26

Charlotte Inn, The
🆕 Il Tesoro/Terrace | **MV** — –

Chatham Bars Inn
Chatham Bars | **CC** — 22

Chatham Wayside Inn
Wild Goose | **CC** — 21

Colonial Inn
Merchants Row | **Concord** — –

Colonnade Hotel
Brasserie Jo | **Back Bay** — 20

Winnetu Oceanside Resort
Lure | **MV**   21

XV Beacon Hotel
Mooo... | **Beacon Hill**   24

LATE DINING

(Weekday closing hour)

NEW Abby Park | 12 AM | −
Milton

Anchovies | 1 AM | **S End**   20

Apollo Grill | 4 AM | **Chinatown**   17

Assaggio | 12 AM | **N End**   24

BarLola | 1 AM | **Back Bay**   18

Bar 10 | 12 AM | **Back Bay**   17

NEW Big Papi's | 12 AM | −
Framingham

Billy Tse | 12 AM | **Revere**   20

NEW Bistro Chi | 1 AM | **Quincy**   −

Bluestone Bistro | 12:45 AM | 17
Brighton

Border Cafe | varies | **multi.**   19

Boston/Salem Beer | 12 AM | 18
multi.

Bricco | 2 AM | **N End**   25

Brighton Beer | 1 AM | **Brighton**   −

Brownstone | 2 AM | **Back Bay**   15

Bukowski | varies | **multi.**   17

Café Belô | varies | **multi.**   20

Cafe Escadrille | 1 AM | **Burlington**   19

Caffe Paradiso | varies | **N End**   17

Cambridge Common | varies | 17
Harv Sq

Cambridge 1 | 12 AM | **multi.**   22

Chapin's Fish/Beach Bar | −
1 AM | **CC**

Charlie's Kitchen | varies | **Harv Sq**   17

Chau Chow | 3 AM | **Chinatown**   21

Church | 12 AM | **Fenway**   20

NEW City Table | 2 AM | **Back Bay**   −

Coolidge Corner | 1:15 AM | 17
Brookline

NEW Coppa | 12:45 AM | **S End**   −

NEW Corner Tavern | 12 AM | −
Back Bay

Cornwall's | 12 AM | 15
Kenmore Sq

Cottonwood | 12 AM | **Back Bay**   18

NEW Danny Quinn's | 12 AM | −
MV

Deep Ellum | 12 AM | **Allston**   18

NEW Ducali | 1 AM | **N End**   −

NEW Farm Bar | 1 AM | **Essex**   −

NEW Federal | 2 AM | **Beacon Hill**   −

Flash's | 12 AM | **Park Sq**   18

Franklin | 1:30 AM | **S End**   26

Z Fugakyu | 1:30 AM | **Brookline**   25

Gaslight Brasserie | 1:30 AM | 21
S End

Geoffrey's Cafe | 1 AM | 19
Roslindale

NEW Ginger Ex. | 12 AM | −
Inman Sq

Golden Temple | 1 AM | **Brookline**   21

Halfway Cafe | 12:30 AM | 17
Dedham

Harry's | 1 AM | **Westborough**   20

Haru | 12 AM | **Back Bay**   20

Harvard Gardens | 1 AM | 17
Beacon Hill

John Harvard's | 12 AM | 16
Harv Sq

Jumbo | 1 AM | **Chinatown**   23

NEW Kama | 1 AM | **Quincy**   −

Kayuga | 1:30 AM | **Brookline**   24

Kaze | 12 AM | **Chinatown**   23

Kingston | 2 AM | **D'town Cross**   20

Kowloon | 1 AM | **Saugus**   17

NEW Lansdowne | 1 AM | −
Fenway

Living Room | 12 AM | 15
Waterfront

NEW Lord Hobo | 1 AM | −
E Cambridge

Lucca | 12:15 AM | **N End**   25

Lucca Back Bay | 1:30 AM | 21
Back Bay

Middle East | 12 AM | **Central Sq**   17

Miracle of Science | 12 AM | 19
Central Sq

Mission B&G | 12 AM | **MFA**   19

Z Oishii | 12 AM | **S End**   27

Other Side | 12 AM | **Back Bay**   19

Parish Cafe | varies | **multi.**   22

Peach Farm | 3 AM | **Chinatown**   25

Poe's/Rattlesnake | 12 AM | −
Back Bay

Post Office | 1 AM | **CC**   16

Punjabi Dhaba | 12 AM | 24
Inman Sq

Red Fez | 12 AM | **S End**   18

Red Sky | 1 AM | **Faneuil Hall**   18

Rist. Damiano | 12 AM | **N End**   −

Rist. Villa Francesca | 19
12:30 AM | **N End**

Salvatore's | 12 AM | 20
Seaport Dist

Santarpio's Pizza | 12 AM | 25
E Boston

Sharky's | 12:30 AM | **MV**   21

South St. Diner | varies | 16
Leather Dist

Stella | 1:30 AM | **S End**   24

Suishaya | 2 AM | **Chinatown**   21

Sunset Grill/Cantina | 1 AM | 20
multi.

Taiwan Cafe | 1 AM | **Chinatown**   23

ⓩ Tangierino | 12 AM | **Charlestown** 24

Temple Bar | 12 AM | **Porter Sq** 20

ⓩ Top of Hub | 1 AM | **Back Bay** 20

Townsend's | 12 AM | **Hyde Park** 19

Trident | 12 AM | **Back Bay** 19

NEW Trina's | 12 AM | **Inman Sq** -

UBurger | 12 AM | **Boston U** 23

Via Matta | 1 AM | **Park Sq** 25

Vlora | 1 AM | **Back Bay** 22

MEET FOR A DRINK

ⓩ Abe & Louie's | **Back Bay** 26

Alchemist | **Jamaica Plain** 17

Alchemy | **MV** 22

Aqua Grille | **CC** 19

ⓩ Aquitaine | **Dedham** 23

Asana | **Back Bay** -

Atlantic Fish/Chop | **MV** -

Audubon Circle | **Kenmore Sq** 21

Bambara | **E Cambridge** 20

Bar 10 | **Back Bay** 17

Baxter's | **CC** 18

Bayside | **Westport** -

Beacon St. Tavern | **Brookline** 20

Beehive | **S End** 18

Bella Luna/Milky Way | **Jamaica Plain** -

NEW Big Papi's | **Framingham** -

Bina Osteria | **D'town Cross** -

Bin 26 | **Beacon Hill** 21

NEW Bistro du Midi | **Back Bay** -

Black Cow | **multi.** 19

Blue22 | **Quincy** 19

Boarding House | **Nan** 21

NEW Bobby's | **Wellesley Hills** -

Bokx | **Newton Lower Falls** 23

Bond | **Financial Dist** -

Bouchée | **Back Bay** 21

Bricco | **N End** 25

ⓩ Bristol Lounge | **Back Bay** 24

Burren | **Somerville** 14

Butcher Shop | **S End** 25

Cactus Club | **Back Bay** 16

NEW Cafe 47 | **Back Bay** -

Cambridge 1 | **multi.** 22

Casablanca | **Harv Sq** 22

Chez Henri | **Harv Sq** 24

Church | **Fenway** 20

Clink | **Beacon Hill** 19

Club Cafe | **S End** 18

Club Car | **Nan** 20

Comfort | **Watertown** -

NEW Corner Tavern | **Back Bay** -

Cottage | **Wellesley** 19

Cottonwood | **Back Bay** 18

Daedalus | **Harv Sq** 17

NEW Danny Quinn's | **MV** -

Dante | **E Cambridge** 24

ⓩ Davio's | **multi.** 25

Delux Cafe | **S End** 21

Dillon's | **Back Bay** 16

District | **Leather Dist** 17

DJ's | **W End** -

Dog Bar | **Gloucester** 23

Doyle's | **Jamaica Plain** 15

Drink | **Seaport Dist** -

ⓩ Eastern Stand. | **Kenmore Sq** 22

Ecco | **E Boston** -

NEW 88 Wharf | **Milton** -

Erbaluce | **Park Sq** -

Estragon | **S End** -

Firefly's | **Quincy** 20

Flash's | **Park Sq** 18

Franklin | **multi.** 26

Gaslight Brasserie | **S End** 21

NEW Ginger Park | **S End** -

Glenn's | **Newburyport** 23

Good Life | **D'town Cross** 17

Grafton St. Pub | **Harv Sq** 17

ⓩ Grill 23 | **Back Bay** 25

Harvard Gardens | **Beacon Hill** 17

Highland Kitchen | **Somerville** 23

Houston's | **Faneuil Hall** 22

ⓩ Hungry Mother | **Kendall Sq** 27

NEW Il Casale | **Belmont** -

Independent, The | **Somerville** 18

James's Gate | **Jamaica Plain** 16

Jasper White's | **Hingham** 21

John Harvard's | **multi.** 16

Joshua Tree | **multi.** 15

NEW Kama | **Quincy** -

Kingston | **D'town Cross** 20

NEW Lansdowne | **Fenway** -

Lavender Asian | **Sudbury** -

La Voile | **Back Bay** 23

NEW Ledge | **Dorchester** -

Les Zygomates | **Leather Dist** 22

Littlest | **Financial Dist** -

Living Room | **Waterfront** 15

Local | **W Newton** -

Lo La 41° | **Nan** 21

NEW Lord Hobo | **E Cambridge** -

LTK | **Seaport Dist** 20

Lucky's | **Seaport Dist** 18

Mantra | **D'town Cross** 18

Market | **Financial Dist** 16

NEW Market | **Theater Dist** -

Marliave | **D'town Cross** 22

Masa | **multi.** 23

Matt Murphy's | **Brookline** 22

Restaurant	Rating
Max/Dylan | **multi.**	–
McCormick/Schmick | **multi.**	21
NEW Mediterranean | **MV**	–
Met B&G | **Natick**	21
Metropolitan | **Chestnut Hill**	21
NEW Milestone | **Wellesley**	–
Miracle of Science | **Central Sq**	19
Mission B&G | **MFA**	19
Z Mistral | **S End**	27
M.J. O'Connor's | **multi.**	–
Z Morton's | **Seaport Dist**	25
Nebo | **N End**	21
Z No. 9 Park | **Beacon Hill**	28
NEW Nourish | **Lexington**	–
Oceanaire | **Financial Dist**	24
Olivadi | **Norwood**	–
Om | **Harv Sq**	19
Orleans | **Somerville**	17
Orta | **Hanover**	–
NEW Pairings | **Park Sq**	–
NEW Palio's | **Lexington**	–
Parish Cafe | **Back Bay**	22
NEW Pazzo | **Back Bay**	–
Poe's/Rattlesnake | **Back Bay**	–
NEW Pomodoro | **Needham**	–
NEW Post 390 | **Back Bay**	–
Publick House | **Brookline**	21
Red Fez | **S End**	18
Redline | **Harv Sq**	17
Rocca | **S End**	24
Roobar | **CC**	21
Ross' Grill | **CC**	22
NEW Rowes Wharf | **Waterfront**	–
Rudi's | **Roxbury**	–
Z Ruth's Chris | **D'town Cross**	24
Sanctuary | **Financial Dist**	19
Scampo | **Beacon Hill**	22
Scollay Sq. | **Beacon Hill**	19
Z Sel de Terre | **multi.**	23
Sensing | **Waterfront**	–
Silvertone B&G | **D'town Cross**	21
NEW Six Burner | **Back Bay**	–
606 Congress | **Seaport Dist**	21
NEW Sofia | **W Roxbury**	–
Solea | **Waltham**	23
Sonsie | **Back Bay**	20
Z Sorellina | **Back Bay**	27
Stella | **S End**	24
Stephanie's | **multi.**	20
Stix | **Back Bay**	17
NEW Stork Club | **S End**	–
Straight Wharf | **Nan**	25
Studio 3 | **multi.**	–
NEW Suffolk Grille | **Canton**	–
Sunset Grill/Cantina | **Boston U**	20
NEW Symphony 8 | **Fenway**	–
Tavern in Sq. | **multi.**	17
Tavern/Water | **Charlestown**	13
NEW Tavolino | **Foxboro**	–
Tavolo | **Dorchester**	–
Temple Bar | **Porter Sq**	20
33 Rest. | **Back Bay**	20
Z Top of Hub | **Back Bay**	20
NEW Tory Row | **Harv Sq**	–
NEW Town | **Nan**	–
Townsend's | **Hyde Park**	19
NEW Trina's | **Inman Sq**	–
Z Troquet | **Theater Dist**	27
28 Degrees | **S End**	20
NEW Twenty8 Food | **Foxboro**	–
21st Amendment | **Beacon Hill**	17
Z 21 Federal | **Nan**	24
Union B&G | **S End**	24
Via Matta | **Park Sq**	25
Vinalia | **D'town Cross**	17
Vlora | **Back Bay**	22
Vox Populi | **Back Bay**	16
Washington Sq. | **Brookline**	22
Water St. | **MV**	–
West End Johnnie's | **W End**	17
West/Centre | **W Roxbury**	18
West Side | **Porter Sq**	22
Wild Goose | **CC**	21
NEW Woodward | **Financial Dist**	–

OFFBEAT

Restaurant	Rating
All Star | **Inman Sq**	23
Baraka Cafe | **Central Sq**	26
Barking Crab | **Seaport Dist**	16
Betty's Wok | **MFA**	19
B. Good | **Back Bay**	19
Bukowski | **multi.**	17
Butcher Shop | **S End**	25
Café Polonia | **S Boston**	24
Centre St. Café | **Jamaica Plain**	25
Z Cuchi Cuchi | **Central Sq**	22
Dalí | **Somerville**	25
Z Galleria Umberto | **N End**	26
Green St. | **Central Sq**	24
Z Helmand | **E Cambridge**	26
Karoo Kafe | **CC**	24
LTK | **Seaport Dist**	20
Masala Art | **Needham**	23
Merengue | **Roxbury**	–
Paramount | **Beacon Hill**	23
Prose | **Arlington**	24
Publick House | **Brookline**	21
Punjabi Dhaba | **Inman Sq**	24
Redbones | **Somerville**	22
Rest. Cesaria | **Dorchester**	–

Santarpio's Pizza | E Boston — 25
Shabu-Zen | Chinatown — 22
Sidecar Café | MV — -
Stone Soup | Ipswich — 25
Strip-T's | Watertown — 22
Trident | Back Bay — 19
Vinny's/Night | Somerville — 23
Wine Cellar | Back Bay — 20

OUTDOOR DINING

(G=garden; P=patio; S=sidewalk; T=terrace)

🅉 Abe & Louie's | S | Back Bay — 26
Academy Ocean | P | CC — 22
Adrian's | T | CC — 16
Alberto's | S | CC — 20
Ashmont Grill | P | Dorchester — 22
Atasca | P | Kendall Sq — 23
Atlantica | P | Cohasset — 15
Atlantic Fish | S | Back Bay — 23
Atria | P | MV — 25
Audubon Circle | P | Kenmore Sq — 21
Back Eddy | P, T | Westport — 22
🅉 B&G Oysters | G | S End — 26
Bangkok Blue | P | Back Bay — 21
Barking Crab | T | Seaport Dist — 16
BarLola | P | Back Bay — 18
Baxter's | T | CC — 18
Beacon St. Tavern | P | Brookline — 20
Birch St. Bistro | P | Roslindale — 19
NEW Bistro du Midi | P | Back Bay — -
Black Cow | T | Newburyport — 19
Blarney Stone | P | Dorchester — 16
Bluestone Bistro | P | Brighton — 17
Boarding House | P | Nan — 21
Bookstore & Rest. | P, T | CC — 19
NEW Boston Burger | P | Somerville — -
Bottega | P | Back Bay — 24
Bouchée | P | Back Bay — 21
Brant Point | T | Nan — 21
Bravo | T | MFA — 21
Brotherhood/Thieves | P | Nan — 18
Bubala's | P | CC — 16
Bullfinch's | P | Sudbury — 21
Cactus Club | S | Back Bay — 16
Cafeteria | P | Back Bay — 17
Caffe Tosca | P | Hingham — 24
Canestaro | S | Fenway — 19
Capt. Frosty's | P | CC — 21
Capt. Linnell | P | CC — 22
Casa Romero | P | Back Bay — 23
Charley's | G | multi. — 18
Charlie's Kitchen | P | Harv Sq — 17
Ciao Bella | P, S | Back Bay — 19

Cinco | P | Nan — 26
🅉 Clam Box | T | Ipswich — 26
Clancy's | T | CC — 22
Columbus Café | P | S End — 19
Cooke's | P | CC — -
Cottonwood | P | Back Bay — 18
Daily Catch | P | Seaport Dist — 24
Dante | P | E Cambridge — 24
🅉 Détente | G | MV — 27
Devlin's | P | Brighton — 20
Dillon's | P | Back Bay — 16
Dog Bar | P | Gloucester — 23
Dunbar Tea | P | CC — 22
NEW Dune | P | Nan — -
🅉 Eastern Stand. | P | Kenmore Sq — 22
NEW 88 Wharf | P | Milton — -
Enzo | P, T | CC — 24
Even Keel | P | Nan — 19
NEW Farm Bar | P | Essex — -
Fifty-Six Union | G | Nan — 22
Finz | T | Salem — 20
Firefly Woodfire | S | CC — 20
🅉 Galley Beach | P | Nan — 24
Gardner Museum | G | MFA — 20
Grafton St. Pub | P | Harv Sq — 17
Grapevine | G | Salem — 25
Green Briar | P | Brighton — 17
🅉 Hamersley's | P | S End — 27
Harvest | P | Harv Sq — 25
Henrietta's | T | Harv Sq — 23
Hi-Rise | P | Harv Sq — 24
Hungry I, The | G | Beacon Hill — 24
NEW Il Casale | S | Belmont — -
NEW Il Tesoro/Terrace | T | MV — -
James's Gate | P | Jamaica Plain — 16
🅉 J's Nashoba | P | Bolton — 26
Karoo Kafe | T | CC — 24
KingFish Hall | P | Faneuil Hall — 22
La Casa/Pedro | P | Watertown — 21
La Cucina/Mare | P | CC — 25
Landing | multi. — 16
Lattanzi's | G, P | MV — 21
La Voile | P | Back Bay — 23
NEW Ledge | P | Dorchester — -
Le Languedoc | P | Nan — 26
L'Étoile | P | MV — 26
Lo La 41° | P | Nan — 21
Lure | MV — 21
Mac's | S | CC — 24
McCormick/Schmick | P | Faneuil Hall — 21
NEW Mediterranean | P | MV — -
Miel | G, P | Waterfront — 21
Mother Anna's | P | N End — 21

Neighborhood Rest. | G | **Somerville**	23
NEW North 26 | P | **Faneuil Hall**	–
Z Oleana | P | **Inman Sq**	28
Orinoco | S | **S End**	25
Orleans Inn | T | **CC**	17
Other Side | P, S | **Back Bay**	19
NEW Pairings | S | **Park Sq**	–
Parish Cafe | P | **Back Bay**	22
NEW Pazzo | P | **Back Bay**	–
Piattini | P | **Back Bay**	23
Poe's/Rattlesnake | T | **Back Bay**	–
Porcini's | P | **Watertown**	22
Red Fez | P | **S End**	18
Red House | P | **Harv Sq**	20
Red Rock | G, P | **Swampscott**	20
Rist. Fiore | P, T | **N End**	21
Riva | P | **Scituate**	26
Ropewalk | P | **Nan**	–
NEW Rowes Wharf | T | **Waterfront**	–
Rustic Kitchen | P | **Hingham**	20
Z Ruth's Chris | P | **D'town Cross**	24
Salvatore's | P | **Seaport Dist**	20
Scampo | P | **Beacon Hill**	22
Scollay Sq. | P | **Beacon Hill**	19
Scoozi | P | **Back Bay**	18
Sibling Rivalry | P | **S End**	24
Sidecar Café | P, S | **MV**	–
Siena | P | **CC**	21
Siros | T | **N Quincy**	19
NEW Six Burner | P | **Back Bay**	–
Sol Azteca | P | **multi.**	20
Sophia's | P | **Roslindale**	23
South End Buttery | P | **S End**	21
Stanhope Grille | P | **Back Bay**	23
Stella | P | **S End**	24
Stellina | G | **Watertown**	22
Stephanie's | S | **Back Bay**	20
Straight Wharf | P | **Nan**	25
Summer House | **Nan**	20
Sweet Life | G | **MV**	25
Tantric | S | **Theater Dist**	20
Tapéo | S | **Back Bay**	22
Tavern/Water | P | **Charlestown**	13
Temple Bar | P | **Porter Sq**	20
Z Topper's | T | **Nan**	27
NEW Town | P | **Nan**	–
Tratt. Il Panino | P | **N End**	23
Tremont 647 | P | **S End**	21
Trevi Café | P | **CC**	–
28 Degrees | P | **S End**	20
29 Newbury | P | **Back Bay**	20
Z 21 Federal | P | **Nan**	24
224 Boston St. | G | **Dorchester**	22
Via Matta | P | **Park Sq**	25
Village Sushi | P | **Roslindale**	23
Vox Populi | S | **Back Bay**	16
Winslow's Tavern | P | **CC**	20
Wonder Spice | P | **Jamaica Plain**	21
Woodman's | G | **Essex**	23
NEW Woodward | P | **Financial Dist**	–
Zen | P | **Beacon Hill**	24

PARKING

(V=valet, *=validated)

Z Abe & Louie's | V* | **Back Bay**	26
Al Dente* | **N End**	22
Amarin Thailand* | **Newton**	22
Antico Forno* | **N End**	23
Z Aquitaine | V | **S End**	23
Asana | V | **Back Bay**	–
Atlantica | V | **Cohasset**	15
Atlantic Fish | V | **Back Bay**	23
Aura* | **Seaport Dist**	22
Avenue One | V | **D'town Cross**	18
Avila | V* | **Theater Dist**	24
Bacco* | **N End**	21
Bambara | V | **E Cambridge**	20
Z B&G Oysters | V | **S End**	26
Bar 10 | V | **Back Bay**	17
Beehive | V | **S End**	18
Bertucci's | V* | **multi.**	17
NEW Big Papi's | V | **Framingham**	–
Billy Tse | V | **Revere**	20
Bin 26 | V | **Beacon Hill**	21
Blu* | **Theater Dist**	21
NEW Blue Canoe | **MV**	–
Blue Room* | **Kendall Sq**	25
Bokx | V | **Newton Lower Falls**	23
Bombay Club | V | **S End**	20
Bond | V | **Financial Dist**	–
Bouchée | V* | **Back Bay**	21
Brasserie Jo | V | **Back Bay**	20
Bravo* | **MFA**	21
Bricco | V | **N End**	25
Z Bristol Lounge | V* | **Back Bay**	24
Butcher Shop | V | **S End**	25
Café Fleuri | V | **Financial Dist**	22
Cafeteria | V | **Back Bay**	17
Caffe Paradiso* | **N End**	17
Caliterra | V | **Financial Dist**	16
Cantina Italiana* | **N End**	22
Z Capital Grille | V | **multi.**	26
Casablanca* | **Harv Sq**	22
Chart House | V | **Waterfront**	21
Chart Room | V | **CC**	20
Chatham Bars | V | **CC**	22
Chau Chow* | **Chinatown**	21

Menus, photos, voting and more – free at ZAGAT.com

Restaurant	Rating
Cheers* | Faneuil Hall	14
☑ Cheesecake | V* | multi.	18
Ciao Bella | V | Back Bay	19
Clink | V | Beacon Hill	19
☑ Clio/Uni | V* | Back Bay	27
Club Cafe | V | S End	18
Coonamessett | V | CC	18
Cottonwood* | Back Bay	18
☑ Cuchi Cuchi | V | Central Sq	22
Dante | V | E Cambridge	24
Davide Rist. | V | N End	24
Da Vinci | V | Park Sq	22
☑ Davio's | V* | Park Sq	25
District | V | Leather Dist	17
Donatello | V | Saugus	24
Douzo* | Back Bay	24
Durgin-Park* | Faneuil Hall	17
☑ Eastern Stand. | V | Kenmore Sq	22
East Ocean* | Chinatown	24
☑ Elephant Walk | V | Fenway	23
Exchange St. Bistro* | Malden	20
Figs | V | Charlestown	23
Fire & Ice* | Harv Sq	16
Fishmonger's* | CC	18
Fleming's Prime | V* | Park Sq	24
☑ Fugakyu | V | Brookline	25
☑ Giacomo's | V | S End	25
Golden Temple | V | Brookline	21
Grafton St. Pub | V | Harv Sq	17
☑ Grill 23 | V | Back Bay	25
☑ Hamersley's | V | S End	27
Haru* | Back Bay	20
Harvest | V* | Harv Sq	25
Henrietta's | V* | Harv Sq	23
House of Siam | V | S End	24
Houston's* | Faneuil Hall	22
Hungry I, The | V | Beacon Hill	24
☑ Hungry Mother* | Kendall Sq	27
Incontro | V | Franklin	22
Ivy Rest. | V | D'town Cross	20
Jacob Wirth* | Theater Dist	17
Jae's | V | S End	20
Jasper White's* | Back Bay	21
Jer-Ne | V | Theater Dist	20
Joe's American | V | N End	16
Joe Tecce's | V | N End	19
John Harvard's* | Harv Sq	16
Joshua Tree | V | Allston	15
Jumbo* | Chinatown	23
Kashmir | V | Back Bay	23
KingFish Hall* | Faneuil Hall	22
KO Prime | V | D'town Cross	24
La Fam. Giorgio* | N End	23
Lala Rokh | V | Beacon Hill	23
La Morra | V | Brookline	24
L'Andana | V | Burlington	25
La Voile | V | Back Bay	23
Left Bank | V | Tyngsboro	21
☑ Legal Sea | V* | multi.	22
Le's | V | Chestnut Hill	21
☑ L'Espalier | V | Back Bay	28
Les Zygomates | V | Leather Dist	22
Lineage* | Brookline	23
Living Room | V* | Waterfront	15
Locke-Ober | V | D'town Cross	24
L'Osteria* | N End	23
Lucca | V | N End	25
Lucca Back Bay | V | Back Bay	21
Lucia | V | N End	21
NEW Lyric | V | CC	-
Maggiano's | V | Park Sq	19
Mamma Maria | V | N End	25
Mantra | V | D'town Cross	18
Marco Romana* | N End	26
Mare* | N End	26
NEW Market | V | Theater Dist	-
Marshside | V | CC	15
Masa | V | S End	23
Ma Soba* | Beacon Hill	20
Maurizio's | V* | N End	25
McCormick/Schmick | V | Park Sq	21
Melting Pot | V | Park Sq	20
☑ Meritage | V* | Waterfront	27
Metropolis | V | S End	23
Metropolitan | V | Chestnut Hill	21
Midwest | V | Inman Sq	20
Miel | V | Waterfront	21
☑ Mistral | V | S End	27
Mooo... | V | Beacon Hill	24
☑ Morton's | V | multi.	25
Mother Anna's* | N End	21
Nico | V | N End	-
9 Tastes* | Harv Sq	20
☑ No. 9 Park | V | Beacon Hill	28
☑ Oak Room | V | Back Bay	25
Oceana | V* | Waterfront	24
Oceanaire | V | Financial Dist	24
Ocean House | V | CC	25
☑ Oishii | V | S End	27
☑ Olives | V | Charlestown	25
Om | V | Harv Sq	19
Osushi | V | Back Bay	23
Paddock | V | CC	20
NEW Pairings | V | Park Sq	-
Palm | V* | Back Bay	23
Papa Razzi | V | Back Bay	18
Parker's | V* | D'town Cross	22
Peach Farm* | Chinatown	25
Penang* | Chinatown	22

Z Petit Robert | V | S End — 24
P.F. Chang's | V | Theater Dist — 19
Pigalle | V* | Theater Dist — 26
Z Pisces | V | CC — 27
Plaza III* | Faneuil Hall — 21
NEW Post 390 | V | Back Bay — -
Z Prezza | V | N End — 27
Z Radius | V | Financial Dist — 26
Red House* | Harv Sq — 20
Z Red Pheasant | V | CC — 27
Rendezvous | V | Central Sq — 26
Z Rialto | V* | Harv Sq — 26
Rist. Fiore | V | N End — 21
Rist. Toscano | V | Beacon Hill — 24
Rist. Villa Francesca | V | N End — 19
Roadhouse | V | CC — 20
Rustic Kitchen | V | Theater Dist — 20
Z Ruth's Chris | V | D'town Cross — 24
Salvatore's* | Seaport Dist — 20
Sandrine's* | Harv Sq — 24
Saraceno* | N End — 23
Scampo | V | Beacon Hill — 22
Scarlet Oak | V | Hingham — 20
Z Sel de Terre | V | multi. — 23
Sensing | V | Waterfront — -
75 Chestnut | V | Beacon Hill — 21
Shabu-Zen* | Chinatown — 22
Sibling Rivalry | V | S End — 24
Sidney's | V | Central Sq — 21
606 Congress | V | Seaport Dist — 21
Skipjack's* | Back Bay — 20
Sky | V | Norwood — 19
Smith/Wollensky | V | Back Bay — 23
Sonsie | V | Back Bay — 20
Z Sorellina | V | Back Bay — 27
Sorriso | V | Leather Dist — 20
Stanhope Grille | V | Back Bay — 23
Stella | V | S End — 24
Stephanie's | V | Back Bay — 20
Stix | V | Back Bay — 17
Strega Rist. | V | N End — 21
Sunset Grill/Cantina* | Boston U — 20
Z Tangierino | V | Charlestown — 24
Tanjore* | Harv Sq — 22
Z Taranta* | N End — 27
Tasca | V | Brighton — 23
Tavern in Sq.* | Porter Sq — 17
Teatro | V | Theater Dist — 24
Terramia* | N End — 26
33 Rest. | V | Back Bay — 20
Z Top of Hub* | Back Bay — 20
Z Toro | V | S End — 26
Townsend's | V | Hyde Park — 19
Z Tratt. di Monica/Vinoteca | V* | N End — 26

Tremont 647 | V | S End — 21
Tresca | V | N End — 23
Z Troquet | V | Theater Dist — 27
Turner Fish | V | Back Bay — 21
28 Degrees | V | S End — 20
Umbria Prime | V | Financial Dist — 23
Union B&G | V | S End — 24
Z Union Oyster | V* | Faneuil Hall — 20
Z Upstairs/Square | V* | Harv Sq — 24
Via Matta | V | Park Sq — 25
Vlora | V | Back Bay — 22
Vox Populi | V | Back Bay — 16
West End Johnnie's | V | W End — 17
Wine Cellar | V | Back Bay — 20
Zócalo Cocina | V | Brighton — 22

PEOPLE-WATCHING

Z Aquitaine | Dedham — 23
Asana | Back Bay — -
Atlantic Fish/Chop | MV — -
Bayside | Westport — -
Beehive | S End — 18
Bella Luna/Milky Way | Jamaica Plain — -
NEW Big Papi's | Framingham — -
Bina Osteria | D'town Cross — -
NEW Bistro du Midi | Back Bay — -
Blu | Theater Dist — 21
Boarding House | Nan — 21
Bouchée | Back Bay — 21
Bricco | N End — 25
Butcher Shop | S End — 25
Cafe Edwige/at Night | CC — 26
Cafeteria | Back Bay — 17
Caffe Paradiso | N End — 17
Charley's | multi. — 18
Ciao Bella | Back Bay — 19
Z Clio/Uni | Back Bay — 27
Club Cafe | S End — 18
Cobie's Clam | CC — 19
Cottonwood | Back Bay — 18
NEW Courtyard/Boston Library | Back Bay — -
Z Cuchi Cuchi | Central Sq — 22
NEW Danny Quinn's | MV — -
Dante | E Cambridge — 24
Z Davio's | multi. — 25
Drink | Seaport Dist — -
Z Eastern Stand. | Kenmore Sq — 22
NEW 88 Wharf | Milton — -
Florentine Cafe | N End — 21
Franklin | S End — 26
Gaslight Brasserie | S End — 21
NEW Ginger Park | S End — -
Z Grill 23 | Back Bay — 25
Highland Kitchen | Somerville — 23

NEW Il Casale	Belmont	–
Jetties	Nan	14
KingFish Hall	Faneuil Hall	22
NEW Lansdowne	Fenway	–
Laureen's	CC	23
NEW Ledge	Dorchester	–
Living Room	Waterfront	15
Lo La 41°	Nan	21
NEW Lord Hobo	E Cambridge	–
LTK	Seaport Dist	20
Mantra	D'town Cross	18
NEW Market	Theater Dist	–
Masa	Woburn	23
Max/Dylan	Charlestown	–
NEW Mediterranean	MV	–
Z Mistral	S End	27
Z No. 9 Park	Beacon Hill	28
NEW Pairings	Park Sq	–
Parish Cafe	Back Bay	22
Pearl	Nan	24
Piattini	Back Bay	23
Poe's/Rattlesnake	Back Bay	–
NEW Post 390	Back Bay	–
Z Radius	Financial Dist	26
Rodizio	Somerville	22
Roobar	CC	21
Ropewalk	Nan	–
NEW Rowes Wharf	Waterfront	–
Scampo	Beacon Hill	22
Scollay Sq.	Beacon Hill	19
Sibling Rivalry	S End	24
Sidecar Café	MV	–
Sonsie	Back Bay	20
Z Sorellina	Back Bay	27
Sportello	Seaport Dist	–
Stephanie's	multi.	20
NEW Stork Club	S End	–
Studio 3	multi.	–
Tavern in Sq.	Salem	17
NEW Tavolino	Foxboro	–
Teatro	Theater Dist	24
NEW Technique	E Cambridge	–
Temple Bar	Porter Sq	20
NEW Tory Row	Harv Sq	–
Tremont 647	S End	21
Trident	Back Bay	19
28 Degrees	S End	20
29 Newbury	Back Bay	20
Z 21 Federal	Nan	24
Via Matta	Park Sq	25
Vox Populi	Back Bay	16
Wagamama	Back Bay	18
Water St.	MV	–
West End Johnnie's	W End	17

PRIVATE ROOMS

(Restaurants charge less at off times; call for capacity)

Belfry Inne	CC	25
Brotherhood/Thieves	Nan	18
Z Capital Grille	multi.	26
Capt. Linnell	CC	22
Chanticleer	Nan	25
Chatham Bars	CC	22
Chau Chow	Chinatown	21
China Pearl	Chinatown	21
Coonamessett	CC	18
Dan'l Webster	CC	20
Z East Coast	Inman Sq	25
Z Eastern Stand.	Kenmore Sq	22
Z Elephant Walk	multi.	23
Filippo	N End	21
Fleming's Prime	Park Sq	24
Z Fugakyu	Brookline	25
Golden Temple	Brookline	21
Z Grill 23	Back Bay	25
Harvest	Harv Sq	25
Hungry I, The	Beacon Hill	24
Z Il Capriccio	Waltham	27
Ivy Rest.	D'town Cross	20
Kashmir	Back Bay	23
Kowloon	Saugus	17
Lala Rokh	Beacon Hill	23
Z Legal Sea	multi.	22
Z L'Espalier	Back Bay	28
Locke-Ober	D'town Cross	24
Lure	MV	21
Mamma Maria	N End	25
Mantra	D'town Cross	18
McCormick/Schmick	multi.	21
Metropolitan	Chestnut Hill	21
Z Mistral	S End	27
Z Morton's	Back Bay	25
Òran Mór	Nan	24
Pearl	Nan	24
Z Radius	Financial Dist	26
Regatta/Cotuit	CC	25
Saraceno	N End	23
Sibling Rivalry	S End	24
Smith/Wollensky	Back Bay	23
Stella	S End	24
Z Tangierino	Charlestown	24
Z Taranta	N End	27
Z Topper's	Nan	27
Tremont 647	S End	21
Turner Fish	Back Bay	21
Z Upstairs/Square	Harv Sq	24
Vinalia	D'town Cross	17
Whitman Hse.	CC	21

RAW BARS

Arnold's Lobster | **CC**	23
Atlantic Fish/Chop | **MV**	-
Back Eddy | **Westport**	22
🗹 B&G Oysters | **S End**	26
Barley Neck Inn | **CC**	20
Bookstore & Rest. | **CC**	19
🗹 East Coast | **Inman Sq**	25
🗹 Eastern Stand. | **Kenmore Sq**	22
Finz | **multi.**	20
Five Bays | **CC**	25
Jasper White's | **multi.**	21
Jetties | **Nan**	14
KingFish Hall | **Faneuil Hall**	22
Larsen's Fish | **MV**	27
🗹 Legal Sea | **multi.**	22
Lobster Pot | **CC**	22
Locke-Ober | **D'town Cross**	24
Mac's | **CC**	24
McCormick/Schmick | **multi.**	21
Moby Dick's | **CC**	23
Naked Oyster | **CC**	25
🗹 Neptune Oyster | **N End**	27
Oceanaire | **Financial Dist**	24
Orleans Inn | **CC**	17
Oyster Co. | **CC**	23
Port | **CC**	23
Red Inn | **CC**	24
Ropewalk | **Nan**	-
Skipjack's | **multi.**	20
Summer Winter | **Burlington**	24
28 Degrees | **S End**	20
🗹 Union Oyster | **Faneuil Hall**	20
Village Fish | **Needham**	20
Woodman's | **Essex**	23

ROMANTIC PLACES

Alberto's | **CC**	20
Amari | **CC**	22
🗹 Aquitaine | **S End**	23
Ariadne | **Newton**	21
Asana | **Back Bay**	-
Assaggio | **N End**	24
Atasca | **Kendall Sq**	23
Atria | **MV**	25
Barker Tavern | **Scituate**	23
Barley Neck Inn | **CC**	20
BarLola | **Back Bay**	18
Beach Plum | **MV**	25
Belfry Inne | **CC**	25
Bin 26 | **Beacon Hill**	21
Bistro/Crowne Pointe | **CC**	22
🆕 Bistro du Midi | **Back Bay**	-
🗹 Bistro 5 | **W Medford**	27
Boarding House | **Nan**	21

Bon Savor | **Jamaica Plain**	20
🗹 Bristol Lounge | **Back Bay**	24
Buca's Tuscan | **CC**	23
Cape Sea | **CC**	26
Capt. Linnell | **CC**	22
🗹 Carmen | **N End**	26
Casa Romero | **Back Bay**	23
Casino Wharf | **CC**	20
Chanticleer | **Nan**	25
Chez Henri | **Harv Sq**	24
🗹 Chillingsworth | **CC**	27
🆕 Chilmark Tavern | **MV**	-
Cinco | **Nan**	26
🗹 Clio/Uni | **Back Bay**	27
Comfort | **Watertown**	-
🗹 Company/Cauldron | **Nan**	28
🆕 Coppa | **S End**	-
🗹 Craigie/Main | **Central Sq**	27
🗹 Cuchi Cuchi | **Central Sq**	22
Daily Catch | **Brookline**	24
Dalia's Bistro | **Brookline**	19
Dalí | **Somerville**	25
Dalya's | **Bedford**	23
Da Vinci | **Park Sq**	22
🗹 Détente | **MV**	27
🆕 Dune | **Nan**	-
Erbaluce | **Park Sq**	-
Estragon | **S End**	-
Euno | **N End**	24
Figs at 29 Fair | **Nan**	-
Finale | **multi.**	23
Fleming's Prime | **Park Sq**	24
🗹 Front St. | **CC**	27
🗹 Galley Beach | **Nan**	24
G Bar | **Swampscott**	21
Gennaro's Five N. | **N End**	-
Ghazal | **Jamaica Plain**	-
Glory | **Andover**	21
Grain & Salt | **Allston**	-
Grapevine | **Salem**	25
Grezzo | **N End**	23
Grotto | **Beacon Hill**	25
Haveli | **Inman Sq**	-
🗹 Helmand | **E Cambridge**	26
Hungry I, The | **Beacon Hill**	24
🗹 Il Capriccio | **Waltham**	27
🆕 Il Casale | **Belmont**	-
🆕 Il Tesoro/Terrace | **MV**	-
🗹 J's Nashoba | **Bolton**	26
🗹 La Campania | **Waltham**	28
Lala Rokh | **Beacon Hill**	23
Lambert's Cove | **MV**	25
L'Andana | **Burlington**	25
La Voile | **Back Bay**	23
Left Bank | **Tyngsboro**	21

Le Languedoc | **Nan**	26
☑ L'Espalier | **Back Bay**	28
L'Étoile | **MV**	26
Lucca | **N End**	25
☑ Lumière | **Newton**	27
Lure | **MV**	21
Mamma Maria | **N End**	25
Marliave | **D'town Cross**	22
Mews | **CC**	27
☑ Oak Room | **Back Bay**	25
☑ Oishii | **S End**	27
☑ Oleana | **Inman Sq**	28
Olivadi | **Norwood**	-
Òran Mór | **Nan**	24
Orta | **Hanover**	-
Osteria/Civetta | **CC**	-
☑ Outermost Inn | **MV**	25
Pagliuca's | **N End**	22
Pierrot Bistrot | **Beacon Hill**	24
Pigalle | **Theater Dist**	26
☑ Prezza | **N End**	27
Red House | **Harv Sq**	20
Red Inn | **CC**	24
Rist. Damiano | **N End**	-
NEW Rist. Pavarotti | **Reading**	-
Salts | **Central Sq**	26
☑ Sel de Terre | **multi.**	23
Sensing | **Waterfront**	-
75 Chestnut | **Beacon Hill**	21
Sol Azteca | **Fenway**	20
Solea | **Waltham**	23
Sorriso | **Leather Dist**	20
Spiga Trattoria | **Needham**	-
NEW State Road | **MV**	-
Stephanie's | **S End**	20
Straight Wharf | **Nan**	25
Sweet Life | **MV**	25
NEW Tajine | **Harv Sq**	-
☑ Tangierino | **Charlestown**	24
☑ Taranta | **N End**	27
Tasca | **Brighton**	23
☑ Top of Hub | **Back Bay**	20
☑ Topper's | **Nan**	27
Tosca | **Hingham**	25
NEW Town | **Nan**	-
Townsend's | **Hyde Park**	19
Tresca | **N End**	23
Trevi Café | **CC**	-
NEW Trina's | **Inman Sq**	-
☑ Troquet | **Theater Dist**	27
Tryst | **Arlington**	22
☑ 28 Atlantic | **CC**	26
☑ 21 Federal | **Nan**	24
Umbria Prime | **Financial Dist**	23
☑ Upstairs/Square | **Harv Sq**	24

Via Matta | **Park Sq**	25
Vlora | **Back Bay**	22
Water St. | **MV**	-
West/Centre | **W Roxbury**	18
Wine Cellar | **Back Bay**	20
Zebra's Bistro | **Medfield**	24

SINGLES SCENES

☑ Abe & Louie's | **Back Bay**	26
Atlantic Fish/Chop | **MV**	-
BarLola | **Back Bay**	18
Bella Luna/Milky Way | **Jamaica Plain**	-
Blue22 | **Quincy**	19
Boston Sail | **Waterfront**	15
Cactus Club | **Back Bay**	16
Cafe Escadrille | **Burlington**	19
Casino Wharf | **CC**	20
Chatham Squire | **CC**	18
Club Car | **Nan**	20
Cottage | **Wellesley**	19
David Ryan's | **MV**	15
Dillon's | **Back Bay**	16
Fleming's Prime | **Park Sq**	24
Glenn's | **Newburyport**	23
Glory | **Andover**	21
Grafton St. Pub | **Harv Sq**	17
Houston's | **Faneuil Hall**	22
John Harvard's | **Harv Sq**	16
Joshua Tree | **Somerville**	15
NEW Kama | **Quincy**	-
NEW Lansdowne | **Fenway**	-
Living Room | **Waterfront**	15
Max/Dylan | **D'town Cross**	-
Middlesex | **Central Sq**	17
M.J. O'Connor's | **Park Sq**	-
Orleans | **Somerville**	17
Poe's/Rattlesnake | **Back Bay**	-
Redline | **Harv Sq**	17
Sanctuary | **Financial Dist**	19
Sunset Grill/Cantina | **multi.**	20
NEW Symphony 8 | **Fenway**	-
Tavern in Sq. | **Porter Sq**	17
Temple Bar | **Porter Sq**	20
33 Rest. | **Back Bay**	20
28 Degrees | **S End**	20
Village Fish | **Needham**	20
Vox Populi | **Back Bay**	16
West End Johnnie's | **W End**	17

SLEEPERS

(Good food, but little known)

Abbondanza | **Everett**	23
Academy Ocean | **CC**	22
Amari | **CC**	22
Amelia's Kitchen | **Somerville**	22

Amelia's Trattoria | **Kendall Sq**	22
Angelo's | **Stoneham**	26
Atria | **MV**	25
Aura | **Seaport Dist**	22
Bangkok Bistro | **Brighton**	22
Barker Tavern | **Scituate**	23
Belfry Inne | **CC**	25
Bhindi Bazaar | **Back Bay**	22
Bia Bistro | **Cohasset**	24
Bistro/Crowne Pointe | **CC**	22
Bistro 712 | **Norwood**	24
Bite | **MV**	26
Blackfish | **CC**	24
Blue Moon | **CC**	24
Bokx | **Newton Lower Falls**	23
Bon Caldo | **Norwood**	22
Brenden Crocker's | **Beverly**	25
Bridgeman's | **Hull**	26
Cafe Barada | **Porter Sq**	23
Café Brazil | **Allston**	23
Cafe Edwige/at Night | **CC**	26
Café Polonia | **S Boston**	24
Caffe Tosca | **Hingham**	24
Cantina Italiana | **N End**	22
Cantina la Mexicana | **Somerville**	24
Capt. Linnell | **CC**	22
Catch of the Day | **CC**	25
Chanticleer | **Nan**	25
Chapoquoit Grill | **CC**	22
Chesca's | **MV**	23
Cinco | **Nan**	26
Clancy's | **CC**	22
Cottage City | **MV**	22
Courthouse | **E Cambridge**	22
Davide Rist. | **N End**	24
DeMarco | **Nan**	22
Devon's | **CC**	24
Dog Bar | **Gloucester**	23
Donatello | **Saugus**	24
Don Ricardo's | **S End**	23
Dunbar Tea | **CC**	22
El Sarape | **Braintree**	25
Enzo | **CC**	24
Erawan/Siam | **Waltham**	22
Euno | **N End**	24
Fifty-Six Union | **Nan**	22
Five Bays | **CC**	25
Flat Iron | **W End**	22
Friendly Fisherman | **CC**	24
Glenn's | **Newburyport**	23
Grapevine | **Salem**	25
Green St. | **Central Sq**	24
Grezzo | **multi.**	23
Haley House | **Roxbury**	24
Himalayan Bistro | **W Roxbury**	24
Hot Tomatoes | **multi.**	22
Incontro | **Franklin**	22
Jasmine | **Brighton**	24
Jimmy Seas | **MV**	23
Karoo Kafe | **CC**	24
Karoun | **Newton**	22
Kathmandu Spice | **Arlington**	22
Kayuga | **multi.**	24
Kaze | **Chinatown**	23
La Cucina/Mare | **CC**	25
La Fam. Giorgio | **N End**	23
La Galleria 33 | **N End**	26
L'Alouette | **CC**	26
Lambert's Cove | **MV**	25
La Summa | **N End**	22
Laureen's | **CC**	23
Le Grenier | **MV**	23
Le Languedoc | **Nan**	26
Le Lyonnais | **Acton**	23
L'Étoile | **MV**	26
L'Osteria | **N End**	23
Mac's | **CC**	24
Marliave | **D'town Cross**	22
Masona Grill | **W Roxbury**	25
Massimino's Cucina | **N End**	23
Mela | **S End**	24
Misaki | **CC**	24
MuLan Taiwanese | **Kendall Sq**	23
Muqueca | **Inman Sq**	24
Namaskar | **Somerville**	23
Navy Yard | **Charlestown**	23
Neighborhood Rest. | **Somerville**	23
Net Result | **MV**	25
NewBridge | **Chelsea**	24
New Dong Khanh | **Chinatown**	22
New Jang Su | **Burlington**	23
New Mother India | **Waltham**	22
North St. Grille | **N End**	23
Oceana | **Waterfront**	24
Òran Mór | **Nan**	24
Out of/Blue | **Somerville**	22
Oyster Co. | **CC**	23
Pagliuca's | **N End**	22
Paris Creperie | **Brookline**	22
Parker's | **D'town Cross**	22
Pellana | **Peabody**	26
Pho Hoa | **multi.**	22
Piccola Venezia | **N End**	22
Piccolo Nido | **N End**	24
Pi Pizzeria | **Nan**	23
Ponzu | **Waltham**	23
Porcini's | **Watertown**	22
Port | **CC**	23
Prose | **Arlington**	24
Qingdao Gdn. | **Porter Sq**	24

Queequeg's	**Nan**	25	Fire & Ice	**multi.**	16
Regatta/Cotuit	**CC**	25	Jacob Wirth	**Theater Dist**	17
Riva	**Scituate**	26	Kowloon	**Saugus**	17
Rodizio	**Somerville**	22	Optimist Café	**CC**	21
Ross' Grill	**CC**	22	⊠ Union Oyster	**Faneuil Hall**	20
Sabur	**Somerville**	22		
Sakurabana	**Financial Dist**	25		

Queequeg's | **Nan**	25
Regatta/Cotuit | **CC**	25
Riva | **Scituate**	26
Rodizio | **Somerville**	22
Ross' Grill | **CC**	22
Sabur | **Somerville**	22
Sakurabana | **Financial Dist**	25
Saporito's | **Hull**	26
Saraceno | **N End**	23
Sea Grille | **Nan**	22
Seiyo | **S End**	25
Seoul Food | **Porter Sq**	22
Sfoglia | **Nan**	24
Shanghai Gate | **Allston**	24
Shangri-La | **Belmont**	23
Shawarma King | **Brookline**	22
Ships Inn | **Nan**	24
Shogun | **Newton**	23
Sichuan Garden | **multi.**	22
Sir Cricket's | **CC**	24
62 on Wharf | **Salem**	24
Sofra Bakery | **Huron Vill**	26
Soma | **Beverly**	22
Sophia's | **Roslindale**	23
Sorella's | **Jamaica Plain**	26
Sorelle | **Charlestown**	23
St. Alphonzo's | **S Boston**	22
Stanhope Grille | **Back Bay**	23
Stir Crazy | **CC**	23
Stone Soup | **Ipswich**	25
Strip-T's | **Watertown**	22
Super Fusion | **Brookline**	27
Sushi by Yoshi | **Nan**	25
Sweet Life | **MV**	25
Tacos El Charro | **Jamaica Plain**	23
Tanjore | **Harv Sq**	22
Taqueria Mexico | **Waltham**	22
Tartufo | **Newton**	22
Terra Luna | **CC**	24
Vicki Lee's | **Belmont**	25
Village Sushi | **Roslindale**	23
Vining's | **CC**	24
Vlora | **Back Bay**	22
Volle Nolle | **N End**	26
Woody's Grill | **Fenway**	22
Wu Chon | **Somerville**	22
Xinh Xinh | **Chinatown**	25
Yama | **multi.**	22
Zabaglione | **Ipswich**	22
Zen | **Beacon Hill**	24

THEME RESTAURANTS

Cheers | **multi.**	14
Durgin-Park | **Faneuil Hall**	17
Fire & Ice | **multi.**	16
Jacob Wirth | **Theater Dist**	17
Kowloon | **Saugus**	17
Optimist Café | **CC**	21
⊠ Union Oyster | **Faneuil Hall**	20

TRENDY

Alchemy | **MV**	22
Alta Strada | **Wellesley**	21
Ashmont Grill | **Dorchester**	22
Avila | **Theater Dist**	24
⊠ B&G Oysters | **S End**	26
Beehive | **S End**	18
Bin 26 | **Beacon Hill**	21
Bouchée | **Back Bay**	21
Bricco | **N End**	25
Butcher Shop | **S End**	25
Cafeteria | **Back Bay**	17
Caffe Tosca | **Hingham**	24
Cambridge 1 | **Harv Sq**	22
Church | **Fenway**	20
Cinco | **Nan**	26
Clink | **Beacon Hill**	19
Dante | **E Cambridge**	24
District | **Leather Dist**	17
Douzo | **Back Bay**	24
⊠ Eastern Stand. | **Kenmore Sq**	22
Exchange St. Bistro | **Malden**	20
Five Bays | **CC**	25
Gargoyles | **Somerville**	24
Gaslight Brasserie | **S End**	21
Jerusalem Pita | **Brookline**	–
NEW Kama | **Quincy**	–
KO Prime | **D'town Cross**	24
La Verdad | **Fenway**	22
Lineage | **Brookline**	23
NEW Lord Hobo | **E Cambridge**	–
LTK | **Seaport Dist**	20
Mare | **N End**	26
Max/Dylan | **D'town Cross**	–
Mooo... | **Beacon Hill**	24
Myers + Chang | **S End**	23
Om | **Harv Sq**	19
Osushi | **Back Bay**	23
Pearl | **Nan**	24
Pops | **S End**	22
Port | **CC**	23
Rendezvous | **Central Sq**	26
Rocca | **S End**	24
Sibling Rivalry | **S End**	24
Sonsie | **Back Bay**	20
Sophia's | **Roslindale**	23
⊠ Sorellina | **Back Bay**	27
Sorriso | **Leather Dist**	20
Stella | **S End**	24

Stix | **Back Bay**	17
NEW Symphony 8 | **Fenway**	-
Tavolo | **Dorchester**	-
Teatro | **Theater Dist**	24
Temple Bar | **Porter Sq**	20
⨯ Toro | **S End**	26
NEW Tory Row | **Harv Sq**	-
Tremont 647 | **S End**	21
NEW Trina's | **Inman Sq**	-
28 Degrees | **S End**	20
29 Newbury | **Back Bay**	20
224 Boston St. | **Dorchester**	22
⨯ Upstairs/Square | **Harv Sq**	24
Via Matta | **Park Sq**	25
Vox Populi | **Back Bay**	16
Wagamama | **Back Bay**	18

VIEWS

Adrian's | **CC**	16
Anthony Cummaquid | **CC**	18
Anthony's | **Seaport Dist**	18
Aqua Grille | **CC**	19
Ardeo | **CC**	20
Asana | **Back Bay**	-
Atlantica | **Cohasset**	15
Atlantic Fish/Chop | **MV**	-
Audubon Circle | **Kenmore Sq**	21
Back Eddy | **Westport**	22
Barking Crab | **Seaport Dist**	16
Baxter's | **CC**	18
Bayside Betsy's | **CC**	15
Beach Plum | **MV**	25
Bistro/Crowne Pointe | **CC**	22
Black Cow | **Newburyport**	19
⨯ Black Dog | **MV**	19
Blu | **Theater Dist**	21
NEW Blue Canoe | **MV**	-
Bombay Club | **multi.**	20
Bookstore & Rest. | **CC**	19
Boston Sail | **Waterfront**	15
Brant Point | **Nan**	21
Bravo | **MFA**	21
Bricco | **N End**	25
Bridgeman's | **Hull**	26
⨯ Bristol Lounge | **Back Bay**	24
Bubala's | **CC**	16
Bukowski | **Inman Sq**	17
Café at Taj | **Back Bay**	20
Cape Sea | **CC**	26
Capt. Kidd | **CC**	18
Capt. Parker's | **CC**	18
Casino Wharf | **CC**	20
Chart House | **Waterfront**	21
Chart Room | **CC**	20
Chatham Bars | **CC**	22

Clancy's | **CC**	22
Daily Catch | **Seaport Dist**	24
Dante | **E Cambridge**	24
David Ryan's | **MV**	15
Devon's | **CC**	24
Dolphin | **CC**	21
Enzo | **CC**	24
Fanizzi's | **CC**	20
Finz | **Salem**	20
Fireplace | **Brookline**	21
Fishmonger's | **CC**	18
⨯ Galley Beach | **Nan**	24
Gardner Museum | **MFA**	20
⨯ Gibbet Hill | **Groton**	24
Grafton St. Pub | **Harv Sq**	17
Hemisphere | **CC**	17
Home Port | **MV**	20
⨯ J's Nashoba | **Bolton**	26
Landing | **Marblehead**	16
Left Bank | **Tyngsboro**	21
⨯ Legal Sea | **Waterfront**	22
Liam's | **CC**	20
Lobster Pot | **CC**	22
Marshside | **CC**	15
⨯ Meritage | **Waterfront**	27
Mews | **CC**	27
Miel | **Waterfront**	21
Net Result | **MV**	25
No Name | **Seaport Dist**	19
⨯ Not Average Joe's | **Newburyport**	18
Oceana | **Waterfront**	24
Ocean House | **CC**	25
⨯ Olives | **Charlestown**	25
Om | **Harv Sq**	19
Orleans Inn | **CC**	17
⨯ Outermost Inn | **MV**	25
NEW Post 390 | **Back Bay**	-
Red Inn | **CC**	24
⨯ Red Pheasant | **CC**	27
Red Rock | **Swampscott**	20
⨯ Rialto | **Harv Sq**	26
Ropewalk | **Nan**	-
Ross' Grill | **CC**	22
Saltwater | **MV**	-
Salvatore's | **Seaport Dist**	20
Sherborn Inn | **Sherborn**	19
Sidney's | **Central Sq**	21
Siros | **N Quincy**	19
Sonsie | **Back Bay**	20
Summer House | **Nan**	20
Tavern/Water | **Charlestown**	13
Tom Shea's | **Essex**	20
⨯ Top of Hub | **Back Bay**	20
⨯ Topper's | **Nan**	27

Menus, photos, voting and more - free at ZAGAT.com

NEW Tory Row | **Harv Sq**	-
Z Troquet | **Theater Dist**	27
Turner Fish | **Back Bay**	21
Z 28 Atlantic | **CC**	26
Water St. | **MV**	-
Woodman's | **Essex**	23

WATERSIDE

Adrian's | **CC**	16
Anthony Cummaquid | **CC**	18
Anthony's | **Seaport Dist**	18
Aqua Grille | **CC**	19
Atlantica | **Cohasset**	15
Atlantic Fish/Chop | **MV**	-
Back Eddy | **Westport**	22
Barking Crab | **Seaport Dist**	16
Baxter's | **CC**	18
Bayside Betsy's | **CC**	15
Black Cow | **Newburyport**	19
Z Black Dog | **MV**	19
NEW Blue Canoe | **MV**	-
Bookstore & Rest. | **CC**	19
Brant Point | **Nan**	21
Bridgeman's | **Hull**	26
Bubala's | **CC**	16
Capt. Kidd | **CC**	18
Casino Wharf | **CC**	20
Chart House | **Waterfront**	21
Chart Room | **CC**	20
Chatham Bars | **CC**	22
Clancy's | **CC**	22
Daily Catch | **Seaport Dist**	24
Dante | **E Cambridge**	24
NEW 88 Wharf | **Milton**	-
Enzo | **CC**	24
Finz | **Salem**	20
Fishmonger's | **CC**	18
Z Galley Beach | **Nan**	24
Hemisphere | **CC**	17
Jetties | **Nan**	14
Landfall | **CC**	18
Landing | **multi.**	16
Left Bank | **Tyngsboro**	21
Z Legal Sea | **Waterfront**	22
Liam's | **CC**	20
Lobster Pot | **CC**	22
Lure | **MV**	21
Mews | **CC**	27
Miel | **Waterfront**	21
No Name | **Seaport Dist**	19
Oceana | **Waterfront**	24
Ocean House | **CC**	25
Orleans Inn | **CC**	17
Z Outermost Inn | **MV**	25
Red Inn | **CC**	24

Red Rock | **Swampscott**	20
Riva | **Scituate**	26
Ross' Grill | **CC**	22
Sensing | **Waterfront**	-
Siros | **N Quincy**	19
Slip 14 | **Nan**	18
Straight Wharf | **Nan**	25
Summer House | **Nan**	20
Tavern/Water | **Charlestown**	13
Tom Shea's | **Essex**	20
Z Topper's | **Nan**	27
Z 28 Atlantic | **CC**	26

WINNING WINE LISTS

American Seasons | **Nan**	25
Angelo's | **Stoneham**	26
Anthony's | **Seaport Dist**	18
Atria | **MV**	25
Bin 26 | **Beacon Hill**	21
NEW Bistro du Midi | **Back Bay**	-
Blue Room | **Kendall Sq**	25
Z Bramble Inn | **CC**	27
Bravo | **MFA**	21
Butcher Shop | **S End**	25
Z Caffe Bella | **Randolph**	26
Chanticleer | **Nan**	25
Dante | **E Cambridge**	24
NEW Dune | **Nan**	-
Z Grill 23 | **Back Bay**	25
Z Hamersley's | **S End**	27
Z Il Capriccio | **Waltham**	27
NEW Il Casale | **Belmont**	-
Z La Campania | **Waltham**	28
Z Legal Sea | **Park Sq**	22
Z L'Espalier | **Back Bay**	28
Les Zygomates | **Leather Dist**	22
Z Lumière | **Newton**	27
Lure | **MV**	21
Mamma Maria | **N End**	25
Mantra | **D'town Cross**	18
NEW Market | **Theater Dist**	-
Z Meritage | **Waterfront**	27
Z Mistral | **S End**	27
Z No. 9 Park | **Beacon Hill**	28
NEW North 26 | **Faneuil Hall**	-
NEW Pairings | **Park Sq**	-
Z Prezza | **N End**	27
Z Radius | **Financial Dist**	26
Ross' Grill | **CC**	22
Salts | **Central Sq**	26
Silvertone B&G | **D'town Cross**	21
Smith/Wollensky | **Back Bay**	23
Taberna/Haro | **Brookline**	23
Tomasso | **Southborough**	24

Z Topper's | **Nan**	27
Tresca | **N End**	23
Z Troquet | **Theater Dist**	27
Z 21 Federal | **Nan**	24
Z Upstairs/Square | **Harv Sq**	24
Vinalia | **D'town Cross**	17
Wine Cellar | **Back Bay**	20

WORTH A TRIP

Belmont
NEW Il Casale	-
Shangri-La	23

Cape Cod
Z Abba	27
Z Bramble Inn	27
Buca's Tuscan	23
Z Chillingsworth	27
Z Inaho	27
Mews	27
Z Red Pheasant	27
Regatta/Cotuit	25
Z 28 Atlantic	26

Edgartown
Water St.	-

Hull
Bridgeman's	26
Saporito's	26

Ipswich
Zabaglione	22

Martha's Vineyard
Atria	25
Beach Plum	25
Z Détente	27
Lambert's Cove	25
L'Étoile	26

Nantucket
American Seasons	25
Chanticleer	25
Z Company/Cauldron	28
Òran Mór	24
Z Topper's	27

Natick
Z Maxwell's 148	26
Oga's	26

Randolph
Z Caffe Bella	26

Revere
Floating Rock	-

Scituate
Barker Tavern	23

Stoneham
Angelo's	26

Wellesley
Z Blue Ginger	26

Wellfleet
Mac's	24

Westport
Back Eddy	22

THE BERKSHIRES RESTAURANT DIRECTORY

	FOOD	DECOR	SERVICE	COST

TOP FOOD

28	Old Inn/Green	*Amer.*
27	Wheatleigh	*Amer./French*
	Blantyre	*Amer./French*
25	Gramercy	*Amer./Eclectic*
	Elizabeth's	*Eclectic*

TOP DECOR

28	Wheatleigh	*Amer./French*
	Blantyre	*Amer./French*
27	Old Inn/Green	*Amer.*
25	Jae's Spice	*Amer./Asian*
23	Mezze Bistro	*American*

Aegean Breeze, The *Mediterranean*   19 | 15 | 18 | $39

Great Barrington | 327 Stockbridge Rd. (bet. Cooper & Crissey Rds.) |
413-528-4001 | www.aegean-breeze.com

Great Barrington Grecophiles breeze into this "casual", "fairly priced" Mediterranean for "luscious broiled fish" and other "delicious" "traditional" Hellenic fare proffered by a battalion of "hospitable" servers; although some find the blue-and-white taverna-style digs "uninteresting", the "attractive" patio is "pleasant" "in warm weather."

Allium *American*   22 | 22 | 19 | $46

Great Barrington | 42-44 Railroad St. (Main St.) | 413-528-2118 |
www.mezzeinc.com

"Food mad" Great Barrington gets a fresh "big-city dining" experience by way of this "sophisticated" New American, a "cool sibling of Williamstown's Mezze"; the "limited" but "intriguing" market-based menu served in "chic", "modern" environs impresses most, and though the fussy fume it's "more show than go" with "erratic" service and "pricey" tabs, overall it's a "winner."

Alta *Mediterranean*   20 | 18 | 21 | $37

Lenox | 34 Church St. (bet. Housatonic & Walker Sts.) | 413-637-0003 |
www.altawinebar.com

"Wonderfully nice owners" set a "friendly" tone at this "fine" Lenox restaurant and wine bar where "terrific" Mediterranean eats are matched by a "great selection" of "reasonably priced" wines; if the "informal" interior is a tad too "young and lively" (read: "noisy"), it's "lovely to eat on the outdoor porch" when weather permits.

Aroma Bar & Grill *Indian*   21 | 14 | 22 | $30

Great Barrington | 485 Main St. (bet. Maple Ave. & Pope St.) |
413-528-3116 | www.aromabarandgrill.com

A "refreshing alternative" in Great Barrington, this "traditional" Indian offers "generous portions" of "well-priced", "delicious" dishes "spiced to your taste" and served by a "conscientious" staff that "tries hard to please"; as for the decor, some call it "kitschy" and some bill it bland – but "who cares?"

Baba Louie's Sourdough Pizza *Pizza*   24 | 12 | 18 | $21

Great Barrington | 286 Main St. (bet. Elm & Railroad Sts.) |
413-528-8100 | www.babalouiespizza.com

"Waiting crowds are a testament" to the "outstanding" "crunchy", organic thin-crust pizzas purveyed at this "rockin'" Great Barrington destination; add "fresh, novel" toppings, "marvelous salads", "first-rate" Italian sandwiches, a "competent staff" and "value" prices, and no wonder it's a "family favorite."

	FOOD	DECOR	SERVICE	COST

Barrington Brewery & Restaurant *American*

| 15 | 15 | 19 | $24 |

Great Barrington | 420 Stockbridge Rd./Rte. 7 N. (Old Stonebridge Rd./ Rte. 183) | 413-528-8282 | www.barringtonbrewery.net

Though it's certainly "not fancy", the "basic" American grub at this "family-friendly" Great Barrington microbrewery "hits the spot" "after a day of leaf peeping" or skiing; "large servings for little cash" come dished up "fast" in a big, "cheerful", "lively" space with working vats on view – oh, and "the beer ain't bad either!"

NEW Berkshire Harvest *American*

| - | - | - | M |

Lenox | 55 Pittsfield Rd. (bet. Dugway Rd. & Main St.) | 413-637-9777 | www.theberkshireharvest.com

Aptly named, this Lenox newcomer relies on regional farmers, bakers, vintners and even chocolatiers to supply ingredients for its New American menu, on which surprises such as tandoori chicken turn up alongside updated comfort classics like roast turkey, mac 'n' cheese and meatloaf; all come served in a casual, sunlit dining room adorned with local photos or a spacious taproom, with affordable rates a bonus (the under-$10 daily blue-plate specials are a particular boon for the budget conscious).

Bistro Zinc *French*

| 22 | 22 | 19 | $48 |

Lenox | 56 Church St. (Housatonic St.) | 413-637-8800 | www.bistrozinc.com

It's all "trendy" "urban chic" at Lenox's "popular" "replica of a French bistro", where "young and old" gather for "delightful" fare in "sexy" surroundings that include a "cool bar"; if only the prices weren't so "steep", the service were "warmer" and the "tight room" weren't so "zoo-y" in high season (remember, "reservations are a must").

Bizen Restaurant *Japanese*

| 22 | 17 | 17 | $42 |

Great Barrington | 17 Railroad St. (Rte. 7) | 413-528-4343

"Yummy", sometimes "edgy" sushi and Japanese grilled dishes make up the "encyclopedic menu" at this "rather pricey" spot in Great Barrington; a "small space" plus "bustling" "crowds" equals often "harried" staffers, so cognoscenti "sit at the bar" and "schmooze" with "knowledgeable" chef-owner Michael Marcus (he also "makes the pottery" on view) or retreat to a tatami room for the prix fixe kaiseki dinner.

Z Blantyre *American/French*

| 27 | 28 | 27 | $163 |

Lenox | Blantyre | 16 Blantyre Rd. (Rte. 20) | 413-637-3556 | www.blantyre.com

A true "grande dame", this "ritzy" hotel dining room with "a magnificent setting" in Lenox exudes the "luxury" of "a bygone era", from the "fabulous" French–New American à la carte lunches and prix fixe dinners to the "thoroughly professional", "refined staff" to "gorgeous", "romantic" environs filled with "fresh flowers" and soft piano music; yes, the whole "pampering" experience is "over-the-top", just like the "out-of-sight prices" – but this is "one splurge that's really worth the dough"; N.B. jacket and tie required, children under 12 not admitted.

	FOOD	DECOR	SERVICE	COST

Bombay ⓜ *Indian*
23 | 14 | 19 | $30

Lee | Quality Inn | 435 Laurel St. (Rte. 20) | 413-243-6731 |
www.fineindiandining.com

"Spicy food"-favorers find "wonderful" renditions at this "festive" Lee
Indian appreciated for "considerate service" and a weekend brunch
buffet deemed "one of the best buys anywhere"; if the plain decor
seems "peculiar", "sit at a window" and enjoy the "lovely lake view."

Brix Wine Bar ⓜ *French*
22 | 21 | 23 | $40

Pittsfield | 40 West St. (bet. McKay & North Sts.) | 413-236-9463 |
www.brixwinebar.com

"Fine" French bistro fare and "a smart wine list" make for "a winning
combination" at this "appealing" Pittsfield "hangout" where the "expensive" food tabs are tempered by "good-value flights"; an "attentive" staff works the "intimate" gold-and-burgundy room, which some
say gets too "noisy" when everyone else is having too much "fun."

Cafe Adam *European*
22 | 15 | 19 | $36

Great Barrington | 325 Stockbridge Rd. (bet. Cooper & Crissey Rds.) |
413-528-7786 | www.cafeadam.org

"Imaginative", "well-prepared" contemporary European fare is
served "at reasonable prices" alongside an "amazing wine list" at
this "casual", "out-of-the-way" Great Barrington cafe where toque-
owner Adam Zieminski "settled down" after some swanky cheffing
across the pond; diners settle in the minimalist "New York–style interior" with its black accents and matching blackboards (for specials) or nab an umbrella table on the porch when it's nice out.

Café Lucia ⓜ *Italian*
21 | 17 | 20 | $51

Lenox | 80 Church St. (bet. Franklin & Housatonic Sts.) | 413-637-2640 |
www.cafelucialenox.com

"If you love osso buco, make a beeline" for this Lenox veteran where
the "chef's signature" is the highlight of the "pricey" menu of "reliable" Italian "classics"; even admirers admit the "ordinary" interior
of the 1839 house gets too "crowded" and "noisy", but they just ask
the "pleasant" staff for a table on the "pleasurable" deck.

Castle Street Cafe *American/French*
19 | 17 | 20 | $44

Great Barrington | 10 Castle St. (Main St.) | 413-528-5244 |
www.castlestreetcafe.com

"Popular with transplanted New Yorkers and locals" alike, this "dependable" Great Barrington American-French bistro serves up "old
favorites done well" in lighter preparations at the "lively" bar – which is
"enhanced by cool jazz on weekends" (nightly in summer) – and
"more pricey" full dinners in the "spacious" dining room; a "courteous" staff is another reason it packs an "invariably full house."

Chez Nous ⓜ *French*
24 | 18 | 23 | $50

Lee | 150 Main St. (Academy St.) | 413-243-6397 |
www.cheznousbistro.com

"Half the time it's excellent, the other half it's out of sight" pronounce
pleased "picky locals" of Gallic chef Franck Tessier's "mouthwatering"

French fare and his American wife Rachel Portnoy's "luscious desserts" (she also offers "warm welcomes" as hostess) at this "comfy", costly "country house" in Lee; there's also a "quality wine list", from which the "efficient" staff can suggest "perfect complements."

Church Street Cafe *American* | 21 | 17 | 20 | $43 |

Lenox | 65 Church St. (bet. Franklin & Housatonic Sts.) | 413-637-2745 | www.churchstreetcafe.biz

A "tried-and-true" "standby for Lenox residents" (as well as tourists heading to Tanglewood), this "relaxed" New American employs an "accommodating staff" to deliver "attractive, delicious food" that's "a bit pricey but worth it"; patrons pick from three "peaceful" rooms, or sit on the "delightful" porch in summertime to "enjoy the scenery" "in the middle of town."

Coyote Flaco Ⓜ *Mexican* | ▽ 21 | 18 | 20 | $30 |

Williamstown | 505 Cold Spring Rd. (Bee Hill Rd.) | 413-458-4240 | www.mycoyoteflaco.com

"Come hungry" for "real Mexican" "served with flair" advise amigos of this Williamstown branch of the fairly priced, "family-owned" chainlet; even those who declare it "generally mediocre" find places in their hearts for "not-to-be-missed" margaritas, live flamenco guitar on Friday nights and a "mariachi serenade" on Cinco de Mayo.

Cranwell Resort, | 20 | 23 | 22 | $51 |
Spa & Golf Club *American*

Lenox | 55 Lee Rd./Rte. 20 (Rte. 7) | 413-637-1364 | www.cranwell.com

"What a beautiful place" declare dazzled guests of Lenox's "lovely" Tudor-style mansion resort, where "attentive" staffers serve "wonderful", "expensive" New American fare in the "romantic" Wyndhurst room or Music Room Grill; the less enthused tut it's a tad "hoity-toity" and suggest "sticking to Sloane's Tavern", the home of "good burgers and shareable salads" "at moderate prices", or the spa cafe and its "fresh" light fare.

Dakota *Steak* | 18 | 17 | 19 | $34 |

Pittsfield | 1035 South St. (Dan Fox Dr.) | 413-499-7900 | www.steakseafood.com

A "family atmosphere" pervades the Pittsfield branch of this "large, popular" steakhouse chain known for its "huge menu" of "predictable", "plentiful" protein in various guises, "amazing salad bar", "magnificent" Sunday brunch and "value prices"; the "pseudo" "big-game-hunter theme" (realized through mounted "elk and moose heads") is "disconcerting" to some, but the "warm", "caring staff" "never disappoints."

Dream Away Lodge Ⓜ⌗ *American* | - | - | - | I |

Becket | 1342 County Rd. (Stanley Rd.) | 413-623-8725 | www.thedreamawaylodge.com

Legendary in the Berkshires, this New American eatery/bar/ performance venue buried in Becket's backwoods has hosted acts from Bob Dylan to Liberace in a laid-back old farmhouse as colorful as its brothel/speakeasy past; a small affordable menu of comfort classics (think chicken, pot roast, mac 'n' cheese) is served in a comfy room, where all is so mismatched it matches, but remember, it's cash only, just weekends in winter and get good directions.

Elizabeth's Ⓜ⊅ *Eclectic*

25 | 13 | 22 | $33

Pittsfield | 1264 East St. (Newell St.) | 413-448-8244

Practically a "cult classic", this "offbeat" Pittsfield Eclectic offers a "limited", "lovingly prepared" menu of "unbelievable pastas" and "bountiful", "spectacular salads", plus one fish and one meat dish (both "amazing") per night; "foodies" "sit in the kitchen" of the "homey" space to watch "scene-stealer" chef Tom Ellis, then marvel at the final "quirk": only checks, cash "or IOU – and they mean it."

Fin *Japanese*

23 | 13 | 18 | $38

Lenox | 27 Housatonic St. (Church St.) | 413-637-9171 | www.finsushi.com

"Tiny but tony", this Lenox "hole-in-the-wall", co-owned by Bistro Zinc's Jason Macioge and his brother, Nick, serves "inventive, yummy sushi" and other "complex" "Japanese" dishes "with twists"; while the "roar" and "cramped", "diner"-style digs are negatives, fans find greater comfort at the red-lacquered bar – or when they get it to go.

Firefly *American*

17 | 17 | 15 | $39

Lenox | 71 Church St. (Housatonic St.) | 413-637-2700 | www.fireflylenox.com

Pros proclaim this "casual" "neighborhood place" in Lenox a "fine choice" for "interesting" New American fare, while cons criticize an "unfocused menu" and "amateur", "disappearing servers"; however, come summer, everyone appreciates the "busy", "pretty bar" and "wonderful porch."

Flavours of Malaysia Ⓜ *Asian*

- | - | - | I

Pittsfield | 75 North St. (McKay St.) | 413-443-3188 | www.flavoursintheberkshires.com

Now in Pittsfield after a move from Lenox, this easygoing Asian owned by chef Sabrina Tan turns out the tastes of China, Malaysia, India and Thailand, so expect everything from dim sum to chicken satay to samosas (with a few American dishes thrown in for good measure); spacious burgundy surroundings create a warm, relaxed vibe, while inexpensive tabs keep the mood happy.

Frankie's Ristorante Italiano *Italian*

- | - | - | M

Lenox | 80 Main St. (Cliffwood St.) | 413-637-4455 | www.frankiesitaliano.com

Chef-owner Stephane Ferioli creates a classic mom-and-pop vibe at this casual Lenox Italian where family photos on red felt walls and golden ceilings fashion a cozy backdrop for traditional recipes from his *nonna* (think lasagna with spinach dough, ragout bolognese and seafood fra diavolo); spouse Molly meets and greets, and moderate tabs add another friendly note.

Gala

▽ 21 | 24 | 23 | $41

Restaurant & Bar *American/Continental*

Williamstown | Orchards Hotel | 222 Adams Rd. (Main St.) |
413-458-9611 | www.galarestaurant.com

This Williamstown New American–Continental's "calm setting" includes "spacious" rooms bedecked with "dark-wood paneling" and a "lovely" courtyard; an "eager staff" conveys the "beautifully presented" fare, and while it's somewhat pricey, a lighter menu is available in the bar area where "seats by the fireplace are coveted."

⚡ Gramercy Bistro *American/Eclectic*

25 | 21 | 23 | $40

North Adams | 24-26 Marshall St. (Rte. 2) | 413-663-5300 |
www.gramercybistro.com

The "thoughtfully prepared", "updated" bistro classics made with "local, artisanal" ingredients "exceed expectations" at this "welcoming" chef-owned American-Eclectic in North Adams; factor in "luscious desserts", "personable service" plus a "warm" vibe, and it's no surprise locals "love it"; N.B. in spring 2010, it's slated to move into the old Café Latino space at Mass MoCA up the block.

Haven *American/Bakery*

- | - | - | I

Lenox | 8 Franklin St. (Main St.) | 413-637-8948 |
www.havencafebakery.com

This casual American cafe and bakery in Downtown Lenox serves freshly prepared fare featuring local/organic ingredients for breakfast, lunch and, occasionally in the summer, dinner; gin, rum and vodka come from a local distillery, and everything's served in simple surroundings with wainscoting and dark hardwood floors.

Hub, The 🅼 *American*

- | - | - | M

North Adams | 55 Main St. (Center St.) | 413-662-2500

Culinary couple Matthew and Kate Schilling (he chefs, she greets) create a country-diner mood at their North Adams American where the storefront space sports stools at a counter, a black-and-white-tiled floor and vintage photos on the walls; it's a convivial hub for locals looking for affordable light fare like burgers and sandwiches or heartier offerings such as the signature spicy jambalaya.

Isabella's 🅼 *Italian*

- | - | - | M

North Adams | 869 State Rd. (bet. Georgia & Hawthorne Aves.) |
413-662-2239 | www.isabellasrest.com

Professors, businessmen and families mingle merrily at this affordable North Adams Italian that's named after the daughter of chef-owner Drew Nicastro and his front-of-house spouse Leigh-Anne Jones; set in an 1890s farmhouse, the environment includes soothing moss-green-and-khaki rooms and a summertime dining porch.

Jae's Spice *American/Asian*

21 | 25 | 19 | $38

Pittsfield | 297 North St. (bet. Summer & Union Sts.) | 413-443-1234 |
www.eatatjaes.com

Creating "buzz" in a "dramatic" old-department-store space in Pittsfield, this Jae Chung venture proffers the "Pan-Asian food he's famous for" as well as "mainstream" New American dishes, all at "remarkably modest prices"; the "gorgeous" decor features scattered Asian doodads and a sushi bar, and once the sometimes "disorganized" service "smoothes out", all will be "terrific."

John Andrews *American* 25 | 21 | 22 | $55

South Egremont | Rte. 23 (Blunt Rd.) | 413-528-3469 | www.jarestaurant.com

"You want classy in the Berkshires?" – this "charming", "off-the-beaten-track" South Egremont New American is it declare devotees; an "elegant" dining room sets the mood for "masterfully prepared", "sophisticated" cooking "that'll warm your heart", served by a staff that "knows how to keep fussy New Yorkers happy"; wallet-watchers who find it "on the expensive side" opt for the bar where the less expensive, "simpler menu is just as delicious."

Jonathan's Bistro *American* - | - | - | M

Lenox | 55 Pittsfield Rd. (bet. Dugway Rd. & Main St.) | 413-637-8022

New American cooking that runs the gamut from wraps and grilled pizza to fancier fare keeps a diverse crowd coming to this midpriced Lenox spot; all nestle into bistro-style digs tricked out in shades of pumpkin with gold curtains and a copper bar or head to the patio when it's warm.

Marketplace Kitchen *American/Sandwiches* - | - | - | I

Sheffield | 18 Elm Ct. (Main St.) | 413-248-5040 | www.marketplacekitchen.com

An offshoot of the Marketplace, the popular specialty foods store down the road, this casual Sheffield American serves creative sandwiches, salads and soups in a sunny storefront done up in hues of coffee and butternut squash; locals pile in for cheap breakfasts and lunches and for Tuesday's family dinner, an ever-changing theme meal where a mere $20 buys enough homey favorites to feed a family of four.

Mezze Bistro + Bar *American* 25 | 23 | 23 | $45

Williamstown | 16 Water St. (Rte. 2) | 413-458-0123 | www.mezzeinc.com

Expect "love at first bite" at this "upscale" New American "surprise" in "the northern Berkshires wilderness" (aka Williamstown), where "refined", "inventive" tastes are matched by a "superb wine list" and "professional service"; the "attractive setting", tricked out in chocolate and cream tones, is "the place to be seen", or come summer, "get an eyeful, if you're into star-watching."

Mill on the Floss, The M *French* 23 | 22 | 23 | $49

New Ashford | 342 Rte. 7 (Rte. 43) | 413-458-9123 | www.millonthefloss.com

"An old favorite" in New Ashford, this "time-tested" French spot offers "sophisticated", "pricey" fare in a "lovely, unpretentious" 18th-century farmhouse; sure, it's "a bit dated", but "romantics" "take comfort in the warmth" of its wood-beamed, "cozy", candlelit rooms, while "friendly, helpful service" is another reason it's an "enjoyable" "standby for special occasions."

Mission Bar & Tapas ●🗷 *Spanish* | - | - | - | M |

Pittsfield | 438 North St. (Maplewood Ave.) |
www.missionbarandtapas.com

Perhaps this Spanish tapas specialist is kind of an "arty place" for Pittsfield, but "young hipsters and older couples" alike pile in for "superb" small plates, charcuterie, "tangy salads" and Iberian wines; works by local artists brighten deep red walls in the long and narrow room where "musicians playing live" add to the "mellow, unrushed atmosphere."

Morgan House *New England* | 16 | 15 | 17 | $37 |

Lee | Morgan House | 33 Main St. (Mass. Tpke., exit 2) | 413-243-3661 |
www.morganhouseinn.com

Lee locals report the newish owners are "really trying to better" this "quaint" early-19th-century inn, starting with "updating" the decor with fresh paint and a mural of the town; originally, the New England "comfort food" remained "pretty much the same" ("bargain priced" for the Berkshires but "pedestrian") – however, the menu has been updated post-Survey, outdating the Food score.

Napa *Eclectic* | 19 | 18 | 17 | $43 |

Great Barrington | 293 Main St. (Church St.) | 413-528-4311 |
www.napagb.com

This Great Barrington eatery and wine bar offers "interesting", "well-prepared" Eclectic dishes alongside "inexpensive wines" (a contrast to the somewhat pricey fare); high ceilings, peach walls and a long bar create a "nice" setting that helps patrons overlook the "noisy sound level" and "needs-improvement" service; N.B. there's live cabaret or jazz Tuesdays, Fridays and Saturdays.

🆕 Nudel 🅼 *American* | - | - | - | M |

Lenox | 37 Church St. (bet. Housatonic & Walker Sts.) | 413-551-7183 |
www.nudelrestaurant.com

Young chef Bjorn Somlo, a Berkshires native, launched this Lenox New American newcomer in the spot once occupied by Dish Café Bistro after transforming the narrow space into a bright, warm room with an open kitchen, wood floors and benches and a bar fashioned from recycled church pews; the seasonally driven, daily changing and reasonably priced menu spotlights 'nudels' (as in 'pastas') paired with innovative accoutrements.

🇿 Old Inn on the Green *American* | 28 | 27 | 25 | $65 |

New Marlborough | Old Inn on the Green |
134 Hartsville-New Marlborough Rd./Rte. 57 (Rte. 272) |
413-229-7924 | www.oldinn.com

"Worth every minute of the drive" to "remote" New Marlborough, this New American "jewel" set in an "exquisite" 1760 inn is "a fabulous find" for chef-owner Peter Platt's "outstanding" cuisine, matched by "stellar service" and "wonderful wines"; the "impossibly romantic" dining rooms "lit only by candles and fireplaces"

	FOOD	DECOR	SERVICE	COST

might "leave you drowsy with satisfaction", while the tabs will definitely cause your wallet to be considerably lighter – unless you've come on Wednesday, Thursday or Sunday for the "bargain" $30 prix fixe.

Old Mill American | 24 | 23 | 25 | $50 |

South Egremont | 53 Main St. (Rte. 41) | 413-528-1421 | www.oldmillberkshires.com

"Wonderful", "lovingly prepared" American cooking, "gracious" service and a fireside "atmosphere that makes you feel warm and cuddly" explain why this "well-worth-the-cost" "rustic charmer" in a "beautiful" 1797 South Egremont mill has been "a must" for more than 30 years; the one teeny "turnoff" is the no-rez policy for fewer than five, but even that's made up for by the "delightful bar to wait in."

Once Upon a Table American/Continental | 21 | 15 | 23 | $38 |

Stockbridge | The Mews | 36 Main St. (bet. Elm St. & Rte. 7) | 413-298-3870 | www.onceuponatablebistro.com

"Simple, well-cooked" eats are the attraction at this "adorable" Continental-New American "tucked in the mews" next to Stockbridge's Red Lion; a "friendly, efficient" staff works the "pleasant" but "tiny" room, which is "great" for lunch and quickly "full at night" ("reservations are a must").

NEW Perigee Eclectic/New England | - | - | - | M |

Lee | 1575 Pleasant St. (bet. Church & Willow Sts.) | 413-394-4047 | www.perigee-restaurant.com

At this midpriced Lee newcomer, New England classics meet the rest of the culinary world to create an Eclectic assemblage that the proprietors have trademarked as Berkshire cuisine; the neat brick exterior with periwinkle shutters gives way to a bistro-style downstairs with a cozy beamed bar and a quieter, softly lit, wainscoted upstairs.

Pho Saigon Vietnamese | ∇ 19 | 10 | 18 | $24 |

Lee | 5 Railroad St. (Main St.) | 413-243-6288

"Traditional" "homestyle" Vietnamese comes in "good, plentiful" and cheap supply at this "authentic", owner-operated Lee spot; most don't mind that bamboo accents are the only things notable in the no-frills digs, the "cheerful" servers "hardly speak English" or the "kitchen's slow when it gets busy."

NEW Point at Thornewood Inn, The ⑤Ⓜ American | - | - | - | M |

Great Barrington | Thornewood Inn | 453 Stockbridge Rd. (Rtes. 7 & 183) | 413-528-3828 | www.thornewoodinn.com

Comfort's the point of this Great Barrington Traditional American dispensing crowd-pleasers like pork tenderloin, mac 'n' cheese, grilled salmon and a regular whimsical chicken-something, all at affordable rates; patrons at the sprawling Dutch Colonial–style inn pick from three dining spaces: a pubby taproom, a cozy area done up in creams or a larger environment with soft-green walls, a dance floor and Palladian windows overlooking a garden.

	FOOD	DECOR	SERVICE	COST

Prime Italian
Steakhouse & Bar *Italian/Steak* | 20 | 20 | 20 | $57 |

Lenox | 15 Franklin St. (Rte. 7A) | 413-637-2998 |
www.primelenox.com

It may "not blow your socks off", but the menu at this "solid" Lenox
Southern Italian steakhouse mixes "simple meat and potatoes" with
chef-owner Gennaro Gallo's homemade gnocchi and the like; manned
by a "pleasant" staff, the setting features "smoked glass" dividers on
the booths, a lit-from-beneath bar and bright red banquettes.

Red Lion Inn *New England* | 18 | 22 | 21 | $45 |

Stockbridge | Red Lion Inn | 30 Main St./Rte. 102 (Rte. 7) |
413-298-5545 | www.redlioninn.com

This 1773 "quintessential New England inn" – a Stockbridge "icon" –
trots out "warhorses like roast turkey" on its "fine", "old-fashioned"
menu; a "courteous" staff serves in the "genteel", "high-priced"
main dining room, "cozy", "less expensive" Widow Bingham's Tavern
or "fun", "reasonable" Lion's Den pub, and even the debonair who
decry it's "dowdy" and "stuffed with tourists" declare it's "lovely to
eat in the courtyard."

Rouge Ⓜ *French* | 23 | 18 | 16 | $50 |

West Stockbridge | 3 Center St. (Rte. 41) | 413-232-4111 |
www.rougerestaurant.com

"A charming couple" runs this "lively" West Stockbridge bistro: chef
William Merelle cooks up "exceptional", somewhat pricey French
fare (and "inventive" tapas, served in the bar), while spouse Maggie
greets in the "homey" space; *les négatives* are "lapses in service" on
"busy" nights, when it's "noisy as a Paris subway", and "cramped"
conditions that should be helped by a relatively recent expansion.

Route 7 Grill *American/BBQ* | 23 | 17 | 21 | $33 |

Great Barrington | 999 S. Main St. (bet. Brookside & Lime Kiln Rds.) |
413-528-3235 | www.route7grill.com

"Lip-smacking ribs, succulent pulled pork" and other "fantastic"
BBQ tops a menu of "delicious" American "comfort food" at this
"hopping joint" in Great Barrington; "locavores" love its "commitment to regional farmers", while everyone "gives three cheers" for
the "festive", "child-friendly" vibe, "cordial" service and "reasonable" tabs; a two-sided fireplace warms up the "spare decor", and
there's "a jolly bar too."

Shiro Sushi & Hibachi *Japanese* | ∇ 20 | 19 | 22 | $34 |

Great Barrington | 105 Stockbridge Rd. (bet. Blue Hill Rd. & Brooke Ln.) |
413-528-1898

Shiro Lounge *Japanese*
Pittsfield | 48 North St. (School St.) | 413-236-8111 |
www.berkshiro.com

"Enthusiastic, goofy chefs" perform a "typical hibachi show" at this
Great Barrington Japanese offering "fresh sushi" in addition to the
"theatrical" experience; aficionados advise "don't overlook it" just because of its plain digs "next to a bowling alley"; N.B. post-Survey, a

sports bar was erected on one side of the dining room, and Shiro Lounge, a hibachi-less, more upscale offshoot in Pittsfield, premiered.

Siam Square Thai Cuisine *Thai* | 18 | 15 | 19 | $27 |

Great Barrington | 290 Main St. (Railroad St.) | 413-644-9119 | www.siamsquares.com

"Thai food is hard to come by" in the Berkshires, so this "reliable", "welcoming" Great Barrington "landmark" "does the trick" when "noodle cravings" hit, dispensing all "the basics as well as a few unusual options" for "cheap"; the space is "modest and quiet", while the staff is "sweet."

Stagecoach Tavern Ⓜ *American*   ▽ | 20 | 23 | 22 | $41 |

Sheffield | Race Brook Lodge | S. Undermountain Rd./Rte. 41 (Berkshire School Rd.) | 413-229-8585 | www.stagecoachtavern.net

"A warm hearth beckons" at this "rustic" roadside tavern in Sheffield, where seasonal American fare made with local and organic ingredients comes full of "flair and flavor"; the staff is "friendly", while "inviting" decor reflects the inn's 1829 vintage with "beautiful wood" beams and floors, candlelight and "cozy corners for quiet talk."

Sullivan Station Restaurant *New England*   ▽ | 15 | 15 | 19 | $33 |

Lee | 109 Railroad St. (Mass. Tpke., exit 2) | 413-243-2082 | www.sullivanstationrestaurant.com

"Weekend crowds, even off-season" confirm that Lee's "delightful" "converted train station" is on the right track with its "variety" of simple, "solid" New England "comfort fare" "at the right price"; it's a "family-friendly" spot that's "literally a hoot" when the Berkshire Scenic Railway tourist ride rolls by.

Sushi Thai Garden *Japanese/Thai* | 20 | 14 | 19 | $28 |

Williamstown | 27 Spring St. (Rte. 2) | 413-458-0004 | www.sushithaigarden.com

"A nice surprise in staid Williamstown", this Thai turns out "fresh", "spicy" "standards" – and the "sushi isn't bad either"; the decor is "typical", staff "helpful" and rates "reasonable", so no surprise it's a "favorite of faculty and students", with just a fussy few shrugging it's "nothing special."

Taylor's Ⓢ *American* | - | - | - | M |

North Adams | 34 Holden St. (Center St.) | 413-664-4500 | www.taylorsna.com

Housed in the storefront once occupied by Gideons, this American restaurant in underserved North Adams offers "nicely presented" classic steaks and seafood at moderate prices; "helpful" staffers preside over the brick-walled space, which underwent a massive renovation recently, adding a new mahogany bar next to an open kitchen.

Trattoria Rustica *Italian* | 23 | 21 | 20 | $45 |

Pittsfield | 27 McKay St. (West St.) | 413-499-1192 | www.trattoria-rustica.com

"Turn on your GPS" to find this "little corner of Naples" "hidden in the backstreets of Pittsfield", where chef-owner Davide Manzo's "delectable", "pricey but worth-every-penny" Southern Italian meals come via "congenial", "well-paced" service; add a wood oven and "low-lit", "romantic" ambiance in the "pretty" stone-and-brick-walled room and you've got a "winning combination."

Trattoria Il Vesuvio *Italian* ▽ 18 | 17 | 20 | $39

Lenox | 242 Pittsfield Rd. (bet. Lime Kiln & New Lenox Rds.) | 413-637-4904 | www.trattoria-vesuvio.com

Pros claim "you can't go wrong" with the "red-sauce" classics at this "popular" Lenox Italian presided over by an "accommodating", "down-to-earth" family that "appreciates your company"; cons complain the eats are "simply so-so", but even they're pleased that the "rustic", converted century-old stable is made "cozy" by a wood-fired brick oven.

Truc Orient Express *Vietnamese* 21 | 18 | 19 | $34

West Stockbridge | 3 Harris St. (Main St.) | 413-232-4204

"Super" Vietnamese cooking at "fair prices" keeps customers coming "year after year" to this family-run West Stockbridge "standby" that's been "doing something right" for three decades now; an "efficient", "polite" staff plus a "really nice gift shop" are other reasons it's "worth a detour", so though the digs decorated with art from the motherland are "a bit dated", it's "no matter."

Viva Ⓜ *Spanish* ▽ 23 | 19 | 21 | $44

Glendale | 14 Glendale Rd. (Rte. 102) | 413-298-4433 | www.vivaberkshires.com

"Finally, a real Spanish" spot in Glendale cheer those "pleasantly surprised" to find this nook near the Norman Rockwell museum; "authentic tastes" can be found in "to-die-for paella", "terrific tapas" and other "fabulous" fare in a "comfortable", casual mustard-and-terra-cotta setting jazzed up with a Picasso-esque mural.

🄴 Wheatleigh *American/French* 27 | 28 | 26 | $97

Lenox | Wheatleigh | 11 Hawthorne Rd. (Hawthorne St.) | 413-637-0610 | www.wheatleigh.com

It's "heaven on earth" avow the "wowed" at this "gorgeous" Italianate mansion in Lenox, where "truly lovely" rooms form an "elegant" backdrop for "superb" French–New American cuisine and "extraordinary", "formal service"; it strikes a few as "somewhat stuffy", but most are "left sighing" by the whole "spectacular" experience, and though you may have to "sell your house" to pay the bill, this is one "splurge" that's "worth every penny"; N.B. jackets suggested.

Xicohtencatl *Mexican* 21 | 18 | 21 | $35

Great Barrington | 50 Stockbridge Rd. (Rte. 7) | 413-528-2002 | www.xicohmexican.com

"Upscale", "real Mexican" is the deal at this "colorful" Great Barrington cantina serving "scrumptious" "regional specialties" in "generous" amounts and for relatively "modest costs"; a "staggering selection of tequilas" ensures everyone has "a blast" in the "festive" digs, while "dining on the terrace at sunset is sublime"; P.S. don't sweat the name, just call it "'shico.'"

THE BERKSHIRES
INDEXES

Cuisines

Includes names, locations and Food ratings.

AMERICAN

Allium	**Great Barr**	22
Barrington Brew	**Great Barr**	15
NEW Berkshire Harvest	**Lenox**	-
Z Blantyre	**Lenox**	27
Castle St.	**Great Barr**	19
Church St.	**Lenox**	21
Cranwell Resort	**Lenox**	20
Dream Away	**Becket**	-
Firefly	**Lenox**	17
Gala	**Williamstown**	21
Z Gramercy	**N Adams**	25
Haven	**Lenox**	-
Hub	**N Adams**	-
Jae's Spice	**Pittsfield**	21
John Andrews	**S Egremont**	25
Jonathan's	**Lenox**	-
Marketplace	**Sheffield**	-
Mezze Bistro	**Williamstown**	25
NEW Nudel	**Lenox**	-
Z Old Inn/Green	**New Marl**	28
Old Mill	**S Egremont**	24
Once Upon	**Stockbridge**	21
NEW Point/Thornewood	**Great Barr**	-
Route 7	**Great Barr**	23
Stagecoach Tav.	**Sheffield**	20
Taylor's	**N Adams**	-
Z Wheatleigh	**Lenox**	27

ASIAN

Flavours/Malaysia	**Pittsfield**	-
Jae's Spice	**Pittsfield**	21

BAKERIES

Haven	**Lenox**	-

BARBECUE

Route 7	**Great Barr**	23

CONTINENTAL

Gala	**Williamstown**	21
Once Upon	**Stockbridge**	21

ECLECTIC

Elizabeth's	**Pittsfield**	25
Z Gramercy	**N Adams**	25
Napa	**Great Barr**	19
NEW Perigee	**Lee**	-

EUROPEAN

Cafe Adam	**Great Barr**	22

FRENCH

Z Blantyre	**Lenox**	27
Castle St.	**Great Barr**	19
Mill on Floss	**New Ashford**	23
Z Wheatleigh	**Lenox**	27

FRENCH (BISTRO)

Bistro Zinc	**Lenox**	22
Brix Wine	**Pittsfield**	22
Chez Nous	**Lee**	24
Rouge	**W Stockbridge**	23

INDIAN

Aroma B&G	**Great Barr**	21
Bombay	**Lee**	23

ITALIAN

(S=Southern)

Café Lucia	**Lenox**	21
Frankie's Rist.	**Lenox**	-
Isabella's	**N Adams**	-
Prime Italian	S	**Lenox**	20
Tratt. Rustica	S	**Pittsfield**	23
Tratt. Il Vesuvio	**Lenox**	18

JAPANESE

(* sushi specialist)

Bizen*	**Great Barr**	22
Fin*	**Lenox**	23
Shiro*	**multi.**	20
Sushi Thai Gdn.*	**Williamstown**	20

MEDITERRANEAN

Aegean Breeze	**Great Barr**	19
Alta	**Lenox**	20

MEXICAN

Coyote Flaco | **Williamstown**   21

Xicohtencatl | **Great Barr**   21

NEW ENGLAND

Morgan Hse. | **Lee**   16

NEW Perigee | **Lee**   -

Red Lion Inn | **Stockbridge**   18

Sullivan Station | **Lee**   15

PIZZA

Baba Louie's | **Great Barr**   24

SANDWICHES

Marketplace | **Sheffield**   -

SPANISH

(* tapas specialist)

Mission Bar* | **Pittsfield**   -

Viva | **Glendale**   23

STEAKHOUSES

Dakota | **Pittsfield**   18

Prime Italian | **Lenox**   20

THAI

Siam Sq. Thai | **Great Barr**   18

Sushi Thai Gdn. | **Williamstown**   20

VIETNAMESE

Pho Saigon | **Lee**   19

Truc Orient | **W Stockbridge**   21

THE BERKSHIRES

CUISINES

Locations

Includes names, cuisines and Food ratings.

BECKET

Dream Away | *Amer.* -

GLENDALE

Viva | *Spanish* 23

GREAT BARRINGTON

Aegean Breeze | *Med.* 19
Allium | *Amer.* 22
Aroma B&G | *Indian* 21
Baba Louie's | *Pizza* 24
Barrington Brew | *Amer.* 15
Bizen | *Japanese* 22
Cafe Adam | *Euro.* 22
Castle St. | *Amer./French* 19
Napa | *Eclectic* 19
NEW Point/Thornewood | *Amer.* -
Route 7 | *Amer./BBQ* 23
Shiro | *Japanese* 20
Siam Sq. Thai | *Thai* 18
Xicohtencatl | *Mex.* 21

LEE

Bombay | *Indian* 23
Chez Nous | *French* 24
Morgan Hse. | *New Eng.* 16
NEW Perigee | *Eclectic/New Eng.* -
Pho Saigon | *Viet.* 19
Sullivan Station | *New Eng.* 15

LENOX

Alta | *Med.* 20
NEW Berkshire Harvest | *Amer.* -
Bistro Zinc | *French* 22
Z Blantyre | *Amer./French* 27
Café Lucia | *Italian* 21
Church St. | *Amer.* 21
Cranwell Resort | *Amer.* 20
Fin | *Japanese* 23
Firefly | *Amer.* 17
Frankie's Rist. | *Italian* -
Haven | *Amer./Bakery* -
Jonathan's | *Amer.* -

NEW Nudel | *Amer.* -
Prime Italian | *Italian/Steak* 20
Tratt. Il Vesuvio | *Italian* 18
Z Wheatleigh | *Amer./French* 27

NEW ASHFORD

Mill on Floss | *French* 23

NEW MARLBOROUGH

Z Old Inn/Green | *Amer.* 28

NORTH ADAMS

Z Gramercy | *Amer./Eclectic* 25
Hub | *Amer.* -
Isabella's | *Italian* -
Taylor's | *Amer.* -

PITTSFIELD

Brix Wine | *French* 22
Dakota | *Steak* 18
Elizabeth's | *Eclectic* 25
Flavours/Malaysia | *Asian* -
Jae's Spice | *Amer./Asian* 21
Mission Bar | *Spanish* -
Shiro | *Japanese* 20
Tratt. Rustica | *Italian* 23

SHEFFIELD

Marketplace | *Amer./Sandwiches* -
Stagecoach Tav. | *Amer.* 20

SOUTH EGREMONT

John Andrews | *Amer.* 25
Old Mill | *Amer.* 24

STOCKBRIDGE

Once Upon | *Amer./Continental* 21
Red Lion Inn | *New Eng.* 18

WEST STOCKBRIDGE

Rouge | *French* 23
Truc Orient | *Viet.* 21

WILLIAMSTOWN

Coyote Flaco | *Mex.* 21
Gala | *Amer./Continental* 21
Mezze Bistro | *Amer.* 25
Sushi Thai Gdn. | *Japanese/Thai* 20

Menus, photos, voting and more - free at ZAGAT.com

Special Features

Listings cover the best in each category and include names, locations and Food ratings. Multi-location restaurants' features may vary by branch.

ADDITIONS

(Properties added since the last edition of the book)

Berkshire Harvest	Lenox	-]
Flavours/Malaysia	Pittsfield	-]
Haven	Lenox	-]
Hub	N Adams	-]
Isabella's	N Adams	-]
Jonathan's	Lenox	-]
Marketplace	Sheffield	-]
Nudel	Lenox	-]
Perigee	Lee	-]
Point/Thornewood	Great Barr	-]

BRUNCH

Alta	Lenox	20]
Bombay	Lee	23]
Cafe Adam	Great Barr	22]
Dakota	Pittsfield	18]
⚡ Wheatleigh	Lenox	27]
Xicohtencatl	Great Barr	21]

BUSINESS DINING

Allium	Great Barr	22]
Cranwell Resort	Lenox	20]
Gala	Williamstown	21]
Jae's Spice	Pittsfield	21]
Napa	Great Barr	19]
Taylor's	N Adams	-]

CATERING

Bizen	Great Barr	22]
Bombay	Lee	23]
Castle St.	Great Barr	19]
John Andrews	S Egremont	25]
Mezze Bistro	Williamstown	25]

CHILD-FRIENDLY

(Alternatives to the usual fast-food places; * children's menu available)

Aegean Breeze	Great Barr	19]
Baba Louie's	Great Barr	24]
Barrington Brew*	Great Barr	15]
Bistro Zinc*	Lenox	22]
Café Lucia	Lenox	21]
Castle St.	Great Barr	19]
Church St.*	Lenox	21]
Coyote Flaco*	Williamstown	21]
Dakota*	Pittsfield	18]
Elizabeth's	Pittsfield	25]
Marketplace	Sheffield	-]
Morgan Hse.	Lee	16]
Old Mill	S Egremont	24]
Once Upon	Stockbridge	21]
Red Lion Inn*	Stockbridge	18]
Rouge	W Stockbridge	23]
Route 7*	Great Barr	23]
Shiro	Great Barr	20]
Siam Sq. Thai	Great Barr	18]
Sullivan Station*	Lee	15]
Sushi Thai Gdn.	Williamstown	20]
Tratt. Il Vesuvio*	Lenox	18]
Xicohtencatl*	Great Barr	21]

DINING ALONE

(Other than hotels and places with counter service)

Alta	Lenox	20]
Baba Louie's	Great Barr	24]
Fin	Lenox	23]
Napa	Great Barr	19]
Once Upon	Stockbridge	21]
Pho Saigon	Lee	19]

ENTERTAINMENT

(Call for days and times of performances)

⚡ Blantyre	varies	Lenox	27]
Castle St.	jazz/piano	Great Barr	19]
Mission Bar	folk/indie rock	Pittsfield	-]
Red Lion Inn	varies	Stockbridge	18]

FIREPLACES

Aegean Breeze | **Great Barr**	19
Barrington Brew | **Great Barr**	15
Z Blantyre | **Lenox**	27
Cranwell Resort | **Lenox**	20
Dakota | **Pittsfield**	18
Dream Away | **Becket**	-
Gala | **Williamstown**	21
John Andrews | **S Egremont**	25
Mill on Floss | **New Ashford**	23
Morgan Hse. | **Lee**	16
Z Old Inn/Green | **New Marl**	28
Old Mill | **S Egremont**	24
Red Lion Inn | **Stockbridge**	18
Route 7 | **Great Barr**	23
Stagecoach Tav. | **Sheffield**	20
Truc Orient | **W Stockbridge**	21
Z Wheatleigh | **Lenox**	27

GAME IN SEASON

Allium | **Great Barr**	22
Alta | **Lenox**	20
Bistro Zinc | **Lenox**	22
Z Blantyre | **Lenox**	27
Brix Wine | **Pittsfield**	22
Café Lucia | **Lenox**	21
Castle St. | **Great Barr**	19
Church St. | **Lenox**	21
Cranwell Resort | **Lenox**	20
Elizabeth's | **Pittsfield**	25
Firefly | **Lenox**	17
Z Gramercy | **N Adams**	25
John Andrews | **S Egremont**	25
Jonathan's | **Lenox**	-
Mezze Bistro | **Williamstown**	25
Napa | **Great Barr**	19
NEW Nudel | **Lenox**	-
Z Old Inn/Green | **New Marl**	28
Red Lion Inn | **Stockbridge**	18
Rouge | **W Stockbridge**	23
Stagecoach Tav. | **Sheffield**	20
Z Wheatleigh | **Lenox**	27

HISTORIC PLACES

(Year opened; * building)

1760 | Old Inn/Green* | **New Marl**	28
1773 | Red Lion Inn* | **Stockbridge**	18
1797 | Old Mill* | **S Egremont**	24
1817 | Morgan Hse.* | **Lee**	16
1829 | Stagecoach Tav.* | **Sheffield**	20
1839 | Café Lucia* | **Lenox**	21
1840 | Jae's Spice* | **Pittsfield**	21
1841 | Chez Nous* | **Lee**	24
1852 | Church St.* | **Lenox**	21
1890 | Mezze Bistro* | **Williamstown**	25
1893 | Sullivan Station* | **Lee**	15
1893 | Wheatleigh* | **Lenox**	27
1894 | Cranwell Resort* | **Lenox**	20
1900 | Tratt. Il Vesuvio* | **Lenox**	18
1903 | Gramercy* | **N Adams**	25
1924 | Brix Wine* | **Pittsfield**	22
1945 | Dream Away | **Becket**	-

HOTEL DINING

Blantyre

Z Blantyre | **Lenox**	27

Morgan House

Morgan Hse. | **Lee**	16

Old Inn on the Green

Z Old Inn/Green | **New Marl**	28

Orchards Hotel

Gala | **Williamstown**	21

Quality Inn

Bombay | **Lee**	23

Race Brook Lodge

Stagecoach Tav. | **Sheffield**	20

Red Lion Inn

Red Lion Inn | **Stockbridge**	18

Thornewood Inn

NEW Point/Thornewood | **Great Barr**	-

Wheatleigh

Z Wheatleigh | **Lenox**	27

Menus, photos, voting and more - free at ZAGAT.com

JACKET REQUIRED

(* Tie also required)
☑ Blantyre* | **Lenox** — 27

MEET FOR A DRINK

Alta | **Lenox** — 20
Bistro Zinc | **Lenox** — 22
Brix Wine | **Pittsfield** — 22
Castle St. | **Great Barr** — 19
Chez Nous | **Lee** — 24
Gala | **Williamstown** — 21
☑ Gramercy | **N Adams** — 25
Jae's Spice | **Pittsfield** — 21
Mission Bar | **Pittsfield** — –
Napa | **Great Barr** — 19
Old Mill | **S Egremont** — 24
Prime Italian | **Lenox** — 20
Red Lion Inn | **Stockbridge** — 18
Stagecoach Tav. | **Sheffield** — 20

MICROBREWERIES

Barrington Brew | **Great Barr** — 15

OFFBEAT

Barrington Brew | **Great Barr** — 15
Elizabeth's | **Pittsfield** — 25

OUTDOOR DINING

(G=garden; P=patio; T=terrace)
Aegean Breeze | P | **Great Barr** — 19
Alta | P | **Lenox** — 20
Barrington Brew | G | **Great Barr** — 15
Cafe Adam | P | **Great Barr** — 22
Café Lucia | G, T | **Lenox** — 21
Church St. | P | **Lenox** — 21
Firefly | P | **Lenox** — 17
Gala | P, W | **Williamstown** — 21
John Andrews | T | **S Egremont** — 25
Jonathan's | P | **Lenox** — –
☑ Old Inn/Green | T | **New Marl** — 28
Red Lion Inn | P | **Stockbridge** — 18
Rouge | T | **W Stockbridge** — 23
Shiro | P | **Great Barr** — 20
Sullivan Station | T | **Lee** — 15
Tratt. Rustica | P | **Pittsfield** — 23

Tratt. Il Vesuvio | T | **Lenox** — 18
Xicohtencatl | T | **Great Barr** — 21

PEOPLE-WATCHING

Allium | **Great Barr** — 22
Alta | **Lenox** — 20
Bistro Zinc | **Lenox** — 22
Mezze Bistro | **Williamstown** — 25

POWER SCENES

Bistro Zinc | **Lenox** — 22
Mezze Bistro | **Williamstown** — 25

PRIVATE ROOMS

(Restaurants charge less at off times; call for capacity)
Bizen | **Great Barr** — 22
☑ Blantyre | **Lenox** — 27
Castle St. | **Great Barr** — 19
Church St. | **Lenox** — 21
Cranwell Resort | **Lenox** — 20
Dakota | **Pittsfield** — 18
Gala | **Williamstown** — 21
John Andrews | **S Egremont** — 25
Mill on Floss | **New Ashford** — 23
Red Lion Inn | **Stockbridge** — 18
Rouge | **W Stockbridge** — 23
Stagecoach Tav. | **Sheffield** — 20
☑ Wheatleigh | **Lenox** — 27

PRIX FIXE MENUS

(Call for prices and times)
Bizen | **Great Barr** — 22
☑ Blantyre | **Lenox** — 27
Bombay | **Lee** — 23
☑ Old Inn/Green | **New Marl** — 28
☑ Wheatleigh | **Lenox** — 27

QUIET CONVERSATION

☑ Blantyre | **Lenox** — 27
Gala | **Williamstown** — 21
☑ Gramercy | **N Adams** — 25
John Andrews | **S Egremont** — 25
Mill on Floss | **New Ashford** — 23
Stagecoach Tav. | **Sheffield** — 20
Taylor's | **N Adams** — –
☑ Wheatleigh | **Lenox** — 27

RESERVE AHEAD

Bistro Zinc | Lenox	22
Z Blantyre | Lenox	27
Z Old Inn/Green | New Marl	28
Once Upon | Stockbridge	21
Z Wheatleigh | Lenox	27

ROMANTIC PLACES

Z Blantyre | Lenox	27
Cranwell Resort | Lenox	20
John Andrews | S Egremont	25
Mill on Floss | New Ashford	23
Z Old Inn/Green | New Marl	28
Taylor's | N Adams	-
Tratt. Rustica | Pittsfield	23
Z Wheatleigh | Lenox	27

SENIOR APPEAL

Aegean Breeze | Great Barr	19
Cranwell Resort | Lenox	20
Gala | Williamstown	21
Morgan Hse. | Lee	16
Red Lion Inn | Stockbridge	18
Taylor's | N Adams	-

SINGLES SCENES

Alta | Lenox	20
Brix Wine | Pittsfield	22
Castle St. | Great Barr	19
Jae's Spice | Pittsfield	21
Napa | Great Barr	19
Prime Italian | Lenox	20
Sushi Thai Gdn. | Williamstown	20

SLEEPERS

(Good food, but little known)

Bombay | Lee	23
Brix Wine | Pittsfield	22
Cafe Adam | Great Barr	22
Fin | Lenox	23
Z Gramercy | N Adams	25
Mill on Floss | New Ashford	23
Rouge | W Stockbridge	23
Tratt. Rustica | Pittsfield	23
Viva | Glendale	23

TAKEOUT

Aegean Breeze | Great Barr	19
Baba Louie's | Great Barr	24
Barrington Brew | Great Barr	15
Bistro Zinc | Lenox	22
Bizen | Great Barr	22
Café Lucia | Lenox	21
Castle St. | Great Barr	19
Church St. | Lenox	21
Dakota | Pittsfield	18
Gala | Williamstown	21
John Andrews | S Egremont	25
Marketplace | Sheffield	-
Morgan Hse. | Lee	16
Once Upon | Stockbridge	21
Rouge | W Stockbridge	23
Shiro | Great Barr	20
Siam Sq. Thai | Great Barr	18
Stagecoach Tav. | Sheffield	20
Sushi Thai Gdn. | Williamstown	20
Truc Orient | W Stockbridge	21

TEEN APPEAL

Baba Louie's | Great Barr	24
Barrington Brew | Great Barr	15
Coyote Flaco | Williamstown	21
Dakota | Pittsfield	18

TRENDY

Allium | Great Barr	22
Bistro Zinc | Lenox	22
Bizen | Great Barr	22
Brix Wine | Pittsfield	22
Cafe Adam | Great Barr	22
Castle St. | Great Barr	19
Fin | Lenox	23
Jae's Spice | Pittsfield	21
John Andrews | S Egremont	25
Mission Bar | Pittsfield	-
Napa | Great Barr	19
Z Old Inn/Green | New Marl	28
Prime Italian | Lenox	20
Rouge | W Stockbridge	23
Xicohtencatl | Great Barr	21

Menus, photos, voting and more – free at ZAGAT.com

THE BERKSHIRES

SPECIAL FEATURES

Wine Vintage Chart

This chart is based on our 0 to 30 scale. The ratings (by U. of South Carolina law professor **Howard Stravitz**) reflect vintage quality and the wine's readiness to drink. A dash means the wine is past its peak or too young to rate. Loire ratings are for dry whites.

Whites	95	96	97	98	99	00	01	02	03	04	05	06	07	08
France:														
Alsace	24	23	23	25	23	25	26	23	21	24	25	24	26	-
Burgundy	27	26	23	21	24	24	24	27	23	26	27	25	25	24
Loire Valley	-	-	-	-	-	23	24	26	22	24	27	23	23	24
Champagne	26	27	24	23	25	24	21	26	21	-	-	-	-	-
Sauternes	21	23	25	23	24	24	29	25	24	21	26	23	27	25
California:														
Chardonnay	-	-	-	-	23	22	25	26	22	26	29	24	27	-
Sauvignon Blanc	-	-	-	-	-	-	-	-	25	26	25	27	25	-
Austria:														
Grüner V./Riesl.	24	21	26	23	25	22	23	25	26	25	24	26	24	22
Germany:	21	26	21	22	24	20	29	25	26	27	28	25	27	25

Reds	95	96	97	98	99	00	01	02	03	04	05	06	07	08
France:														
Bordeaux	26	25	23	25	24	29	26	24	26	24	28	24	23	25
Burgundy	26	27	25	24	27	22	24	27	25	23	28	25	24	-
Rhône	26	22	24	27	26	27	26	-	26	24	27	25	26	-
Beaujolais	-	-	-	-	-	-	-	-	24	-	27	24	25	23
California:														
Cab./Merlot	27	25	28	23	25	-	27	26	25	24	26	23	26	24
Pinot Noir	-	-	-	-	24	23	25	26	25	26	24	23	27	25
Zinfandel	-	-	-	-	-	-	25	23	27	22	22	21	21	25
Oregon:														
Pinot Noir	-	-	-	-	-	-	-	26	24	25	26	26	25	27
Italy:														
Tuscany	24	-	29	24	27	24	27	-	25	27	26	25	24	-
Piedmont	21	27	26	25	26	28	27	-	25	27	26	25	26	-
Spain:														
Rioja	26	24	25	-	25	24	28	-	23	27	26	24	25	-
Ribera del Duero/ Priorat	26	27	25	24	25	24	27	20	24	27	26	24	26	-
Australia:														
Shiraz/Cab.	24	26	25	28	24	24	27	27	25	26	26	24	22	-
Chile:	-	-	24	-	25	23	26	24	25	24	27	25	24	-
Argentina:														
Malbec	-	-	-	-	-	-	-	-	25	26	27	24	-	

Menus, photos, voting and more - free at ZAGAT.com